Warfare and the Human Condition

Ernest Dyer

Published by New Generation Publishing in 2023

Copyright © Ernest Dyer 2023

First Edition

The author asserts the moral right under the Copyright, Designs and Patents Act 1988 to be identified as the author of this work.

All Rights reserved. No part of this publication may be reproduced, stored in a retrieval system or transmitted, in any form or by any means without the prior consent of the author, nor be otherwise circulated in any form of binding or cover other than that which it is published and without a similar condition being imposed on the subsequent purchaser.

ISBN: 978-1-80369-637-9

www.newgeneration-publishing.com

New Generation Publishing

Contents:

Introduction 1

Chapter 1 'Prehistory to Civil Life: the origins of human conflict' 16

Chapter 2 'The Bloody Middle Ages' 111

Chapter 3 'The Early Modern Period' 162

Chapter 4 'The Modern Period: industrialized warfare' 225

Chapter 5 'Post-World War II: the institutionalization of international hegemony' 319

Conclusion 437

Appendix 1 Global governance and re-imagined United Nations 506

Appendix 2 Information 512

Appendix 3 Artificial intelligence – a possible scenario? 521

galaxies spread across an immense and seemingly eternal universe. An expansive spatiality that we now assume was initially created at some point of singularity approx 13.8 billion years ago with a predicted life projecting into the future for billions more. Within this profound conjunction of space/time immensity, our own life-times of 70 odd years (if fortunate) seem to be but a brief flicker of consciousness, of singular irrelevance. What can my own existence mean within such awesome dimensions?

My own tiny 'window' of consciousness, during which I can contemplate the Reality within which my life unfolds, is of fundamental relevance to me. Is this time of my being alive but a mysteriously random 'gift', or for too many a life of generally relentless travail or even suffering? Is this time offered to bear witness as our history continues to unfold? Have I emerged into an exercise involving some metaphysical absurdity – the absurdity of a purposeless existence within a wider existential context for which I am merely irrelevant? Why am I being taunted by life's absurdity? As bare questions these are unanswerable, but as irrepressible stimulants to thinking they can prompt me to reflect beyond the social relativities and more philosophical conundrums that I have been born into.

I feel that I have in a sense 'found myself' in existence. As an initial encounter this was an existence of my growing up in a comfortable family setting within a proudly working class community in post WWII South-East London. Up until my teenage years I took the values and guidelines for acceptable behaviour experienced during this time pretty much for granted as being 'normal'. I was socialized into a normality of post-war 'Britishness'. I was enculturalized within a mass of people mostly offering a bovine acceptance of class-based division and social circumstances of marked inequalities of wealth and of opportunity.

At about the age of 15 I began to realize two 'facts': God was a fictional construction and that my own life will end – that the world turns without any god beyond the imaginations of believers and will in due course turn without me. Absorbing the implications rather than living as if denying these facts is the challenge that each one of us

Introduction

'If civilization is to survive, the expansion of understanding is a prime necessity'

A.N.Whitehead 'Modes of Thought' (1938, p63)

As the world's people drift relentlessly towards our own destruction we might ask.... is this end for our species the inevitable outcome of evolved human nature expressed and influenced by about 150,000 years of social become civil life? Or can the world's international institutions and nation-state relationships be re-imagined in the image of the possible, in ways that can resolve the many conflictual issues currently confronting us?

These are the existential questions whose brooding presence is central to defining the future of humanity.

We are each born into a world within a set of circumstances usually including a nexus of familial and social relationships. For most this includes at least one active parent and some close and perhaps some extended family, beyond these to childhood friends and neighbours. As we grow, links of varying emotional strengths are made with teachers, work colleagues, adult friends, and more intimate partners. Across these thread a complex mesh of more instrumental interactions with numerous unnamed others whose lives interact with our own, mostly but briefly.

In spatial terms we are aware of a home, a locality, perhaps a village, town, or city, and these within a region, a country; as we grow we gain a wider sense of an awareness of being in a global world. Then later we might learn about our world being but a planet within a solar system, and this drifting languidly within one of the billions of faces. Many people chose to adopt a perspective that accepts their death but they then invoke the idea of a god to offer the hope of some form of life beyond death. To assume a truth in some more formal religious structure that allows a level of cognitive resolution to the more emotional idea of personal death.

The founding 'fathers' of religions set out certain practises required by believers for them to gain access to a life beyond death. Throughout civil life these have included various forms of supplication, a commitment based on faith-related ideas proposed by men (if these claim to mediate a god's commands – collected in various holy texts), and for some of them: animal or human sacrifice, self-flagellation, child abuse both physical (medically unnecessary male circumcision, female genital mutilation[1]) and psychological, as when a child is saturated in a single religion throughout childhood, so attempting to deny a child the freedom to consider all religious and non-religious metaphysical perspectives. And for a belief in miraculous occurrences usually happening in a distant past and not authentically repeated since, set in circumstances that deny the laws of nature as we have come to know them.

My own socialization was but one form of the many possible social contexts within which children gain early experience of the world. Seeping steadily into my consciousness as I grew towards adulthood was the realization that many people living elsewhere in the world were suffering at the hands of others, or due to economic circumstances created by others.

I could daily: on T.V., the radio, in newspapers and in recent years the internet, learn of evil being expressed all across the world and yet the all knowing, all powerful, all good, god that I had been taught to believe cared deeply for 'his' followers was silent. An enigmatic

---

[1] And for some females the experience of even more barbaric forms of circumcision than practiced on male babies, such as the practice of sewing up a woman's labia majora to leave an opening just wide enough to urinate through but making penetrative sex impossible.

shadowy figure that has from the earliest historical times been cast across much of the civilized world, taking various now codified forms as its assumed presence has mesmerised the faithful. The followers of this or that religion who so often believe that they – whether Christian, Jew, Moslem, Hindu, Buddhist, whatever - have had the amazing good fortune to have been born and socialised into knowledge of the one 'true' religion. And have not simply been the victims of a form of emotional abuse inflicted upon them by their parents and a local community. If the leaders of the world religions were to be sufficiently confident in their god's authenticity why do they determinedly refuse to allow children to grow up free from the relentlessly constraining propaganda of just one religion, and not allow them to experience a wide range of metaphysical beliefs (including agnosticism and atheism)? And so for them to be 'drawn to' a belief rather than, in effect, have one imposed on them by the arbitrary circumstances of birth and the insidiously powerful influence of socialization?

If faith is so strong, why I wonder have so many 20th and 21st century leaders of religions - the Popes, Bishops, Rabbis, Mullahs, Imams, Patriarchs, Ayatollahs, Swamis, Shamans, and various other types of 'cleric' - who have often gained high social status and comfortable material lives from their religious roles - when coming to their natural end, allow the determined deployment of expensive medical technology as they so embarrassingly cling tenaciously to life. When we might expect that they would embrace their passing with open arms and bright eyes willingly looking beyond the earthly travails as they accept their 'god-given' natural mortality and pass into the form of heavenly terrain (for some peopled with accommodating virgins for others a land flowing with milk and honey,....) that they have reassured so many others would be the glorious fate awaiting a true believer.

Would so many young men have marched to war without some expectation of the afterlife that they had from early childhood been assured would be their fate if they were killed? A supposed afterlife it seems that so many religious leaders try to avoid for as long as possible. Would so many have throughout history accepted gross economic and social inequality if they were not socialized to accepting these conditions as the will of some or other god?

As a teenager I would sometime gaze out to sea or across some heath- or down- land focused on the why of my existence.... why am I here and why am I here at this time and not before or in a time to come: Why did I not experience existence huddled in some prehistoric cave, or seated in some Greek forum listening to Socrates, or in the shelter of a Bodhi tree absorbing the wisdom of Siddhartha Gautama, or hearing the swish of the whip as I crouch over the oars in a Roman galley, toiling in some medieval field, herding goats in the Gobi Desert in the tenth century or making porcelain in some Chinese pottery at about the same time, crossing the Atlantic on the 'middle passage' as a prisoner wrenched from my west African tribal homeland soon to be sold as a slave in some West India market-place to face a future of relentless toil, or picking hemp in some nineteenth-century English work-house or, or, or.... the millions of other circumstances in which young men have found themselves since civil life began. Why now? Why here? Why not at some other time and place did I not experience the unique conjunction of individual awareness cast loose within a lived experience of the world rather than the one that I felt was laid-out before me.

When a child why was I merely due to an accident of birth-place able to live in relative comfort, whereas millions of other children were being denied even the basic requirements for reasonable lives. Yes, obviously historical circumstances have provided the relatively comfortable economic conditions for 20th/21st century Britain. Even if these were to some extent the outcome of the exploitation of peoples living within the British Empire and countries where British political and economic hegemony produced conditions of asymmetric power in trade. Famously so with the African slave trade and with China in the nineteenth-century Opium Wars.

But these are post-birth considerations whereas my focus here is on the randomness of when and where we were actually born; the time and place that we 'find ourselves' in life. The writer Blaize Pascal highlighted the uniqueness of being human and alive with his asking '....there is no reason why here rather than there, why now rather than then......The eternal silence of these infinite spaces frightens me.' (cited in Theodosius Dobzhansky, 1976, p.346)

I feel more in awe than frightened at this uniqueness and its possible implications. Just thinking about the earthly why 'here' rather than 'there' leads me to reflect on my own safe, secure, upbringing within a supportive South-London working class community, compared those born into poverty, economic exploitation, or within a zone of military conflict; communities in turmoil, and in otherwise unsafe locations.

I suspect that all of us have at times in our lives glimpsed aspects of a path towards a different alignment between the world and the lives within which we have found ourselves. Towards the end of this book I seek only to elaborate on this. This reflective exercise would not involve a personal journey from a-to-b, in the sense of seeking to take the reader from some assumed state of ignorance towards some ultimate state of Enlightenment. It is instead a form of journeying designed to stimulate a self-reflective transformation of one's approach to life. Hopefully, as a process of self-affirmation wedded to the commitment to a possible future for humankind more generally. A future we have all surely considered if but in a dream, now understood as a necessary condition for the survival of future generations if they are to avoid a future involving slavery to depersonalized identities that seems to be facing us – with the relentless advance of the stilted being of consumerism, of but instrumental relationships, and a pattern of continuously recursive self-reference; and that's only if we can avoid a thermo-nuclear holocaust and the impending environmental catastrophe facing the world.

As a more empirical framework to my endeavouring to understand the evil that threatens our existence, I am going to posit two key 'facts' about the Reality within which we all live; within which all of our life-journeys - lived reflectively or unreflectively - unfold. The first is that a process we know as evolution has led to humankind becoming aware of its presence on Earth (and increasingly during the last 3000 years, as a presence in a Universe), the product of reflective self-consciousness attuned to learning as a bio-cultural adaptation. This evolutionary process can be understood as being essentially the development of levels (or modes) of consciousness; of biological processes that gave rise to organisms able to process evermore 'information'. And here we have the second key fact – since life on Earth began the sum total of information available (especially as more formal knowledge) to be accessed by consciousness has increased significantly, and the rate of its accumulation is now exponential.

The outcome of the complex interrelationship between rising levels of consciousness and increasing amounts of information has been the progressive widening of the Reality within which we humans live – Reality being that aspect of Being that we can potentially access. We live within what can be termed an 'ecology of information' – a situation at least partially expressed in the vast store of texts that have been past down to us and in the huge data-bases now available; with programmers able to design algorithms that can nimbly identify significant patterns and processes within this vast store.

The question of evil touched on earlier, presumes the presence of human beings and this in turn invites the underlying question of what it means to be human. In order to gain some understanding of the human condition – this strange entity we know in some reflective consideration of ourselves, of what we observe in others, and of what we have learnt about our ancestors – it would be useful to consider the human in the context of its evolution. Biology is the study of life and, as the renowned geneticist Theodosius Dobzhansky suggested, everything in biology makes sense in terms of evolution. If this is perhaps an over confident generalization the sciences, especially those of geology, zoology, palaeontology and genetics, have provided an accumulating body of knowledge offering convincing evidential substance to the initial work of those such as Gregor Mendel, Charles Darwin, and Alfred Russell Wallace. Allowing some confidence in a meta-theory suggesting that human life has evolved from an initial conjunction of molecular complexity and environmental conditions that pertained on Earth about 3.8 billion years ago.

And, as a result of the characteristics of organic molecules developing, initially via energetic self-replicating molecular change (liable to tiny replication errors) become more clearly genetic transmission, along with changing environmental conditions, have generated the appearance of a wide range of types of organic life-forms. Forms, as both plant and animal life, that have spread throughout the world's oceans and across its landmasses. I will be considering the bio-mechanisms providing the dynamic for the evolutionary process in more detail in the concluding chapter but here I just want to highlight an aspect of evolution that relates to my own perspective on an implication of evolution as this links to the human condition and so to the question of why evil.

As already noted (Dyer, 2021), I want to suggest that the primary direction of evolution – its most creative aspect – has been the appearance of life-forms able to process ever-increasing amounts of information. And this 'amounts' is in terms of both quantitative and qualitative information, so in detail and in complexity. My own understanding of information is that it provides the fabric of the Reality within which all life exists – a non-material (non-baryonic) substance that pervades the whole Universe. Information can be understood as that which arises from the resolution of uncertainty in experience – but I would suggest that the uncertainty here is just the level of 'difference'. Where there is difference within some stimuli there is information. Most obviously with differences such as the arithmetical 1,2,3, or the coding language of computing 0100111, or with an atom of carbon losing an electron to a neighbouring atom of oxygen a 'difference' takes place. Our DNA contains masses of information as does an image of a flag, a tree, or the 'dance' of a bumblebee identifying the location of a food source. If you can imagine nothingness then the stuff of information would be its very opposite in terms of semantic content.

Similar to energy, mass, and space-time, information is another primary entity involved in the fundamental expression of the Universe – information is best understood as having energy but no mass (similar to photons), its energy being observed in action because its energy is context-dependent. What is ostensibly the same information can energize different reactions in different situations. (see Appendix 2 below for more detail on information)

Enigmatically, information is not necessarily out there waiting to be discovered as life-forms develop into new species. A useful perspective can be gained from viewing information as being both out there waiting to be discovered and also as being created as new knowledge accumulates – Reality, as we can know it, is an outcome of the interweaving of both discovery and creativity. At the start of this last sentence I noted 'useful' – a word that gets to the very nub of this text. I eschew any idea of some ultimate truths about the world – science at its best allows some level of confidence in how it describes and explains our experience and the best of philosophy can offer guidance in relation to personal morality and ethics more generally; as to a limited extent can religion (the limitation here being the veracity of the claimed source of wisdom). But truths, however informed (if this 'informed' can be critically important), are human constructions and as such can only be provisional, being based on knowledge available at any time. In recognition of the ontological conditionality of truths I more often use the term 'useful', which implies a sense of purpose. My own purpose, as noted above, being to gain some understanding of the human condition primarily as this relates to the expression of evil in humankind's history. I will translate useful into heuristic devices, and other linguistic tools, designed to provide the conceptual implements posited to enable understanding; so truths framed as being more instrumental conditions used to support the validity of my extended outline.

The conceptual implements, identified as 'modes' of evolutionary developmental stages, that I use to describe my own focus on developing consciousness, as the condition for information processing, are quite crude – those such as: instinct, sentience, consciousness, awareness, self-consciousness, world consciousness.

The boundary (as this relates to information processing capacity) between each of these is vague, and more about how behaviours are subjectively defined than anything more precise. The neuro-philosophers Patricia and Paul Churchland (1986 – and more recently Edouard Machery 2008) are particularly critical about the use of what they term traditional 'folk language' (commonsensical) to describe states of thinking and the description of mental states. Their views, noted as a form of 'eliminative materialism', include the suggestion that '…..future scientific developments will show that the way we think and talk about the mind is fundamentally flawed.' They argue the need to focus on observable brain processes, and they advocate a more informed set of descriptive/explanatory discriminations, to move beyond the: '….primitive psychological taxonomy of current ordinary language, to some more penetrating and extraordinarily more fertile taxonomy of states drawn from that more advanced neuro-functional account of our brain activity.'

For my own central purpose I do feel that the use of 'folk' concepts, such as sentience, awareness, and self-consciousness, even given their conceptual fuzziness, would be sufficient to understand the theory outlined. The fuzziness only really becomes apparent at the boundaries between my information processing modes and their associated behaviours, which are:

- response - instinctual/or closely pre-programmed behaviours – e.g. bacteria, plants, sponges
- sentience as guiding more mobile activity - moving around an environment seeking food or favourable conditions – e.g. beetles, flies, as well as starfish, and primitive fish.
- awareness - a more developed mode of mobile activity – where behaviour patterns become more complex – e.g. higher fish, lizards, amphibians.
- a level of conscious awareness with more developed sentience but continuing to be focused on quite local habitats, accepting migration, e.g. grazing and hunting terrestrial animals such as cattle, jaguars, rats, hyenas, bears - as well as birds.

- a more developed form of consciousness observed in a wide range of behaviours where some elements of planning and interactive social activities, up to more complex forms of vocal and physical communication, are exhibited e.g. whales, other cetaceans, and some early evolved primates such as lemurs, loris and tarsiers.
- self consciousness – present at a more basic level in chimpanzees, gorillas, orang-utan, baboon, and bonobos, but most obviously in Homo sapiens and some extinct species of the genus Homo, including habilis, rudolfernsis, floresiensis, neaderthalensis, denisovans, and erectus.

This last mode of self-consciousness as it developed, in behavioural terms, with its most advance species (Homo sapiens) has been the conduit by which evil has primarily found expression in the world, and my purpose is to endeavour to identify aspects of self-consciousness that have led to this.

Another, more quantitative, way of illustrating this evolutionary progression would be based on the fairly valid assumption that consciousness is more developed in animals with bigger brains (in terms of neuron numbers and network complexity). I am not considering consciousness within any species only identifying a reasonable 'marker' of how the consciousness exhibited by sentient beings has evolved. So, with this reservation see the list below starting with organisms evolving from the time known as the Cambrian Explosion (from about 550 m.y.b.p.) when life began to become more complex:

- Roundworm   –   302 neurons   550 m.y.b.p.
- Cockroach   –   1,000,000   320 m.y.b.p.
- Frog   –   16,000,000   200 m.y.b.p.
- Racoon   –   2,149,000,000   135 m.y.b.p.
- Brown Bear   –   9,586,000,000   30 m.y.b.p.
- Fin Whale   -   15,000,000,000   25 m.y.b.p.
- Chimpanzee   –   28,000,000,000   18 m.y.b.p.
- Homo Sapien –   86,000,000,000   150,000 y.b.p. (modern form from about 50,000 y.b.p)

Although quite crude as a measure the order of this list does, if roughly, correlate neuron numbers with the time of the appearance of these life-forms. Of more relevance is the information-processing capacity of each type of life-form and this can be assessed by the study of the complexity (range) of an animal's behaviour.

Accepting reservations in relation to the relevance of neural interconnectedness and whole body involvement in consciousness, I suggest that if it were possible to identify the sequential line of species leading from the Last Universal Common Ancestor (LUCA - of about 3.8 b.y.b.p., possibly even earlier) of all cellular life to modern Homo sapiens and the relationship between neuron numbers and time of species appearance, then the progressive nature of evolution (in terms of information processing power) would become quite obvious. Neuronal numbers and their patterns of interconnectedness is a robust indicator of information processing capacity and we can see that this capacity has evolved in stages (modes) over time.

This list above takes us to the human mode of 'self-consciousness' but I also want to posit another biological stage of information processing, that which I would very loosely term 'world-consciousness'. A mode where, if human life is to continue, then certain behaviours, linked to novel ways of processing information, will be necessary. Each information-processing mode incorporates behaviour patterns of the prior mode and will have species at the upper end of its mode's information-processing capacity that show elements of the next higher mode.

Even given the relative imprecision of these modes, and the generality of the examples I have included to allow some idea of the information processing capacity relevant for each, I think the reader should be able to see that there has been a steady development in the information-processing capacity of life-forms on earth. And that it is possible to loosely identify various stages (I note as modes) along the way. In themselves the stages are less relevant than the proposition that information-processing has been the dynamic for evolutionary development itself; which is of fundamental importance.

If biological evolution has been (and continues to be) the appearance of species so adapted to be able to process evermore information then obviously the modern form of the species Homo sapiens is in the vanguard of this development. An anatomically modern form of which appeared about 50,000 y.b.p., initially living in small-groups (bands) sustained by hunter-forager-gatherer types of lifestyle and progressively developing into what is termed civilization, with the social and economic practices and institutions necessary to support this. Nearly four billion years to progress from some relatively simple self-replicating molecules perhaps forming in some alkaline hydrothermal vents deep within the sea to the phenomenon that is twentieth-first century civilization.

It is the mode of consciousness I note as 'self-consciousness' that has given rise to civil life and with it the most awful expressions of evil.

As I grew up I became uneasily aware of the evil that has pervaded (indeed at times actually characterised) humankind's history from the earliest time of civil life. Yes, no doubt there was inter-group conflict prior to the development of towns and cities, but it was civil life and associated technologies that elevated localised conflict into wide-ranging warfare.

What do I mean by evil? A working definition would be 'any act that causes unnecessary harm to a human-being'. So the types of harms that could have been avoided if different conditions had pertained; importantly including decisions being made that contributed to forming the conditions. I feel that I should add harm to any animal or other aspects of the living environment but do not want to get distracted, so my focus is on humanity. I want to suggest that we should view evil as acts, not as some essence residing within individuals - a key consideration. This perspective would not absolve individuals for their part in an evil act, but it does prompt the consideration of a wider context involving the social conditions in which the expression of evil is more rather than less likely to occur. And in this sense, offers the grounds for understanding in relation to causation beyond this or that individual or group and so offering the grounds for a more realistic strategy for its possible alleviation.

Let's not get entangled in some over-abstracted philosophical debate, on the meaning of unnecessary, or what constitutes harm. I mean an act that causes harm when there is a clear alternative course of action (including inaction). Just think about any act that could cause harm for or your family that 'could have been avoided' whether this is a drunken motorist, a polluted atmosphere, or a thermonuclear explosion, all realistic threats in today's world. But 'could have been avoided' would also apply to famines, and the various types of natural disasters to which some people – usually the poor - are more vulnerable than others.

Identifying the conditions of could have been avoided for each particular expression of evil is a profound challenge to humanity. The question of could have been avoided links to the political and economic conditions that set the circumstances within which significant harms are liable to take place. Consequently, would it be possible to reform the current national and international economic and political systems, so that these are designed to eliminate the worst expression of evil – the massacres, ethnic cleansing, mass rape, gross economic exploitation, all forms of modern-day slavery, the 5/6 million displaced people living in refugee camps, the millions of children living in poverty, the homeless children endeavouring to survive on the street, the thousands dying in famines due more about access to markets rather than food shortages .... etc. etc. I want to leave this matter for the final chapter of this essay.

I suggest four obvious sources of evil in today's world, each of which threatens the future of humankind:

- Environmental degradation.
- Artificial Intelligence – who controls it and its potentially dramatic implications.
- Gross economic inequality – especially in relation to poverty
- Conflict – various forms of warfare.

Whilst these are interrelated, I will be primarily focusing on 'warfare', not least due to my view that if we can tentatively begin to design the international conditions conducive for ending warfare and reducing all forms of intergroup conflict to a minimum, then the political and economic conditions necessary for this will impact positively on our ability to focus on alleviating the other three threats.

In order to consider warfare I will need to go to a very dark place. The dark place is encapsulated in the very concept of 'war' – the basis of harms between and within nation-states. By my own broad definition the latter would also include within nation ethnic cleansing, which can hardly be termed civil war in the conventional sense as only one side is usually an immediate aggressor, excepting that the one side aggressor can also be an aspect of war involving nation-states when one invades another – The US-led alliance invading Afghanistan (2001) and Iraq in 2002(3) or the Iraq invasion of Iran (1980-88) and Kuwait (1990), or the Russian invasion of Afghanistan (1979-89) and Ukraine (2022) – just to note some more recent examples – if historically, few countries have not invaded another (usually a neighbouring) country.

I will now offer an overview of evil in human history primarily as expressed in conflict. This in order to provide an evolutionary become historical context to better enable the consideration of ways in which the expression of evil can be significantly reduced, or even if possible eradicated.

Chapter 1 'Prehistory to Civil Life: the origins of human conflict'

War is a concept that does not need to be precisely defined – we can just note it as a violent form of human activity undertaken by one group, or a coalition of groups, against another group, or coalition of groups (in modern terms a group being a state or a nation or a religious or otherwise ethnic-based collective). The word 'against' expresses the conflictual nature of this type of behaviour. A voluntary activity involving conflict and one that usually causes quite significant harm. In modern terms we can also distinguish between conflict both between and within nation-states (as in civil conflicts).

If you consider the most terrible harms that human-beings can do to each other – man, woman, child, baby - then this has been perpetuated time and time and time.......again. Any type of injury – shooting, stabbing, burning, strangling, disembowelling, skinning, drawing and quartering, torture, deliberately starved to death, deliberately infected with disease, rape, beheading, crushing, drowning, burying alive, poisoning by chemicals or gas, being blown into bits or burnt to cinders by the impact of nuclear or conventional explosives delivered by cannon, missile, or aeroplane ..... indeed, if you can think of any action by which one human-being can kill another human-being it has probably been carried out in conflict.

As already noted, humankind is a species of life that first evolved from about 150,000 y.b.p., taking its modern anatomical form from about 50,000 y.b.p. A species having progressively evolved from earlier species of primates that had in turn evolved from earlier forms of mammal that in turn had evolved from earlier species of amphibians.....and so on, and so on, far back to some single-celled organism that first developed on Earth about 3.8 billion years ago. A progressive density of evolution with anatomical and behavioural differences allowing classification into individual 'species', even accepting that there is grounds to consider an underling unity to all life at a primary biological level.

It was from about the time of the demise of the large dinosaurs circa 65 million years ago that a type of creature emerged to provide the immediate ancestor of all later primates. These, the 'prosimians', spread throughout tropical forests that flourished in regions with warm, moist, climates – the fossil record contains 28 species from Europe and 41 species from North America.

Prosimia are classified as a sub-order of the primate order – one of what are today 29 orders of mammals, including: Rodentia (squirrels, rats, beavers, voles), Carnivora (bear, dog, cat), Perissodactyla (horses, donkey, zebra, rhinoceros), Cetacea (whale, dolphin) – The earliest primates (the prosimians) were rodent-sized, tree-living, insectivorous creatures and, although these early primates became extinct, their evolutionary species legacy is categorized within three sub-order categories of Prosimia, Tarsoidea, and Anthropoidea. And it is types of creatures from the latter group that would evolve into modern species of monkey, apes, and the one species of human-beings – Homo sapien - surviving from the approximately fourteen species of Homo that have lived on Earth from about 2 million years ago.

From the Miocene period (23.3 – 5.3 m.y.b.p) the remains of 'ape-like' but hominid creatures become relativity common; fossil evidence from approximately 500 individuals is available to study. Although most of these remains are limited to teeth and parts of jaws and skulls these are some of the most useful body-parts by which to assess primate relationships and stages of development.

There are few signs of wounds caused by conflict on these skeletons, but given what we know of other Anthropoidea species, such as: Chimpanzee (our genetically nearest living relative), Bonobo[2], Orang-utan, Baboon, and Gorilla, some level of conflict was

---

[2] It is fairly widely accepted that Bonobos are the least aggressive species amongst these, more often engaging in quite promiscuous sexual intimacy as a displacement

quite likely to have been an integral aspect of early homo's behavioural repertoire. But within small hunter-gatherer-forager primate groups most conflict would probably have been over access to available food sources and to females which, if there were a sufficiency of each then we might assume more threats than actual fights. Even when resources were limited, threat and submission or brief engagements would be more common than fights to the death. Afterall, small groups of 10-50 individuals would have relied on each other for social interaction and for defending territory from other groups; with fatality to prominent members being potentially costly to each competing group.

Anthropological evidence of tribal life suggests that this rather benign assessment of prehistoric group relations might significantly underplay just how aggressive tribal peoples can be. Studies of groups such as the Yanomamo in Amazonia, [3]the Dani in the highlands of New Guinea, the harsh treatment of Bushmen (including Pygmy and !Kung) by neighbouring tribes in Southern Africa, and the traditional raiding for cattle, women, and slaves, and similar with intertribal conflict between Aboriginal groups in Australia, throughout the Americas, and the quite extreme violence of South Sea Islanders. Clearly, wherever in the world tribal groups have been studied we have evidence of conflict. We cannot of course assume that prehistoric groups and 19th/20th century tribal conflicts can be easily compared. But, given similar environment and social conditions for tribal-based groups between these two periods the balance of evidence, - from both anthropology and ethnology – and what we do understand as human nature, is persuasive of some types of conflict being a common characteristic of humankind since the species first evolved.

I think that from the earliest time of its evolution, we can at least

---

activity when managing conflict.

[3] For the anthropologist Napoleon Chagnon (2013, p275) his extensive1988 study of the Yanomamo suggests that: 'Approximately 45 per cent of all the living adult males in my study were unokais, that is had participated [directly] in at least one killing.' A statistic that for Chagnon '...might not be unusual among pre-contact tribesmen'.

conclude that human groups would have exhibited a 'tendency' for violent behaviour directed towards members of their own species – with 'tendency' suggesting, as we also know, that violence is not inevitable. But that certain forms of social, cultural, and subsistence, conditions need to prevail for the tendency to be expressed or indeed inhibited.

For prehistoric groups, within-group conflict was probably also common but would, at least for some groups, have been contained with threats, shunning, and minimal actual physical violence within an assumed social hierarchy. Although ethnographic evidence from studies of similar sized hunter-gather-forager tribal groups surviving into the 19th and 20th centuries does suggest that any individual causing disruption within a group could be swiftly and permanently dealt with perhaps by expulsion, but also by being killed.

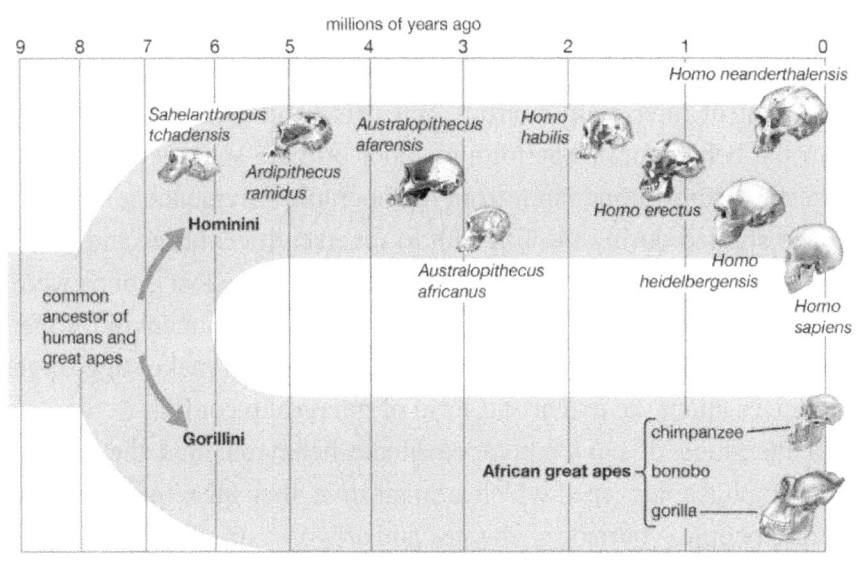

Species of the genus Homo were able to extend their behavioural repertoire in a significant way when some of these began to develop the imaginative (cognitive) sense and the eye-hand co-ordination skills to enable tool-making. The earliest stone tools are associated with Homo habilis from about 2 m.y.b.p. And during the long period of prehistory when small bands of humans lived various types of hunter-gatherer-forager lifestyles it is difficult to definitively identify if such implements as spears, flint arrow heads, stone or flint hand-axes, bolas, and similar advancing stone-age tools were used for hunting or for conflict. I would assume that each could and would have been engaged in depending on the setting.

A primary feature of primate group living is of a fairly loosely circumscribed territory over which a group gains its subsistence and it would have been when members of one group trespassed on the assumed territory of another that the more destructive forms of inter-group conflict would have ensued. There would have been a lack of specific territorial boundaries, but each group would have had quite a clear idea of its own territory. As well as trespass in order to gain access to food or water sources there would also at times have been raiding parties seeking females. Given species breeding priority, women would have been an on-going valued resource for these groups. We cannot know from direct evidence the reasons for, or even the extent of intergroup conflict. But it is valid to make inferences from the behavioural repertoire of other primate species genetically closest to humankind and from ethnographic evidence of native groups studied during the fifteenth to nineteenth centuries and those surviving into the twentieth century. Although these last groups were studied 10,000 years on from the time of Neolithic humankind, so an extended period for cultural enrichment, we can still make suggestive inferences about the extent and form of intergroup conflict. [4]

If the study of contemporary primate behaviour and the human ethnographic evidence of which is suggestive, then the remains of pre-historic people – burials, skeletons, and artworks do offer some more direct information.

One of the earliest more substantial pieces of evidence of conflict is

---

[4] A level of caution is necessary when making assumptions about a range of activities undertaken by groups of Homo sapien during the time we define as prehistoric – see especial Graeber and Wengrow, 2021 for a less conventional interpretation of this time.

of the Homo species Homo neanderthal, with the skeleton of a young man who met a violent end about 36,000 y.b.p. He must have been a member of one of the very few groups still surviving in Europe at that time. It was very soon after this that the Neanderthals became extinct as a species; if the presence of Neanderthal genes in human-beings does indicate at least some interbreeding with modern humans. The Neanderthals (along with Homo denisovans[5]) seem to have been a successful Homo species occupying numerous sites in central and northern Europe and across Asia to the Far East from about 400,000 y.b.p. until their demise by about 35,000 y.b.p.

It has been generally agreed that the most significant radiation period of modern human-beings out of Africa began around 65,000 y.b.p. (if some pre-Homo sapien types had travelled to southern Asia perhaps as early as 150,000 y.b.p. and) and led to the Neanderthals (and Denisovans) being displaced and eventually wiped out. An outcome probably due to competition for territory with more aggressive Homo sapien competitors and to their living in smaller groups than the incomers. Their relatively low population density and some suggestive evidence of inbreeding making the species vulnerable.

During the early Prehistoric period there is a lack of hard evidence to confirm extensive violence between groups of humans, other that is, than the clearly suggestive demise of Homo groups such as the Neanderthals and the Denisovans, which indicates the possibility of their being unable to compete for resources when in competition with the more efficiently adapting Homo sapiens.

Included in early Homo toolkits were weapons suitable for hunting and also for intergroup violence. It seems that bows and arrows, as well as spears, could have being used 20,000 y.b.p in the area of the Fa Hien Cave in Sri Lanka, or even earlier in 48,000 y.b.p. in the area of the Sibudu Cave in South Africa. The evidence (bone arrow-heads)

---

[5] Home denisovan diverged from the Homo neanderthal and the Homo sapien line about 1,000,000 y.b.p surviving down to 50,000 y.b.p. - showing some genetic evidence of inter-breeding with Neanderthals.

of these being used for inter-group conflict rather than just hunting is arguable. But as we move into the period from about 30,000 y.b.p. we can see cave art possibly depicting human archers attacking each other – so we can from then acknowledge the clear development of weapons that allow the killing of human-beings at a distance. There is even more substantial evidence from Morella de Velos in Spain circa 10,000 y.b.p. with cave-art showing a scene of a fight also involving archers. Bodies excavated at Jebel Sahaba in northern Sudan (Nile Valley) circa 12,000 y.b.p, suggest conflict between peoples of two cultures. When people of the Natufians culture appear to have attacked people of the Qadan culture; 61 skeletons were unearthed with 38 of these showing indications of trauma, a significant number (16) of these being injured at the time they died – 21 individuals sustained injuries by pointed projectiles, either arrows or spears. At Nataruk, Turkana, in Kenya circa 10,000 y.b.p. the were the remains of 27 people showing evidence of violent deaths – clubbed or stabbed...two male skeletons had stone projectiles embedded in skulls. The 'Talheim Death Pit', southern Germany 7,000 y.b.p. contains 34 skeletons in a mass grave including 16 children, all of the skeletons had signs of significant trauma caused by clubs or sharp weapons, with two injured by arrows. There is also some native Australian rock art circa 10,000 y.b.p. depicting a violent scene.

Prehistoric conflict was an aspect of a behavioural repertoire shared by primate species (whether all species or only some groups within a species and only some types within each group is irrelevant here) but peaceful co-existence is also an aspect of primate group behavioural repertoire. Attempts to identify whether conflict is an outcome of human nature (humankind being inevitably evil) or the outcome of nurture (socialization), initially within small groups seems to be rather fruitless and indeed unnecessary to understand the conflict we see around us in today's world which is the primary aim of this book. But consideration of this early time does provide a genealogical context for what followed in humankind's history.

From what evidence we do have, the pre-historic small kin-based groupings (more 50-100 strong 'bands') would probably have settled disputes between individuals (perhaps in league with confederates) by confronting each other with threats and possible violence or with the whole group ganging up on individuals judged to have transgressed some or other normative expectation. This invariably leading to expulsion from the group or at least some violent punishment (either of which being a probable death sentence). It might be that pre-the Holocene (before circa. 11,700 y.b.p.) a home territory was not so significant due to more of it generally being available if a group is challenged by a more powerful neighbours. Fight if you are able, raid when opportunity allows, but if the very survival of a group is threatened then just 'up-sticks' and move on. 'Up-sticks' being appropriate as a group would have had comparatively few goods to carry – some clothes, a range of stone tools, no doubt some wooden, flint or stone weapons, and perhaps a few of the less-mobile elderly; and these bearing the store of a group's cultural history and mythic/religious beliefs. Cultural history and beliefs stored in the memories of the elderly, and the material goods being fairly easily carried or dragged in a travois.

This is obviously just a generalised explanation offered for evidence of Palaeolithic conflict. Using behaviour patterns observed in surviving primate species, Palaeolithic evidence, and what we have seen since early recorded history – we might also fairly assume that at times and in places some types of leaders (or an elite section within a group) might have used conflict to enhance their control over a group or to impose it on others. Or to engage in, or threaten, conflict to enhance an individual's social status and perhaps their control over more females. A form of ego (status) – enhancement sought through violence or the threat of it.

Given what followed when evolutionary development became civil history any Prehistoric and Paleolithic violence is of general interest rather than directly relevant to finding the means to bringing an end to today's, and to prevent future, wars. But there is fairly persuasive evidence that competition for valued resources was common throughout humankind's species development since Homo sapiens first emerged into the evolutionary story. And if from fairly minimal evidence of significant intergroup conflict pre-10,000 y.b.p. we can at least assume some level of within group and inter-group violence similar to our closest primate species – so lots of threatening behaviours, territorial trespassing for resources, some raiding for females and the occasional killing – and perhaps at times some more organized intergroup conflict.

Again, given the paucity of evidence, it is speculative to suggest that significant intergroup violence became more common from the time of humans moving to settled lifestyles based on agriculture and living in villages, some of these growing into towns and some of these becoming cities. But it does seem that intergroup violence (in terms of impact on populations) was ramped up during the Neolithic and in the first larger towns and in some cities there is evidence of defensive walls and watch-towers (e.g. Jericho circa 9,000 y.b.p.). It is the case that having the attention of an aggressor – seeking some valued resource – can have a devastating impact on the attacked group, hence placing a premium on defence.

Since it appeared as a presence on earth, humankind (the species Homo sapien) has progressed from various forms of prehistoric subsistence adaptation (hunter-gatherer-forager – with advancing types of stone-age technology) whilst living in small bands. Spreading to occupy habitable areas of the world, many such groups settled into more simple types of agricultural subsistence that in places developed into quite sophisticated, and highly productive, types of farming – and this especially for those settled in fertile river valleys including: Tiger/Euphrates (Middle East, 4,000 BCE), Nile (Egypt 4,000 BCE), Huang He (northern China 2,000 BCE), Indus River Valley (now covering parts of what is now northeast Afghanistan, Pakistan and northwest India circa 2,250 BCE), and a bit later close to fertile valleys of some large rivers of Meso-America (1500 BCE).

This progressive transition for some groups from hunter-gather-forager to forms of early civil life also witnessed an incremental change in the way in which humans settled conflict within and between groups.

By about 10,000 y.b.p the species had adapted in various ways, which by each group depending on a number of factors including habitat conditions, cultural influences and no doubt to some extent a tendency to favour certain lifestyles by leading group members. Broadly we can identify four primary adaptations: continuing as hunter-gatherer-forager, nomadic herdsman, pastoralist, and farmer. But of course there would have been a significant range of variations within each of these, and no doubt some groups moved between types of adaptation as habitat changes made this necessary or it became an option.

When we move into the time of civil life, and populations living in towns and cities, the surplus made possible by agriculture, trading, and at times no doubt by raiding and warring, provided the means to support a range of skilled and unskilled workers, craftspeople, and artists, as well as a priestly class/caste as administrators and religious leaders, weapon and tool- makers, all overseen by an elite composed of some of these and various types of 'royal' grouping. Early civil life not only created the surplus resources required for its own support it also provided a store of the valued goods to be so often competed for. Be these manufactured goods, fertile land, precious minerals and metals, women, or slaves. Setting out to gain the valued goods belonging to others could also enhance the status of a leader. The history of civilization suggests that the ambitions of leaders can be a powerful element in pursuing the activity of warfare. If also the prospects of a share in the spoils of warring can provide a clear incentive for the common soldier.

In addition, warring over valued goods could not only foster group cohesion, but the military capability necessary for making war, also provided the means to control disaffected populations.

Human beings are complicated in terms of biological become cultural adaptations (and so the generative intentionality they bring to any issue) and history tells us of certain groups (stereotypically..... Vikings, Mongols, Spartans, Zulus) for whom warring had become a primary cultural trope (so an important source of social status) – with material rewards being gained on earth and/or spiritual rewards being expected in an afterlife.

We can see with the Middle-Eastern large town of Jericho evidence of how early civil life was developing. The lowest levels of the Jericho site contains human materials dated as early as 8,350 BCE and amongst the slightly newer detritus has been found obsidian (volcanic 'black-glass') which provided one of the best cutting stones and must have been transported 700km from its source in Anatolia. There is evidence of trading (and perhaps exchanging presents or offering tributes between groups) even earlier, indeed at least some Kebaran peoples of the region traded in colourful sea-shells, and possibly also in salt. These types of shell were also found in the lowest Jericho levels.

Jericho by around 7,500 BCE was a town with a population of about 2,000 living in dwellings made partly of brick and partly of wattle and daub. The presence of a large ditch and an enclosing wall suggesting the need for defence against marauders. Apart from the wall and traces of a circular tower, no evidence has been found of communal buildings, whether for religious or civic purposes. But even these (wall and tower) would have required a significant level of co-operative commitment, with organized labour and sufficient food to support them during construction.

There was an early hiatus in the occupation of Jericho when, at about 7,300 BCE, the people deserted the town. Given that there is no clear evidence of destruction we might assume that it was caused by a risk element associated with reliance on agriculture and a semi-urban life. Perhaps a significant local change in climate, disease, or crop pest (such as locusts), occurring over a number of years would have been enough to persuade any surviving Jerichoans to move on.

After a break of about three centuries the Jericho site was re-occupied by a people who rebuilt with more robust and more ornate buildings, and with matting being used on floors. We have evidence of the domestication of goats conveniently providing, milk, meat, skins, and hair, being bred from more docile hybrids of wild species. Of interest from this time of occupation there are clear signs of reverence of the dead, skulls were removed from the skeletons and placed in 'shrines'. In some cases a plaster 'face' of the deceased was moulded onto the skull, and echoing the high value placed on shells earlier, these were placed in the plaster as eyes. One skull had a moustache painted on, which is apparently the earliest evidence of facial hair used for adornment. The evidence we do have suggests that Jericho was by far the largest 'village' (first town) amongst what must have been many farming villages scattered across the central area of the Middle-East and southern Turkey. We can also clearly see that at the community level humankind's social organization is now centred on 'tribal identity'.

There is a convincing body of evidence (cowry shells found a long way from their marine origins, distinctive types of pottery, metals from Anatolia etc.) of pre-civil and early-civil trading and/or gift-exchange over quite long distances. But the increase in the range of productive farming surpluses available to support crafts-people and traders made possible by civil life led to a significant increase in the variety of trade-goods and in the volume of trade. A developing network of primarily trading relationships are in place, both city to city and beyond the Middle-East region; at a minimum this encompasses fairly regular trading over wide-ranging geographic connections. Encompassing the vast Euro-Asian landmass, so taking in Egypt, northern Anatolia, the tip of the Arabian Peninsula, and the Indus valley.

These contacts also favoured the transmission of technological developments and ideas (including religious), to the promotion of genetic diversity as peoples intermix, and to conflict between peoples. Conflict caused by those pre-disposed to covet their neighbour's wealth, be it land, material possessions, women, or to gain slaves. One might wistfully hope that some interactions took the form of co-operative activities. Ones not simply of two or more groups forming alliances to attack another group, but perhaps co-operative arrangements to engage in mutually beneficial activities, such as large-scale irrigation or construction projects.

Across the more fertile areas, beside rivers, larger oasis, or on hillsides favoured with a sufficient amount of sunshine and rainfall (warmth and precipitation), the development of agriculture continues. This area of the Middle-East was increasingly, down towards 5000 BCE, a productive land, with growing populations made up of interacting peoples. With some out-group breeding and cultural intermixing that would have helped to stimulate the human mind to further cultural enrichment and technical advance. In the 5,000 years between 8,000 BCE and 3,000 BCE the world population grew from 5 to 14 million people.

By about 3000 BCE there is evidence of more serious inter-city conflict, usually involving disagreement over boundaries; with depictions of chariots engaged in a pitched battle between these and helmeted, spear carrying, troops; dated 2,600 BCE

Uruk, the Sumerian name for the city that the Warka phase is named after can be taken as a typical. By 3,000 BCE Uruk covered 600 acres and was protected by a wall six miles round, containing a population of possibly up to 40,000. The central focus here is on a number of large buildings most (if not all) being temples dedicated to a pantheon of the City's gods, with these being surrounded by residential districts. Districts being initially loosely arranged according to trade (tribe- and/or caste-based) specialization that included smiths, carpenters, potters, boat-builders, workers in reed and textiles, masons, seal engravers, sculptors and other artists. The sculptors being responsible for high quality statues and the artists being responsible for the ornate wall decoration which became known as cone mosaics. The seal engravers made seals with images which, when pressed into soft clay, would make a permanent mark that might have recorded parties to an agreement, or perhaps represented a religious motif. These early cylindrical seals bore many of the signs and symbols that were to develop into the pictograms of early writing. Along with the crafts, we could fairly infer the presence of many traders, fortune tellers, medical 'advisers', and perhaps prostitutes, soldiers-of-fortune, thieves, and others drawn to the growing City, all adding to the rich cultural and genetic mix from which cities were to develop into even more socially complex civilizations.

Overseeing these early cities were the 'priests' that administered a city (assumed to be on behalf of the gods), managing the storage and distribution of the substantial surplus of the farmers; those whose agricultural activities made all of the rest possible. Able-bodied men from most social groups would be required to give up some time of their working year to work on community projects, including constructing religious buildings, bridges, and maintaining or expanding irrigation networks. On the site of Uruk were found a mass-produced type of vessel, the 'bell-pot', which is considered to have served to contain rations handed out to those working on community projects. From the evidence available it appears that life at Uruk over the 500 years down to about 3,000 BCE was relatively peaceful. Although there does seem to have been some, at least low-level, inter-city conflict during this time.

Early on the Mesopotamian cities had the land available to expand their agricultural areas, and seem generally to have achieved a certain level of peaceful co-existence, with growing networks of trade between regions beyond Sumer. William H. McNeill (1963 p68) noted that: 'Even in the fourth millennium B.C., ships from the land of Sumer sailed through the Persian Gulf to Arabia and into the Red Sea, thus making contact with the ancient Egyptians.'

There is no direct evidence of contact with the Indus civilization (where Harrapan civil life was organized from circa 3,300 BCE) but it seems that suitable ships and sailing skills were available to make the journey east possible.

Having to manage agricultural surpluses, the division of land, sharing water resources, predictions of seasonal changes, and similar types of 'measurement' (quantification) presented the mostly priestly administrators with problems. Ones which increased almost year on year as the amounts needing to be collected and distributed increased. As was often the case in humankind's history problems stimulate solutions, and those found were to have a history-long impact on the future of humankind, on its collective ability to process 'information'.

For some considerable time various images and other marks had been 'scratched' onto pottery-ware. Indeed, from as early as 20,000 y.b.p. we have evidence of marks being scratched onto various clay and stone objects. It was a socially evolutionary rather than a revolutionary step from the marking of pottery to keeping 'tallies' by means of marks made in soft clay tablets that could be preserved as they dried and hardened. From early in city life 'symbols' were used to refer e.g. standing for something such as a sheaf of wheat or a cow, or their owner, or measures of their lands i.e. llll (or other symbols) for four sheaves of corn, four cows, etc. Gordon Childe (1942) notes specific uses of seals from Ubaid culture: the outline of a certain size of jug = a given measure - the same outline with two diagonal lines across it = a measure of barley - the same jug with three diagonal lines across it = a measure of beer, and so on.

A technique possibly serving as an intermediate step between designs on pottery and writing upon clay tablets was the use of seals with relief symbols on them. Seals would, when pressed into soft clay, leave the associated sign such as the mark of an individual to 'seal' a transaction or a promise. An abstract sign pointing beyond itself to a concept, this 'mark' refers to that 'object', a profound step in communication and in humankind's ability to preserve, and subsequently to create, information. Looking at the inventory of occupational groups living in Uruk we can see that of seal-maker being included; such was their importance to early city life.

In order to gain a more coherent understanding of the beginning of writing, numeracy, and proto-science, I will range over the period from 3,500 to 2,500 BCE. This means overlapping the time when the first more obvious civilizations began circa 3,000 BCE, a more general development to be returned to. The activity of farming was the underlying stimulus for both technical innovation (including ox-harness for ploughing, irrigation systems, building techniques, etc.) and the finding of ways to calculate and measure the produce of agriculture and stockbreeding as well as the land this production was based on.

This basic economic condition indirectly stimulated human imagination into ambitious building projects, and again, as a consequence, to improve knowledge of the strengths and potential uses of various materials; the weight that different types of supports could bear, the stresses managed by various architectural forms, etc. Buildings pushed up towards the sky. Notably the ziggurats from the top of which the movements and patterns of the celestial bodies could be studied. The importance of celestial bodies was enhanced with more regular notice being taken of their movements, relative brightness, the seasonal patterns being formed, and of novelties such as 'shooting stars' (meteorites burning up as they enter the Earth's atmosphere). Quite early in civil life the movements of certain celestial bodies could be seen to correspond to the seasonal changes so important for a farming community.

Out of a whole range of symbols inscribed on seals came the early pictographic script, which began to be scratched onto clay tablets freehand, rather than impressed by seals. This early (proto-writing) developed during the latter part of the Uruk stage ('Uruk' represents a culture as well as an individual city), from about 3,000 BCE. Three main linguistic groups were present - Japhetites, Semites, and Sumerians - but it was a broadly Sumerian language that was to emerge as the dominant written form. The first tablets were marked with both pictograms (abbreviated representations of pictures) and with the numerals used to calculate and record accounting information. Early pictographic scripts could expand their range of application in two main ways. They could become ideographic with a particular 'symbol' representing an object, activity, or idea in the world, a process requiring the continuous generation of new symbols. A form of script that would reach its fullest development in China. The alternative, and the one taken by the Sumerian script (a fundamental 'choice' for subsequent intellectual and scientific development/progress in the 'West'), was the use of single words (many of which had only one syllable in Sumerian) used to represent spoken sounds. A basic range of these 'phonograms' could, in different arrangements (potentially unlimited), be joined together to represent a multiplicity of objects, ideas, or activities.

It was now possible to represent conceptual information by combining sounds into compound (more than one syllable) words. Taking this route quickly improved the linguistic efficiency of the developing Sumerian script. At circa 3,200 BCE there is evidence of approx 2000 individual 'signs' in use, by 3,000 BCE it is down to 800 and by 2,500 BCE, when the Sumerian script becomes fully intelligible to scholars, it is reduced to a relatively efficient 600.

From about 2,500 BCE towards the end of the period of the primacy of Sumerian culture, instead of writing by employing the technique of signs scratched (traced) onto clay tablets, 'writing' was impressed onto the tablets by use of a reed stylus with a wedge-shaped tip. Mesopotamian writing from this time being known as 'cuneiform' (wedge-shaped). The reduction in the number of symbols continued throughout most of the subsequent period of the script's use.

Contemporary with the development of a written script, the demands of administering a growing city also gave rise to numerical notation. Simple linear marks representing quantities on a one-to-one basis, then marks representing multiples. Calculation including addition-subtraction-division-multiplication would have been easy to grasp with the earlier fairly simple numerical marks. Two forms of numbering are evident, one using decimal (1,10,100,1,000, etc.) the other sexagesimal (1,10,60,600,3,600, etc. an alternating progression of 10s and 6s) notation. Interestingly, for the applications required in Sumer circa 3,500-2,500 BCE each was as efficient as the other; either seems to have been employed depending on circumstances. It was the sexagesimal system with a base of 60 that was developed by the early Babylonian/Sumerian priest-astronomers.

It seems that from perhaps as early as 3,000 BCE priests were recording the movement of the heavenly bodies - by 2,350 BCE we have the daughter of Sargon the Great (of Akkad), En Henduanna, appointed Chief priestess of Babylon (as Moon Goddess and a renowned poetess) and as part of her duties she was overseeing the recording of the movement of the stars. There was also an agreement to divide day and night into two twelve-hour periods, so formally establishing the 24 hr day. With the sexagesimal notation being used to divide each hour and with time being measured by types of sundial and water-clocks.

By 1,800 BCE Babylonian astronomers were able use the by then long-recorded movements of the stars and planets to note the procession of equinoxes and the regular appearance of eclipses (initially lunar, then later solar). There was a focus on the movement of the Sun and the Moon, and from these observations they were able to establish a lunar calendar of 12 months (354 days). The discrepancy between this and a solar calendar was overcome in the 8th century with a 'leap month' being added (7 years in every 19 years were 'leap month' years) to the lunar year. The calendars drawn up by the early civilizations - Babylonia, Egyptian, and Chinese by 1136 BCE - measured the length of a solar year at 365 and 1/2 days. These, along with other propitious 'sign/omens', were used as guides for the time of sowing and harvesting various crops, so justifying a high status for the priest-astronomers.

The use of numerical calculation was, with the Sumerians and the subsequent civilization in Mesopotamia, specifically related to more practical uses. Early on the Sumerians discovered the constant relationship between the diameter of a circle and its circumference, 'pi', but they only used the rough approximation of 3:1 (rather than the more accurate 3.14:1). This being all that was required for practical purposes, such as the calculation of the amount of grain in a cylindrical store; this is an example used by Gordon Childe (1943) of how need can drive invention. The only approximate accuracy of this particular notation (pi) should not be taken as a guide to other uses of mathematics. The records show that the seasonal predictions taken from astronomical observation indicate quite precise calculation and careful recording.

With the society constituted by various peoples subsumed under the name of Sumerians we are rolling back the historical record to the beginning of science, and the idea of a more 'objective' form of knowledge. But also revealed is that individuals responsible for the significant, more scientific, innovations and their development also believed in astrology with its twelve 'signs of the zodiac' and in divination using such entities as the shape of a sheep's liver.

The development of writing during the 3-4,000 year history of pre-common era Mesopotamia would itself justify an extended focus going well beyond my limited aims. A development that shows an almost industrial approach to recording many of the activities that characterized early civil life, undertaken by a succession of priestly scribes. Professionals spending much of their time collating and detailing original information and also in the production of countless copies of many 'documents' (clay tablets and clay cylinders), and this copying continuing over millennia. A continuity that, to a considerable extend, explains the longevity of the forms taken by Mesopotamian scribal scholarship, initially Sumerian in linguistic form then reflecting Akkad influences, with a later Amorite contribution.

Sumerian administrative texts covered many aspects of civil life including: prayers to various gods, hymns, royal inscriptions, laws, mythical stories, as well as the thousands of more mundane records of contracts, property ownership, tax collection and corvée service, in addition to information on crops and animal husbandry. One has only to consider what is known of the Library of Nineveh with its accumulation of an estimated 1500 cuneiform clay tablets assembled by the Assyrian King Assurbanipal (668-627 BCE) to gain some idea of the breadth and the continuity of nearly 3,000 years of Mesopotamian history. Here was a monumental marker of the means of storing an accumulation of humankind's knowledge, including a mass of information gained by scribes sent out to foreign lands to gather information. A. Leo Oppenheim (1977 ed. p15) noted this library as having '......every right to be called the first systematically collected library in the ancient Near East'. Oppenheim highlights an interesting feature of this body of written material, one that reflects a change in perception of the ruling elites. He notes that initially the texts focus on quite local, city-based, concerns (taxation and city administration as well myths, hymns, etc.) and records ownership of land within a city's environs and prescribed acceptable behaviour between citizens, but increasingly, we see evidence of the widening horizons of a ruling group's interests. There is information relating to long-distance trading links, of military conquests in regions beyond just neighbouring cities, and treaties suggesting political hegemony over extensive areas of the Middle-East. Overall changes that

Oppenheim (1977 ed.) suggests as a change of perspective from city-state to the idea of a territorial state.

Of course this written material (although early flagging up the advancing production of information as knowledge) was in effect unavailable to the illiterate majority of the population but what was available to the masses (and preceded the written versions by up to 1,000 years) was the oral transmission of similar, if popularized, versions of hymns to the gods, as well as story and news telling.

Taking in the whole body of Mesopotamian literature, we can gain some idea of the advance in the ways in which civilizing humanity was managing and seeking to understand and engage with the world within which they lived.

In terms of managing, we have today access to more than 100,000 texts from this time and these show quite an efficient approach to administering an empire - Each of the tablets was dated, and placed ('filed') in baskets according to the type of business being recorded, with labels attached to many of these. The business covered included commercial activities, legal agreements (involving sale or rent of land or sale of slaves), and even letters from kings to their subjects and on occasion to the gods. The names of individuals involved in the various transactions are noted, as is the name of the responsible official.

Medical texts, advice to craftsmen, descriptions of various types of artwork, and omens also form part of this corpus of written texts. The medical texts are especially interesting in that they show a mixture of the magical and the rational that reflects the level of medical knowledge of the time. We see an increasingly prescriptive process of diagnosis, with prognosis linked to suitable treatments. Treatments could be of two main types......the more rational, using a wide range of herbs (roots, leaves, stems) of smearing wounds with animal fat or the ingestion of blood or ground bones and..... the more magical, using a range of spells, and specific directions on how to administer herbal remedies e.g. propitious numbers, such as seven drops of a particular liquid, or the assistance in preparation of a virgin. The reliance on apotropaic magic to ward off illness (indeed misfortune in general) and also magical incantations, spells, and other actions as cures reflects the fact that diagnosis often gave the cause of disease as 'evil magic'.

The development of literate societies enabled the recording of conflict. If mostly couched in narratives glorifying some or other victorious leader rather than recording the devastation caused by the bloody business of warfare. It is with the written documents that we learn more about specific disputes/conflicts, the when and how, including the numbers involved and at least some aspects of the outcomes.

Some notable literary works include the Epic stories: 'The Epic of Gilgamesh' (the version stored in the library of Assurbanipal had 3,000 lines on 12 clay tablets), the Creation epic 'Enuma elis' (a more sacred text of up to 170 lines), another epic 'When the gods were men' (1245 lines on three tablets), the 'Epic of Irra' (a poem taking in war, peace, pestilence, and prosperity), plus a number of shorter epic stories are known. From Phanaronic Egypt circa 3,200 BCE we have the Narmer Palette (the 'Great Hierakonpolis Palette') perhaps the earliest known example of Egyptian hieroglyphic inscription. On this ceremonial tablet there is outlined a great battle, with victory going to the First Dynasty King Narmer, gaining the approval of the gods for the consequent unification of the kingdom of Egypt.

Over the 1000 years between 3,500-2,500 BCE the systems of script and numerical notation were developed and improved, they also spread with the priests and traders that travelled between Mesopotamian cities and more distant regions. Now that writing and the means of calculating and recording the products of agriculture and trade was in the hands of an elite group of priests, a more structured form of education had to be introduced in order to control the transmission of this powerful knowledge, and so as another means of consolidating the power of the ruling elite.

An interesting example of using authority in the service of maintaining elite privileges within hierarchical systems of social class, was introduced by the priesthood of Babylon. They announced that the senior god Enlil had made it a law that sons should follow the trade of their fathers. This had traditionally been a generally accepted practice but as cities became more socially complex the customs of breeding and of families working within specific trades were beginning to be eroded as the increasingly intermixing groups formed the populations of cities. The rulers reacted and ordered that endangered customs, such as the practice of tribe/clan trade specialization that contributed to reinforcing social hierarchy, had to be codified and so liable to enforcement. Even accepting that for the most part it was the community view that considered the priests to be working for a city's god/s: gods who were generally assumed to be actually housed in the temple. For the priests to be just below the apex of a hierarchy at the top of which stood the gods, and under which were arranged the various socio/economic classes. All co-existing within networks of economic and social relationships forming, down to circa 3,250 BCE, generally fairly well-ordered and 'relatively' peaceful city-based societies.

So now, at about 3,000 BCE, we see cities of Mesopotamia growing in size and in the complexity of their related social and economic structures. The population of Eruch has grown to 50,000 and this was only one of a number of leading cities in the region. In Eruch we see laid-out streets lined with rows of generally uniform mud-brick housing then, at the centre of the city, usually sited on elevated mounds, are monumental buildings, including temples and granaries. There is also the division of the city into districts according to occupational category as well as social status; a common feature of cities down to at least medieval times. As well as locally produced foodstuffs, reed baskets, pottery, carpets and other textiles, being traded in street-markets that were also offering an increasingly more varied range of goods, mostly produced within the city, but with some imported via extensive trade-links. The economic structure is based on class-differentiation and consequent unequal distribution of wealth. A distribution based primarily on some combination of the social-economic-religious-political-military 'power' that any group can deploy. An arrangement that was to pertain as the general economic structure for all 'civilized' societies down to today. [6]

Social stratification was for Arnold Toynbee (1976 ed. p57) the first "social evil", and the price paid for civilization in Sumer; his second social evil was "warfare". No doubt changing self-perceptions of each group's power would have resulted in some level of conflict between different interest groups vying for control within any city. This being in addition to the more defensive violence used to defend the rich cities from bands of marauding nomads as they struck at tempting targets in the border areas of Sumer.

The Temple was the focus for the administration of the agricultural wealth and also a range of basic services such as weaving, baking, butchery, – and of course for the spiritual guidance of the population. For Gordon Childe: '……the temple appears as a sort of divine *household*, an enormously enlarged version of the patriarchal household of barbarism.' (Childe, 1942, p103)

Collectively, humankind now had much going for it, with writing, numeracy, and forms of proto-science. New intellectual tools were being forged to assist in shaping its future. The accumulation of knowledge is probably the most significant emergent property of civil development. Not just in the area of technological invention and proto-scientific discovery (both practical and theoretical) but also in music, painting, sculpting, and story-telling. In theory, the future of humankind in the third millennium BCE looked bright, bursting with the potential to become ever more civilized, and what we might idealistic consider to be more 'human'. The world was spread before them, its environment still relatively unsullied, heavy with the

---

[6] The authors David Graeber and David Wengrow (2022) offer an evidence-based challenge to what has mostly been the conventional view of early civil life – amongst other differences they suggest that some early cities had more democratic, community-centred, forms of governance, rather than the more elitist/hierarchical systems generally on offer that all agree did later came to characterise civil life. And this in locations such as Mesopotamia (Uruk 3,300 BC, Meso Amaerica (Teotiuacan 1150 AD), The Indus River (Mohenjo-daro 2,600 BC) and some cities of pre-Shang China (pre-1,200 BC).

potential for unifying exploration; which could have been motivated by benign curiosity rather than rapacious greed. Although there was conflict between groups it does seem that pre 3,000 BCE the massacres of large populations and the horrors of organized warfare were as yet unknown (or perhaps only unrecorded). But there was no 'supra-consciousness' that could offer a guide for humanity and its future; the gods were silent and the people ignorant.

As I now begin to outline the central developments that arose in the following 5,000 years, I want to note the significance of the time roughly around 3,200-2,000 BCE When for Hugh Thomas (1995, p.58): "By 3,000 B.C. war had assumed a familiar shape". Prior to this yes humanity bled here and there from the wounds of local inter-group conflicts, and local massacres probably occurred, but humankind had not been witness to the extent of the carnage that would spill scarlet on the millennia to come.

The intelligence that had created the potential for agricultural surpluses sustaining civilizing humankind was also applied to wrest from the earth the raw materials from which the tools - both useful in the plough, axe, and various means of transport, and the less useful in 'weapons' - that would take us into the future were forged. Since the earliest times in humankind's self-conscious life bright metal material found on or just below the ground has attracted attention. For a long period such objects mainly served decorative purposes. The process of turning metal-bearing ore into shaped tools and weapons requires a succession of skilled steps, and the means to gain sufficient raw-materials fostered progress in mining techniques beyond the basic hole-digging of stone quarrying. From the evidence it seems that the elements of this process were first developed in the highlands of southern Anatolia.

Of the first metals used, gold and silver were too soft for any utilitarian uses, but their resistance to corrosion, in addition to their brightness and relative rarity, made them attractive objects of ornamentation and as a sign of social status. But with copper, initially found on or near the surface, a metal had been found that was both malleable and when hammered became hardened. Copper was being worked in Sumer as early as 3,000 BCE; presumably introduced by craftspeople whose origins were in Anatolia. Anatolian peoples are also credited with inventing the technique of glass making by 2,500 BCE, a skill past on to Egypt by 1,500 BCE. The nature of the ornaments, tools, and weapons, produced suggest that casting had been used since 3,500 BCE. It was not long before some perceptive individuals realised that if a copper ore containing casiterite was heated to a sufficiently high temperature then any tin present in the casiterite alloyed with the copper to form the even harder metal bronze. This technological advance was introduced into Mesopotamia by a second wave of Anatolian metal workers in about 2,600 BCE. It was bronze tools and weapons that early civilizations relied upon to carve out the first empires. Bronze served as the primary metal for tool and weapon making down to 1,300 BCE when the even harder iron began to gradually supersede bronze for these uses. Invariably cities, federations of these, and later on empires, ultimately asserted their power on the battlefield. Underlying this power was the extent of the 'surplus' wealth a political entity could deploy to pay for the very best weapons and/or the most able indigenous and/or mercenary fighters.

Before moving on to consider advancing civilization beyond about 3,000 BCE, I would briefly note another development that accompanied early civil life. The practice of slavery, of human beings being 'owned' by others, (often by the temple) if having to engage in forced service was probably an occasional aspect of human communities for a long time before the first cities. Captives, as a by-product of raiding, or purposely rounded up, when strong groups preyed on weaker neighbours, would have served as forced labour in some communities. With city life slavery progressively became an integral feature – an 'institution' for much of civilization. Perhaps with any slaves surplus to a city's own needs being traded for other goods. By city-life circa 1,000 BCE slavery would become an institution and slaves but another commodity - used as labour on public building construction, and later rowing galleys, and working as miners and road makers - and has continued in different forms, in spite of attempts at abolition, down to the present day.

In contrast to the more rational history in humankind's development we know that peoples within the city walls believed in many forms of predicting the future by consideration of the condition of the internal organs and viscera of various domestic animals (extispicy). Indeed predictions were even based on the behaviour of some animals, e.g. the flight pattern of birds at certain times of year, behaviour of animals in particular locations such as at the entrances to a city, as well as identifying deformed animals and humans as presages of important events. The pseudo-science of astrology arose in the earliest cities, serving as a means of predicting the fortunes of individuals. The position and movements of the heavenly bodies had long been recorded as a way of determining seasonal cycles as well a source of a wide range of 'omens'. Omens were divined in many natural features such as cloud formations and more extreme weather patterns, as well as numerous aspects of human and animal bodies, including hair colour and the shape of fingernails and of moles. The practice of divination was both a religious and secular trade specialization; reflecting its intrinsic connection to civil life. The interpretation of various 'omens' (even omen gods, see Oppenheim, 1977) undoubtedly preceded their written record within city bounds but in Mesopotamia it was to develop into a veritable 'industry', accompanying civilization down to the ascendancy of the Romans (circa 300 BCE) and beyond. Divination probably peaked between 2,000-1,000 BCE but with some, such as astrology and tarot cards, being still practiced on the gullible down to today.

But by now, along with cultural and intellectual advances, organised warfare had also emerged into the history of humankind. Just a progressive development of species-long forms of intergroup conflict but once allied to economies supported by agricultural surplus, profits from trade and various forms of taxation, technological innovations in the means of killing, and personal ambitions, the great evil of warfare had become manifest.

At around 2,700 BCE we arrive at an event worth noting in humankind's history, for the first time we have a definite historical figure. The King of Kish, Emmebaragesi, is depicted on fragments of pottery, and mentioned in the Sumerian epic poem 'Gilgamesh and the Agga of Kish' as the father of Agga. Kish must have been a prominent city of northern Sumer during most of this period, the title of 'King of Kish' is one added to that of later kings claiming sovereignty over the north as their own home cities rose to become dominant. The period from about 3,000 BCE down to 2,346 BCE was to be the time of Sumerian supremacy. These were a people with diverse tribal backgrounds as inhabitants of an extended region of southern Mesopotamia that by this time encompassed at least a dozen, if mostly quite modest in size, cities. A people who increasingly identified with a common religion-culture, generally having similar views on how society should be structured, in terms of division of property and differences in accessing valued resources. In general, people sharing a common world-view. Although, given a clear difference in living conditions between the 'educated' elite and the 'uneducated' masses, this common world-view would probably have been seen from two broad but quite different perspectives.

Civil developments in Sumer included monumental architecture, the improvement of literacy and numeracy, trade specialization, social stratification, the abstraction of a common value from goods ('currency') in forms which were easy to store and to negotiate with. The region's religious life was polytheistic in form, with pre-city tribal cults centred on animistic and nature worship continuing to be followed in the early established cities and their surrounding territories; if the primary city-gods themselves progressively undergo subtle changes in form and role.

Even accepting the advances in technological and agricultural improvement, the 600 year period of Sumerian predominance is characterized by yes the further development of civil-society but also, especially during the later stages, by quite extensive inter-city conflict.

Perhaps on occasion the 'masses' within a city rebelled in protest at specific injustices. It would be unusual if this did not happen during times when the mostly unwritten contract between the rulers and ruled, which helped to maintain social stability, was broken by the former. What appears to have been an attempt at social reform was made by King Uru'inimmgina of Largash (2,378-2,371 BCE). During his short (7 year) reign, he introduced measures that, whilst giving support to the priestly caste also went some way towards alleviating the lot of the poorer citizens. It seems that he endeavoured to prevent those in debt from being evicted by wealthy landlords and more powerful creditors, or even having to sell up other property such as their domestic animals. The King introduced measures allowing for delay in the payment of debt, and, in certain circumstances their cancellation. Could it be that the shortness of his reign was brought about as his peers lost patience with what appears to have been a concern with alleviating more obvious social injustice?

Although the temple was an important focus for city-life, there was a shifting balance of power between the temple and wealthy private citizens and, as defensive and offensive conflicts became more prevalent the palace was becoming more important than the temple. The administration and regulation of agriculture, fishing, and trading, was primarily the responsibility of the temple, and the gods who 'resided' there were the ones to which communal obeisance and more formal forms of worship were directed in order to obtain good fortune and the favour of a city's god/s. But the internal dynamics of city life at this time would be misunderstood if too much attention were given to the Temple.

From about 3,000 BCE cities in central and southern Mesopotamia had progressively developed into communities with a single semi-divine monarch. The elevation of one person (or a small elite group) to head the community would have begun much earlier, indeed had long preceded city-life as a 'big-man' or 'corn-god'; probably due to quite practical administrative requirements. That of leading some 'war cabinet', set up to deal with a specific inter-town/tribe (later inter-city) conflict or to defend the home-base from the aggressive attentions of marauding tribesmen sweeping in from lands fringing Sumerian territory. A single leading ruler could have arisen (perhaps chosen or even elected) from a group of city priest-governors who came to control the religious and civil life of any city. At the end of the period being considered the priest-ruler had moved from the temple to become the royal king-ruler in the palace (whilst retaining a god-like mantle), with the right to pass the royal inheritance to his son or favoured relative, soon being firmly established. Even at this early time the records provide evidence of an ideological narrative being promoted by rulers and their accolades suggesting that the leader's activities were determined solely by the unselfish pursuit of the interests of all they ruled over; perhaps the most mendacious claim made throughout history (down to today) by ruling elites of various types of political regimes.

Included in the evidence for a significant improvement in material conditions are increasing amounts of more elaborate and finely worked metal tools, pottery, ornaments, artworks (including sculpture, interior decoration and exterior adornment of prominent buildings), and invariably weapons. The sale of slaves for both household and temple use had become an established 'trade'. Land was a mixture of the lesser amount privately owned and the greater amount owned by the temple, in effect the central part of the state. Even more obvious signs of the increasing prosperity of the city as a whole are the 'grave-goods' that accompany the burial of the rulers and other wealthy citizens. The royal tombs of Ur contained pottery and statuettes, and a range of other more valuable goods, deemed suitable to accompany the deceased into an after-life. These goods depict evidence of economic well-being, and also include wheeled vehicles, such as fairly basic chariots and carts, the latter being drawn by harnessed oxen. The funeral entourage, including, men and women servants, courtiers, and guards, were at times put to death in order that they too would pass into another life and so be able to continue to serve their lord.

The idea of some 'afterlife' (heaven/hell) has been a characteristic aspect of humankind's psychological constitution from the dawn of reflective self-consciousness, one that has had a profound impact on human history and has served as one of the essential pillars supporting most of the enduring religions. Without the expectation of some form of afterlife would not human history have taken a very different course - think of the economic resources devoted to funerary rites, religious buildings, and the material burden of a priestly caste; an extreme example being the gross distortion of the economy of Pharonaic Egypt. Would soldiers have risked their lives so willingly? Would the poorest classes have so often resignedly accepted their allotted economic and social inferiority? Upon Neanderthal practices of gentle suggestiveness arising from sincere confusion of what happened to the 'spirit' of the dead, history has (more often in the interest of ruling elites) elaborated closely related concepts that fed and continue to cater for humankind's attempt to resolve the existential dread of death; of an individual's finality.

The peoples of these early historical times could be excused, they were part of a socio/evolutionary process the metaphysical structure of which they were ignorant, their psychology was circumscribed by their historical circumstances and by the limitation of the imaginative possibilities they had access too.

On a pattern to be repeated throughout subsequent history, the growing wealth of the expanding cities of Mesopotamia attracted the attentions of others; aggressive strangers from regions, mainly to the north and west. It was bands of these, no doubt hardened by inter-tribal conflict (and the generally harsh life of nomadic pastoralism) that, intent not just on opportunistic raiding as previously but on conquest and settlement, displaced the descendants of those who created the relatively peaceful U'baid culture. Although with the incomer's power in cities continued to shift more towards the palace, the importance of the priest-hood was generally maintained. They continued to administer the basic economy of the cities and to control access to formal education. The temple often exercised ownership of a large proportion of the lands and domestic animals. On a more populist level the priesthood, at least for the most part, controlled the influential pseudo-sciences of extispicy, divination, and astrology.

The priesthood generally represented an early type of 'civil service' and had the power to influence, direct, and control any leader, especially those with less interest in the minutiae of administration, and more in recreational activities such as hunting and war-making. The influence of the priestly caste, in what continued to be highly religious communities, would have been ignored at their peril by any short-sighted king.

Throughout this period we have cities in conflict as their expanding hinterlands met to become defined borders (lines on 'maps') producing the delineation of 'our-land' 'their-land' division. There must have been division of land between communities long before city-life, but these were more between neighbours that knew each other and shared similar outlooks. With towns and cities (with their larger populations) the 'others' over the border became increasingly an abstraction, an entity with imagined characteristics commonly generated by prejudice and seen as a threat. Borders, as is common in human history, served to generate a deal of argument, and to provide the ground conditions for conflict.

A.C.Grayling noted that: 'There is scarcely any boundary, any border, in the world that was not drawn in the blood of conflict at some point in history.'(Grayling, 2017, p4)

And conflict there was, becoming evermore costly in human lives, owing primarily to advances in the technology of weaponry and in the general activity of organized warfare; along with, what history suggests was an increased willingness to kill and enslave other human beings.

There is a record, on a stone 'victory stele', of a battle taking place in Mesopotamia (in today's central Iraq) between the Gutians and an army of 360,000 Akkadian soldiers led by King Naram-Sin (reigned 2254 - 2218 BCE) during which, although deemed the victor, 90,000 of his soldiers died.

A general pattern of changing predominance of one or other city (and its associated city-gods), with ever-shifting alliances and short-lived federations, became a central feature of inter-city relationships. The most notable examples being that between Largash and Umma, two neighbouring cities that had engaged in a protracted dispute over an area of fertile land (Gu'edena) that lay between them. A dispute settled for a time when Eannatum, King of Largash made the King of Umma swear an oath to six divinities not to cross a canal that had previously served as a border, the ownership of which was central to the dispute. There is evidence here of a formal agreement to end hostilities, no doubt with difficult negotiations leading to what must have been one of the earliest of 'peace' treaties. However, after a fairly short interlude the conflict was renewed, occasionally including nearby cities taking one side or the other, with even more destructive results than earlier.

It was to take the military strength available to King Lugalzaggisi (c. 2,371-2,347 BCE) to end the factious conflict between Largash and Umma and impose a 'peace' on the cities of Sumer, as city-states were subsumed within a proto-empire. One that Lugalzaggisi extended, mainly by force of arms, from 'sea to sea'; from the Persian Gulf to the Mediterranean. An early exercise in empire building, endeavouring to extend dominion over wide areas of land, incorporating many diverse groups of people, so placing increased emphasis on administrative skills.

It seems that this first 'empire' was but loosely ruled, based in Sumer, with Largash as its principle city, becoming ever-less controlled as it spread to the north-west. This early attempt at empire was based primarily on military strength alone rather than military strength wedded to political and administrative acumen. A combination which was later to become more evident with the activities of Sargon-the-Great (Sharrum-kin). Here we have an interesting and significant historical character. Sargon began his career as a ruler just to the north of Sumer in the land which came to be called Akkad, so named after Agade the city Sargon founded to serve as his capital. It seems that he came to prominence in the city of Kish, rising from relatively lowly beginnings. Legend has it that he was born (in secret) to a high priestess who placed the baby in a reed basket and set him adrift on the river Euphrates. He was retrieved from the river and brought up by a gardener who had seen the basket stuck amongst reeds. The gardener took the infant home and raised him in modest circumstances. More ordered history records that he was a Semitic-speaking officer serving in the civil service or army (perhaps both) who rose to become King of Kish. Lugalzaggisi was a Sumerian who spoke the language of Sumaria, Sargon an Akkadian speaking a Semitic language. The languages of two fairly distinct cultures which were to clash as the general interest of each population became subsumed within the dynastic ambitions of their rulers. Both kings began their rule at the same time about 2,371 BCE but by 2,347 BCE the strength of Sargon (perhaps encouraged by the Akkadian merchant class) and his Akkadian-based army overwhelmed the Sumerians led by Lugalzaggisi, and in doing so joined the Akkadian dominions to those of Sumer, and its already established proto-empire. During this conflict we see mass killing at a distance, as the long-bow, adapted from those used in central Asia, gave victory to the Akkadians over the mainly lance-bearing Sumerian soldiers. According to C.D.Darlington (1971, p95) the conquest of Sumer was undertaken by what were primarily a pastoral people who 'came as conquers'.

The rule of Sargon extended for 56 years during which a general, if on occasion uneasy, peace was imposed over a region which included central and southern Mesopotamia; and at times over quite extensive lands to the north and west. Trading was facilitated by a common currency, certain trading regulations, laws, maps, the introduction of a standardized system of weights and measures, and access to more types of trade goods and larger markets. There was also a move towards religious unity involving the reduction (generally by assimilation) in the numbers of gods. But few peoples accept for long the rule of elite groups they view as outsiders, especially if taxation is heavy, an unacceptable religion is imposed, and elements of a foreign culture are introduced. The history of all empires is interwoven with incidences of conflict resulting from the human wish for self-determination, especially for those united by a sense of shared oppression.

With the emergence of the political entities we term empires we have ruling groups who attempt to provide a continuity of leadership; so-called dynasties. The succession of, usually but not exclusively, related individuals assuming the chief royal office. Dynasties beginning and ending in conflict would become part of the pattern of recorded history.

During the period of Sargon's rule he is said to have fought 34 land battles in southern Mesopotamia in addition to others in the north. He founded a dynasty which would encompass the reign of five Semitic kings, initially his two sons and then to his militaristic grandson Naram-Sin (the self-declared 'God of Akkad'). This empire saw the further elevation of the role of kingship as an embodiment of the 'triumphant warrior'.

Sargon's time as king is considered to have been a productive period during which the absorption of social and cultural elements of Sumerian enhanced Akkadian city-life; improving the descriptive and literary scope of an emerging Akkadian written language. The process of unifying the Akkadian Empire included building and maintaining a powerful mobile army and significantly improving the lines of communication. If these running along already long-trodden routes supported trade in goods that flowed too and from the borders of the Empire and beyond. Goods that included timber, copper, tin, obsidian, lapis lazuli and other precious stones not available within Mesopotamia proper. Along with increasing trade these lines of communication were kept open to facilitate, not only the movement of trade-bearing caravans and soldiers, but also the passage of swift-footed messengers carrying information from across the Empire to the cities, as well as orders from the senior administrators out to the regions. At sea, knowledge of navigation and improvements in shipbuilding enabled trading at some distance; with the risk of storms but without that of attack by pastoral, nomadic, and other land-based raiders. Regular sea-borne trading reached to Persian Gulf ports such as Oman and Bahrain, with some evidence that the trade ships ventured beyond the Gulf as far as sea-ports of the developing Indus-valley civilization. What had long been relatively uncoordinated trade links and inter-city communication was now organized over wide areas to sustain what was politically a relatively unified empire.

Sargon was the product of pastoralist forbears, skilled in the art of warfare and familiar with complex nomadic/semi-barbarism negotiation over grazing rights, bride dowries, blood feuds, etc. With his Akkadian soldiers he had conquered the Sumerians by force of arms, but such was the attractiveness of the rich culture of Sumer that Sargon, and most of the Semitic kings that followed him, adopted much of this as their own. Initially this included the written script, even given the often awkward translation of the Sumerian into Semitic language. This literary contact in turn stimulated an advance in sophistication of the Akkadian written script that, in the following centuries, improved to equal then arguably surpass the literary achievements of the original Sumerian.

The background of the mass of Semitic Akkadians was of generally uncivilized semi-nomadic, more pastoralist, peoples occupying an area adjacent to the civilization of Sumer. Increased exposure to the benefits of regular trading, and to other Sumerian cultural influences, allowed them to see advantages and opportunities in city-life. They had possessed the aggressive tendencies of the barbarian (originally a Greek word, simply denoting a foreigner) allied to the wish to gain access to the accrued wealth, and cultural sophistication, of Sumer. A combination of military aggression and cultural ambition that was to fuel the activities of successive invaders, strengthened by tribal alliances, sweeping in from beyond the border-lands of civilization for millennia to come.

Religion retained its importance in Sumer-Akkad with the, now reduced, pantheon of city gods. There were still many gods arranged in hierarchical order; immortal and together all-powerful, able to take human form and eat, drink, and fight, and even having children and servants. The role of each Sumerian being to serve these gods with: worship, prayer, and sacrifice. The tales of the gods constituted a central aspect of daily life. For the common person religion provided a world-view that was nicely circumscribed, offering an explanation for their birth and death, and for all the vicissitudes and successes in between. For the ruling group it offered all this and in addition served to justify their favoured position and to assist the maintenance of social stability. The priestly caste continued to predominate in the civil service as well as in the still pervasive religious life of the period, but now we see such people as regional governors, senior army officers, and wealthy merchants, becoming more influential.

Naram-Sin, the fourth king of the Sargonied dynasty, not only claimed the title of 'King of the four quarters of the earth', but also assumed the title 'God of Akkad'. Modesty in titles has rarely if ever been a characteristic of monarchs! The general evidence suggests that Mesopotamian rulers, even accepting inflated titles, stood as the god's representatives, a god-like aura attached to them (for public consumption) but the claim to actually be gods if ever believed in fact, was a relatively short-lived aspect of Mesopotamian kingship. As distinct from Pharaonic Egypt, where the Pharaoh being conceived of as a god in his own right, whose immortality was assured, continued until a much later time.

Within the empire established by Sargon a significant advance was made in terms of new possibilities for trade between peoples of different cultural backgrounds including those living at considerable distances from Akkad-Sumer. This last aspect of a vitalized 'empire' reached out to the, by now contemporary civilizations, centred on the Nile valley in the west and the Indus river system in the east. Trading links, if less established, probably extended out to those many large towns growing at a pace on islands (Crete, Minorca, Cyprus) within the Mediterranean Sea. Trade links certainly extended north into Anatolia (an important source of metals, and the valued obsidian) and beyond. Also, the improving network of 'roads' facilitated both trade and the passage of individuals lured by the possibility of better lives in the city. The idea of unwelcome strangers was far less relevant in cities within a multi-ethnic empire than it had been in the more isolated cities of Sumer. Indeed, a body of mobile people possessing craft, administrative, or other skills, was advantageous to any empire's development. The two cultures of Akkad-Sumer fused to create new imaginative possibilities for human communities, including reinforcing the acceptance of an elite group holding dominion, and enjoying the prestige and the wealth drawn from their exercising control over an extensive region.

The acquisition, or defence, of many such 'empires' was to be a salient political feature of developing humankind from that time down to recent years. The increased wealth available to these new political entities, even accepting a deal of dissipation on military spending, monumental construction, and luxurious living for the few, allowed continued material development for humankind as a whole. It's difficult to conceive that progress in early technologies, in mathematics, along with improvements in the possibilities of the written word (alphabets etc.), would have been made without the demands placed on those that administered increasingly more complex economies operating over extensive regions.

It is worth noting that in the Sargonied Empire, as well as in all those that followed down to the modern period, the majority of the population lived an agrarian life-style. Creating the farming and fishing harvests which continued to be the economic mainstay of cities, and so the economic foundations upon which most empires were built. The sturdy, stoical, farmers, and their village-based communities, might perhaps have seen sons go off to war, but they themselves would have had psychological horizons extending little further than those defined by the cyclical demands of agriculture, the mythology of their traditional gods, and some other enduring elements of a traditional local culture.

The period of the Sargonoid dynasty (143 years) was a time of significant advance in complexity of human society, laying the foundations for further advances in artistic, technological, and administrative aspects of social life. But this was a relatively uncontrolled empire, and a deal of tribe-based regional autonomy continued.

During the whole period of the first empire (Sargonoid) its wealth attracted the aggressive attentions of pastoralist peoples on its borders, as had most cities in past times. This became a greater problem from the reign of the fourth Sargoniod, the politically weak if militaristic King Naram-Sin; a factor contributing to the gradual weakening of the Empire. The dynasty came to an end, due a combination of the debilitating effects of internal dissent about succession after King

Shar-kali-sharri (c.2,217 - c.2,193 BCE) and the growing power and ambitions of invaders.

When the last king, Shar-Kali-sarri, of the Akkad/Sumarian Empire died there followed about a century of unrest, with various ethnic groups competing for control, out of which the Gutians emerged as rulers. A rule reinforced by an influx of Gutian people from their traditional base in the Zagros Mountain range to the east.

Early civilizations, and individual city-states, were continually prone to the aggressive attentions of their neighbours. Later on the wealth of empires attracted marauding peoples from much further away. The early civil history of humankind, writ large, contains a central theme of the unifying tendency of civilizations brought down by the aggressive attention of powerful barbarians spilling across borders. And yet the more immediately destructive effects of such contacts were mitigated (for the development of humankind as a whole) by the stimulating effects arising from both the intermingling of cultures, and also the intermingling of genetic constitutions. Mesopotamia and adjacent regions remained the creative hub of humankind's development in the Middle-East, whereas Egypt had for many centuries experienced an intellectual stability bordering on stagnation. Although in the final millennium prior to the common-era, many of the developments made in Babylonian technology, mathematics, and astronomy, were made available via Egyptian scribes.

The arts advanced in Pharaonic Egypt, as did monumental architecture, but little else and those that did advance were mostly minor progressions on traditional practices. Egyptian civilization was, to a considerable extent, a backward looking one (if paradoxically, infused with ideas of a future life after death), in contrast to those based in Mesopotamia that looked much more to the future; if mostly in planning to defend, expand or consolidate empires.

A continual period of internal conflict was effectively brought to an end with the ascendancy of a strong ruler, Narmer (reigned 3,150 BCE - c. 3,273 – 2,987 BCE was the Early Dynastic Period), who came from the City of Hierakonopolis and who established the First

Dynasty to oversee the initial unification of the land of Egypt. A unification that was to last for the next 900 years. There was a priority given throughout the whole period of dynastic rule on ensuring the unity of the Upper and Lower regions of the country; a unification symbolized in the white (Upper Egypt) and red (Lower Egypt) halves of the imperial crown. For a long time there was a continuing diversity of local cultures, including religious beliefs; with it taking most of the next 1,000 years for a distinctive 'Egyptian' culture to emerge.

The internal conflict that a unified Egypt brought to an end was replaced by external conflict as Egyptian leaders sought to expand the territory under their control to the south and west and by war with civilizations to the east. Their worship focused on a range of gods, with importance being increasingly placed on the idea of an afterlife and of rulers being somehow 'in touch' with (or themselves actually being) the gods. Ideas that together found obvious expression later on in massive programmes of monumental building. A phenomenon that for the Egyptologist Heinrich Brugsch-Bey: '…..tell more emphatically than living speech or written words of the miseries of a whole population, which was condemned to erect these everlasting monuments to pharaonic vanity.' (Brugsch-Bey, 1902, p11)

In Sudan (the land then known as Kush/Nubia) and Ethiopia (the land of Punt) the Egyptian influence was definite and enduring. As early as the 12th Egyptian Dynasty (1991-1786 BCE) Egypt began to occupy and administer Nubia, seeking riches, in particular gold and emeralds. Building a chain of forts that, by the time of the completed conquest of Nubia in the reign of Thutmose I (c.1525 - 1512 BCE), ran as far south as Semna. For centuries before this occupation was completed the highly regarded mercenary soldiers from Nubia were fighting alongside Egyptians as the latter sought to expel Hyksos invaders from the northeast that had occupied Egypt. Aspects of Egyptian culture were brought back to Nubia by the returning soldiers. Although there was much inter-breeding, especially between the elites of each society, the Nubians, away from the towns and forts, retained a distinct cultural identity. Generally when Egypt was militarily strong Nubia was occupied, but when Egypt was militarily weak Nubia was self-administered. By the 8th century BCE Nubia, was ruled by its own king; free from direct Egyptian rule or its slightly less onerous suzerainty. Indeed, benefiting from retaining the wealth that had previously been passing to the north, Nubia gradually became militarily strong enough to launch its own military expeditions. The Nubian King Kashta initiated the conquest of Egypt, an ambitious aim which was to be completed by his son Piankhi (c751 -716 BCE) who reached as far north as the shores of the Mediterranean. This conquest was to be fairly short-lived, as the then all-conquering Assyrians armed with superior iron weapons invaded Egypt and drove the Nubians back into their southern homelands.

The Gutian's earlier successful invasion of Akkad/Sumer was mostly just a change of ruling group rather than anything more. What somewhat scanty evidence there is suggests that the Gutians were despised by both Akkadian and Sumerian peoples and after about a century of uneasy reign they were expelled or exterminated when a Sumerian, Utukegal of Uruk, arose in 2,120 BCE to lead a rebellion liberating most of the area of the old empire. Utukegal's reign lasted but seven years, before he was displaced by the city governor made king of Ur - King Ur-Nammu. Who proceeded in short time to re-form much of the old empire, (at least most of southern Mesopotamia) and claim the title 'King of Sumer and Akkad'. This initiated a new (the third) Dynasty of Ur with a succession of five rulers taking us down to the end of the third millennium (Ibbi-Sin 2,028-2,004 BCE) of human history

The evidence suggests that Ur III was a centralized state, with the king firmly established as an absolute ruler. Unusually for Mesopotamia, the king seems to have been fully deified (rather than just being a demi-god), with prayers and sacrifices being made to him in the many temples. The reconstituted empire was divided into forty provinces, each of which was administered by a form of 'governor' (ensis) with both civil and judicial responsibilities. The main responsibility of the provincial governor being to oversee the assessment and collection of taxes which were then paid annually, as 'tribute', to the king. Not surprisingly, most provinces corresponded to areas previously focused on established city-states, but others were new. This is early evidence of the construction of a coherent administrative structure by which to efficiently run an empire. The strength of such a system was the successful theoretical definition and practical implementation of how local provincial interests should be taken into account while their principle purpose remained that of supplying the resources used to support the centralized 'ruling groups'. Included amongst these being the many servants, slaves, crafts and arts people, soldiers, and various types of 'hangers on', serving the royal and priestly aristocracies.

The benefits of empire were not entirely one-sided, the power of empire gave an amount of protection to the population, and growing cities offered opportunity to those such as the surplus sons and daughters of farm-based peasant and village-based artisan. Add to this the psychological comfort of a supposedly powerful religion continually reinforced by the extensive priestly caste who continued as the main body of scholars and civil servants. The 'truth' of Mesopotamian religion was a reflection of the power of the Empire, with military success assumed to be due to the benevolence of the gods. Gods were still closely connected to localities, with most cities retaining a local god of their own, each begin assigned a place in a hierarchy overseen by the city god of Ur. Taken all together, life in an efficiently administered, and benevolently overseen, empire had its comforts and more stimulating attractions as well as its systemic forms of inequality, exploitation, and injustice.

When sufficient advantages were not on offer local unrest was evident, and on occasion provincial governors would try to gain more local autonomy. Rarely in early history did the combination of royal benevolence and administrative efficiency pertain for long, excepting perhaps as a certain archaic form in Pharaonic Egypt. The increasing weight of the materially parasitic 'ruling groups', and the insistent and heavy demands of the always active military, eventually weakens empires; with a consequent vulnerability to internal rebellion or foreign invasion. Ur III, for over a century, appears to have gotten the balance of interests required for successful government about right. It was a centralized state with an administration assisted by a fairly efficient form of bureaucratic civil service, inter-connected by a well-ordered network of foot messengers.

From literary sources written close to the time we have knowledge of how Ur III came to an end during the reign of the fifth ruler, King Ibbi-Sin (reigned c, 2028-2004 BCE). Whilst this king was engaged in warfare in Elam the land to the east of Mesopotamia one of his regional governors, Ishbi-Erra, persuaded the King of imminent danger to cities such as Nippur and Isin from marauding Amorites. Having then been granted the right to protect these important cities and the surrounding area Ishbi-Erra entered upon a series of skilful negotiations with the Amorites. He formed a federation with other rebellious regional governors and, taking advantage of the King Ibbi-Sin's 'depression', the would-be usurper gradually extended his own kingdom. Within twelve years he and his followers had control over southern Mesopotamia, including the previous capital Ur. The power of religious belief can be seen in this series of events, with sources supporting the claim that the depression suffered by King Ibbi-Sin was brought on because he came to believe that the premier god Enlil disliked him. Whereas Ishbi-Erra believed that he was Enlil's favorite, a belief partly sustained by the fact that Nippur was the city of Enlil. Indeed contemporary literature recorded that the sacking of Ur by invading Elamite tribesmen and the end of the ruling dynasty was the consequence of its invoking the anger of Enlil.

Throughout historical time when men go to war they prefer to believe that gods have stood at their shoulder, victory in battle justifying such belief, defeat being explained by having in some way invoked their gods anger or perhaps just due to its disinterest in their cause.

Now the Empire was to be broken up with the greater part, Isin, to be ruled for over 200 years by a dynastic succession began by Ishbi-Erra, most of the rest being divided between a number of local governors that had emulated Ishbi-Erra in expanding their own territorial control. The new king maintained continuity with the previous Ur III civilization, to the extent of driving the Elamites out of Ur and re-establishing its position as the premier city. The new rulers also adopted the Akkad/Sumerian 'king as deity' model, along with the system of administration, and much of the culture.

Even accepting an uneasy level of political continuity in the dynasties established by King Isbi-Irra in Isin and King Naplanum in Lasa for southern Babylonia, political fragmentation was to characterize the rest of the region. For civil Mesopotamia at this time, there seems to have been little progress in the cultural, intellectual and administrative development of civilization beyond those inherited from the dynasty established by Sargon. Communities outside of Isin and Lasa included city-states effectively operating as self-governing entities, with some lose and temporary federations of these. There were some more ambitious attempts at more formal federations in Eshnunna, Assyria, Babylonia, Mari, Carchemish, Yamkhad, Qatna, and Elam.

For McNeill (1963, p50) the period from the time of the end of the Akkad-Sumer dynasty to the time of Hammurabi (c 1800 BCE) was one of no strong central control and with cities across the empire becoming vulnerable to raiding over its borders, the temporary occupation of some outlying regions, as well as from internal revolt.

All around the more civil areas, tribal groupings sought local control as their influence 'waxed and waned' in line with fluctuations in power that the civil collectives were able to deploy against them. From written evidence this seems to be a time when social conditions for the majority of the city- and town- based civil populations were quite poor. Relations between cities, city-states, would be empires, and the many tribal and clan-based groupings, seem to be ones of suspicion, uneasy alliances, and quite regular conflict; with spying and other forms of covert information gathering being evident as the conflict became endemic.

As has been seen above, since the time of the earliest cities evidence of fighting between city-dwellers and adjacent barbarian tribes-peoples was a regular source of conflict. The forms of conflict can be seen by their representation in ancient literature. One of these being the Mesopotamian epic poem outlining the life of the wise priest-king Gilgamesh, an individual credited with having direct access to mystical areas of existence. The tale gives dramatic form to conflict between those dependent on city-life and the barbarians inhabiting the mountains, deserts, and steppes, within reach of civilization. This epic, in its numerous versions, is a precursor to other epic stories produced by civilizations such as in Egypt, the Indus Valley, of the Greek Homeric tales, and in certain books of Hebrew texts, some of which were included in the Old Testament of the Holy Bible. Many centuries before it began to be set down in written form the Gilgamesh Epic (Sumerian in origin) was a central aspect of cultural transmission past down the generations by skilled story-tellers. Some more common aspects of life were included along with colourful accounts of problems between humans and the gods, and of struggles with the forces of nature.

From about 2,100 BCE, the seeds of a new civilization had been growing in lands to the north of the region. There had been a gradual but continuous infiltration into the region of Amorite tribes-people, many of whom had forsaken the pastoralist lifestyle, had taken to trading, and had been for many centuries in close contact with the cities. Unlike the barbarian types such as the Gutian peoples, the Amorites (a Semitic-speaking people) appear to have appreciated the benefits of civil life and rose to become the dominant group in important cities such as Babylon, Nippur and Kish, by 1990 BCE. This Babylonian state, containing many interbreeding ethnic groups, would later on produce King Hammurabi, who would rule from 1792-1750 BCE. His reign would see a rapid expansion of the Babylonian Empire and consequent significant increase of the size and political status of the City of Babylon. An expansion that was to re-unite most of the original Sumer-Akkad Empire and even to extend it to encompass part of the emerging civilization of Assyria to the north and Elam and Zagros to the west.

In the land bordering Mesopotamian around 2,000 BCE, a number of tribal peoples had developed the primary characteristic of early civil life, peoples that included Hittites, Hurrians, Canaanites, Assyrians, Kassites, Elamites. William H. Mc Neill suggested that: '.....all [of these] evolved something approaching civilization; and with the exception of the Canaanites, they all laid the groundwork for the rise of militarily formidable states.'(Mc Neill, 1963)

Seemingly inevitably, as civil life developed the increasing focus on more organised conflict created an 'arms industry' mostly focused on more specialised sections of the military itself, whose remit was to seek to improve the battle strategies and the killing technology of warring. A development out of what must have been an extended history of specialist weapons-making going back to the earliest time of human life when a stick became a spear, a flint became a knife an axe-blade or an arrow point, and a rock became a bludgeon.

The weaponry of the civilized world, and many groups of its immediate pastorialist enemies circa 2000 BCE, included all of the stone-age weapons but with most now also made from bronze metal (an alloy of copper and tin), the powerful composite bow, and the use of horses rather than donkeys to pull chariots carrying soldiers into battle. Various types of shield, helmets and other body armour designed to allow protection of vital body-parts and some degree of relative freedom of movement. As towns and cities came under attack the means of taking them would see the introduction of siege equipment such as battering rams and catapults – prompting defensive measures – stockades, walls, lookout towers, ditches, and moats, were introduced along with more aggressive means of repelling attackers including burning oil and rocks being poured down on attackers along with a rain of arrows. The history-long 'arms race' had clearly begun, as would-be combatants set out to produce evermore devastating weaponry – what one side had the others also sought.

The expansionist King Hammurabi successful in war, also outlined an (for the time) enlightened legal code, he oversaw a period of relative peace across much of Babylonia. His legacy contributed to a three hundred year period of general civil unity based on Babylon when a deal of progress was made in areas of humankind's intellectual life. As mentioned above, writing spread further but it also became more refined when used in documents related to law, trade, and literature, mathematics, and astronomy. The technology of warfare and increasing trade gave impetus to improvements and innovations in shipping, wheeled vehicles, and in the use of metals for tools. Incremental improvements were also made in many other areas of city life such as the construction of buildings, in irrigation systems, as well as in animal husbandry and selection of crop plants.

This period of sustained progress ended quite abruptly when new ethnic groups appear on the historical landscape of Middle-Eastern civilization. A decline began when a force from 'Sealand' moved to expel the Amorites from the region of Assyria (to the north of the Empire). The Empire's end being sealed when in 1595 BCE tribesmen led by the Hittite King Mursilis swept in force into Mesopotamia to sack Babylon and overthrow the last Amorite ruler, King Samsu-Ditana. It seems that the Hittites were raiders rather than occupiers, soon withdrawing with their loot back to their homelands.

Instead of taking over but maintaining a civilization it appears that in the north the 'Sealand' peoples led by King Ilumael (Iluma-ilum), were much more of an 'occupying force', sacking city after city. Creating an enmity in the population that resurgent Kassites, who had already began to fill the political vacuum in the south and central regions created by the Hittite invasion and withdrawal, were able to take advantage of. They defeated (or rather displaced) the Sealand people and so began a long period of unsettled and culturally fairly stagnant rule. A new 'dark age' (G.Chile, 1942) now descends over Babylonia for centuries to come but the seeds of advancing humankind that the Babylonian civilization had broadcast across the Middle-East were taking root and growing. The intellectually most important aspects of this dispersal of civil-ideas included: literature, mathematics, and astronomy.

If the Fertile Crescent was the primary birth-place of western civilization it had been a difficult birth – one characterised by conflict between competing groups, the uneasy polarity of 'them' and 'us', and the formation of systemic conditions for social inequality and economic exploitation. On the other side of the balance we have times when people come together for communal projects, the creation of systems of law (if not all aspects of these have been systems of justice), advances in areas of knowledge such as mathematics, civil administration, medicine, astronomy, agriculture, and some primary elements of the mechanical sciences. Civil life dramatically extended the horizons of available 'information', so expanding the Reality within which humankind was evolving but doing so at the cost of the evils that had become an inherent feature of human community life.

Further east, the Indus civilization that had arisen after that of Sumer, was similarly centered on a great river (the Indus), made up of numerous tributaries threading through and so irrigating an extensive area of fertile land. This civilization had been developed following continuous occupation by humankind (initially by Homo erectus) of the Indian subcontinent for at least 250,000 years. A subcontinent that, with its extensive shoreline, fertile plains and well watered uplands, offered a variety of attractive habitats. For most of this time diverse patterns of shifting hunter-gatherer-forager lifestyles had provided the means of subsistence allowing the population to slowly increase. Then, beginning around 5,500 BCE we have evidence from across the subcontinent of small groups adapting variations of Neolithic lifestyles. It was in the potentially productive region centred on the Indus river valley that different tribal groups, both pastoralists and hunter-gatherers took to agriculture and animal husbandry as they settled to build villages, some of which grew into towns and some of these into the cities that made up the Indus civilization. Repeating the pattern of development seen earlier in Mesopotamia, and quite probably at the emergence of Indus city-life the influence of this older civilization to the east was present in the form of adventurous immigrants or perhaps disaffected craftsmen who had migrated to take up residence in the emerging cities further east. The connections that brought these migrants from Mesopotamia were possibly those initially formed by trade routes established from early on.

The Indus civilization lasted from c. 2,350 to c 1,700 BCE. With about eight sites so far identified as reaching the size of small cities, principally Harrappā and Mohenjo-Daro. Each of these two having buildings extending to cover an area of about a mile square, housing populations of between 40-50,000 at their high point. In each city, housing was primarily in mud-brick or burnt-brick built homes, ranging in size from two or three rooms to quite impressive multi-roomed residences. The roadways dividing up the residential, commercial, religious, and administrative sections of the cities were based on quite formal grid patterns. There were some impressively large communal granaries storing the harvests and also temples housing the priests who primarily administered the cities. At later times fortified 'citadels' grew to overlook the cities. At Mohenjo-Daro there are the remains of a large communal bath, early evidence of the ritual washing that would later become an important feature of the Hindu religion. These two larger cities, separated by about 300 miles, show other signs of civil life, with specialized crafts, stratified societies, - including a ruling elite dominated by the priestly class early on and by the warrior class later - extended trading relations within and beyond the civil region and its supporting lands, and of course drains!

The uniformity of the style of both pottery and seals, and a system of weights and measures, as well as widespread trade across the region (covering 500,000 square miles), point to this being a civilization with centralized political control overseeing its economic and religious administration. The arable land was mostly amenable to a light plough with the wide floodplain and an intricate network of tributaries reducing the need for much large-scale irrigation works.

The factors which brought such an extensive civilization to ruin are not known in much detail but there is evidence that over-population caused deforestation (a shortage of the wood essential for building and heating), which in turn accelerated destructive flooding of the river system. It is possible that tectonic shifts in this geologically unsettled region might have changed the course of the Indus River, increasing flow-rate and so reducing the amount of arable area. And there is always the possibility that disease caused survivors to move on. It has also been suggested that the consumption of the surplus produced by the masses, but mostly consumed by the ruling elite, reached an unsustainable level (monumental buildings, military adventures, luxurious living, etc.) – plus the cost of maintaining military units across the region in order to control an economically exploited population.

Whatever changes reduced the economic viability of the cities there is also evidence that barbarian invaders from the north-east (probably pastoralist tribes from today's Iran) swept in to take advantage. These invaders would have been made up of a coalition of tribes who called themselves Aryan (Noble Folk), perhaps more culturally primitive than the peoples of the Indus civilization but also more aggressive and more heavily armed. For the most part these invaders did not linger long in the Indus Valley but swept on to occupy central and eastern northern India. Gradually settling down to lead a civilization that was to rise in the Ganges Delta from around 1,000 BCE. Where the lighter-skinned Aryans constituted the ruling elite and the darker-skinned 'natives' making up the majority of the population.

From now on the history of India, its culture, religion, as well as its written and spoken languages was to be strongly influenced by the descendants of the Aryans (the Aryan legacy). Here were to be the Indian beginnings of the insidious and in civil development terms constricting, caste system. Initially being comprised of far fewer castes, with only warrior, priest, and the common people (traders, craftsmen, farmers, etc.) dividing the Aryans; with the native peoples constituting the fourth caste whose primary role was to serve the basic needs of the three higher castes. Given the range of skin-colour now in evidence it is obvious that there would have been a significant amount of interbreeding (social mobility) early on and its seems that as Indian society developed the caste system became increasingly more complex (0000s of sub-castes – the 'jatis') and allowed progressively less social mobility; the caste system being but another socially constructed form of maintaining social and economic inequality based on clan and class hegemony.

In China.....Up to the appearance of the Shang, who it seems were but the leading tribe among a loose alliance of pastoralist incomers, the area seems to have been relatively peaceful, characterised by limited local conflicts rather than organized warfare. The beginning of the

Shang dynasty is dated at about 1,600 BCE when a supposedly virtuous leader, Cheng Tang, overthrew the cruel King Xi to become the first of about 30 Shang kings.

With the Shang the cities and towns have defensive earthen ramparts and in the grave-goods we can observe the evidence of an increasingly more violent society. The Shang dynasty lasted to about 1,100 BCE (possibly as late as 1025) during which the capital city moved at least three times. Settling from 1400 BCE on the City of Anyang, by when Shang leaders ruled over an Empire that had been gradually extended to reach as far south as the Yangtze.

This Chinese civilization had a population composed of peoples of diverse ethnically based clan-groups, which would have provided the differential basis for the markedly stratified society that it became. At the base of Shang society was a more or less oppressed peasantry supporting an aristocratic warrior and priestly class, the leaders of which represented the apex of the social hierarchy. In between were the various craftspeople, merchants, and others that were a central characteristic of civil life. The position of emperor was somewhat unstable, with the person holding the position being the leader of but one clan among others, each with their own chieftain. Given the unstable nature of the royal succession within this aristocratic elite, it is likely that numerous small 'wars' occurred as clans sought to take over areas of land, and co-opt the surplus wealth produced by peasant farmers. In Anyang, as we have seen elsewhere, the city was divided up into the various areas in which each occupational group would have lived. There was little social mobility, with craft and trade skills being passed down within clans. An interesting suggestion from one scholar is that the grid-like layout of Anyang is "reminiscent of charioteers' encampments" (McNeill, 1963), and so perhaps a reminder of the importance of these weapons of war to the ruling groups

The socially stratified and economically unequal society of Anyang was supported by the surplus of an agriculture based on millet, wheat, and rice, and on the products of animal husbandry practiced on goats, cattle, pigs, sheep and domesticated fowl. Variety was available in the products of 'garden types' of produce, supplemented with wild animal flesh including that of fish. Cast bronze was utilized for fish hooks, knives, a range of farming tools and various ornaments, ritual bowls, and weapons. The latter were added to by the advanced compound bow, tipped with bronze, bone, or flint arrow-heads. Trading extended over large areas within and beyond the Empire's border, indeed the name Sheng Jen (Shang man) became synonymous for trader.

The extent to which the two, generally related, features of human communities, social stratification and conflict, pertained in North America circa 1,500 BCE cannot be clearly outlined but we do have some evidence of both. In terms of social stratification we can identify a range of burial sites with significant amounts of grave goods for some individuals, chieftains and their 'royal' families/moieties, to take into the afterlife. For conflict, there is evidence of continuous raiding (and indeed slavery) from early on - just as the study of history has taught us to expect given human beings having neighbours identified as 'different'; here it was primarily based on tribal-type distinctions.

To the south, the Olmec civilization can be identified as developing civil life by about 1,150 BCE. The Olmecs were quite warlike, for Clive Ponting: '....the monuments show numerous scenes of warfare and conquest which may have been an important part of the way in which the elite controlled Olmec society' (Ponting, 2000, p112). There does not seem to have been any formal script (although there is some evidence of 'hieroglyphic' inscriptions) but it is likely that a calendar was in use.

The next distinct civilization of South America was that of the Mayans. Martin Empson has Mayan civilization being politically based on '....a loose empire of independent city states.' States located within the agricultural land surrounding cities such as Chichen Itza and Uxmal. For Empson: 'Maya farmers developed many different ways of irrigating their fields: dams, terracing, raised fields, canals and reservoirs.' (Empson, 2014, p53) As ever in civil life, the powerful elites of Mayan civilization drew their own vast wealth from the surplus created by peasant-type agricultural and the occupational specialization and trading that this can in turn support. Although the Mayans had previously been thought to have been a fairly peaceful civilization Margaret MacMillan (MacMillan, 2021) has highlighted how more recent the translation of the Mayan script reveals a society often at war with others.

The Mayan Empire would collapse at about 900 CE, from what seems to have been primarily due to internal conflict (a peasant's revolt has been suggested) but this was also the time that saw the rise of the Aztecs. And it was the Aztecs who gave the name Teotihuacan to the ancient city that had once flourished in the area of the Valley of Mexico. It seems that, although the active time of this city corresponds to the period of the Mayan civilization (to the east) there are differing views as to whether it was a Mayan city or an independent expression of civil life. It does seem that culturally it was a mix of Mayan, and some other more local cultures. This city grew (from late 100 BCE to about 650 CE) to cover about 8 square miles, with extensive residential areas and numerous 'pyramid' temples and a wide central thoroughfare: The Street of the Dead. In the area of one temple it seems that 260 individuals had been sacrificed with their bodies being buried in ways that were purposefully aligned. The temples were decorated with a range of colourful artworks including the repeated image of a goddess with claws in place of hands, her headdress being decorated with painted human hearts. A grisly early indicator of the exuberant sacrificial bloodletting that would come to characterize Aztec religious practices later on.

In the southern Pacific islands....The more adventurous could venture out onto the seas, at first travelling to nearby islands but later (from circa 300 BCE) to develop the more efficient single outrigger canoe, utilizing a sail when feasible; with skilful navigation by the stars enabling journeys of perhaps thousands of miles. Unfortunately, even with paradise-like material conditions, such is the proneness of the human psychological constitution to create in-group out-group delineation's that there were also the conditions for conflict. At later times (as population pressure increased) the South Seas were to see some of the bloodiest forms of man-to-man fighting that humankind has devised. In some of the more habitable of the 1,000 islands across the south-Pacific at this time were settlements of tribal groups, led by chieftains, each group expressing their own versions of tribal culture.

A distinctive feature of humankind's early civil development was the piecemeal transformation of how societies are controlled. During the earlier, more village-based, agricultural period it does seem that community control was significantly more co-operative, with power being diffused throughout any circumscribed (primarily tribal) group. Extreme power of any group could operate when a hallowed normative value had been transgressed; but normative was generally drawn from a shared set of values. Yes, some individuals - religious leaders, medicine men, those skilled in hunting, in building, and no doubt fighting, and the few surviving elderly (wisdom - and more able to transmit tribal mythology and history) - in each group probably could be identified as especially valuable (perhaps also considered to be favoured by a god) and so becoming prominent in any society. But if we leap forward a few thousand years we see determinedly hierarchical societies and the term 'ruling elite' becomes more easily appropriate - a politico/religious pyramid of control with: chieftains, kings, pharaohs, princes, priests, and their families or clans at the apex. Figures whose power becomes legitimized by a socially constructed interweaving of myths, religion, and political machinations, reinforced if necessary by outright brutality.

    These elite sub-groups gained extraordinary power (indeed of life and death) over populations and were able to garner a staggeringly disproportionate share of the wealth produced by any community. Wealth that expanded substantially with the progressive adoption of farming as the primary means of economic subsistence.

It appears from the evidence that Europe before about 1,500 BCE was a 'relatively' peaceful region[7] with different tribes (and clans) adapted to lifestyles ranging from fairly primitive stone-age (hunting/gathering etc) to the monument building peoples organized and directed by incoming migrants (the megalithic people) and their descendants, with the skilled work being carried out by these and no doubt some indigenous artisans. The communities were economically supported by the farming activities of native peoples who were themselves the fusion of early groups of hunter-gatherers and those who, from about 4,000 BCE, had perhaps brought knowledge of the Neolithic revolution from the Middle-East. The relatively peaceful co-existence early on was no doubt partly to do with low population levels, room for expansion, and the variety of available ecological niches; as well as the need to rely on cruder stone-age weapons. In the period just before 1,500 BCE this was to change markedly in at least one European region where the attributes of three identifiable groups of people came together.

One of these groups was pastoralist, probably with herds of cattle, located in east-central northern Europe. They were armed with heavy polished stone axes and appear to have been quite aggressive; similar to pastoralists elsewhere. They can be identified in eastern Russia from about 2,500 BCE. But starting about 2,000 BCE they were reached by the megalithic peoples from the south-east, and seem to have initially been receptive to the incomer's ideas. From about the same time another identifiable group began to appear. They were traders and metal-workers who had probably originated in Iberia (but possibly south central Europe) and spread via mountain passes and river valleys throughout Europe seeking metals, amber, and gold. They also traded in 'worked goods', especially their yellow/red pottery with its distinctive 'corded' designs; establishing trade routes that would be used for millennia to come. For the most part they kept to

---

[7] The 'relative' is valid given clear evidence of conflict from the early Neolithic – Including defensive walled encampments by 3,500 BCE in Britain and elsewhere, and bodies found in a number of long barrow burials of individuals killed by blows from axes, clubs, and having been shot with arrows.

themselves as an interbreeding group. But it seems that in the areas occupied by the intermingling megalithic, and later the Battle-Axe peoples, they found communities that had become aware of the potential of metalworking. Here it seems that they established more permanent relationships, if perhaps never to the extent of freely interbreeding. These three peoples, plus surely others and hybrids of all, brought their diverse traditional abilities together to fuse into an effective fighting force. Organized, administered, and led in religion by the heirs to the megalithic folk; fed, motivated and led in mobile warfare by the pastoral Battle-Axe people; and in trading by Beaker-Folk (who were also noted for their skills in archery). They had gained the skills to produce bronze, and later iron, weapons and tools from incomers; miners and metal-workers travelling up the Danube River from Anatolia. Metal axe-blades could more easily fell the extensive forests and metal plough blades could open up the heavier soils; both enabling the extension and increased productivity of farming.

The Battle-Axe people had already domesticated the horses that would carry warriors into battle and later on pull their chariots. Groups of these diverse but unified peoples (perhaps 'federated' would better reflect the arrangement) became the core of the barbarians ('foreign people') that from about 1,700 BCE, spread and later became associated with a culture (or rather cultures) known as the 'Urnfield'. This due to their burying the ashes of their dead in elaborately decorated urns; with the form of decoration differing across Europe.

They were initially armed with the powerful stone battle-axe, then later with bronze weapons; especially effective was a type of sword with a flange grip protecting the handle. They travelled across Europe; from Iberia to Eastern Europe and Italy to Scandinavia, in successive waves and were to represent the dominant European culture whose warriors would intermittently swoop down on the civilizations to the south and east. At first settling to establish themselves in loose confederations in the border regions of the early Middle-Eastern empires but gradually, as their power increased and the older empires continued their relative decline, more determinedly pursuing their incursions into the heart of Mesopotamia. They were raiding as far south as Egypt by 1,300 BCE. Perhaps the most long-lasting impact, and a way of tracking the spread, of these aggressive incursions has been the transmission, over wide areas, of languages with their roots in the Aryan language of these barbarians. Linguistically, these peoples drew on landlocked origins in central and Eastern Europe, their native language having no word for sea.

In Anatolia they were known as Hittites, in Persia as Mitanni. The Anatolian settlement is of particular significance. Here, beginning in the central region, five barbarian tribes, connected to the more general barbarian movements out of east central Europe, established a confederation, with one tribe being elevated above the others. During peaceful times they traded and exchanged crafts-people and ideas with cities of the Middle-East. But, taking advantage of times of internal turmoil, they also raided deep into the heart of the old empires. By 1500 BCE the use of bronze for weapons and tools was beginning to be superseded by those made of iron. The use of charcoal in small furnaces enabling the higher temperatures required, and so the 'Iron-Age' had begun. Although iron could still not be melted sufficiently to cast (this had already been achieved in China but not really exploited there) but it could be softened and so enable it to be beaten into shape and then hardened by forging.

As Hittites these peoples ruled over an Empire extending from the Black Sea to the Near East. They were the first to show, in quite dramatic form, how effective Iron Age weapons would be when deployed against enemies armed only with Bronze Age weapon technology.

With the collapse of the Hittite Empire around 1200 BCE, their metal-smiths dispersed across the Mediterranean region but also to the east. These metal-working techniques reaching India by 519 BCE, at the same time as the army of Darius the Persian.

The use of iron for weapons added to the killing power of armies and the political power of those motivated by ideas of conquest and the control of other peoples. It was the barbarian tribes living on the fringes of civil life that initially most successfully exploited the advantages of iron with their mobile forces mounted on horseback or transported on fast sailing ships. Often these invaders brought a new vigour to civil life as they replaced decadent aristocracies that had become politically and socially separated from the masses of city people. Iron was an addition too, rather than a replacement for, bronze-age technology.

The period, from 1,500 BCE, is still known as the Iron-Age, but J.D.Bernal points out that 'More bronze was made and worked in the Iron-Age than ever in the Bronze Age itself.' (Bernal, 1954, p147). Iron did not really show its predominance in weapons for war and tools for production until about the 13th century BCE. What we then see is the spread and take-up of various forms of metallurgy in a similar way that the techniques of agriculture had spread thousands of years before. But instead of contributing to producing a benefit (as in food production and improved construction), iron as a material for weapons contributed to even more ferocious levels of war-making.

My somewhat sweeping 'look across the world', very loosely taken circa 1500 BCE, brings me back to the eastern Mediterranean where the two regions of Mesopotamia and Egypt (the extended 'Fertile Crescent') in which civil-life first arose are under increasing pressure from predatory peoples. Most of Mesopotamia succumbs to and falls under various combinations of Hittite, Kassite, Hurrian, and Assyrian, hegemony. But Egypt (made more secure partly at least by distance) after Pharaoh Ahmose had expelled the Hyksos in about 1,570 BCE (the Semitic Hyksos had invaded Egypt from the Levant in about 1783 BCE) and reinstated his Theban Royal family to the throne of a united country, has embarked upon "Five brilliant centuries of Egyptian civilization" according to D.H.Trump (1980, p160).

This last significant efflorescence of Egyptian civilization would see expansion into Palestine, first undertaken by Ahmose as he pursued the Hyksos north in order to exhaust their power and so reduce their threat. Over these five centuries Egypt would retain more or less military dominance over the area to its north-east. Whilst impressive in terms of monumental buildings, and artistic endeavour, there was little in the way of technical or intellectual advance in Egypt during these 500 years.

A civil focus for iron-age warfare was the city of Babylon and the wide-spread region that often fell within its administrative control. At about 1,450 BCE, the Kassite King Ulamburiash annexed Babylonia, thereby unifying most of Mesopotamia. This king and his immediate successors were in contact with Egyptian, Mitanni, Canaanite, and other kings, amongst other things arranging a succession of political marriages as part of a more extensive pattern of diplomacy. The Kassites engaged widely in trade, in particular the exchange of their lapis lazuli for Egyptian gold. In Anatolia the Hurrians, who had been in some form of alliance with the Mitanni (then controlling the area roughly covered by today's Syria), absorbed other indigenous peoples to become the Hittites, ruling an empire from their capital Boghazköy. During the 16th century they raided south into Syria and northern Mesopotamia, reaching as far as Babylon. But repeatedly having to retreat back to their homeland when it came under pressure from the Mitanni and the Kassites. The Hittites enjoyed a resurgence during the 14th century, suppressing the Mitanni in 1370 BCE, and capturing Cyprus.

The island of Cyprus was a site of early urbanization in the eastern Mediterranean, a development underpinned initially by the extensive exploitation of rich copper deposits. But Crete (to the west) was to become the administrative centre for the region's first identifiable civilization. A Bronze-Age civil life began to emerge here soon after 2000 BCE in what seems at first to have been a relatively peaceful period. Even as late as 1700 BCE there is little evidence of defensive fortifications, suggesting that the sea gave some protection in that significant forces did not have ships of a size that enabled successful sea-borne invasions. Sea-borne aggression at that time seems to have been more the activities of pirates and small-scale raiding rather than invasion. An attraction to the early settlers of Crete was its sizeable forests of cedar and cypress and down to the middle of the second millennium BCE wide tracts of these were cleared. The Island's river valleys would within a few centuries become denuded of most trees. The hardy olive tree did survive the axe and was cultivated and selectively improved to produce one of the Mediterranean region's most prized and enduring crops. This civilization, although geographically restricted, gave rise to a sophisticated culture, including impressive palaces (16 palace sites have been identified) some with under-floor drainage and at least one with a flushing lavatory in the queen's 'megaron'. Water was supplied to the main palace of Knossos via an aqueduct and distributed (gravity fed) throughout the palace by a series of terracotta pipes. These basic facilities for bodily needs enabled the inhabitants to better enjoy the colourful artistic productions of the Minoan culture that decorated the more substantial buildings.

The Minoan city of Knossos had developed into a metropolitan trading port, the activities of which were overseen from its magnificent palace with walls 150m long, wide sweeping staircases, and particular areas given over to workshops, storerooms, religious practices, sleeping, communal quarters, and a central court adjacent to which was a throne room. Parts of this building might have been five stories high. Coloured images of birds, wild monkeys, leaping bulls, dancers, finely dressed goddesses, and similar, graced the decorated plaster interior walls, ceilings, and floors. Along with these frescos were plaster reliefs, some fine pottery vases, figurines, and clay and glass seals, all produced by highly skilled craftspeople, as well as large quantities of other decorations, pottery, and seals, produced by less skilled artisans. To store the produce needed to support those occupying or visiting this building there were long galleries containing jars for grain, olive oil, and other produce. One area has been identified as the domestic quarter, evidence of a significant servant (probably including slaves) class having emerged. The Palace of Knossos could be taken to represent the highest level of material culture reached by the Minoan civilization.

Whilst the elite groups enjoyed luxury living they were merely at the apex of a stratified society composed of families of peasants, herdsman, farmers, fishermen, craftspeople, artists, fortune-tellers, merchants, builders, slaves, and many others, all part of a rent, tithe, tribute and trade, based economy. The class-based occupational differentiation related in part to different skills, aptitudes and traditional practices, of the mixture of early settlers and later migrants, living on the island. Anatolian, Egyptian, and Phoenician influences have been identified, with each group of immigrants tending to follow particular trades. This was a literate (at least for elite groups) society with two identifiable scripts, both pictographic. One used for administration and trade the other, being more impressive, was engraved on seals of jasper and rock crystal possibly used for magical purposes; some of these showing the influence of the seal engraving of Anatolia, as did their religion.

The craftspeople produced high quality goods: Including the original ('revolutionary', for B3 Vol.1 p117) fragile light-on-dark eggshell-ware pottery skilfully painted in white, red and orange, with both abstract and naturalistic studies. Metalwork, of silver, gold, and bronze, objects that show advances in technical and artistic skill. The common human practice of burial accompanied by grave goods has preserved some fine examples of the Minoan craft skills. Trade reached out across the Mediterranean, and especially with Egypt. The fine polychrome Minoan Kamáres ware pottery has been found in burial sites in Cyprus, Egypt, and the Levant. Copper daggers based on Cretan designs (influenced by earlier Syrian ones) have been found as far to the west as Italy and Spain. These two examples support the view that trade for Minoan cities was wide-ranging, involving manufactured goods rather than raw materials; although there was also some trade in metals, olive oil, timber, leather-work, and perhaps even opium.

The civil authority of the Minoans did not extend much further that the main island (Crete), and some others that could be viewed on its horizon. If not a colonizing civilization in terms of armed occupation, it did have a wide-ranging influence on the culture of other peoples. It seems, from evidence such as colourful frescos depicting sports and dancing, to have been a people, or possibly only an elite group, who enjoyed life. During the Minoan time we also see developments in weaponry: large spears (javelins) used for stabbing and throwing, innovations in body armour, and a small round shield that combined effectively with the short, stabbing and cutting, bronze sword.

From about the middle of the second millennium BCE we begin to have ships more obviously designed for war rather than trade, with raised platforms at bow and stern to assist boarding parties, and some having a fearsome ram protruding from the prow. These warships were probably not Minoan in origin but their design did spread throughout the Aegean and beyond during the active period of this civilization.

As Minoan civilization reached a peak at around 1500 BCE another empire was rising to the north in southern Greece, and when two centuries on the former went into decline the latter was well placed to take advantage. This decline has been attributed to a number of contributing factors. Once most of the extensive forests had been cleared the shallow-rooted fruit and olive trees, and other vegetation that replaced the trees, could not for long hold the rich soil, within a few centuries soil erosion was having a marked impact on agricultural productivity. Over the horizon came sea-borne raiders, grown strong enough to attack and loot Minoan towns. A series of natural disasters added to the general decline of Minoan civilization, with earthquakes, tidal waves, and volcanic eruptions, occurring around 1500 BCE.

The magnificent Palace of Knossos had already been destroyed about 1,700 BCE either by an earthquake or perhaps by invasion of people from Anatolia. The palace was rebuilt, on a larger scale, destroyed again in a volcanic eruption about 1,600 BCE, then rebuilt again to be deserted when the Minoan Empire came to an end, with invasion by Mycenaeans from mainland Greece.

What we do know from our knowledge of early civilizations is that they have but a limited period of ascendancy and pre-eminence before some combinations of factors – climate change, reduced soil fertility, invaders, disease, overconsumption of the surplus wealth and neglect of military forces, overbearing exploitation of a civilization's primary producers – being just some more obvious factors that could consign a civilization, rather than its peoples, to history.

During the more settled times, the Hittite skills in administering their own loosely controlled primarily Mesopotamian empire (with client local kings) encouraged much intermixing of peoples, exchanging trade-goods, and the passing on of ideas. Metals, with copper and iron being the most prominent, came in abundance from the Anatolian highlands (as well as from Cyprus), some to be traded on and some to be made into iron tools and weapons. The latter seem to have been the weapons of only the highest military and noble elites and on rare occasions given as gifts to other rulers. Iron weapons were sent to Egyptian pharaohs, one of which was placed in the tomb of Tutankhamen. Other than later contacts with Egypt, little is known about Hittite civilization. This due mainly to the determination of their conquers, the Assyrians, to completely destroy any material trace of them. We do know that they were able administrators and generally skilled warriors. Their cities were finely stratified socially and usually economically quite successful. If in the countryside within which the cities and towns were set the mass of people mostly lived lives of relentless toil.

From early in the second millennium barbarian tribes identified as Luwian and Hittite, along with others, had moved from eastern-Europe into Anatolia. Some stayed to found small kingdoms whilst others moved on south and west. One group, probably a branch of the Luwians, settled on some islands to the east of mainland Greece, city names such as Carchemish, Melid, and Wilusa (possibly the Troy of the Homeric tales), providing a clue to the origins of their founders. On one island, Siros, they built a fortified city.

Another people, the Achaeans, moved in from the north. These were aggressive patriarchal tribal groups, primarily descendants of nomadic herdsman, familiar with the use of light chariots. They had established the city of Mycenae which would become the centre of a new civilization and also bequeath to it a name. During the first half of the millennium other tribal peoples (Ionians, Aeolians, immigrants from Phoenicia and the original Neolithic natives, the peasant Pelasgoi) settled on the mainland and some other offshore islands in this region. And it would be the descendants of these peoples, as ever with some intermixing with the indigenous populations, that were to found the civilization known to us as Mycenaean. As the Mycenaean's rose they encroached progressively upon Minoan trade until by around 1400 BCE supremacy was theirs, one dramatically confirmed when in around 1350 BCE they had captured the city of Knossos.

In general most of what was good, in terms of administrative skill and culture, came from the Minoan inheritance being absorbed by the Mycenaeans. The latter were a war-like people of, as has been noted, diverse origins. It seems that the principle ruler, a king, was but the chosen leader of a prominent tribal group, advised by a council of headmen. The Mycenaean civilization extended over most of the area previously controlled by the Minoans. Its trading links were similar, if becoming even more extensive, with beads from Britain and amber from the Baltic being found in Mycenae, illustrating its reach.

One notable stage in humankind's development took place in the city of Ugarit around 1300 BCE (near modern Beirut) during the period when it was ruled by a Phoenician king. Fourteenth century Ugarit (Ugarit-Ras Shamra) was a colourful trading port subject to Mycenaean, Phoenician, Egyptian, Mesopotamian, and even perhaps Anatolian, influences. A city suggested by David Trump as being: '…..one of the most stimulating cities of the ancient world.' (Trump, 1980, p167)

Due partly to this cosmopolitanism, at least six different scripts ('Akkadian, Sumerian, Hittite, Hurrian, Egyptian, and Cypriote', McNeill 1963, p145) were in use, causing some difficulty and at times confusion. Need generated a solution to this problem and some (for us anonymous) Ugarit scribes produced an 'alphabet' reduced to thirty signs, an alphabet considered to be have been based on a Canaanite one that had preceded it. Although similar needs-led innovations in writing mediums were taking place in other parts of Mesopotamia it was to be the alphabet produced by the scribes of Ugarit whose use was to prove the more enduring. Perhaps the most significant result of having a simplified script was that it became more accessible for wider groups in the communities of the time. The written word was moving out of the temples and palaces and its restricted use by traders, and into increasingly more literate sections of the population. Learning to write, using this alphabet-based script, now ceased to require years of study, and a reasonable facility could be gained in months rather than years. From now the great 'epics' that had been orally transmitted down the generations (early on most having themes originating in Mesopotamia) were increasingly to be written down. The new literary productions soon extended beyond the epics to include poetry, dramas, and more philosophical commentaries. But this extended literary use of the new alphabet would be made in other lands in which the Phoenician alphabet would be adopted.

The Phoenicians as a people appear to have successfully negotiated their way through the period of aggressive Mycenaean hegemony that covered most of the Mediterranean and indeed of the Sea-people who would later displace the Mycenaeans as the dominant military force in the Mediterranean; even if in one period about 1,500 BCE they are recorded as paying tribute to Egypt. The Mycenaeans and the Phoenicians were trading peoples and each made advances in the technical aspects of ship-building. They also enabled the spread of civil-life across the Mediterranean - the Mycenaeans mostly by conquest but also trading, the Phoenicians mostly by trading and occasionally by conquest. But culturally, this was a form of Mediterranean civil-life that had for the most part been the original creation of the Minoans. The Mycenaeans left little of material note; some monumental buildings and sites of the characteristic 'beehive' tombs of their nobles, and some finely made gold objects (masks). But their war-like tradition endured into Greek history as later Homeric literature looked proudly, if mistakenly, back to the early Mycenaeans as being representative of an 'Heroic' age.

For McNeill (1963) p58 '....individuals arose who, like Homer and Hesiod in Greek times, took the old mythical materials and re-worked them into new and lengthy works of art.' The Iliad and the Odyssey are epic-length poems that offer an heroic view of the Mycenaean nobility as they liked to be imagined circa 1,500 BCE – poems that in some variations had initially been past down by an oral tradition.

By the end of the 13th century Mycenaean civil power had extended north into central and northern Greece and it was outposts here that first felt the effects of a new wave of barbarians moving in from central Europe. This was the period from which events were to be included in the 'Homeric' literature of later times. One event, the siege of Troy, provided the factual material around which Homer's powerful imagination wove the Iliad. A sequel to which, The Odyssey, tells of the problems faced by returning warriors. The whole period recorded as the 'Trojan War' coincided with incursions from aggressive Dorian people. It seems that the passage of these invaders was facilitated by confusion caused by a series of quite severe earthquakes, and perhaps a population debilitated by plague. By 1200 BCE the principle Mycenaean cities had been sacked and the civilization had fallen to invaders. A civilization which, perhaps more than any other up to that time had ruled by force of arms fell to others even stronger. It would be the rulers of numerous mini kingdoms into which Greece fractured that would pertain as most of the Aegean region entered a 'Dark Age' characterized by internal strife and cultural stagnation.

Since 2000 BCE the people later identified as Phoenicians (noted above) had settled and developed cities (such as Tyre, Sidon, Arwad, and Byblos) along the coast of the Levant ; a narrow stretch of fertile plain between the coast and the mountain range, on the eastern side of the Mediterranean. The name Phoenicia derives from the Greek word (*phoinix*) for the colour purple and this relates to a dye made by using an extract from the murex sea-snail. A dye used by dyers to colour, deep red or purple, the fine textiles which were highly valued at the time, especially by Mesopotamian nobility. Interestingly, the name Canaan derives from the Semitic word for purple, a connection which gives a clue to a common identity of these peoples. As ever, when a name is given to a people it rarely if ever identifies a people with common ethnic origins and/or racial homogeneity. In general, it seems that the people called Phoenicians were from Canaanite stock (a people themselves of diverse Semitic origins), but they would have interbreed with many different groups of over-sea and over-land immigrants. The growing prosperity of Phoenician cities attracted skilled people from across the region, some of the most significant of these being residues of Minoan and Mycenaean civil-life such as artists and crafts-people moving from decline to opportunity.

By 1300 BCE the bustling cities of Tyre, Byblos, Sidon, and Ugarit, provide evidence of the success of these ship-building, sea-faring, peoples. They had survived and prospered in spite of, (and perhaps sometimes in co-operation with), the periods of Minoan and then of Mycenaean power. A survival due to astute political strategy, and a prosperity based upon extensive trading relations. As the two older civilizations declined the Phoenicians would enjoy a period of ascendancy (".....a brief golden age" Roberts, 1993, p87). Even though the period of actual ascendancy would not last long, the Phoenicians were to claim an important place in history for many centuries to follow. Their principle cities were thriving by 1100 BCE and when the Hebrew King David led his armies to defeat the Philistines the Phoenicians were freed of restraints and able to further expand their trading and colonizing activities. By the end of the 9th century at least 25 and possibly as many as 50 sites (including Carthage, Valletta, and Cadiz) across the length of the Mediterranean and beyond to Britain, were either Phoenician trading ports or had developed into one of their colonies (some such as Carthage were colonies brutally taken from indigenous peoples). They used timber from the forests of cedar that covered areas of the mountains in the hinterland of their homeland to build the great ships that would carry sailors, settlers, trade-goods, and a culture, across the seas. Trade goods included the cedar valued for shipbuilding and a range of manufactured products including, jewellery, glass, ivory carvings, and of worked-metal ornaments, utensils and tools.

Phoenician trade-routes served as conduits along which passed many different types of economic migrants, including most significantly miners and metalworkers of Anatolian heritage, who would stimulate and accelerate economic development in many regions of the Mediterranean. One example of the legacy of these economic migrations being the tin miners who travelled in Phoenician ships to settle in the south-western tip of England. Along these routes would also pass the simplified alphabet, and its later modifications, which had originated in Ugarit. The Greek historian Herodotus notes that when in 600 BCE the Egyptian Pharaoh Necho wished to enhance his reputation by sponsoring the circumnavigation of Africa it was Phoenicians that he paid to undertake the three year long expedition.

We might admire the ship-building, sea-fairing - cloth dying, glass-making, fine metalwork, quarrying and masonry, carpentry, ivory carving, although most design and artistic styles were derivative, if taking novel forms - and trading skills of the Phoenicians but other aspects of their culture are less appealing to the modern mind. Their religion derives mainly from Babylonia, worshipping the same gods in similar temples. The latter being administered by priests who organized both women and boy prostitutes. Child infanticide was not uncommon in the Mediterranean world (during the second millennium) at this time, usually for eugenic (see Plato's 'Republic'), or fairly selective religious, purposes. But for the Phoenicians the ritual burning of live infants became a common practice, amounting according Darlington (1971, p177) to "......undiscriminating sacrifice, a religious orgy".

The generally recognized demise of the Phoenicians as a significant force was completed in the 7th century BCE when their homeland was invaded by the Assyrians and the daughters of the then King of Tyre were transported to be imprisoned in the harem of the victorious Assyrian King. Some of the colonies endured under local Phoenician rule and their skills, as sea-farers would see them noted many times in the subsequent history of the Mediterranean. They would also feature in another passage of history, that concerning the Hebrews, when they are known (by themselves) as Canaanites. These were mainly the peoples that lived inland from the coast in parts of today's Palestine/Israel.

So, similar to many peoples and their cultures, with the Phoenicians there was a mixture of stimulation to humankind's advance and the retention of less admirable practices. The most significant positives for my purposes were the simplification and spread of an alphabet, the improvement in navigational and other maritime skills, a general stimulus to economic advance, and spreading administrative and cultural aspects of civil-life to new areas across the Mediterranean region. Lastly, we might recognize that during the time of Phoenician ascendancy the Aegean was in general decline, and it was in Phoenicia and its colonies that other Aegean Bronze Age artistic traditions were preserved.

Somewhat in contrast to the Phoenicians (although they might at times have been mistaken for each other) there was another maritime 'nation' active in the Mediterranean during the later part of the 2nd millennium - these became known as the Sea-Peoples. Possibly originating from the western coast of the Aegean Sea as descendants of as many as nine identifiable tribal groups from western/central Anatolia; but, in fact, their specific origins remains a mystery. The primary sources of information of these people are from Egyptian records which refer to them as 'tribal peoples' and more obviously as 'coming from the sea in their warships…..' They do seem to have been a confederation of different groups active in the region (the eastern Mediterranean) between about 1276-1000 BCE. The contrast with the Phoenicians was in the way they chose to interact with others - the Phoenicians generally focused on trade whereas for the Sea-Peoples the focus was on military conquest and looting. Their relationship with the Phoenicians seemed to have had some basis of cooperation and on the occasion that the Phoenician island city of Arvad was invaded by the Hittites the Sea-People are said to have ejected the invaders and returned Arvad to the Phoenicians. In 1,208 BCE a force composed of Sea-People and Libyans attempted to invade Egypt but were repelled by an army led by Ramses II ('.....great builder and valiant solider.' For Brugsch-Bey, 1996, p293). As they were by the later pharaohs, Ramses III and Mernepath, during subsequent attempts at invasion. It has been suggested that the Sea-Peoples settled in Libya, Sicily, and southern Italy, and also in Palestine (the Philistia of the Hebrew Bible). A derivation of the latter being a name subsequently given to them, as the Philistines, a name to pass into history as synonymous with cultural stagnation and artistic ignorance.

The so-called Sea Peoples, groups of raiders who "live on ships" and appear in records from Egypt, Syria, and Anatolia, have traditionally borne at least some of the blame for the decline of Pharaonic Egypt.

Scheidel quotes Ramses III reflecting on their attacks on Egypt from 1207 BCE '…all at once the lands were removed and scattered in the fray. No land could stand before their arms…..They laid their hands upon the lands as far as the circuit of the earth.'

Although history frames the Sea-Peoples as the most aggressive nation during a period when inter-group conflict was common, some historians take the, perhaps rather sweeping, view that the Mediterranean-wide activity of the aggressive Sea-Peoples helped to clear the way for the rise of the Greeks the Romans, and so of Western civilization. Little comfort for those many who suffered at their hands.

At about this time the Hittites (their Empire ran from 1,600 - 1,178 BCE) had for a century been gnawing away at the northern borders of the Egyptian Empire, especially attacking down the Levant. The Egyptians, under Ramses II, confronted the Hittites led by King Muwatalli in 1,285 BCE at Kadesh (in today's Syria). When the dust on the battlefield had cleared each side claimed victory but, although the lighter more manoeuvrable Egyptian chariots proved more effective than the heavier ones of the Hittites, the balance of evidence suggest something of a bloody draw; with the Hittites remaining in control of the land they had already taken but extending no further. A peace treaty was agreed in 1,260 BCE (presumable one of the earliest written peace treaties ever signed between two 'nations') and this seem to have been sealed (or at least reinforced) by the marriage in 1,256 BCE of a Hittite princes to Ramses II. It does seem that these two empires never again faced each other on the battlefield.

We are now to consider, if only briefly, perhaps the greatest imperial power yet to stride across the stage of Middle-Eastern history. The Assyrians, although noted from as early as 3,500 BCE, they come more fully into historical view from about 1,420 BCE when they seem to have controlled a small semi-autonomous region of the Mitanni Kingdom (lying on the border with Babylonia), being locally administered from the City of Ashur. This city beside the River Tigris had a strong heritage of Akkadian influences showing in the names of its early rulers. And yet even earlier we have knowledge of a civilized 'ghetto' in a suburb of the then thriving southern Anatolian city of

Kanesh housing a colony of merchants from Assyria in 1,950 BCE. It seems that an Assyrian community developed and thrived in the region of Ashur.

Around 1,350 BCE the Assyrian ruler Ashur-uballit I (self-styled 'Great King'), perhaps in alliance with King Suppiluliumas of the Hittites, successfully rebelled against King Tushratta ruler of the Mitanni. Ashur-uballit I is generally considered to be the king who established the Assyrian empire. He and others of the Assyrian ruling group, as had other Mesopotamian rulers before them, admired aspects of Babylonian culture and it remained influential. There is also evidence of royal family interbreeding between the two civilizations.

Once established the Assyrians became an aggressive and expansionist force. By 670 BCE they would control an Empire that included Mesopotamia, west to Egypt, the eastern coast of the Mediterranean, the Island of Cyprus, north to Anatolia and south into the Arabian Desert. Their aggression was partly at least in reaction to the similarly aggressive and oppressive behaviour of the Mitanni and the Hittites. With Assyrian kings regularly leading expeditions west against Semitic tribes of a group called the Akhlamu and south into Babylonia. At about the turn of the 13th century King Adad-nirari I, by defeating both Kassite and Mitanni armies, was able to rule over the whole of Mesopotamia.

With Assyrian royalty's characteristic lack of modesty Adad-nirari I styled himself 'King of All'. These sort of titles were not uncommon in past Mesopotamian royalty,[8]*and due to their, albeit superficial, 'aura' they served a propaganda purpose, in relation to both those ruled over and for potential enemies. The Assyrians seem well aware of the value of propaganda for enhancing imperial status as can be seen from their style of stone carving (primarily battle and hunting scenes), and in numerous written texts. One of the latter claimed that King Shalmaneser I, following a successful battle with the remnants

---

[8] Indeed almost all royalty down to today freely offer each other various grand titles, awards, and meaningless medals, to decorate their robes and uniforms and otherwise contribute to supporting their aching sense of self-importance.

of the Mitanni, ordered the blinding in one eye of 14,400 prisoners, sending a message of impressive power supposedly allied to relative leniency.

During this time we see the Assyrians able to field awesome armies; as well as their own professional officers and soldiers they were also prepared to conscript any able-bodied male citizen. The Assyrian deployment of large infantry-based fighting forces was to prove successful, and they devised a battlefield strategy that would be adopted by many others (Persians, Romans and, even much later, Napoleon). Assyrian kings also adopted the practice of incorporating whole sections of defeated armies into their own forces, paying them by imposing extra taxes on subjected populations. This was a policy that would sow the seeds of Assyria's downfall when by 612 BCE most of the Assyrian army was composed of subject, poorly paid, men with little sense of loyalty to their masters.

From the evidence available, it seems that the Assyrians of these times were feared by their neighbours. Some of whom (such as the Hittites and Babylonians) formed alliances to mitigate Assyrian economic or military power. In the later period of the 12th century King Tukulti-ninurta had to fight the Hittites in the north and also suppress a Babylonian rebellion in the south. Here we see a method of dealing with opposition that would assist Assyrian rule over other territories, the practice of transporting large numbers of the defeated; thus dislocating potential enemies, as well as unintentionally stimulating the interbreeding of diverse peoples.

Another significant Assyrian king was Tigath-Pileser I, whose army not only beat off a series of would be invaders but also pushed most of the Empire's boundaries outward and in general consolidated Assyrian direct or indirect rule over northern and central Mesopotamia (sacking Babylon circa 1100 BCE), north into Anatolia and west to control most of Syria as far as the Mediterranean coast. His reign also saw improvements in civil administration and in the management of agriculture.

With the death of Tigath-Pileser I Assyria experienced increasing difficulty defending itself and entered a period of relative decline. It was King Adad-nirair II (ruled c. 911-891 BCE) who began to reverse declining Assyrian fortunes, his scribes keeping meticulous accounts of the King's exploits in warfare, in particular in repelling repeated incursions of tribal peoples from northern Arabia. Adad-nirair's son, Tukulti-Ninurta II (ruled 891-884 BCE), continued the expansionist policies of his father, along with the practice of keeping detailed records of his military exploits.

Throughout most of the following two and a half centuries following the reign of Tukuls-Ninurta II, the Assyrian Empire was led by a succession of more or slightly less terrible leaders.

Notable ones being: Tiglath-Pileser III (746-727 BCE - a general made king as a result of military rebellion), Sargon II (721-705 BCE), Sennacherib (704-681 BCE), and Ashurbanipal (668-627 BCE).

In Ashurbanipal we have a typical Assyrian King but 'writ large', a combination of cruelty in warfare allied to quite enthusiastic support for the arts. He was cruel even by the standards of the Middle-East at this time, liberally: "flaying, beheading, and impaling" captured enemies. An inscription on a monument erected following his crushing of an internal revolt reads: 'Their young men and old I took prisoners. Of some I cut off their feet and hands, of others I cut off the ears and nose and lips.......The male children and the female children I burned in flames; the city I destroyed.'

At the borders hostile and increasingly bolder peoples raided and generally withdrew, decreasing the state's revenue and extending its army. When the Medes of Iran settled their long-lasting enmity with the Scythian barbarians to the north they formed an alliance able to deploy powerful, highly mobile armies. The Scythians moved swiftly into Syria and Palestine, and the Medes set about the destruction of the Assyrian homelands. It was they who dealt the final blow to the Assyrian Empire. An empire which is effectively at an end when Mede soldiers sacked Nineveh in 612 BCE, with the victors being merciless in ensuring that Assyria would be unable to rise again.

In this overview of developments I wish to include a people active at this time whose literary and social unity has made them stand out in history, if in an uneven continuity, down to today. These were the Hebrews (later to be named as Israelites) who were the principle ancestors of the group that became known as the Jews. These also arose from a coming together of a mixture of peoples from Semitic tribal groups. We have to go back to about the turn of the second millennium to pick up the origins of the Hebrews. One significant group of those who would later be identified as Hebrews were mostly nomadic shepherds eking out a sparse living as they ranged across northern Arabia and the Sinai as far west as Egypt. By about 1500 BCE a relatively small group (of the tribes) had settled in Egypt paying 'tribute' to the Hykos who were then ruling as pharaohs[9]. It has been suggested that these migrants were seeking grazing land and refuge during a time of famine in their home region.

In Egypt many of the settlers seem to have gradually changed from nomads to farmers. Similar to Egyptian citizens, they were also expected to undertake labour on public works during seasonally slack times of working on the land. By about the middle of 1300 BCE, for a number of reasons (including possibly a high birth-rate causing concern amongst Egypt's rulers), life in Egypt became less attractive and an exodus took place. It was highly unlikely that this was a mass migration of a single large group in one event, and was more probably a process taking place over a period of years (even decades) during which most of the Hebrew tribal population of Egypt - now composed of the product of some level of interbreeding with Egypt's then indigenous peoples - moved east. The Jewish story (written down many centuries after the event) has it that a leader, Moses, led his people back towards the east, along the way re-adopting the nomadic tradition of their forefathers. But whilst in Egypt many of these people had seen the benefits of the farming life and had developed a hunger

---

[9] Biblical tradition has Abraham, the 'first' prophet/leader leaving Sumerian Ur in about 1950 BCE and moving into Palestine - McNeill (1963) suggests that The God of Abraham possibly had its origins as a family god, one of many that different tribes had adopted in Sumer.

for land to settle on rather than just graze over as had their ancestors.

A new approach to religion does seem to have been an important factor in holding the migrating tribes together during their time of wandering in the region of Sinai (the Biblical 40 years), drawing other Semitic tribal peoples to join them. It is difficult to believe that a single man, Moses, would take it upon himself to propose a monotheistic religion to a people worshiping a range of tribal gods. But perhaps this was facilitated due to their having already been exposed to the idea of a single god in the elevation of a primary Egyptian god Ra during the reign of Akhenaten, who had ruled Egypt from about 1,335 BCE.

By the time that the Hebrews and their allies entered Palestine they were a more cohesive people, led by a priestly caste with convictions of adherence to a single god in 'Yahweh'. It was to be increasingly zealous and shrewd, if often cruel and demanding, Hebrew priests, later added to by the prophets (when later on these two groups were in conflict, the priests tended to support kings the prophets to support the masses) that from the earliest times of the exodus, determined a national and religious identity that would endure like few others. Ponting notes the 'invented' and 'idealized' aspects of their claimed traditions: 'The narrative of the Old Testament is clearly written to give a particular religious message and is of limited historical value.' - and he suggests that the wandering in the dessert and the story of conquest under Joshua '.....seems to have been invented to justify the right of Israel to the area.' (op cit, 2000, p212)

It was from about 1,100 BCE, that serious conflicts began as the Hebrews endeavoured to expand into Palestine and so 'rubbed against' the settled Philistines and Canaanites, who were also having to deal with the nomadic Midianites raiding from the west. The most significant factors which led to the military success of the Hebrews was their unity, one due partly to a shared religion and also the migration story which became enshrined in mythology as being an escape from tyrannical rule. These alongside a more obvious shared ambition to gain the land of others.

Early victories provided momentum as they progressively (with occasional setbacks) suppressed Palestine, nominally in the name of Yehweh. When victorious it was attributed to this god's favour with his 'chosen' people, when a setback was suffered it was not due to any diminution of Yahweh's power but only to his dissatisfaction with his chosen ones. This led to a stoical attitude of acceptance, of defeat as being God's will. As noted above, the Hebrew monotheism was not entirely new, Amen-hotep IV (later to be Khu-n-aten 'splendour of the Sun's disk') had preceded this with his elevation of the 'Sun-disk' which symbolized the god Aten to be the one and only god of Egypt. A god accessible to all people and not just those of the priestly caste. Prof. Ninian-Smart quotes Amen-hotep IV: 'How numerous are Thy works. They are concealed from the vision of men, O sole God, other than whom there is no other. Thou hast created the earth according to thy heart, with men and flocks and all the animals......Thou dost apportion to each man his place, thou providest for his needs: each has his nourishment, and the hour of his death is fixed.......' (Ninian-Smart, 1969, p289). From as early as 2,500 BCE Ra (Aten) had been a primary god (the Sun-disk representing the body or the eyes of Ra) - In the Egyptian way, the Ra concept was blended with a range of other gods (Horus, Amun, Osirus) - a common representation of Ra being as a human body with a hawk's head topped by a Sun-disk with a snake curled around it.

Inland of the region adjacent to the Mediterranean, the tribal Hebrews tenaciously fought to displace people of Semitic origins similar to their own. They were, by the admission of their own scribes, often ruthless in war and in settling the fate of those they defeated. At the beginning of their campaign they had more success against the less developed hill peoples than against the iron armed tribes of the valleys and plains. Their leaders surveyed the task of conquest that they had given themselves and they set (or gave it to Yahweh's voice) grim conditions for the treatment of their foes. For the Amorites, Hittites, and Canaanites, living in the areas coveted by the Hebrews, nothing left after the capture of a city was to be allowed to live including men, women, and children. For others, generally the men were to be put to death with the women and children taken to serve the needs of the victors. This was not an uncommon approach adopted by other armies in dealing with the defeated, but the Hebrews codified it as a god's direction and appear to have applied it with a cruel determination (Bible, Numbers 21 "*So they* [Moses people] *slew him* [Sihon king of the Amorites] *and his sons; and all his people, until there was not one survivor left to him; and they possessed his land.*" Also Numbers 31, Deuteronomy 21 "*But in the cities of these peoples that the Lord your God gives you for an inheritance, you shall save nothing that breaths, but you should utterly destroy them, the Hittites and the Amorites, the Canaanites, and the Per'izzites, the Hivites and the Jeb'usites, as the Lord your God has commanded;*"

Gradually the Hebrews ruthlessly gained control of their 'Promised Land' (an imagined veneer of religious justification over what was clearly land they had promised themselves) and military success led to economic progress; the cities became more Jewish and a generally uneasy peace was restored. As conflict eased, Phoenician and other traders returned to trade. As often happens when peoples come into mutually beneficial contact different amounts of fusion takes place, and undoubtedly many of the peoples engaged in trade (and indeed in war) were genetically and culturally absorbed into the Jewish movement.

Even down to 1,000 BCE, all the tribes which would become known as Hebrews/Jews[10] did not quite have the cohesion of a nation and there was some antipathy towards the idea of kingship. It took until the reign of the second Israelite king, David, that national unity was more fully established. As a young man David, a member of the tribe of Judah, is said to have incurred the wrath of the then king, Saul, and was forced into exile. For a time he fought as a mercenary in the army of the Philistines and when Saul died he gained their approval of his bid for the throne of Judah. Following years of bitter tribal

---

[10] The idea of 12 tribes is certainly an invention, see below re. how this conveniently allows the 'Ark of the covenant' to be looked after by a single tribe for one month per year.

conflict David, mainly supported by southern tribes, defeated the Jesubites to take possession of Jerusalem.

David was recognized as king of all Israel/Judah in 1002 BCE. A clever and ambitious king, leading his army against the Philistines, Moabites, and other neighbouring peoples. By the end of his reign he ruled over all of the Canaanite lands, southern Syria, and the land to the east of the Jordan River from the Orontes River in the north to the Gulf of Aquaba in the south. David and his ruling group had taken a disparate mix of Semitic tribes with a fairly loose sense of historic identity beyond the narrative of exodus from Egypt, and managed to unite them in defence of the land their forefathers had conquered by force of arms; it was a unity that forged them into a nation…...the Jewish nation.

When later on aggressive neighbours took advantage of Israel's internal divisions its empire was reduced to the mutually antagonistic kingdoms of Israel in the north and Judah in the south. The following three centuries were characterized by conflicts between the two (Jewish) kingdoms and, especially for the richer Israel also against most of their neighbours. By 722 BCE the army of Sargon II had overrun Israel, and in the Assyrian way large numbers of the Israelites were deported to be replaced by migrants from the north and the west. After its conquest Judah became a vassal state of Assyria until King Josiah successfully rebelled, taking advantage of a time of Assyrian weakness which was primarily due to the aggressive intentions of the Scythians and Medes, culminating in the destruction of the Assyrian Empire as noted above.

Soon after this a re-invigorated Babylonia, also rebelled against the Assyrians and had driven them back north to then take control of the whole of territory of the old Babylonian Empire. They then, in 609 BCE, invaded Judah. A Judah already weakened by having to fight the Egyptians earlier in this year resulting in King Jehoiakim ruling Israel pretty much as a suzerainty of Egypt until the Babylonian take-over. Following a rebellion against them led byKing Jehoiakim, the Babylonians returned to crush the rebels, destroy Jerusalem (587 BCE) and other cities in the region, and deported considerable numbers of the Judeans to Babylonia. Thus all the aristocracy and leading sections of the principle tribes of the Hebrews were now in exile. This might well have consigned a people to historical obscurity, but for the Jews it would serve as a defining event ('the Diaspora') for their national identity over the 2,500 years, down to the forced establishment of the state of Israel at a cost to the relatively peaceful peoples that had long been settled there.

The Jews were no more nor less culpable for fictionalizing their origins than other peoples, but belief in theirs, coupled with the idea that they are in some way 'chosen', has endured down to today. Along with the religious advance to a personalized monotheism was a god who would not be represented in any craven image, thus gaining in numinous power in the minds of worshippers. His material invisibility meant that no conquerors could symbolically cast down any statues of this god, exposing their weakness as they were crushed into rubble and dust. An act long held as dramatic proof of the weakness of any conquered people's gods.

Hebrews, just as many other 'nations' of those times, were often exceedingly and unnecessarily cruel, covetous over the lands of others, and in their writings they mostly idealized or even directly falsified their history. So why do I highlight the development of what only ever became a relatively small empire. The primary reason for this is that the Jewish peoples themselves can be identified throughout history becoming influential in the subsequent history of lands far from the Middle-East - often to the benefit of the peoples they lived amongst, and regularly bred with - especially in areas such as politics, trade, finance, music, medicine, law, education, and the social and natural sciences.

Conflict spread religions and in the Far East the influence of Buddhism received a significant impetus when the Mauran Emperor Ashoka (ruled c 269-232 BCE) embraced the religion and did so as a guide for his life rather than just as a political expedience. Ashoka was said to have been a militarily cruel and aggressive emperor but he then (in 263 BCE) became committed to Buddhism, it is recorded, as a reaction to his witnessing the death and destruction that was the outcome of his warring in the northern state of Kalinga, when 100,000 soldiers died. At this time it is noted that Ashoka said that he would never again go to war unless it was in defence of his people.

It was in the land that became Greece that forms of civil life developed in ways that both enhanced human life (philosophy, mathematics, and the sciences...and arguable perhaps governance) but also continued on the path of hegemonic conflict – initially between city states. In the Greek city-state of Sparta where we see the military state become actual, rather than just serving as the material of myth. The serfs/helots, virtual slaves, of the Spartans were forced to work the land and produce the surplus to allow the *Homoroi* (or free-citizens) to focus their attention on military training and related matters. This was a society where captives in war served as slaves and could be killed - as could helots - during autumn - '......with impunity by any Spartan'. The classical Spartan state developed a system of education into which children taken from their families were introduced at the age of seven. An education focusing on physical exercise but which also included music and poetry. Up to about the age of 12 years girls followed the same education programme as boys, prior to their then taking up domestic duties. At 18 the boys underwent two years of intensive military training before entering a unit composed of 15 members that slept, ate, and fought, together. Such concentration on military training led to Sparta having the most powerful of the Greek military phalanxes. The Spartans expanded into neighbouring areas of Lacedaemon and the Peloponnese, displacing tyrannies but in many places, such as Corinth, allowing oligarchies to take power and lead regimes where a group of the rich citizens repressed most of the population. But the Spartans had little enthusiasm for empire-building and generally settled to be a strong city-state leading a Peloponnesian League of states during times of wider-ranging conflict.

From the 6th century political upheavals occurred in the Middle-East involving hostile invaders such as the Persians and the Medes. A succession of Mede kings had already taken control of the neighbouring provinces of Armenia and Persia to form the basis of what would later become the Persian Empire when, in about 559 BCE, Cyrus II the Great established himself as dual king of the two equal peoples, the Medes and the Persians. In doing so in effect establishing the first Persian 'The Achaemenid' Empire. Cyrus claimed a range of titles, including: 'King of Kings', 'King of the Four Corners of the World', 'King of the Universe', and similar.....no lack of ambitions here! As he expanded and consolidated his rule he ranged widely across much of the Middle-East, at some cost in lives and destruction of civil infrastructure. But history also credits him with some enlightened thinking in relation to human rights, cultural respect, and developing an advanced system of administration covering his empire.

The third King of the Achaemenid Empire Darius the Great gained a foothold on some outlying Greek islands and launched a poorly planned invasion of the mainland only to be defeated by an Athenian-led army at Marathon in 490 BCE, when Greek military tactics and their disciplined phalanxes gave them victory over a much larger (30,000 strong) Persian army. For this expedition the Persian army had been transported to Greece in a fleet of ships.

Ten years after the defeat at Marathon the Persians returned now led by Darius's son Xerxes I (reigned 486-466 BCE) with a much larger army (at least 100,000, possibly 150,000, men and up to a thousand ships – with possibly up to a million men being involved in engineering projects including the construction of bridges, a canal to make the passage of the troops and sailors easier, and others tasked with organising the supplies for the fighting units. This time the Persian forces first crossed from Asia Minor to Europe by building a bridge of pontoons across the Dardanelles. The Persians then moved slowly but relentlessly down through the mainland. An alliance of Attic and Peloponnesian city-states (of about 6-7,000 men), with Sparta (King Leonia's of Sparta) taking the lead, moved north to face the invaders. For a number of days the Greeks, aided by their long stabbing spears and clever defensive tactics, were able to hold the Persian advance in a narrow pass at Thermopylae. Then, following their being outflanked (due, according to legend, to a Greek traitor showing the Persians a path that went around the narrow valley), the Greeks decided on a managed retreat. One aided by a small force made up of all the men from Sparta and some from the two Greek cities of Thespian and Thebes being charged with holding the Persians at Thermopylae for as long as possible. In this famous engagement the 300 Spartans and their other Greek comrades held the pass for two whole days of battle (allowing the rest of the Greek army time to retreat) before they were defeated; all killed, each dying with 'sword in hand'. This act of heroism significantly reinforced the reputation of the Spartans.

The Persians pressed on, taking Athens in 478 BCE but not before the Athenian fleet had sailed to seek shelter further south in the bay of Salamis. It would be here later in the year where the larger Persian fleet would be decimated by the Athenians operating in difficult waters with which they were more familiar. The destruction of their fleet and their uneasy presence amongst a hostile population led to the Persians beginning to withdraw. In the following year a second Persian fleet was defeated at Mycale and its army defeated on land at Plataea, with the Spartans again playing a decisive role.

The news of these battles rapidly spread throughout occupied parts of Greece and numerous local rebellions flared up against the Persians. Finally their defeat by a confederation of Greek cities (the Delian League, with Athens taking the lead) at the Battle of Eurymedon (a battle that took place on both land and at sea) effectively ended Persian rule over the outlying Greek regions and islands and its threat to the central heartlands.

Following the wars with the Persians, Athens progressively gained a sound economic base in manufacturing, commercial agriculture, silver-mining; along with a commitment to 'democratic' government. A democracy which, during its best period, extended the vote to landless citizens, but still only free native males could be citizens. The sea-going ability of Athenian sailors, added to which the fleet was considerably enlarged by order of Themistocles (200 boats paid for in silver) meant that they controlled the Aegean Sea and were a force to be reckoned with far beyond the immediate Greek sphere. Their fearsome Triremes were usually manned by Athenian citizens and the importance and prestige of the fleet, added to the democratizing tendencies of the time, meant that these oarsmen were of political significance. The Athenian oarsman gained a similar status to the hoplite and had the same right to address the assembly.

The Greeks can be seen to represent, at least symbolically, a high point of city life in the west. They introduced innovations in philosophy, theatre, architecture, engineering, mathematics, and the natural sciences, so a significant body of learning to advance civil life. Even if most of these drew more or less heavily from the work of non-Greek predecessors. Here was a florescence of humankind's distinctly human cognitive attributes. As the Greeks flowered in the third century BCE other, more hostile peoples to their west were stirring up embers that from about two century later were to burn and light up the growth and development of another significant empire. One that was to leave an indelible mark on civil life to the extent that the concept of 'civilization', from their ascendancy onwards, would have clear defining features.

Prior to this in 338 BCE a Macedonia led by Philip II, a ruthless but clever leader, was able to take advantage of internal conflict in Greece. Philip, with his reorganized and well-trained army, progressively advanced his own perception of Macedonian interests. By a mixture of clever diplomacy and military strength he took control of northern and central parts of the mainland. In 338 BCE '....the Macedonian phalanx routed the ill-led allied troops. It was the end of Greek liberty'.

Philip was murdered in 336 BCE (aged 48) and his son, Alexander, became king, an outcome that would have a significant impact on the future of the civil world. Alexander consolidated and further expanded the empire that his father had begun to establish and on his death (in 323 BCE, aged 33) the empire would reach from Greece through most of the Middle-East, including Egypt, and east to northern India (the Indus river).

Alexander, whilst he could be ruthless, even personally cruel, was also an intelligent ruler. One sensible enough to maintain a pragmatic balance between reminding subject peoples of Macedonian military strength whilst allowing them to pursue some of their traditional ways of life. He endeavoured to unite the diverse peoples of his empire rather than simply to invoke fear; even his self-appointed status as a god could have been as much about unification as reflecting an excess of egoism.

But perhaps the most important legacy we can attribute to the Macedonians was the extent to which they Hellenized the Empire (Aristotle had been one of a thirteen year old Alexander's tutors). Along with improvements in transport links and a common currency, both of which led to an increase in trade, there was also the spread of Greek crafts-people and of scholars, and with them technical, philosophical and cultural ideas. Of most significance in relation to fostering the addition of 'novel' information (to humankind's bio-cultural 'genome') was the spread of the Greek language. According to Encyclopaedia Britannica (1974 ed.) - 'The three centuries from Alexander to the establishment of the Roman Empire under Augustus were among the most productive and influential in the whole of Greek history.' Whilst Macedonian rule would end with the rise of Rome, its impact on spreading Greek ideas and culture would to an extent endure.

As the Greek intellectual florescence began to fade a small state to its west had been rising. And it would be due to the rise of Rome that Greece itself, having gifted so much to the world's cultural and intellectual heritage, would from now be relegated to the status of civil backwater down to the modern era. Continuing as a part of the civil world but one contributing little to its advance in relation to my concept of accumulating 'novel information'. It is with the Romans that the basic material infrastructures of civil life were established in forms that continue down to our day.

Apart from occasional fragments, Roman history only really begins to be recorded around 230 BCE when it was already the most militarily powerful single grouping in the Mediterranean world. Owing to this, and the tendency of all empires to write their history more as they would have liked it to have been rather than it actually was, we have mythical origin stories with the Romans focusing on the ravishment of a noblewomen, Rhea Silvia. Rhea was the daughter of Numitor, king of Alba Longa. Numitor's younger brother Amulius seized the throne and killed his brother's son. He then forced Rhea to become a Vestal Virgin (priestess of the god Vesta). As such, she was forced to take a vow committing her to thirty years of celibacy, thus ensuring there would be no other royal offspring to threaten the inheritance of Amulius's own son. But it is said that Rhea was ravished by an unknown stranger that she claimed to be the embodiment of the god Mars. The result of this sexual communion being the twins, Romulus and Remus. The Roman historian Titus Livy (b. circa.59 BCE) expressed some scepticism of this story, noting that the imaginative veil of mythology can be a useful cover for mundane sexual impropriety.

When Amulius learnt of the birth of the twins he had the mother thrown into prison and the brothers cast adrift into the river Tiber. But the King's intentions were thwarted by the receding tide which left the baskets carrying the twins to settle on the drying river-banks. And it was here that they were found by a she-wolf attracted by their cries. The wolf suckled and comforted them until the shepherd Faustulus came along and carried them home to his wife Larentia for her to raise. And it was Romulus who 18 years later, as the leader of a band of brigands, founded a small town on a Palatine hill that was to expand over six other hills to become the City of Rome. The site was favoured, not only by its central position on the potentially fertile farmland of the Po-basin but it was also favoured by being just far enough from the sea (20miles) to have reasonable access to sea-borne trade but also at a sufficient distance to be able to defend itself against any attempt at a surprise attack from sea-borne raiders.

I mention the fanciful Romulus story so show the propensity of peoples to wish to write their own version of their history. A propensity that can be seen in such texts as Gilgamesh (Assyrian story), Homeric writings, the Bible (both Christian and Jewish elements), the Koran, Hindu holy texts, along with numerous tales involved in more 'primitive' religions. Indeed most religious stories of creation and of the lives of prophets, other holy men, shaman, and ancestors, are infused within myths and miraculous happenings. Happenings embellished with all sorts of colourful ideas involving angels, devils, and gods assumed to take an active part in human affairs – in sum ideas that were sourced in human imagination and which involve the suspension of the laws of nature as currently understood. Bear in mind that the well-springs of religious beliefs were primarily motivated by the wish to explain that which could not be understood, to fill the anxiety inducing existential 'gaps' in our knowing, and probably also as some attempt to induce a sense of control over natural events and of the harvest by using sacrifice, prayers, supplication, and similar practices. In the context of the certainties in life such motivational sources of religious beliefs are understandable.

After its founding Rome was ruled by a succession of chieftains become kings; mostly aggressive leaders keen to expand their kingdoms or retain their lands in the face of hostile neighbours. But even by the time of the establishment of the Republic (509 BCE) Rome covered only about 15, mostly hard fought over, square miles. A census taken around the time of the last king gives the population of Rome as 83,000 and a later one in 320 BCE gives the population as 250,000. As the Roman historian Eutropius wrote of the Roman Empire's beginnings '….human memory can hardly recall an empire smaller in its beginnings or larger in its growth throughout the whole world'.

By any historical standard the breadth of Roman influence was to place an indelible mark upon human history. By 264 BCE Rome was in control of a federation of city-states that had conquered the rest of the Italian peninsula and had established colonial control over Sicily. A mixture of more or less explicit threat underpinned by favourable marriages enabled the Roman leadership to, relatively peacefully, co-exist with oligarchic neighbours. During this period it also built a navy that soon came to control the western Mediterranean, eclipsing the power of the once mighty Carthage. As it expanded outwards, the Roman areas of influence drew people in. Along with a rag-bag of opportunists, entertainers, traders, and mercenary soldiers, came many others with valuable craft-skills including the arts, metallurgy, general building and the design and construction of civil amenities. The latter begun in earlier centuries by Estruscan masons who provided the means of building amenities such as drains, and buildings whose impressive roofs, towers and domes, could now rest on vaulted arches. The Empire attracted miners and smiths from Anatolia to mine and forge the iron ore of the island of Elba and the copper ore of the Italian mainland. A combination that was to give the 'metallic strength' to Roman legions.

By 43 BCE slavery was a prominent feature of Roman life and, as well as their place as domestic servants to the patrician class, they also served as gladiators, miners, rowers in the galleys, and undertook relentless work in the fields. The numerous slave revolts (the one led by Spartacus being the most well-known) showed that the human spirit could only be oppressed for so long.

When the Republic was established, it progressively evolved a system of government based loosely on constitutional checks and balances - this was enabled partly by the pairing of the highest offices, including that of Consul; each appointee only serving for one year, with the handover taking place on the 'Ides of March'. The patrician class, embodied in the Senate, nominated the candidates for the position of Consul even if the electors were themselves not just patricians but all of the free male citizens. This gave the population some scope to show its displeasure but little if any opportunity for political reform. It took over two hundred years to when, in 172 BCE, candidates from the plebeian class held the role of Consul. But the plebs who, along with patricians, could now look forward to political careers, were only those that had become people of some property. Property, for the most part gained in trade, but now to be used to purchase influence and advance personal interests within civil government and military commands. The Empire was constructed with a mostly carefully judged mixture of armed conquests, trading control, agreements with foreign oligarchs, and favourable marriages. In terms of the Empire's reach, China sent its first ambassadors to Rome in 130 BCE, by when Roman ambassadors had already made their way to the Imperial court in 166 BCE.

The Romans had first invaded Greece in 229 BCE and by 146 BCE Rome ruled an empire covering the whole of the Mediterranean - during the third century (264-146 BCE) the eastern Mediterranean had been controlled by Carthage, whose military was defeated by Rome in the 'Punic Wars'. By the end of the following century Rome had taken control of almost all of Alexander's Empire; except for Egypt which eventually came under Roman rule following the battle of Actium in 31 BCE.

If, taken overall, the long period of the militaristic Roman Empire did inhibit further progress in the sciences that might have been made if Roman elites had not been so antipathetic towards most aspects of Greek civilization. More generally, whilst they adopted much of Greek culture they pretty much came to despise Greek science. The elite Roman mind-set tended to value the practical over the theoretical and military aggression over peaceful co-existence. For their leisure time it would be entertainment and self-indulgence rather than considered reflection on abstract ideals and theoretical ideas on subjects similar to what had been of keen interest for a broad section of the Greek elite.

However, advances made during the time of the Greek become Roman period – philosophy, mathematics, and science, as well as poetry and drama - were in large part at least preserved by the Romans and past into central and western Europe during the period of Roman rule. From about the 1st century BCE there was a period of consolidation of some Greek philosophy and early science by scholars who did recognize its value: with some more modest contributions to these made by individual Romans such as Lucretius and Pliny the Elder.

Significant specifically Roman contributions to advancing civil life would be in architecture, transport, agriculture, and indeed the spread of civil life itself. But it would be Arabic scholars of the early medieval period that would return to and build upon the foundations established by Hellenistic science.

During this time we see trade in a wide range of goods conducted across an extensive geographic area. Grain from Egypt, Spain, and Sardinia - papyrus from Egypt and parchment from Pergamum - gold from Nubia - silver from Spain - quick-silver from Cappadocia.....as well as pottery, oils, wines, chesses, dried fruit, salted fish, iron, ivory, stone, timber, nuts, glass, bitumen, marble, granite, textiles, purple dye, precious stones, spices, and frankincense, from India and Arabia.........and of course slaves from wherever that can be captured or traded (a trade centred in slave markets on the island of Delos from 160 BCE) – were all to be found in Rome.

Sea trade reached out across the Mediterranean and south at least as far as the Horn of Africa - To Britain (Massilia circumnavigated Britain in about 300 BCE) and beyond to Jutland and Norway - east to India, further east to China – along with land-based trade to most regions accessible by caravans of donkey, camel, or horse. It was this movement that contributed to the spread of Greek/Roman cultures, including advances in reason applied to experience, that characterized much of this period.

As Rome the City became Rome the Republic, the concept of Rome as representative of power, civilization, and settled government (administration and justice) became part of a collective consciousness when as the Roman historian Livy wrote '......... a sense of national unity emerged'. In previous centuries there had been proud peoples but these had more often found pride in conquest, the more warlike the better, whereas for Rome, although suited to and enthusiastic for warring in the beginnings, had evolved to become for many a source of pride in most aspects of civilization and settled government. A perspicacious strategy of setting up semi-autonomous regions, between which contact was discouraged, meant that all roads carrying administrative communications and trade led directly to Rome. The City was the axis round which the Empire moved and from which radiated the well made, well organized routes marched by armies and along which peoples and trade-goods flowed. With Roman records we read of a pride in diplomacy, along with the traditional pride in courage shown when wielding strength of arms.

Although there was considerable opposition to Roman rule there was also an element of subject peoples that saw themselves not as being conquered by Rome but rather as becoming protected by it. We can see with evidence from the British Isles - a Roman colony on the western frontiers of its control – that the indigenous elites often willingly adopted the manners and culture of their occupiers.

As the proto-empire grew, Rome itself became the focus of a class divided society with associated underlying tensions between competing class interests. The use of slaves in agriculture produced increased wealth for the large landowners (whose interests were also strongly represented in governance), but their use significantly undercut the income and working conditions of 'free' labour. With poverty amongst non-slaves being widespread, leading to infanticide, the abandonment of children to slavery, and an amount of civil conflict. By the 1st century BCE 2 million slaves in Rome and the surrounding area were serving the interests of the wealthy in a population of 3.25 million free citizens. Strabo notes 10,000 slaves a day passing through the slave market at Delos. Food production for Rome was primarily dependent on their labour.

Famously, the brothers Tiberius and Caius Gracchus campaigned for social and political reform, not least the breakup and redistribution of the vast estates that came to categorize the pattern of Roman land ownership. The brothers were especially angered by the plight of the families of ordinary soldiers who had fought for Rome. Tiberius noted that: '…..the men who fight and die for Italy enjoy nothing but the air and light; without house or home they wander about with their wives and children' and '…..they fight and die to protect the wealth and luxury of others; they are styled master of the world and have not a clod of earth they can call their own…' (N.Lewis and M.Reinhold, eds.1951 vol.1, p236) Tiberius proposed a maximum size for any individual holding to be 500 iugera (125 acres). Unsurprisingly, their politically progressive group *Popularies* drew implacable opposition from the wealthy landowners and enthusiastic support from plebs, slaves, and landless peasants. Tiberius was killed during a riot in 133 BCE (some authorities suggest he was murdered by a group of senators using the riot as cover) and not long afterwards, when faced with the possibility of execution, his brother committed suicide. The government then moved decisively to rid Rome of any threat from below by arresting and executing thousands of the brother's followers; most being dispatched by strangulation.

At the end of the second Punic war, when the rival city of Carthage had been reduced to ruins and any survivors enslaved, the great continent of Africa lay open to Rome. This was yet another source of raw materials and trade goods available to enrich the Empire further, and it was around this time that the Roman 'Empire' surpassed all those that had preceded it, and it was still growing.

But even in ascendancy, the seeds of the Republic's downfall were sown as the vast imperial army become less one made up of conscripted citizens and more one of professional soldiers and mercenaries who came to identify more with their legions and its leading generals rather than the government back in the often distant Rome. From 100 BCE, legions had their own 'Eagles', carried by standard bearers as badges of honour, helping to instil a collective identity within each legion. For some time the expanding frontiers of Empire had enabled the deep division of political factions back in Rome to exist without the downfall of the whole. But this expansion would have its logistical (and other) limits as the cost of further conquest came to outweigh any potential economic benefits.

By 50 BCE Roman control extended across the Mediterranean, much of mainland Western Europe, most of northern Africa and east to the Black Sea coast. But by now the tensions between the mainly provincial based armies and the corrupt and increasingly badly governed Rome were at a critical point. Aided partly by extra powers granted during frontier emergencies, one general came forward to 'save' Rome from itself. Julius Caesar had served as a general whose army had tamed, enlarged, and controlled the province of Gaul; successfully engaging in hard-fought battles with those such as Germanic and Helvetian fighters. Over his seven years in this province he had gained considerable personal wealth and political influence; his loyal soldiers also prospered and in return gave their allegiance to their general. Aware of the disarray into which the central government in Rome was falling, Julius gathered his army, and marched south. In 49 BCE, in direct defiance of Roman law, he led them across the river Rubicon and marched on Rome. Over the following four years of civil war he overthrew the government of Rome and with it, in all but name, the Republic; himself assuming the role of Consul and that of a dictator. He retained the Senate but made sure that it was controlled by senators favourable to his aims. During his time in office he introduced a range of reforms including: measures to relieve debt, making the senate slightly more democratic, reform of the calendar, and introducing land reforms in favour of army veterans. He reigned as a dictator for the rest of his life but it was a life cut-short when in 44 BCE his enemies, a group of about 60 senators led by Cassius and Brutus, conspired together and murdered him. His chosen successor, Octavian, took over where Julius left off, making it clear that control in Rome and of the Empire had been irrevocably shifted away from the traditional republicans and into the hands of those who could deploy military force. It was at this time that the wide-ranging entity known as 'Rome' was established as the Roman Empire. A succession of 'Caesars' followed Julius and Octavian and although they had taken traditional Republican titles they all effectively ruled as dictators.

The Roman army suffered a shock defeat in 9 CE when fierce Germanic tribes-people wiped out three whole legions at the Battle of the Teutoberg Forest (out of a total Roman military across the Empire of 28 Legions) with surviving but captured officers being killed or ransomed and common soldiers being enslaved. Then followed a more settled period 14 - 192 CE, that has been termed a civil golden age; the period of Pax Romana (Roman Peace). As Epictetus noted '…there are no longer wars nor battles nor extensive brigandage nor piracy, but at any hour we may travel the roads or sail from the rising of the sun to its setting'. Epictetus was somewhat partial in his observation and, as is usually the case with historical claims of peace, the term 'relative peace' would more accurately describe this period of time. Relative peace, because for many in the Empire including persecuted Christians (even if rather exaggerated by later Christian authors), slaves and most of the lower classes, for whom life was at times bleak and prospects poor during this period. This period of relative political stability, and so of relative peace, was followed by a gradual descent into repeated crisis with, as Dio Cassius noted, a change from a golden time to one of 'iron and rust'.

Although the Romans mostly adapted the technological inventions or innovations of others their organizational efficiency ensured that these were exploited to the benefit of the Empire. An impressive architectural legacy included baths (the complex in Bath, England, survives to today) drains, flushing toilets, the domed roof supported by vaulted columns, numerous triumphal arches, amphitheatres; building in concrete as well as stone. They used windlasses and a range of iron tools. Their corps of surveyors progressed the construction of roads, canals, aqueducts (one of which still carries water to Segovia in Spain), viaducts, and a range of public buildings to order. Their roads traced mostly straight lines out to the further reaches of the Empire and according to J.M. Roberts 'Between the age of the Caesars and that of the railway train there was no improvement in the speed with which messages and goods could be sent overland'. (Roberts, 1993, p141)

For all of the 900 odd years of ascendancy, relative stability, and then decline, the Roman army was engaged in conflict in some or other part of the Empire. An empire that was mostly carved out and sustained by violence or of its threat. In the new millennium the Empire was increasingly beset by conflict on its European borders with approx 25% of tax income being spent on maintaining the military.

From the reign of Marcus Aurelius (161-180 CE) the Empire was having to cope with conflict in parts of the Middle-East and along much of the border on the Danube and the Rhine. A border that was becoming increasingly more porous due to the depredations of tribal peoples (such as Franks, Huns, and Visigoths); now more often seeking land for permanent settlement rather than a quick strike into the Empire for pillage. The Empire was vulnerable due to weak leadership, onerous levels of taxation, high inflation, and general economic recession. In addition, a significant proportion of the

Roman army was made up of mercenaries who were more likely to make a rationally calculated assessment between personal danger and possible financial reward than would a volunteer. In 137 CE the emperor, Septimius Severus, had to grant special privileges to soldiers in order to ensure their loyalty: increasing their grain rations, allowing them to wear gold rings instead of the insignia of the equestrian order and to marry whilst in service; measures that contributed to easing the austerity of military life.

One of the more bloody attempted rebellions took place in Palestine in 135 CE, the 'Bar Kokhba' revolt, which would end with thousands of Roman soldiers and an estimated six hundred thousand Jewish rebels (including many civilians) being killed.

During the fifth century CE the eastern Empire was able to endure fairly well but in the west relentless assaults on the borderlands continued and over the century a succession of Visigoths, Vandals, Franks, Burgundians, and others, advanced deep into the Empire. Many from these groups were absorbed into the administrative and ruling structures of the Empire to the extent of their leaders often becoming fully 'Romanised'. And when the Huns were repelled in 451 CE at the battle of Troyes the Roman army was commanded by a Visigoth king, leading descendants of the very peoples who had sacked Rome under their leader Alaric in 410 CE.

The western Empire was effectively finished by 500 CE, the last emperor, Romulus Augustus, having been deposed in 476 CE by Odoacer, a barbarian non-Roman mercenary general in the Roman auxiliary. But the eastern Empire endured through various vicissitudes down to the 13th century; even if it was to be as a Byzantine, rather than a Roman, empire.

As in Europe, civilization in China was characterized by internal conflict and external warfare. It has been estimated that, between 535 and 286 BCE there were 358 recorded wars. Walter Scheidel notes that: 'Multi-year campaigns appeared, and operations spread across larger geographic areas……the main states of Qi, Qin, and Chu, could each supposedly draw on up to 1 million soldiers..' he also notes 'Battles involving 100,000 or more combatants...' being mentioned. Scheidel uses the battle of Changping in 260 BCE as an extreme example of early dynastic conflict, where the Qin forces were recorded to have massacred 400,000 soldiers of the Zhao army. (Scheidel, 2017, p184)

During the reign of the Qin King, Ying Zheng, (also known as Qin Shi Huangdi - b.259 BCE) much of China had been unified within an extensive Qin Empire. Zheng acceded to the throne at the age of thirteen and is known as the 'First Emperor'. Going on to build his empire by using the most brutal of methods. He was said to be highly emotional and impetuous, having to be led in political and administrative matters by the clever senior civil servant Li Si.

Another enduring feature of Chinese history of this early time was the barbarian groups, usually nomadic peoples whose lands bordered those of more settled people. Each group of barbarians had their own rich cultural heritage and a tribal-based history that would no doubt have included times (imagined or real) when they felt oppressed by the Chinese.

For the Han, they were to endure continual pressure from the nomadic Haiung-nu who, mounted on horseback, launched swift but regular raids from their northern homeland. These raids were usually repelled and sometimes the nomads would be 'bribed' to stay at home. During the much later Sung Empire of 1041 CE, payment to the Khitan, who controlled most of Manturia, Mongolia, parts of Shansi with the capital of Nanking, had amounted to 200,000 rolls of silk and 100,000 ounces of silver to induce them to remain at home.

Following the demise of the Han (220 CE) until the time of the Jin (western Jin 265-317 CE and eastern Jin 317- 420 CE) China became increasingly divided, as self-seeking warlords and Taoist rebels took advantage of the weakness of a succession of central governments. Three leaders emerged in the three largest regions of the country. Ta'oa in the north, claiming a spurious connection to the Han, with the two other areas, being run by military leaders, each of whom claimed the mantle of emperor. This was the period of the 'sixteen kingdoms'. Although much subsequently written history noted this time as an age of heroism it was in fact one characterized by violent warfare between aggressive warlords.

This time of central political weakness caused, at least partly by factional squabbles of antagonistic clans, weakened the Empire. Yet again the northern nomads, the Hsiung-nu (Hun), took advantage of the great power's vulnerability, swooping south to conquer northern China. A region that once more became divided into a collection of barbarian controlled mini-states.

Most of the remaining period of the T'ang dynasty (to 906 CE) was characterized by short periods of peace between much longer ones of turmoil as disputes between groups whose leaders held competing personal ambitions erupted, and all this against a backcloth of conflict with neighbouring peoples and more popular discontent from within. There was continued banditry and rebellions, with sometimes great loss of life. The bloody outcome of the sacking of Guangzhou in 879 CE by an army led by the rebel leader Huang Chao being but one example.

Chapter 2 The Bloody Middle Ages

Moving back to the Middle East and into the next period to be considered we can see the founding of another religion, Islam completing the pantheon of primary religions that have sustained the religious mindset down to today.

The founder of Islam, Mohammad, was born in 570 CE and within ten years of his death the armies of Islam had carved out an empire that covered most of the Middle-East. By 750 CE the Empire stretched from the Pyrenees in Northern Spain west to beyond the Indian river Indus in the east, north into Armenia and beyond the river Oxus deep into Egypt, west along the northern strip of Africa and of course across the whole of the Arabian Peninsula. An extensive empire, held together mainly by force of arms, but also by the binding aspects of a powerful set of religious beliefs. In places, acceptance was made easier by internal dissent born out of heavy taxation and of peoples already having had unfamiliar religions forced upon them. The new religion of Islam was in essence an Arab religion and many of these peoples had the outlook and sense of identity of Arabs.

What were the origins of this religion – so powerful in the world today, with about one billion believers? The spark igniting a religious fire that was to burn across large parts of the world was struck in the inspired imagination of Muhammad; realised during the time he spent alone in a cave outside Mecca. The dry spiritual tinder of a people hungry for a religion that could keep pace (intellectually and politically) with the monotheism of civilizing people's religious developments but one that was distinctly Arabic, enabled the spark to settle and flare. A people whose own traditional tribal cultures were under threat from rapidly increasing wealth gained in trade and the consequent displacement of respect for tradition, social status, and veneration of the aged. I have used the metaphor of fire as I think this allows a clear, if superficial, understanding of both the rise of Islam, and of the many conflicts that accompanied its spread.

Mohammed was born and grew up in the town of Mecca. A town that had prospered as a centre for caravan-borne trade across southern Arabia. It had grown in stature due to its favourable geographic situation at the intersection of a south to north-west trading route, and a north to south pastoralist summer/winter Bedouin migration trail. At this crossroads where diverse, if mainly Arab, peoples came together, a large black stone had been set up 'in ancient times' (Darlington, 1971). Then around the 3-4th century the stone had been covered in tent-like material, it was by then known as the Ka'abah, and was traditionally associated with sanctuary. Along with this symbolic 'upgrading' (and the increasing power of Mecca) tolls were charged for trade-goods to pass and drinking water was sold to thirsty travellers. The site of the Ka'bah generated significant wealth for the people of Mecca,[11] even if these benefits were differently distributed between the 36 clans (more or less antagonistic towards each other) that inhabited Mecca and its hinterland. The more powerful and wealthy citizens occupied central areas of the City, with the poorest confined to living in the less favoured outskirts. It was in the situation of experiencing a fairly cosmopolitan passing population (bringing ideas along with trade-goods) set within a tribal clan-based hegemony and the social tensions this engendered. With its primarily Arab population practicing a polytheistic faith that was felt by some to be inferior to the monotheistic god of the Jews and Christians who had mostly prospered.

Mohammad married a widow, Khadija, who was herself a fairly wealthy trader and together they would have three daughters. Having married at 26 years of age Mohammad would travel widely across the Middle-East (taking in Egypt and Abyssinia) as he pursued his family's trading interests. He had been orphaned at the age of six so

---

[11] Prior to the stone being covered with the tent-like cube it has been claimed that observers could note that over centuries it had been carved with images of tribal idols that had been added during pre-Islamic times. Many of the original stonemasons were Christians and it is possible that there is an image of the Virgin Mary. I have even read of coarse 'toilet humour' types of carvings.

he relied on his extended family for support and protection in a clannish society. The principle religions of Mecca at that time were Judaism, Christianity, and versions of Arabic polytheistic religions that involved the worship of tribal idols. Social inequalities made Mecca an uncomfortable and unstable place during this time and it was Mohammad's insight into the social problems that led him to call for reform. A call that fell on ears deafened by layers of self-interest. After trying more traditional ways of reforming the society, Mohammed said that he had felt the need to search for the active presence of a god. As he approached middle-age Mohammad is said to have become contemplative and that at the age of 40 there was revealed to him in a series of visionary experiences in which the Archangel Gabriel acted as an interpreter of the will of a one true god (Allah).

Mohammad preached this new religion with three key features:

Allah is the one God
All people, as individuals, must obey the will of Allah (as known by Mohammad)
Allah would judge all human beings at the Day of Judgment

Believers were expected to surrender themselves completely to the will of Allah in the form that it came to be written down and interpreted by men.

The collected interpretations of this god's will, and some other statements and injunctions attributed to Mohammed, were collected together just after he died and constitute the book known as the Quran. The book in its 114 sections (süras) outlines the primary tenants of a religion; in addition a system of law (Shari'a) was added in around the 9th/10th centuries. Mohammad saw himself very much as an ordinary man prone to error, but a man chosen by a god to be his prophet; and this was the miracle from which the faithful are able to learn the certainty of their god's word.

For ten fairly fruitless years Mohammad preached his new religion in Mecca, attracting only a small number of converts. There was some resistance to this new movement from the oligarchy that ruled Mecca; perhaps not surprising given that one of the social implications of Mohammed's teaching was that the rich and powerful should be charitable to the poor and weak. Another interesting aspect of Islam – in relation to the potential for good – is that, unlike Christianity it does not believe in original sin. For Mohammad's Islam human beings are born in innocence and their power to reason allied to their moral conscience allows them to distinguish between evil and good, right and wrong.

When Mohammad's main protector, his uncle Abu Bakr, died Mohammad's fledgling group came under increasing pressure, they were accused of being 'Muslimin' (traitors). They adapted to this pressure by operating as a more secretive 'brotherhood', within which their tribal differences became reconciled. In this turning inwards they became a stronger and more self-sustaining community (the 'ummah'). If more secretive, their reputation as possessors of a powerful new religion spread and, whilst they were distrusted by most of the prominent Meccan tribal leaders, they were gaining respect beyond the City. The opposition they faced in Mecca, and a request made by a delegation of citizens from the hilltop town of Yathrib inviting Mohammed to settle there, initiated the move from Mecca. After his 200 mile journey to Yathrib, Mohammed quickly assumed control of the town and organized attacks on caravans travelling to Mecca.[12]

This guerrilla type hostility lasted for about seven years during which many converts were attracted to the faith, including some Bedouin tribes from the region surrounding Yathrib. It has been suggested (Arnold Toynbee, 1976, p368) that Mohammad turned to violent robbery as the capacity of Yathrib to support his growing band of followers was exceeded by their numbers. At this early time he ordered the Jews to be driven out of the region if they failed to convert

---

[12] This migration was termed the Hegira, 'the emigration', it is from this time that the Muslim calendar begins.

to Islam.

For Toynbee '......robbery, war, and massacre were among the means by which Muhammad won his victory for Islam'

The fairly smooth transitions covering the first two Caliphs' (stewards of Islam) Abu Bakr and Umar ibn al-Khattab[13], was a time of rapid military advance as Muslim (Arab) armies – using surprise tactics and led by fast-moving cavalry mounted on camels – took Damascus in 636, followed by a string of other wealthy Middle-Eastern cities. Within ten years of Mohammad's death Arab armies had overrun much of the land that had seen the birth of western civilization. The wealth that poured back to Mecca was channelled toward the more powerful, now Muslim, families, creating what was in effect a new Arab aristocracy.

There had been a grumbling level of rivalry between the various Muslim armies, and it was some of these (especially the armies garrisoned in Egypt and Iraq) that became sufficiently dissatisfied with their share of the spoils of war, the subsequent unequal distribution of income from taxation, and more generally what they regarded as a dominating approach of the third Caliph Uthman ibn Affen (second cousin and son-in-law of the Prophet, from another prominent merchant family of Mecca) that were the primary dissatisfactions starting a civil war. One triggered by the murder of Uthman in 656.

In terms of theology, this time of internal conflict was to establish a centuries-long schism within the Muslim religious community. A schism at least partly based on the right of succession to lead the caliphate. Following the death of Uthman, another of Muhammad's sons-in-laws, Ali, became the forth Caliph (first Imam, in Shi'ism of the Muslim Ummah). He was considered to have been a fair and just man who endeavoured to bring an end to the internal conflict. For this attempt at moderating between factions he was assassinated by a member of the Kharijite or Seceders sect, noted as using a sword

---

[13] Both from the same wealthy merchant family and elected by the Community itself – Umar was murdered by a slave in 644.

coated with poison. The civil war itself came to an end with the restoration of an, if uneasy, political unity under the powerful Umayyad family and their establishing a dynastic succession, with the position of Caliph becoming based on automatic inheritance. A dynasty that would last until 750 when they were displaced by the Abbasids.

The generally unstable political unity was further undermined by bitter theological differences. A sect, the Shi'ites, accorded Ali the status of martyr (denying the legitimacy of the first three Caliphs), and opposed some Quranic interpretations made by the current leadership of the Muslim Community (Sunni), considering that these had deviated from the original teachings of Mohammad.

For Shi'ites, the legitimate line of succession should have seen the role of Caliph passed from Ali to Hassan, one of his sons and so to a grandson of the Prophet. Among other disagreements there was also a difference in the living status of the Mahdi (the 'right-guided one'); he who is destined to establish the global Caliphate, one characterized by universal justice and peace. For Shi'ites the Madhi is already here but for the Sunni the conventional belief is that the Mahdi has not appeared in historical times. There are also numerous more minor differences that can crudely be noted as the Sunni being more secular and Shi'ite being more orthodox, in terms of interpretation of the Quran; although there are significant exceptions to this general division.

The Quran is of fundamental importance for Islam, but it weakness (similar to the Bible) is that its writings read at times contradictory and at times unnecessarily vague on important issues – it also, in suras such as 'The Night Journey' to Jerusalem and the Ascension to Paradise', offers narratives replete with tales of a series of miraculous happenings. So a belief in the truth of some Quranic stories requires a suspension of belief in the laws of nature as we know them; presumably for believers, laws their god has revealed to humankind.

As with the gods of Moses and of Christ, there is no modesty in the Quranic claims for Allah. The text ends with the assertion that 'Unto God belongeth the sovereignty of the Heavens and of the Earth, and of all that they contain; and he hath power over all things.'

In relation to the main purpose of tracing both positive (humanistic) and negative (evil) aspects of the human evolutionary become historical experience the Quran does offer some enlightened rights to women (mainly involving property) but it also suggests an inferiority of wives to husbands and daughters to fathers and brothers, and offers a series of injunctions that seem to be intended for the control of women. The Quran accepts slavery as a legitimate social institution, only suggesting measures to regulate this activity. A bit later on the Caliph Umar established the rule that only non-believers could be enslaved. Pre and post the time of Mohammad, many Arabs engaged with some enthusiasm in the slave trade, mostly but not solely with sub-Saharan Africa kingdoms.

The scale of the Islamic Empire encouraged the expansion of trade, and banks were established with their central offices in Baghdad and branches in the main cities, where a system was developing that facilitated the use of cheques and letters of credit, so reducing the need for merchants to carry coinage or gold.

For non-believers the Quran, similar to the foundation texts of the other world religions, can be understood as a product of its time and of the motivations of its author/s. Primarily based on Mohammad's interpretations of ideas that he assumed to be revealed to him by the Arch-angel Gabriel, but also an outcome of a detailed editing process overseen by the third Caliph Uthman between 644-56 CE.

The religious scholar and Christian minister G.Margoliouth noted in an introduction to a 1909 translation of the Quran: 'Biblical reminiscences, Rabbinic legends, Christian traditions mostly drawn from distorted apocryphal sources, and native heathen stories, all first pass through the prophet's fervid mind, and thence issue in strange new forms, tinged with poetry and enthusiasm, and well adapted to enforce his own view of life and duty, to serve as an encouragement to his faithful adherents, and to strike terror into the hearts of his opponents.' (Margoliouth, 1909, p.viii)

This appraisal does not make it any less convincing than the earlier religious texts, their all being equally unconvincing to people such as myself i.e. those who consider themselves to be open-minded and committed to reason rather than simply assuming that truth lies in the circumscribed cultural and other ethnic traditions that they grew up within. All of the world's major religions emanate an aura of evil, seen in their foundational texts and embodied at the interface where believers meet the actual world – but they each also have an identifiable core of potential goodness. Within the Quran we can find lines in which the Prophet connects believers with a world as it might be, just three examples being:

- 'Be kind, for whenever goodness becomes part of something it beautifies. Whenever it is taken from something it leaves it tarnished'
- 'You do not do evil to those who do evil to you, but deal with them with forgiveness and kindness.'
- 'Feed the hungry and visit a sick person, and free the captive if he be unjustly confined. Assist any person oppressed whether Muslim or non-Muslim.'

Islam stands on five Pillars.

- To declare ones faith in God and belief in Muhammad

- To pray five times a day

- To give to those in need

- To fast during Ramadan

- To make a pilgrimage to Mecca at least once during a person's lifetime

Measured in quantitative terms the blood that was spilt by Islamists to conquer and convert was probably no more than that of Christianity and Judaism but it did happen over a shorter period of time. And it, and indeed Judaism, differed from Christianity in that those who had established these religions had preached war and destruction whereas the biblical Jesus, preached peace and tolerance. But in terms of the actual outcomes for humankind there is little to choose between these three world religions in relation to their involvement in the historical expression of evil. We might decide that we can distinguish between a god's intentions and the self-serving interpretations made by priests and kings – this is a debate that could bear fruitful enlightenment on how religions have been too often used as vehicles for fulfilling personal, more earthly, ambitions.

Religions more than any other aspect of humankind's history have been expressions of the alternation of whiteness/blackness, darkness/light, good/evil.[14] When, along with inspirational messages that can raise human aspiration for living in peace and harmony there is also the lived reality of evil acts carried out in their name. These three great monotheistic religions also share belief in a 'Book', each being venerated as the very word of their god if, for some unexplained reason, having to be mediated by men.

Historical records suggest that meetings of different peoples was too often based on acquisitive motives and easy aggression which, when allied to technological advances in weaponry, was to widen the fault-line afflicting the human collective psyche. City life, with the concentration of populations, allowed large numbers of men, women, and children, to be included in wars as victims of plunder, bloodlust, or revenge over real or imagined histories. The latter being more often a mixture of the two, as some actual historical event was reinterpreted by collective imagination, contributing its own biased and bitter recollections to collective memories, coalescing down the generations into hatred – polarizing inter-group relations between peoples who usually had more real interest in working together rather than expending energy on kindling their animosity through the centuries.

---

[14] The imagined history of Islam has it that the Kabah stone was originally milk-white but the centuries of absorbing the evils committed by humankind had caused it to turn black.

By the Medieval period forces fighting for control of China were using 'firearms', and the Jurchen Jin defenders at the siege of Kaifeng (1232-1233) had deployed what were either rockets or flamethrowers ('Fire lances') and bombs of gunpowder, against Mongols besieging the City.

In terms of empires, the Mongols themselves deserve highlighting. This due to their creation of a vast empire spanning Eurasia. An empire began in 1206 CE when the assembled Mongolian tribal leaders declared Chenggis (previously known as Temujin – more often known today as Gengis) Khan their supreme chieftain – the Great Khan. A proclamation of leadership assumed to involve the mandate of the senior sky god Tengri, something that infused Mongol self-belief, with each victory being proof of this heavenly favour. Chenggis was a leader who would lead the fierce Mongol armies east and west across Eurasia from their base in the central Asian steppes to lay the foundations of what under his grandson Kublai Khan would become an empire stretching from Poland in the west to the coast of China in the east – an empire forged in blood and terror in but 73 years.

In conflict the initial Mongol strategy was ideally to strike quickly and hard, showing little mercy to the peoples they conquered; the Mongol soldiers were mostly paid out of what could be looted - only once established in a region did they administer efficient forms of taxation systems. These nomadic peoples with a love of horses, sheep, alcohol, and fighting, would transform occasional raiding in neighbouring lands into continuous warfare as they expanded in all four compass directions from their base in Mongolia. As their ambitions grew, and the size of their armies increased, they would more often surround a city, send a delegation to call on the city leaders to surrender (on the promise of lenient treatment) and, if this failed they would lay siege. Using some powerful machines to batter down walls, the Chinese invented triple-crossbow to rain arrows on inhabitants, and with giant catapults hurling rocks at buildings. As their conquest took in much of Northern China they also gained knowledge of artillery and the use of gunpowder.

Once a city fell the killing could be relentless – skilled craftsmen were often spared as were some women and children (to serve as slaves) but most of any resisting city's people would be mercilessly put to death. In the regions of today's Uzbekistan and Turkmenistan it has been estimated that possibly as many as 3 million people were killed over but a two year period.

Chengiss died (cause unknown but he had not been well) in 1226 whilst on campaign against the Tangut Kingdom of Western Xia (North-west of today's China) – to 'honour' their leader's death the Mongols then murdered the entire population of the City of Zhongxing!

In regions such as eastern and south-west Russia they (called Tartars by the Russian chroniclers) were able to take advantage of local divisions. More generally, their military was inventive and flexible, adapting tactics to suit local terrains and the defensive measures they encountered. Using such actions as setting fire to woods and reed beds to allow clouds of smoke to drift across battlefields so confusing their enemies, pretending to raise a siege or to retreat from the battlefield, only to ambush pursuers. They would also use captives as human shields and even on occasion cast captives into moats to ride over their piled bodies.

But perhaps the most telling strategy was the message of terror that preceded the arrival of the Mongol Hordes, a message invariably creating fear throughout populations soon to be engulfed.

On defeating the Jin, Ghenghis's son Ogedei had completed the conquest of northern China with his mother Sorkaktani successfully arguing for the inclusion of most of this within the extensive Mongolian lands she already controlled. Sorkaktani seems to have been a remarkable woman, wife of one Great Khan and mother of two others. For John Man:

'Genghis started the empire: Kublai brought it to its greatest extent; but without Sorkaktani to link the two, without her ambition, foresight, good sense, and a couple of interventions at crucial moments, Genghis empire might have fallen apart.' (Man, 2014, p129)

Sorkaktani's son Kublai would take over northern China and in due course was able to fulfil the long-term Mongol ambition of ruling over a united China. Achieving this when, by 1279 CE the southern Song, then ruling the rich lands of southern China, fell to marauding Mongols led by Kublai, establishing the Yuan dynasty, which would run from 1260-1368. It would be under the Great Khan Kublai that the Mongol Empire would cover its most extensive area – at 12,500 miles from west to east, being twice the size of the Roman Empire at its height.

Whilst ferocious in conquest, and indeed when ruling, Mongol rule did more often adapt to local conditions (even incorporating an alphabet used for record-keeping from the Uighur people of western China), taking advantage of skilled indigenous craftsmen and administrators whilst showing a tolerance to religious practices. On this last, many of the Mongol leaders overseeing territory in the west of the empire themselves adopted Islam, and to the east Gengijis took on the Buddhist faith of his principle wife Sorkaktani, and with one of his sons marrying a Nestorian Christian.

One discovery that I have already mentioned is that of gunpowder, initially (but not only – see above) primarily used by the Chinese for entertainment ('fireworks') rather than warring. The invention of gunpowder and its spread to the west would help to lay the foundations of a massive arms industry – in the making of artillery as well as rifles and handguns. The subsequent history of this industry, dealing specifically in killing, illustrates the influence of military needs in driving innovation and development. Although the discovery of the destructive power of gunpowder was first made in China, in travelling to the west it was to revolutionize warfare and dramatically open up the imbalance in killing efficiency between 'civilized' and 'primitive' peoples. An imbalance that would be taken full advantage of both on the land and on the high seas as the civilized European powers repeatedly fought each other to a blood-soaked stand-still. Perhaps more telling, was the military imbalance favouring European nations as they slaughtered their way across South America, North America, and Africa, to locate the 'killing fields' that saw some of the most callous exploitation of military advantage.

In 771 CE Charles I (Charlemagne), son of the Frankish (Carolingian) Emperor Pepin III, took over what remained of the western Roman Empire and extended its borders. His armies held and then drove the Moslems back on the Iberian Peninsula, as well as similar with the Anglo-Saxons in the north and Slavic invaders in the east. He became a legend, starting out as a warrior-king he increasingly became known for his patronage of scholars and artists. His seal carried the claim of 'Renewal of the Roman Empire'. With the consolidation of a unity between Church and Empire being symbolically confirmed when Charlemagne was crowned and acclaimed as Emperor, and so successor of the Caesars, by the Pope in Rome on Christmas Day 800 CE. But it was to be an uneven partnership in which emperors generally maintained authority over the Church. And the precedent of the Pope having to crown an emperor in order for him to gain full legitimacy was to cause problems down the centuries to come.

More warlike peoples to the north, west and south gradually increased the pressure on the Empire and this, added to 100 years of territorial disputes between the sons of Charlemagne and their successors, caused the Frankish kings to become progressively weaker until the demise of the western Frankish Empire when its last Carolingian king died in 987 CE.

It was a Europe much of which had, for about four centuries, been experiencing the attentions of a people from the north. These 'Norsemen' who were progressively emerging into civil history were mixed peoples who took enthusiastically to trade, although piracy and pillage were also practiced on occasion when motivation and opportunity aligned. These people became known as the Vikings. But the word 'Vik' represented more an activity engaged in rather than being an accurate common descriptor for diverse groups of peoples. A people originating in the countries of Denmark, Sweden, Norway, and adjacent lands, but who were descended from tribal groupings that had been migrating into the region for at least a 1000 years prior to the Viking times.

The stock of the indigenous peoples were added to from about 600 CE, with waves of Scythian pastoralists migrating into Scandinavia from the south and east. Goths from northern central Europe brought a language that was to become the common basis of the more modern Scandinavian languages. Both Scythians and Goths interbred with the increasingly more settled tribal groups that had inhabited the region from much earlier times. Peoples who gained a living by hunting over land or sea, gathering along the foreshore, following migrating reindeer, and undertaking more or less settled farming activities. These diverse peoples shared a collective consciousness that was formed by and expressed in a rich cultural history. Their world saw nature at its rawest and human-beings at their most violent. The struggle for survival in mostly harsh landscapes generally selects the hardiest to survive and leave progeny who, in the case of the Norse peoples, had soaked up mythical tales (Sagas) and had absorbed the values of the warrior.

Fortunately for those more inclined to be warriors there were also the farming types who, for the most part, could actually support the community – although with some individuals there was an overlap as young warriors survived to become farmers in middle age. A central spiritual aspect of this culture were versions of a religion based on fertility, on gods of natural forces, and later as overseas expeditions became an integral aspect of the Norseman's experience, increasingly on a religion of the warrior. For those that engaged in Viking, to die with sword in hand became idealized as a fitting end, allowing them to go straight to Valhalla; the feasting hall of the gods and of heroic warriors that had passed before.

Technically their skill as boat builders and sailors was high, their long-ships with prows at each end, developed from fast rowed vessels in which only the bravely foolish ventured beyond sight of land into sturdy sailing ships that could be rowed when lack of or ill-favoured winds, and/or adverse tides, made this necessary. It was in these ships that the Norse peoples undertook journeys across the North Sea to the British Isles, north to Iceland, and west to Greenland and North America, as well as far up European rivers and along its coastlines.

Not just raping, pillaging and murder, as some of the victims gave testament to but also engaging in trading. Some also settled to farming in places where the balance between survival and life-threatening failure was but a tenuous outcome of weather conditions and disease resistance. Farming that sometimes failed, as in the harsh conditions of Greenland, after a few generations (noted in some Sagas), but succeeding in the relatively more conducive climates of the Britain Isles where they came to rule kingdoms to govern and to extract taxes ('Danelaw'). Hundreds of place names in Britain still today bear testament to the heritage of Norse peoples.

I use the term Norseman to encompass a diversity of tribal peoples moving in and out of as well as being permanently settled in Scandinavia and nearby regions over the 2000 years between 1000 BCE and 1000 CE. Hardly the approach of a serious historian but allowable I think as I attempt to convey a flavour of a group of human-beings who collectively stand out for their adventurousness, cultural originality, physical hardiness, skills in boat-building, seamanship, animal husbandry and crop farming, as well as their extreme (indeed for some the glorification of) cruelty. In these peoples we see the characteristics of much of humanity writ large.

The Vikings did not spring into history as ruthless 'Norsemen'. Some of their ancestors had settled in Scandinavia to a hunting, fishing, life based on a primitive 'stone age' technology as far back as 12,000 years ago. With toolkits that included knifes, axes, various types of scraper, as well as harpoons, spears and boats with skin covered hulls. A technology shaped by the environment's food-bearing characteristics; initially pretty much based on foraging on land and shore, and hunting on the sea. By 1500 BCE (if not earlier) a trade had been established as far south as the Mediterranean in a variety of furs and the much valued amber; the solidified secretions of pine trees. Grave-goods made in bronze, including weapons and ornaments, by craftsman who could match any in the world at the time are testament to show that this period of the Bronze Age was quite a prosperous one in parts of this region. Cave art shows scenes of travel by ships, chariots, wagons, as well as depictions of weapons, along with the festival games, animals, and religious images of the Sun. Peoples pushing up from the south had brought farming to the northern lands. Forests were slowly cleared and by 300 BCE, as the climate turned wetter and colder, Iron Age technology allowed sturdy ploughs, along with hardier types of grain, to realize the potential fertility of heavy soils. At around this time the Greek geographer/traveller Pytheas of Massalia sailed via the North Sea to the western region of Scandinavia and recorded his impressions in a text called 'Of the Ocean'. He is said to have written of the people as 'barbarians' living fairly meagre lives in often harsh climatic conditions. The relative decline from the more prosperous Bronze Age reflects the material evidence left by a range of tribal peoples; some main groups of these being named by Pytheas as: Teutones, Cibri, Gutones (Goths) and Ingvaeones – but there were many other tribes living in a sometimes uneasy co-existence with their neighbours.

In 100 CE the Roman historian Tacitus wrote of a warlike people (probably a reference to Svea, Sweden) able to muster fleets of ships. Trade-based contacts with Scandinavia became increasingly more active on the European scene. When later pushed by increasing population pressure at home and pulled by the attraction of easily accessible booty located abroad, the Norsemen sailed north and west in search of land and south and east in search of more moveable wealth. They were to establish colonies as far west as Greenland and as far east as Kiev. The latter being a city, along with Novgorod, founded by the Rhos, who were Norseman from the area that would become Sweden. These same Rhos penetrated further south and were even able to raid Constantinople in c. 860. They settled down, interbred with, and adopted both the language and the eastern orthodox version of Christianity, of the indigenous people of north-eastern Europe.

Norseman (mainly from Norway) reached Iceland in 874, and Greenland in 985, establishing settlements that survived more easily in Iceland than they were able to in the even more hostile environment of Greenland, this settlement being abandoned about 500 years later. These intrepid and skilled sailors sailed along the coast of America (Vinland) about 500 years before it had gained it modern name.

Both Norwegian and Danish Norseman settled in the British Isles; the former tending to be settlers whilst the latter, at least early on, tended to favour raiding. Although the extent of this - or at least the brutality - was probably somewhat exaggerated for propaganda purposes in the records made by the churchmen, whose institutions were often relieved of their valuables. To read the grisly reports of the monks and other churchmen whose accounts of the attacks have been a significant source of western information from contemporary witnesses, is to read of the Vikings as blood thirsty murderers, raping, pillaging, killing defenceless people and generally of leaving a trail of destruction in their wake. The letters of Alcuin, and the 'Sermon on the Wolf' by Wulfstan, frame the violent activities of the Norseman as God's punishment on a sinful people. The value of gold and silver accrued by rich monasteries and churches were vulnerable targets and this wealth soon became the main attraction for those that went 'viking'. It is claimed that the release of this stored accumulation of capital into the European market gave the continent's economy a significant boost.

The Viking raiding extended south along the western coasts of France, Spain, and Portugal and into the Mediterranean (sacking the City of Seville in 844) and, as in Britain, they raided deep into the country, as they sailed or rowed their long-ships up the principal rivers.

During the ninth century they began to settle and by 851, mainly Danish Norsemen controlled about two-thirds of England; their advance only being halted when the followers of Alfred the Great defeated a Danish army in 871. Even though, as with other parts of the country (and in other European countries), Alfred did agree to pay a tax to the Danes (Danelaw) to maintain an uneasy peace. During the reign of the, in many ways quite enlightened, Danish King Canute (1006-1035 – Cnut) most of England formed part of a Danish empire. Even accepting that they had done much to reduce the wealth of the Church, it seems that the Norseman (at least their nobility) came to find Christianity attractive as a religion. There was a progressive conversion to Christianity by Scandinavian kings. By 1000 Iceland was Christian; in 974 King Harald of Denmark had converted as also in about 998 had King Olaf-Tryggvason of Norway.

At 1000 CE the world's population was around 265 million, Europe's around 40 million; a fairly steady growth since the dawn of history. The next 500 years was to see the foundations of a broad European civilization firmly established, with all the features of advancing civilization. We see the more regular application of technological developments, significant improvements in land and sea communications, and at about this time the intellectual consciousness of humanity takes an important step as the scientific 'method' became formally identified and progressively exploited, for good and for evil.

The Holy Roman Empire, that had been establish by Charlemagne after his coronation in 800 CE, covered a vast swathe of land from the North Sea and the Baltic south across the continent to include half of Italy, west to the coast of mainland Europe and east to the Balkans and Ukraine. An empire containing the numerous more or less subject kingdoms, including those of Poland, Hungary, France, Belgium, Portugal, Romania, Moldova, Austria, and most of North Africa from Algeria to Egypt. The Iberian Peninsula was divided into 5/6 kingdoms, with the Almohad Arabs still occupying the southern half of the region. Peripheral states such as England, Scotland, Ireland, Norway, Sweden, and Denmark, were run as independent kingdoms. From the coronation of Otto I Duke of Saxony in 962 the empire was mostly led by German kings - with it being renamed 'The Holy Roman Empire of the German Nation' from 1512 until its demise in 1806.

Before then barbarians still threatened the eastern borders of Europe and the Christian states of Bohemia, Hungry and Poland, having enjoyed a general peace under Germanic protection, were attacked by the rampaging Mongols in 1240. They were stopped on Polish land but their invasion served to remind the slowly civilizing populations of the European continent of the dangerous potential of central Asian nomads.

So, the primary political units of Europe were the kingdom and the principality, within which grew larger towns and some cities differing in the extent of their autonomy. The other important institutional body was the Christian Church, which vied for power with emperors, kings, and dukes, who were themselves often at each other's throats. Pope Gregory VIII (Hildebrand) struggled throughout his Papacy for the independence of the Church and for a Church that looked to Rome, and so to the Papacy for guidance and authority. Throughout the period 10th-15th centuries we see both of these aims being advanced; the later more successfully than the former. The increasing wealth and obvious opulence of the Church was criticized, both from without by envious kings but also from within, as churchmen such as St. Bernard, St Francis, and St Dominic, suggested a life of poverty to be more appropriate for followers of Christ. But wealth and worldly influence continued to accrue to the Papacy and in 1323 Pope John XXII made a ruling that the suggestion that Christ and his Apostles did not own any property was untrue, indeed heretical, and this 'message from God' was conveniently timed to coincide with a wide-ranging increase in Church owned property.

Even accepting the involvement of the Franciscans in the Inquisition and in the war between Guelfs and Ghibellines, the life of founder of the Order, St Francis of Assisi (1181-1226), was one of an individual with a spontaneous Christian faith expressed in a life of humanistic enthusiasm, personal poverty, and a sincere piety that he extended to all of his god's creation. Christianity (the western Church) managed to remain generally united by the sincerity of believers in a shared faith, as well as the baser recognition of a collective material self-interest. The Fourth Lateran Council of 1215 CE represented the hierarchy of the Church, being attended by 71 patriarchs and metropolitans, 412 bishops, and 900 abbots and priors, from across western Christendom. It was held in Rome and served to consolidate the central role of the Papacy in the leadership of the Church. Not just as a source of spiritual authority but also as the administrative centre of the Church in the world.

From 1050 CE, instead of being appointed by an emperor, Popes were elected by a two-third majority of a group of Church peers 'The Chapter'. This body became the College of Cardinals which still elects Popes, in secret, today. During the $12/13/14^{th}$ centuries the Papacy developed into an even larger bureaucracy. It had sections that dealt with finance, Cannon law, and religious penance. It also launched the 'Inquisition', one of the worst expressions of religious zeal, drawing inquisitors from Dominican and Franciscan monastic orders and also many lay people; presumably anyone with a talent for detecting and suppressing heresy, often violently, wherever it could be found. Many thousands of innocent if naïve Christians were immolated on the sword of Catholic religious hysteria.

In the fifteenth century senior churchmen argued for more power to be vested in the Councils of the Church rather than the Papacy. They re-constituted the Council for a meeting in Pisa, one aiming to seek a resolution to the division caused by having two rival Popes that were contesting each other's legitimacy. Unfortunately the solution arrived at in 1409 was to nominate a third Pope; a solution that not surprisingly was hardly a success; and these three soon excommunicated one another. This 'Great Schism' was not easily resolved, and so the western Church that had been divided since 1378 was not reunited until 1417. But at least the Council had been re-established, and felt that it should have a central role in choosing future Popes, and in Church affairs more generally.

The impact of the Church on the common people was mostly at the local level of the parish; a group of these would be overseen by a bishop or abbot who would have considerably wide-ranging responsibility for their management. A collection of bishops were overseen by an archbishop (or metropolitan) who drew their authority directly from the Papacy, authority signified by a special vestment (the pallium) bestowed on them by the Pope. The value of a parish-living varied considerably, from those being able to support their clergy in luxury to those that offered only a meagre living. All but the most valuable parishes (Catholic 'livings') being generally occupied by clergy drawn from the educated sons of the lower middle-class. Although it was a Church that invited all classes to join, those at the top of its hierarchy came overwhelmingly from the upper classes. Indeed many senior posts were actually reserved for those considered to be of noble birth. Men like the exceptionally clever Thomas Wolsey, the son of a butcher who became Archbishop of York as well as close adviser to Henry VIII of England, were rare exceptions. Bishoprics and the position of abbot provided rich livings (some of these men became fabulously wealthy) even accepting that at times these positions were filled by men motivated by a sincere sense of spirituality that did, at least to some modest extent, become expressed in their lives.

The rising costs of government (including financing of wars – see below) meant the increasing need for higher taxes to be levied and to be efficiently collected. Taxes based on the ownership of land, and on customs duties being widespread on commodities such as wool, wine, and cloth. By the 13th century the collection of taxes came to be arranged on behalf of kings and emperors by important families who were establishing banks. Families such as the Medici in Italy, the Fuggers in Augsburg, and the Jacques Coeur in France. Italian banks became responsible for collecting Papal taxes from the mid. thirteenth century.

In northern Italy at this time free city-states such as Pisa, Venice, Genoa, and Florence, began to prosper on the back of increasing Mediterranean maritime trade and some of the wealth that accrued from this was to sponsor the artistic brilliance that would characterize the Italian Renaissance of 1450-1520. But before this florescence of more attractive aspects of humanity these same cities were to help fund the expression of large-scale brigandage termed the Crusades.

The ground conditions for this European adventure were in the relative peaceful relations with Scandinavian Vikings and eastern European peoples such as Slavs and Magyars now that most of these had been converted to Christianity. But the down-side to this period of relative peace was that there were many armed man-at-arms, lower knights, as well as serfs on the run, roaming Europe as vagabonds or seeking employment as mercenaries serving the courts of various princes, dukes, and kings. Thus stimulating many more minor 'local' conflicts, and civil unrest. There was also an increase in religious piety and in religious affairs more generally as the Church consolidated its hold on the European religious consciousness and the (elite) public mood heightened by such as the Investiture controversy begun in

1075; this being essentially a power struggle between emperor and kings against the Papacy for the right to invest and confer the robes and insignia of office on bishops and abbots. Lying behind this right to in effect, appoint a preferred candidate, lay a covetous struggle for control of the vast wealth of monasteries and other Church owned lands.

There was also a long-held fear of the Islamic world to the south. The ever-present threat of Islamic armies pushing further into Europe and their actual raiding on its fringes, along with regular instances of interference in Mediterranean maritime trade. Add in provocations such as the destruction of the Church of the Holy Sepulchre by order of al-Hakim bi-Amr Allah, the Fatimid Caliph of Cairo (later allowed by a successor Caliph of Cairo al-Hakim to be rebuilt) and the stream of propaganda constructed from some real, but more often invented, hostile acts of Muslim against Christian. A potent mix of conditions coalesced to allow the sad, futile, and bloody drama of the crusades to be played out.

The trigger event for the launch was the appeal in March 1095 of the Byzantine Christian Emperor Alexios I Komnenos to Pope Urban II for mercenaries to be sent to support the defence of his empire against Muslim (Saljuq) Turks, who had recently captured Nicaea on the Empire's southern border. The Pope convened a Council of the Church to meet at Clermont in November 1095. A collection of 250 bishops and a significant number of French noblemen, heard an impassioned appeal from a Pope (the head of a Catholic Church that had reached the peak of its European authority) who pleaded for Christians in Europe to stop fighting each other, unite under the banner of the holy cross, and take up arms against Islamists, both Arab and Turk. To undertake the task, so redolent of Christian religious symbolism, of freeing Jerusalem, the holiest city of Christendom, from the grip of the infidels and heretics.

Along with this appeal for unity was the promise of an 'indulgence' from the Pope such that all who took part in this 'holy war' would be absolved of their sins and an assertion that those who were killed would gain everlasting life in heaven. These more spiritual motivations could find justification in the works of philosophers of the Church including St Augustine who in 'The City of God' had sought to justify the use of force in the service of Christ. Not surprisingly, just to ensure a range of motivating ideas could be covered, Urban also pointedly drew attention to the considerable amount of earthly wealth that was held in the cities of the 'promised land' in the east. Fully aware of the temper of many in the wider audience he appealed for 'robbers to become knights'.

The message of the Pope's appeal spread rapidly across Europe, reaching the receptive ears and feeding the imaginations of thousands of individuals from all classes and, whilst some were undoubtedly motivated by genuine religious indignation at the occupation of the holy land by what they considered to be infidels, the vast majority seem to have been drawn from the sections of society such as the feckless and the otherwise surplus labour of towns with nothing much to lose. There were also the awkwardly placed younger sons of nobility and the mercenary freewheeling 'for hire' soldierly then in abundance across the continent.

Starting with the first, and including by convention eight others over two centuries, the Crusades, as they came to be known, saw a stream of warriors, often accompanied by clergy, together amounting to up to half a million individuals heading east. But it was really only the first crusade that achieved the claimed goal of replacing Muslim with Christian control of Jerusalem. This Christian Crusade was an achievement bathed in the blood of many women and children as the soldiery murdered, raped and pillaged their way too and through Middle Eastern lands; killing Muslims, Jews, and also quite often any Christians who failed to give material support to the enterprise.

An enterprise characteristically culminating when the invaders laid siege to Jerusalem and had completed its capture on 15th July 1099. Over the following 24 hours the crusaders put to the sword almost every inhabitant of the City, whether they be Muslim, Jew, or Christian. During this first (official) crusade the Europeans were able to establish states in Jerusalem, Edessa, Syria, Palestine, and even as far south as Tripoli. Although the next eight Crusades were more or less military failures, the opportunistic invaders made the most of the opportunities for gaining the material rewards that had been promised by the Pope.

The outcomes of this long miss-adventure were that in the short-term the fortunes of many individuals were made (if made in blood and by theft) and a number of northern Italian city-states prospered as the eastern Mediterranean was opened to their trade. Jews had their status as marginal members of European society firmly established by programs of massacre against them, reinforcing their own folk memory of persecution and to historicize their social pariah, scapegoat, role.

The poets, balladeers, and others who recorded aspects of the venture, wove selective facts and mythical ideas together and coloured these with their own imaginative inventions, making heroes out of murderous villains and military triumphs out of moral failures. Probably the worst excess of imagination over actual fact is the overall idea (perpetrated by the Papacy and official histories of western European nation-states) of the Crusades as some sort of heroic battle of Christian good over Infidel evil; such that the very word Crusade is now linked with the idea of the single-minded pursuit of just causes. Men such as Louis IX of France, Richard the Lionhart of England, and Frederic Barbarossa of Germany, are depicted in story-telling as good kings; wise and humane, but also strong and resolute holy warriors, sworn to defend Christian purity. When in fact, a description that encompassed their self-seeking cruelty and greed would be more appropriate for men who squandered vast sums of money as they led motley bands of brigands across south-eastern Europe and into the Middle-East.

Throughout human history military conflict stimulated technical development and the late medieval period, being one of generally wide-spread conflict, was also one of significant development in the means of making war. Three in particular stand out: the use of a long-bow (exploited at Crecy and Agincourt) together with the cross-bow and pike-men (so a light infantry). These innovations making the heavily armed knights mounted upon massive horses effectively obsolete.

The 14/15th centuries saw the introduction of gunpowder, used in firearms and cannon, dramatically changing the nature of warfare. War became considerably more costly, partly owing to the need for large, thicker-walled fortifications (raising the status of civil engineers) to resist cannon-shot and for the larger infantry-based armies that became the norm. The crusaders who had brought back their own experience of building, attacking, and defending, large stone castles; used designs based on models seen during their campaigns – as well as designs for siege equipment - in constructing their own fortifications.

These developments meant that European wars would now be much more likely to be fought on a national rather than a local scale, as only kings supported financially by central governments (and bankers), could afford to wage war by the new means available. Along with the technical developments would be the formation of more reliable and better trained standing armies; a burden on the taxpayer but a significant convenience for those inclined to war. An ordinance of 1445 saw the establishment of a standing army in France and in 1661 one in England.

At sea, the sternpost rudder had made a difference to the efficiency of the sailing boats in China, with this being introduced into Europe during the thirteenth century. This maritime innovation was added to by gunpowder used in shipboard cannon, navigation aided by the cross-staff 'sextant' and the compass, and more efficient forms of rigging and sail-plans. The compass had been long used in China in the form of a short piece of iron attached to a length of wood floating in a container of water. The type of compass that surfaced in the west in the thirteenth century, being an improvement on the Chinese model with its using a thin needle of iron pivoted on a piece of card.

The 15th century discovery of the new lands to the west was suggested by the historian Francisco Lopez de Gomara in 1552 as being the most significant event since the world was created. Rather more modestly, and as such more realistically, the Frenchman Louis Le Roy compared its significance to the invention of printing with movable type.

Following his 'discovery' of the Americas in 1492, Christopher Columbus travelled from island to island and, with the characteristic arrogance of European 'explorers', he freely endowed Spanish names on mountains, capes, rivers, indeed any prominent geographic feature was named, and by implication claimed, for Spain. The sailors first came into contact with indigenous people, later called Tanios, who spoke a language very similar to the Arawaks of the South American mainland to whom they are thought to have been related. These accommodating natives, who met the strangers naked except for gold pendants worn in their noses, and being unarmed and friendly, were just the type that Columbus would have wished to find. They had no conception of private property, were peaceful and, as described by Columbus himself: 'They are very gentle and without knowledge of what is evil: nor do they murder or steal……there are no better people or land in the world'.

Columbus and subsequent European settlers were to take full advantage of these benign, tractable, people who showed their naiveté from the very first contact when they assisted Columbus to provision his ships by showing his men where to find fresh water and even helping to carry the water-barrels. On some islands the sailors did make contact with a more warlike people, the Caribs, who on the basis of no evidence at all, were described by Columbus (who himself had never set foot on an island occupied by Caribs) as cannibals; a misconception that continued to be suggested by some historians into the twentieth century. Columbus, the self-styled 'Captain of cavaliers and of conquests' led four voyages, and on his second trip he took 1200 settlers to establish settlements on Hispaniola. His almost pathological search for gold drove him to issue an order that each Indian over the age of 14 must offer him an amount of gold every three months. Those failing to conform were punished, including for some having their hands cut-off. But even this and other harsh measures were unsuccessful so, if he could not make his fortune by robbing the natives of gold, he would endeavour to rob them of their freedom. By 1545 about 1600 Tanios, those he had called '….affectionate and generous people' were made captive and 550 of these were sent to

Portugal for the slave market, of which 200 died during the passage across the Atlantic.

Labour shortages led to Columbus putting pressure on the settlers, provoking a number of local rebellions against his regime. To the extent that a settler turned Catholic, Friar Bartolome de las Casas, horrified at the treatment of his fellow-countrymen reported his concern (if he also suggested obtaining slave labour from Africa) this, and complaints made by the settlers themselves, contributed to Columbus being relived of the governorship and returned to Spain in chains in order to explain his behaviour. Owing mainly to the intervention of Queen Isabella he was released and soon returned to the West Indies.

There were possibly one million natives living on the island of Hispaniola prior to its settlement by Columbus but within 20 years there were only 28,000 left, and by 1542 this was reduced to 200. Labour shortages, along with the fact that Africa had already become an acceptable source of slave labour, led to the import of African slaves. The first group was landed on Jamaica in 1517; where the trade was to be significantly increased when Jamaica was taken by the British in 1655.

Another Italian (Florentine), Amerigo Vespucci, sponsored by the Portuguese, sailed east to reach South American in 1502 and progressed south to explore the coast. Vespucci gained knowledge of a new continent, one that would be named after him in 1507 by the geographer Martin Waldseemüller. Europeans were to subject the people of the South American mainland to the same cruel process of colonization and exploitation that had been practiced in the paradise islands of the Caribbean Sea.

In 1519, following a couple of slave hunting expeditions to the mainland that had returned to Cuba laden with gold and stories of Indian wealth, Hernando Cortes and a fairly modest force of soldiers (500 men) left Cuba and reached the mainland (on a stretch of coast that is now Mexico). He landed, made camp, and immediately founded a town that was to become Veracruz. By some fluke of good (for them) fortune they had chosen the very day that the Aztec calendar predicted the return of the god Quetzalcoatl, the feathered serpent who favoured peace as opposed to the Aztec tribal god Huitzilopochtli (the 'Hummingbird') worshipped in blood by the warrior ruling class. The Aztecs believed that the peace-loving God would one day return to claim back the Empire. This was probably the reason why the Aztec leader Moctezuma decided not to have the small force slaughtered on the beach when they were at their most vulnerable. Instead he sent a party bearing gifts for Cortes. Among these gifts were a gold disk as big as a cartwheel, a larger one made of silver, and other gold pieces; gifts intended to appease the invaders and to convince them to not move inland. Although it was Cortes's aim to conquer the Aztec Empire[15] he gave no hint of this during the initial meetings with the Aztec ambassadors, merely informing them that he would have to meet with their leader.

The land the Spanish arrived in was not one of a settled happy people. As well as experiencing a period of economic decline the people were also being ruled by an Aztec aristocracy whose authority depended on their creating fear through outright terror. The main means of inducing fear, and the acceptance it generally induced in the peoples of the up to sixteen indigenous tribes in the region the Aztecs ruled over, was the often quite arbitrary selection of native people followed by their ritual sacrifice to the Sun God Huitzilopochtli. Initially prisoners of war were used then subject people were expected to offer their women and children for the gory ritual. But this practice, of sustaining their up to 300 gods by a daily blood sacrifice, fed on itself to become an obsession. The number of people being murdered increased, with possibly as many as 80,000 people being sacrificed over one four-day blood-fest. This was the political situation that Cortes was able to take advantage of; a subject people ruled by terror which in turn induced fear but also hatred. Most of the indigenous population were receptive to the Spanish to the extent that during the battle of Tenochtitlan there were more natives fighting on Cortes's

---

[15] He had burnt the boats they had used to cross to the mainland in order that his men would not be able to consider retreating back to the safely of Cuba.

side than on the side of the Aztecs. A fortuitous decision made by the Spaniards was to take along a native woman called Dona Marina as translator; she was an astute individual, seemingly aware of the regional political situation. According to Arnold Toynbee (1976) without Dona Marina, Cortes: '…would have arrived in Mexico virtually deaf, dumb, and politically in the dark'.

Cortes moved inland, engaging both friends and enemies of the Aztecs in a number of one-sided military engagements. Moctezuma, still fearing that Cortes had come to reclaim the empire on behalf of Quetzalcoatl, sent even more gifts and urged Cortes not to approach the Aztec capital of Tenochtitlan; a plea that was ignored. The first attempt by the Spanish to take the capital, involving a mixture of duplicity and cruelty was repulsed by forces led by a new leader elected by the Aztec tribal council, causing the Spanish to retreat back towards the coast. But they were strengthened by reinforcements from Cuba and the recruitment of Mayan and other natives, constituting a force that returned to take the capital in 1521, following a protracted, bitter, siege. From now the mainland would be open to the Europeans and soon the area today covered by Yucatan, Honduras, Nicaragua, and most of Mexico, effectively came under Spanish rule. And Spanish rule invariably meant a cruel regime determined upon economic exploitation.

To the south another Spaniard, Francisco Pizarro, aware owing to previous sorties to the mainland that there was gold to be found within the Inca Empire, set out with royal authority to explore Peru (Biro) from the end of 1530. He was accompanied by a force of about 200 men, including four of his brothers. Whilst Cortes success had been due to his being able to take advantage of the native population's dislike of their Aztec masters, Pizarro's venture into Peru was favoured by coinciding with a time of conflict between factions each led by the half-brothers Atahualpa and Huascar. Pizzaro pretended to take the side of Atahulpa but, by an act of deception aided by superior arms, took him prisoner after surprising and killing hundreds of his men (2,000 according to the Spanish but 10,000 according to the Incas). He then pretended to accept Atahalpa's offer of a room full of gold in return for his freedom but again reneged on the agreement when the gold was due to be paid. Instead of releasing the Inca leader, Pizzaro put him on trial for the crimes of idolatry, polygamy, and the murder of Huascar. He was found guilty and sentenced originally to be burned at the stake if, when Atahalpa accepted a Christian baptism, the sentence was reduced to strangling.

Holding Peru initially proved to be difficult for the Spanish, with an Inca revolt being led by Huascar's brother Manco. But military supremacy (especially the use of men mounted on horseback) pushed Manco's beleaguered forces into the Andean mountains where they continued to survive until 1572 by when the Spanish finally crushed the last of the Inca resistance with the symbolic beheading of the last Inca leader, Tapac Amaru, in a special ceremony held in Cuzco. But by this time the leading conquerors had turned on each other in a series of clashes that led to the murder of Pizzaro, with open conflict continuing until Viceroy Francisco de Toledo resolved the differences between the opposing factions by a combination of bribes, pardons, and the execution of the more intractable individuals. Following the initial period of conquests – of Columbus, Cortes, and Pizarro – colonial rule of the Americas was to be closely directed from home countries intent on transferring as much wealth as possible from their overseas domains back to Europe.

One aspect of this being the importation of large numbers of Black (African) slaves to make up for the shortfall in labour caused primarily by the murder and death by disease of native peoples. Not mentioned so often was the slave raiding into the interior of the mainland itself as the more easily available native Indians of the coastal regions, and those surviving on the islands, had proved to be reluctant workers who persisted in attempted rebellion and even suicide to avoid enslavement.

Such a glittering prize as the prospect of a steady supply of gold, silver, and other valuable commodities, would not be left to the Portuguese and Spanish to enjoy unmolested, and Dutch, French, and English, governments and merchants, first looked on covetously and then actively fought for control of the West Indian islands and of the wider trans-Atlantic trade. The mixture of official, semi-official, and free-enterprise piracy the late-comers used sat well with the very methods the original, Portuguese and Spanish, colonizers had employed. To illustrate the fabulous wealth that was being fought over.... in 1592 a squadron of English ships ambushed a Portuguese galleon making passage back to Europe. The prize was a cargo of gold, silver, pearls, diamonds, amber, as well as rich cloths, calico, and ebony – there was also a list of spices that included 400 ton of pepper, 45 of cloves, 35 of cinnamon, and 3 of nutmeg, all highly valued commodities in Europe. This cargo has been valued at half a million pounds at 1592 prices; by comparison this would have equated to half of all the annual income of the English exchequer at that time – fabulous wealth in but one cargo.

By 1600, 110,000 Spanish and Portuguese settlers had sought their fortunes in the Americas and by the same period 140,000 African slaves had made a similar journey west; but the passage of the slaves was involuntary, being made to provide the labour upon which the fortunes of many others would be established. Also by 1600, 750,000 pounds weight of gold had travelled the other way back to Spain.

The Pope's comparison of invading and colonising the Americas with the Crusades, seems even more darkly poignant when we see how closely the two periods shared the central characteristic of murder, theft, and pillage, carried out by amoral individuals mostly better armed than their opponents, doing so in the name of the Christian God, with the blessing of the principle clamant to be its representative on Earth.

In Europe at this time divisions caused by the Reformation and the rise of Protestantism led to a number of bitter and costly wars across the continent, only significantly reduced by a series of agreements including the Peace of Augsburg (1555), and the Edict of Nantes (1598), after many thousands had died due to their holding to contested versions of Christianity.

The Catholic Church's response to Protestantism, apart from the liberal use of excommunication, and during the two months following

St Bartholomew's Day 1572 the killing of over 15,000 French Huguenot Protestants[16], was to reform itself into a more hierarchical, even less tolerant, organization.

The Church Council, meeting in Trent (northern Italy) between 1545 and 1563, reaffirmed the supreme authority of the Pope, introduced new regulations for the training of clergy, and clarified the doctrines of Catholicism. At this time another organization was established within the Church that was to serve the Church's purpose well. This was the Society of Jesus (the Jesuits), founded by St. Ignatius Loyola, an organization whose subsequent history was to show the Church at both its very best and at its very worst. Loyola's military background was to influence the close-knit combative approach taken by the Society as it engaged in what amounted to a holy war against Protestantism and operating as a scourge against Catholic 'heretics'. They played a key, indeed enthusiastic, role in the Inquisition. Their focus was to be on training and conversion; especially training priests to go forth and convert the newly conquered people of the Americas. They were often tenacious defenders of the converted to the point of being prepared to sacrifice their own lives. But they also hunted for slaves to work for them.

If we stand back to consider 15th /16th century Europe we can span two centuries rent with religious conflict as well as some opportunity for religious freedom. Most people lived short lives characterized by hard toil whilst they experienced the oppression of employers, whether as workers on the land or in the towns and cities; with many living in poverty. The peasants in most parts of Europe were pushed to the limits and as a reaction there were a series of peasant protests to the point of war from 1524.

The ferment caused by religious divisions gave additional opportunity for longstanding grievances to be acted upon. Peasant armies formed in central and Eastern Europe in what was left of the

---

[16] Pope Pius V, along with 33 cardinals, attended a mass in the Church of St Louis in Rome, during which they gave 'thanks to god' for the massacre.

Empire; generally beginning their fight in the countryside with this spreading to the conurbations. The grievances aired in different localities centred on similar injustices: conditions of serfdom, high tithes or taxes, food shortages, the enclosure of land, removal of the right of the peasants to engage in hunting and wood gathering, and similar. These were more often a protest against the loss of ancient rights than demands for a greater share of the wealth the people were themselves creating. This protest movement was not an organized attempt to overthrow the ruling classes but just a sometimes violent appeal for a level of social justice that would end or at least mitigate the worst effects of lordly rule and of the oppressive Church authority of the time. Although some minor short-term concessions were made, the main reaction being that the ruling classes raised mercenary armies and set them against the protestors. Armies composed of professional soldiers, better trained and better armed than the peasants they faced, proved to be overwhelming; with the result that possibly 100,000 peasants were killed during contests that would be more accurately described as routs rather than battles. Even leading Protestants such as Luther and Zwingli sided with the ruling classes. Luther going so far as to suggest that the peasants should be slain like dogs; writing in a letter to Albert of Brandenburg the then Bishop of Mainz suggesting that: 'Better the death of all the peasants than of princes and magistrates' - suggesting that his adherence to the Bible was based on the worst parts of the Old Testament rather than the somewhat more humanist New Testament and the teachings of Jesus.

The harsh and bloody reaction did not repress the peasants' simmering anger and across Europe during the seventeenth century peasants repeatedly rose against their oppression, literally hundreds of local conflicts are recorded. These uprisings rumbled on over the next few centuries but with few tangible benefits to the peasantry, and indeed they had a reinforcing effect on centralizing the power of the emerging nation-states. It was to be the French revolution that would see the first really significant outcome to an action taken by members of the European lower classes, if more to the longer-term benefit of the classes above them.

Intellectually, during the Reformation scientific ideas were advancing discovery and technical innovation, not least in reinforcing the link between theory and technology were the needs of warfare; driving the improvements in metallurgy, chemistry, and in the large scale mining of the coal that would fuel the transformations required to turn iron ore into guns and cannons (ordnance). In metallurgy, new metals were being smelted including zinc, bismuth, cobalt and kupfernickel. The, new to Europe, high temperature technique of smelting iron to produce 'pig iron', (a form more amenable to casting), had been developed in the mining districts of Germany in the fourteenth century and had spread to most other European countries by the sixteenth.

In terms of governance, it was a Europe that was a network of royal (aristocratic) family connections; more often seeking marriages of convenience rather than love, and military alliances that favoured strength and ambition over principle. The English Tudors, French Valois and Bourbons, and the Austrian Habsburgs, standout in this unsavoury mixture of dynastic aspirations founded in a tracery of elite-group presumptions. The Habsburgs ruled Austria for 600 years and the Holy Roman Empire until its demise in 1806; by when they would be clinging onto but an empty title. When in 1519 Charles V, the Habsburg King of Spain, bribed his way (funded by the Fuggers banking family of Germany) to became Emperor he had united lands from the West to the East Indies.

Before this there had been the contest over an old European power-base, focused on the Italian city-states of Naples, Venice, Milan, and Florence, as well as the Vatican. This region was fought over from 1494-1516. The lead up to this conflict being the emperor-elect Maximilian I's (became emperor in 1508) determination to gain control of alpine passes linking the Austrian branch of the Holy Roman Empire to the northern Italian states. But with a strong Swiss army presenting an obstacle to control of the most easily accessible passes, Maximilian's plan was unrealistic. Ferdinand II of Spain considered that he, through family connections, had a right to parts of northern Italy. A connection that would, given Spanish control of Sicily and Sardinia, seal his control of the north-western Mediterranean.

The French also claimed rights to northern Italian lands going back to thirteenth century, with for example, a claim originating in 1266 by the French House of Anjou to the Kingdom of Naples. In 1494 the young French King Charles VIII set off on an expedition to invade Italy in pursuit of France's historic claims and its more immediate economic interests. Influenced by ideas of knightly chivalry, and a foolishly romantic view of war, Charles framed his expedition as a narrative of crusading. His ambitions saw Italy as but the first step of Angevin expansion to the east. He cleverly bought the neutrality of powerful neighbours, yielding small amounts of disputed territory to Austria and Aragon, and paying an amount of money to England.

The strong French army made fairly easy progress through northern Italy aided by some internal dissent within the city-states. By 1495 Rome, Florence, and Naples, were taken. Other leaders misunderstood Charles's claim to be 'Emperor'- he was apparently referring to the eastern empire and so was reflecting his crusading narrative. But rulers in states to the north assumed he meant the western empire and felt that the French King's ambitions could be a threat to their own interests. An anti-French 'Holy League' was formed by the Papacy (Pope Alexandra VI), Francis II of Aragon, the Holy Roman Emperor Maximilian I, and the city states of Milan and Venice. This formidable alliance forced a French retreat and, by the time the French army surrendered at Atella in 1495, Charles had already fled back to France.

Although a truce was signed it was to prove short-lived when on the early death of Charles his successor, Louis XII, assumed the mantle of French ambition towards Italy. These ambitions were symbolized by his taking Italian titles along with his French kinghood. Louis was careful to form strategic alliances to offset the power of those ranged against him. This time the Papacy, ever looking to favour the side that most favoured the Church's worldly interests, took the French side (if in a fairly neutral way, with little genuine enthusiasm) and an alliance was made with the Swiss Confederation, then at war with Austria, enabling Louis to strengthen his forces by recruiting from the disciplined and well-trained Swiss army.

Henry VII of England and Philip I Duke of Burgundy (also in control of the Low Countries) were brought into the alliance and, when Venice joined this basically anti-Habsburg group, Louise advanced into northern Italy. His army waged a generally successful campaign on land and, echoing the crusading ambitions of his predecessor, he sent a fleet of ships against the Moslem Turks. But sea-borne access for supplying his army in Italy was denied by the ships of Ferdinand of Aragon when the Spanish King broke from an alliance that had seen the French and Aragonese army working together to capture Naples.

Following defeat by the Spaniards the French now sought an alliance with Maximilian I of Austria, the old enemy; an alliance smoothed by arranged marriages and with conditional gifts of French territory offered as dowries. But the King's Council, and later the General Council, prevented an alliance based on the possible loss of French lands and by 1506 the alliance fell apart.

The perception of France as being significantly weakened emboldened some members of the defunct Holy League, along with some others, to continue the conflict. In 1513 the Swiss invaded Burgundy and the English landed an expeditionary force at Calais. But a lack of military power and of political will on all sides to go further, led to a negotiated peace; a peace with England paid for in money and with Austria paid partly by a mutually agreed marriage. Furthermore, minor conflicts involving the French, Spanish, Swiss, and the Venetians, ended in a series of individual peace agreements. The most significant of these being the Treaty of Cambrai (1517) which led to the French, Spanish, and Austrians, overcoming their own differences to combine and turn against the perceived common enemy, the Ottoman Turks. During this period of serial conflict, based on ever-shifting alliances in the pursuit of the self-interest of egoistical rulers, large numbers of the common soldiery lost their lives and most of the people of northern Italy were affected by wide-spread destruction in the towns and countryside.

Within two years of the signing of the Treaty of Cambrai the

French and the Austrians were to renew their squabbles. The trigger event this time being a contest for the imperial throne. A French alliance included German princes and even Ottoman Turks; so long the enemy – but now the 'enemy of my enemy', and so my potential ally. When King Francis I of France claimed the right to become Emperor he was not only following a long French tradition but he also had an eye on his rival Maximilian I's grandson Charles V who was already in control of Spain, Burgundy, and a large part of Austria. Both of the rivals sought to bribe the seven Imperial Electors - three German archbishops, three German aristocrats and the King of Bohemia. But early in the electoral process Francis realized that he lacked sufficient support and instead of pursuing his own ambitions he decided to promote the candidacy of Frederick of Saxony. Although Frederick was elected he feared for his life and resigned within but three hours of his election; Charles was then nominated as 'Emperor Elect' on June 28th 1519. Now in control of what appeared to be the strongest power in Europe he set about the task of regaining territory that had been lost to the Empire; a task that would inevitably mean war with France.

In the European way, each side set about forming militarily pragmatic strategic alliances. An important one being that between Charles and Henry VIII of England, who then invaded France in 1522. The Papacy, judging the Emperor to be the strongest of the rivals, sided with Charles. As did the Constable of Bourbon, who turned against Francis and attacked Provence. Facing defeat by the French, Charles's Imperial Army gave their support to the Bourbons and, in 1525, the French were defeated at Pavia with Francis being taken prisoner. In 1526 Charles added Bohemia, re-named as the Kingdom of Hungry, to the Empire.

France led by Francis's mother, Louise of Savoy, fought on and now a number of European states realized the danger posed by a potentially all-powerful Empire. In response to this threat to themselves, England, the Papacy, and the Venetians, allied themselves with France. A treaty was signed in1526 (the Peace of Madrid) which significantly disadvantaged the French, laid Italy open to Charles, and in which was sown the seeds of future conflict. During the uneasy peace that followed Charles continued his endeavours to bring some order to his rambling empire, but long lines of communication, an economy hampered by large debts and an inefficient tax collection system, made this a challenging task. Even when the internal situation had improved, at least to some extent, Charles did not have long to pause and enjoy his dominions and was soon once again embroiled in conflict with his neighbours.

The uneasy peace ended with Francis's release from imprisonment in Spain and his sworn claim that he had signed the treaty of Madrid under duress, suggesting that he did not have the authority to cede the Dukedom of Burgundy to Charles (a key loss to France under the treaty of Madrid). Viewing the treaty as void, Francis now set about forming the usual conveniently assessed alliances, this time it was to include the Pope and the Venetians in the 'League of Cognac'. He also negotiated with the rulers of Poland and Transylvania and, ignoring significant religious differences, even with the Ottoman Empire (led by Suleiman the Magnificent) with the purpose of presenting an eastern threat to the Empire. But this provocation merely served as an excuse for Charles to attack Rome in 1527; Lutheran mercenaries were fighting alongside an Imperial army that mercilessly looted and sacked the City.

Accepting the military reality, most of the northern Italian states allied themselves with the Emperor. But now England's Henry VIII joined with Francis and his allies and, in 1528, declared war on the Empire. The costs of conflict were high and the morale of the now exhausted Imperial army led to negotiations and in 1529 a peace, the second Treaty of Cambrai, facilitated by Margaret of Austria (the Emperor's aunt) and Louise of Savoy (Francis's mother). Again, we see the fairly piece-meal distribution of some contested lands in ways that generally reflected the reality of territorial possession at the time when hostilities ended. Francis renounced his claims to parts of Italy, even if he would go on to reinstate his claim in later years. The Pope also conceded to the reality of the situation, signing the peace of Cambrai, and in February 1530 he crowned Charles as Emperor.

The Peace of Cambrai was a significant treaty for Western Europe and was a further step towards the formation of the nation states that we have today. The relative peace that followed the signing of the treaty gave Charles the opportunity to reorganize his dispersed dominions. He took steps to centralize the judiciary, as well as the tax collection and other financial arrangements in both Spain and The Netherlands. This included the promotion to key administrative posts of those loyal to himself. These and other changes, also gave some support to advancing the interests of middle-class manufacturing and trading groups. Amongst these changes were financial mechanisms introduced to protect manufacturing industries such as a textile industry at that time suffering from competition with England. These economic policies have been identified by historians as a significant contribution to the early stages of the development of a capitalist economic system. Interesting that protection rather than free-trade was a central characteristic of these economic innovations, but hardly surprising given that the subsequent history of capitalism which has in fact been more about protecting the interests of the powerful (groups, classes, corporations, and nation-states) than it has ever been about genuine free trade.

As with all empires at some time, the Habsburgs were also having to deal with internal dissent as well as external enemies. Internally the most difficult to manage were focused on religious differences with protestant lands in Germany and with the Papacy which, although not internal as a constitutional part of the Empire, it was internal in the sense of its influence on the large Catholic population within its borders. Beyond the border, the Ottoman Turks in the east were the most powerful external enemy. Charles had to confront them at sea in the western Mediterranean and on land in the east as the formidable Turkish army advanced through Hungary, besieging Vienna by 1529.

It wasn't long before Francis, stirred by the Emperor's sponsoring of his own relatives to positions of power in Europe, took action. Throughout the 1530s and 40s he sought opportunities to weaken Charles's hold on his empire; even at times joining forces with the Turks. The combination of the French fleet and a Turkish fleet led by

Barbarossa attacked Nice in 1543. In the late 1540s a French army was in Germany supporting the princes of the Protestant states against the Catholic Emperor. Invariably, after many deaths and widespread destruction, the parties recognized that neither had an overwhelming military advantage; although the balance of power did favour the Emperor's side, a reality recognized in the text of the Peace of Augsburg 1550. A war-weary Charles, assuming that the German princes had learnt a lesson, conceded their right to choose between Catholicism and Protestantism. Charles abdicated as Holy Roman Emperor in 1555, passing the title to his brother Ferdinand I. Then in 1556 he also abdicated as King of Spain, passing this title to his son Philip II. These acts in effect split the western Empire once again into one part centred on Austria and another centred on Spain and the Netherlands; if both parts still ruled by scions of the Habsburg Dynasty who continued to be tied to each other financially and by strategic marriages.

Philip shared the early ambition of his father to lead a united empire as master of Europe. The French King Henry II was but one obstacle to these ambitions. In 1556 Henry's troops entered Italy, ostensibly to defend Papal lands from Spanish-led domination. But a peak in the late 1550s in the financial crisis that affected Western Europe throughout the sixteenth century meant that active conflict could not be sustained by either side. In April 1559, the Treaty of Cateau-Cambresis was signed, outlining the terms of a peace dictated more by financial circumstances rather than any consensus as to the fairness of its terms. Terms that included the return of some disputed territories and an agreed marriage to Philip of Henry's daughter Elizabeth of Valois in June 1559.

The Austrian branch of the Empire had the Ottoman Turks pressing from the east, with Selim II forcing the imperial army to retreat from Hungarian territories, so weakening the political position of the new (1564) Emperor Maximillian II (son of Ferdinand I). Not only were the Turks pushing further into Europe, even as far as Poland, they were also dominant at sea, with Barbary Turk pirates harassing towns along the Spanish coast and on Italian-held islands. It was to take three combined fleets of the Holy League brought together by Pope Pius V (France, Genoa, and Savoy) to defeat the Turkish fleet at Lepanto in 1571. But a Turkish administration led by the clever Selim II, advised by an even cleverer vizier in Mehmed Sokollu, was soon able to build and equip a new fleet that would reverse some to the loses made at Lepanto. A fleet that, from its base in northern African, was able to represent an on-going threat to Spain and to settlements along the northern Mediterranean coast. But the power of the Ottoman Empire, and hence its threat to Europe, did quite soon begin to decline mainly owing to a significant reduction in income from trade and the death in 1579 of Sokollu.

Meanwhile a weak but proud Empire still endeavoured to restore its prestige, with Maximilian II seeking to influence developments in Northern Europe. Here the Scandinavian countries, along with Russia, Germany, and Poland, competed for advantage in the valuable trade in raw materials, furs, timber, hemp, grain, and copper, all highly sought after in the west. Ivan IV ('The Terrible') Tsar of Russia engaged in aggressive action in the eastern Baltic but Sweden, Poland, and Denmark, also fought to maintain or extend their trading interests. A peace of sorts, facilitated by Maximilian II, was established at the end of a devastating seven years war (1561-68) centred on the Baltic. But the death in 1572 of the Polish King Sigismund Augustus led to a period of disruption as a number of aspirants competed for the throne, each of whom was supported by different external sponsors.

Spain's general policy of peaceful co-existence with its neighbours did not extend to the Netherlands, where its rule was maintained by the deployment of the harshest of measures. The Duke of Alba set up the 'Council of Blood'; given this name by history, to acknowledge the methods, involving terror, murder, and looting, that characterized the Duke's approach to suppressing religious dissent and anti-Spanish activities. This provoked a reaction, with an uprising in 1571 that was initially ruthlessly suppressed if, recognizing the failure of this approach, the Spanish withdrew the hated Duke. But this was too little too late to stem the nationalistic fervour that their policy of repression had fostered. In 1576 The States General of Holland was gradually joined by other provinces and after further conflict a new European nation was created in 1581 when the Treaty of Utrecht saw a union of the Low Country and adjoining provinces to form the United Provinces, initially united primarily against Philip of Spain. The final step towards statehood was taken at The Hague where, in July 1581, the States General officially brought an end to Philip's reign as King of the Netherlands.

But now Philip had other enemies, the predominant one being England, whose increasingly more able navy was ravaging Spanish overseas possessions as well as intercepting Spanish and Portuguese treasure ships under a policy that amounted to state sponsored piracy; although one could fairly argue that piracy of the fruits of robbery is merely the squabbling of criminals over ill-gotten gains.

After exposing a Spanish scheme to murder the Protestant Queen Elizabeth I and replace her with Philip's daughter the Catholic Isabella, the English sided with the United Provinces, supplying them with troops and materials with which to harass the Spanish. Philip's attempt to raise the stakes with an invasion of England went famously wrong when, in 1588, ill winds and superior English naval strategy led to the humiliating defeat of the Spanish Armada. A victory which signified the beginning of a long period of naval supremacy that would be experienced by the English (later British), along with a shorter period of decline in the economic fortunes of Spain.

This short overview of European politics during the conflict-ridden sixteenth century was important in that these unseemly machinations were undertaken to suit the economic interests, and egoistical ambition towards aggrandizement, of well-placed individuals and their local cliques. Political developments, and military conflicts, during this period not only contributed significantly to national mythologies but also to consolidating the power base of the ruling elites, in countries such as England, France, and in what would become Germany, and Italy, that were to have such an influence as they progressed into the era of industrialization. It would be the interests of these combinations of traditional and emerging national elites that would shape the political and economic forms that characterized the early, and influenced the later, stages of industrialization. The period also consolidated the assumed ground conditions of inter-nation relationships as being competitive rather than cooperative, conflictual rather than peaceful.

From the 15th century we see a clear trend towards the creation of nation-states across Europe. It is difficult to capture an authentic sense of any country. Countries, or nations, themselves being 'mobile entities' in that they are often invaded, or themselves grow by invading their neighbours – exchanging social and cultural influences as well as blending genes. They are artificial creations with porous borders liable to contract and expand over centuries, with incoming interbreeding peoples enriching the gene-pool as well as often enhancing and developing cultural, economic and political life. The historian's challenge is to endeavour to 'capture' a land with layer upon layer of intertwined complex histories.

That nation-states are synthetic creations would be clear if we followed their roots back into their varied pasts. We would see a range of different sized tribal groups the passage of occasional raiders and more permanent invaders of lands known by the mass of people only as their locality; their loyalty and sense of identity went little beyond the fields, lakes, rivers, swamps, hills, and woodlands of the local chieftain/lordship, and perhaps of immediately neighbouring lands. Yes for most no doubt the idea of wide domains ruled by semi-mythical emperors was an aspect of their perspective (in the West the image of Rome percolated down the centuries) but identity was for the most part confined to the lands they and their immediate ancestors had travelled over and drawn a mostly meagre living from. But deeply embedded into the collective consciousness of Europe's people (as almost everywhere else at this time) was the idea of powerful rulers. This idea might only be embodied for them by their local lord but it was psychologically then easy for people to accept the idea of kinghood (indeed for many touched by Christianity, the Bible is partly a tale of kings and rulers and God himself rules a 'Kingdom of

Heaven'). King (assumed to be blessed by a god) as protector being a more powerful idea than that of some local lord as protector – especially when, along with his local presence, was the immediate impact of a local lord's more immediate oppression.

'States' create nations (not as usually assumed, as some idea of 'natural nations' creating states) and a form of collective tribalism underlies the psychology of nationhood. We generally define a nation as being an entity constituted by a people with at least some sense of a common history, a shared culture, and a collective identity, usually living within with a circumscribed territory. These entities foster a national consciousness that is reinforced as each generation is socialized into the collective sharing of the sources of national identity; including absorbing the mythological roots of a nation. Add shared religion, a common language (primarily post printing), and interbreeding between those of different ethnicity and we have the foundations of a national consciousness. If ethnicity (and tribe, clan, and caste) can be contained within national identity then a state can be unified, if ethnic loyalties clash with national identity then a nation will lack cohesion and can even burst asunder.

The more evil effects of European engagement with the Americas was becoming apparent as the native population declined wherever it came into contact (direct or indirect) with Spanish invaders. The main cause of this decline being the ravages of diseases such as small-pox which spread from 1519, and was a key factor in weakening the defenders of the Aztec City of Tenochtitlan, enabling Cortes to capture the City with relative ease. Later on, it would be diseases such as measles, typhus, malaria, and yellow fever (the last two brought by African slaves) that would add to the overall biological blight inflicted on the indigenous people. The total population of the American landmass in 1500 has been estimated at about 70m, in but one hundred years it was reduced to about 8m; when the whole world context at that time saw an increase of about 20% in population. Millions of the continent's people, mostly victims of disease brought by civilized Europeans, died during the 16th century. Whilst the evils of economic exploitation fuelled by greed were a result of conscious (and so culpable) patterns of behaviour the unforeseen deaths caused by disease took a much heavier toll in human life.

Another result of the individual greed that cast a shadow of evil over human history was (and still is) the slave trade. Whilst slavery had been associated with civil life from the earliest of times the 'industrial' trade in slaves transported from Africa to the Americas took it to a new level of cruelty. Africa had long been a source of slave labour and for centuries the continent's contacts with Islam were characterized by Arabs travelling to central Africa to trade for, or capture, slaves and returning with their human 'cargoes' to north African Mediterranean cities and to those of the Middle-East.

From the fifteenth century black slaves from the African mainland had been used by the Spanish on sugar plantations in the Canary Islands. It was the Spanish priest Bartholome de las Casas who, later to be appalled at the treatment of indigenous people of the West Indies, recommended the importation of twelve African slaves to the islands. This seeming incongruity between the priest's benevolent attitude to the native Arawaks as compared to his unfeeling attitude to black Africans can be explained at least in part by the fact that he initially thought that the former had souls (to be saved) but the latter did not; a view he did change later on. A distinction given the legitimacy of the Papacy by the papal Bull of 1442 which gave religious authorization to the bleak trade in human-beings. Also a view which reflected the European wish to frame the trade in native Africans as a trade in 'goods' rather than in human beings; the then British Solicitor General noted in 1677 that: '……negroes ought to be esteemed goods and commodities'.

Throughout the period of the Atlantic trade a series of pseudo-scientific justifications as well as populist story-telling framed the 'native' (African) as less than human, so reflecting the racism that pervaded all levels of European society and those who ran its colonies.

From the time in the early sixteenth century, when the West Indian islands were shown to be so potentially productive of valuable sugar-cane, the capture and transportation of African slaves became a key element of colonial exploitation of the New World. By the end of the 16th century 275,000 slaves had arrived in the Americas, in the 17th century 300,000, in the 18th 6 million, and in the 19th 2 million. And when we note 'arrived' this does not include the possibly 2-4 million individuals who during this time died on the journey from the point of capture in the inland areas adjacent to the west coast of Africa. The captives were kept in appalling prison-like conditions in the West African coastal towns as ships captains waited for a full-cargo, and more especially on the sea passage itself. A full cargo meant a sufficient number of slaves to fill every spare space below decks. The 'middle-passage' would have been an abominable experience for people wrenched from their homes and communities to be packed tight into the fetid holds of the slave ships. Heads shaved, often striped to their nakedness, and close-packed in conditions where heat, sickness, accumulating excrement and vomit, added to the general awfulness of human bodies crammed together, lacking fresh air, light, fresh water and an even half-decent diet. To complete the degradation and humiliation was the act of selling itself – teeth, eyes, limbs, breasts, and buttocks, were subjected to close examination as if individuals were but stock animals – and when the sale was completed the final inhuman act of being renamed; the last ostensive link to their African home callously erased.

This process of reducing people to their mere commodity-value more easily allowed the inhuman process of maximizing their economic output more acceptable - the 12-18 hour working days, flogging, branding, and for many sexual assault; as but aspects of a daily humiliation of being denied the most basic of human rights. Yes, there was no-doubt the occasional more benevolent master and yes, and the plantations of Maryland and Virginia were, owing to climate and working conditions, an improvement on the conditions in the islands. But benevolence was rare given the economic competition and the felt need to keep order by maintaining a level of terror in a situation where in the islands 80% of the population were slaves and only 20% whites. According to Felipe Fernandez-Armesto (1995) 'Whites preserved order by techniques of selective terror, exploitation of enmity between rival Black nations and copious ministrations of rum and tobacco'.

There were slave revolts for example in Suriname 1757, Haiti (Sainte Domingue) 1790s, Virginia 1800, Brazil and Barbados 1816, Demerara 1823, and Jamaica 1831. All of these (except for Haiti) were eventually brutally put down, with the execution of 000s. On a very few occasions revolts were successful, including those that took place in the Brazilian town of Palmares in the early seventeenth century (1605-1694.....establishing a type of socialist community that lasted for about 90 years), and Haiti in the late eighteenth century.

The fact that throughout the Caribbean colonies the killing of a 'negro' was not considered a crime highlights the callous indifference of European governments to the rights of people whose labour contributed to the economic well-being of the colonial powers. What that contribution was has been the subject of much debate. Some claim that the wealth that accrued by merchants and financiers in European countries such as England provided the capital investment to facilitate the industrial revolution, others that most of the profits were spent on conspicuous consumption of the plantation owners and investors in shipping, and that any surplus on this can be off-set against the high cost of conflict involved in European squabbling over the trade in human beings as well as control of other trade carried to and from the New World.

Although I have focused on the New World trade in slaves we need to acknowledge that the trade went on elsewhere (including China, within the Ottoman Empire, and in other parts of the Middle-East) during this period. Indeed, the Arab trade involving slaves taken from Africa probably increased between 1500-1800. One estimate is of 500,000 people per year being traded out of sub-Saharan Africa to be sold on the markets of Islamic countries. With massive caravans reaching Cairo transporting thousands of slaves in a single trip. Across sub-Saharan Africa the practice of slavery was a common aspect on intertribal life, for Robert C. Allen '……kingdoms like Dahomey and Ashanti, which had long been based on slavery, responded to the external demand for slaves with warfare and raiding.' (Allen, 2011, p99) Aggressive slave using tribes such as these were well-placed to engage with slave-seeking European agents.

During this period merchants and their governments sought opportunities in the Far East as well as in the New World of the Americas. It was mainland European aggressive competition and the resultant conflict that would determine the framework within which the trading contacts were established in the east. First into serious trade with eastern regions were the Portuguese who, following the Papal guidance that they and the Spanish between them might take control of any land not ruled by a 'Christian prince', agreed to divide the world and its trading opportunities to their own mutual benefit. This Papal blessing gave the Portuguese principle rights to lands from a north-south line about 1600 kilometres to the west of the Azores as far east as the Molluccas and the other spice islands – taking in the lands of Africa, Arabia, and others in and adjacent to the Indian Ocean. In turn it gave the Spanish most of the Americas (apart from the west coast of Brazil, this being just east of the original north-south line agreed by the Spanish and Portuguese) and the eastern lands including the Philippines in the Pacific Ocean. It was the rounding of the Capes of Good Hope and Cape Horn that gave the Europeans direct access to the east and to the fabled wealth of the region – tales of which had motivated Christopher Columbus and his royal sponsors when he had set out west from Spain in 1492. The Portuguese reached Java in 1511 and the Spanish (in a fleet setting out from Mexico) reached the Philippines by 1543.

Unlike the New World, the pattern of European involvement in the east was not about large numbers of Europeans emigrating to establish plantations and farms to take advantage of the opportunities on offer. Or of groups fleeing religious and political persecution and economic disadvantage, seeking personal freedom and economic opportunities as in the New World. In the east it was trade that was at the forefront of European actively (at least up to 1800 when plantations such as those for tea and rubber began to be established) and the principle reason that settlements were established in towns and cities in the coastal regions.

The roughly two hundred years from 1600 saw European (including now a French involvement in Indo-China) competition for trade based on the hundreds of forts and trading posts situated along the coasts of the islands and the mainland of the Far East. But also increasingly, from about the end of the seventeenth century, the British (primarily in the form of the 'East India Company') moved inland in order to convert trade into the colonial exploitation of any available resources. The European search for wealth, mostly pursued with single-minded ruthlessness allied to asymmetries in military strength, led to significant trading links being established throughout India, the East Indies, and beyond. This vast region of diverse peoples, rich in natural resources, and in the potential for commercial development, would become a region that would serve to provide the opportunity for individual and corporate fortunes to be quickly made but also as a graveyard for thousands of Europeans; victims of disease and despair as well as military conflict.

The European powers applied the same underlying personal motivation and similar commercial techniques towards gaining trading advantages in the East Indies that had been used in the New World. A New World that had included a northern continent first colonized by Europeans from early seventeenth century: Virginia 1607, New England 1620, the French established a small fort in Quebec, Canada 1606, the Dutch in New Amsterdam 1612 – by 1700 400,000 Europeans had settled in North America, these being primarily from Britain.

By 1625 the town of New Amsterdam on the eastern seaboard of North America was established and defended by the citadel of Fort Amsterdam. A defence that, rather than being required to defend themselves against the natives they had cheated or forced out of the 'ownership' of their traditional lands, was in fact intended as defence against the English whose ships increasingly cruised the eastern seaboard of North America endeavouring to sniff out military weakness and possible booty. By 1674 the English had taken control of this Dutch colonial outpost following a series of protracted negotiations overshadowed with the threat of military action by the more powerful British. The outcome of these negotiations (including the British ceding some trading rights in the far eastern spice islands to the Dutch), led on behalf of the Dutch by the Director General Petrus Stuyvesant, did allow rights and tolerances previously enjoyed by the European settlers of New Amsterdam to be maintained; indeed rights echoed by those that later came to be enshrined in the constitution of the USA via the 1791 'Bill of Rights'.

Colonies were established by farmers, traders and fur trappers, then plantations (cotton, tobacco, rice), and the taking up of mining for precious metals and coal, and working in the timber and fishing industries. Alongside this came the development of transport networks north-south along rivers and via coastal passages, cart-roads, and later wagon trails, cattle trails, and then railways, with these mainly reaching out east-west, following the more accessible overland routes across the continent. Along this network of routes villages and towns were founded, with some of the latter expanding into cities occupied by the financiers, some government institutions, organized religions, and a variety of manufacturing, and farming and food processing industries. The service industries such as, shops, saloons, undertakers, lawyers, medical professions, blacksmiths, builders, prostitutes, entertainers, cart-makers, hauliers, etc. etc. all protected from aggrieved natives by a rag-tag army composed mainly of social misfits, and adventurers seeking excitement and opportunity; but with a disciplined and generally well-trained core. The imbalance in arms and inhuman attitudes towards killing fellow human beings gave a clear advantage to the aggressive, covetous, 'white man'. Civil life developed alongside a frontier mentality; local and state level government structures developed but with a deeply rooted reluctance of many to paying taxes and to the collective provision of services.

The process of clearance (in effect land grabbing) was generated by the wish for self-advancement of thousands of individuals operating, more or less closely, within a legal framework that sought to fiercely protect the property rights of favoured immigrants and the right for these to encroach on land occupied by an indigenous people who had no civil concept of private property; whilst framing the rights of the indigenous peoples in vague and quite general legal terminology. It was a well-armed civil people intent on acquiring land against a people armed for most of the early period of conflict with stone-age weapons technology, following lifestyles that were hunter-gatherer-forager in some places, Neolithic farming in others, and sometimes a mixture of these depending on season.

The relentless slaughter of native peoples by direct violence and or indirectly by disease or starvation began with the annihilation by 1637 of the Pequot tribe whose traditional lands were renamed New England, with Massachusetts as its principle town. It seems ironic that the early stage of the colonization of North America involved the chance to exercise the freedom of religious belief and to earn a living for thousands of poor and some persecuted Europeans - British (Quakers and Catholics), Irish (Catholics), French (Huguenots), German (Moravians), Swiss and Dutch (Protestants) - was at the cost of these same human rights for the numerous 'nations' indigenous to North America.

In the East, trade routes had been extended and the amount of trade in spices and textiles had been significantly increased in quantity. In 1500 commerce was primarily focused on local and regional business activities but by 1800 commerce had extended out to encompass all of the inhabited continents of the globe. There had been a series of minor (incremental) but important improvements in transport technology: wagons and carts on land (and some better roads) and in boats on the inland water-ways that criss-crossed Europe and costal trading boats (e.g. the 'flute' or 'fly boat'), and in the larger ships that ventured across oceans. The international trading predominance of Italian cities such as Genoa, Venice and, later Pisa and Florence, past to their northern European counterparts; first Antwerp then Amsterdam, and later the English cities of Bristol, Liverpool, and London. Further north, the Hansiatic towns of the Baltic region served to allow goods from Scandinavia and Russia (fish, furs, wool, and especially timber) to trade to Western Europe.

Chapter 3 The Early Modern Period

As we enter the seventeenth century a legacy of European dynastic, religious, and political divisions - a complex imbroglio of more earthly ambitions - continued to structure international relationships. In 1618 this continuing pattern of division erupted into a war that was to last for 10 years. What began as a war between fundamentalist Protestantism and conservative Catholicism became one more focused on territorial disputes. Early on France and the Austrian branch of the Habsburgs were the main protagonists but in 1635 the French minister Cardinal de Richelieu, on behalf of the French Government, formally declared war on Spain. The military strength of France and the support of her allies turned early setbacks into a victory of sorts and when the protagonists, as ever bound at some stage to negotiate a peace, met in the towns of Munster and Osnabruck in the province of Westphalia, a detailed basis for peace was painstakingly outlined. It was a peace negotiated on behalf of kings (and the Papacy) and one that would lay the political foundations of a system of national and international governance that would in time lead to their own demise or at least demotion to the role of constitutional monarch.

Negotiations in Westphalia sought to bring an end to both the 80 year conflict between the Netherlands and Spain and the 30 years war between the Holy Roman Empire and initially France and some German principalities, but a conflict that had also drawn in Denmark, Sweden, Poland, Russia and Switzerland. The 30 years war had been fought mainly on German lands, with a devastating impact. The conflict between participants was bitter and bloody, as angry groups of unpaid mercenaries roamed the countryside taking what they wanted as they went along; the lands the war past over were thoroughly plundered and left desolate.

The Treaty that emerged from Westphalia was notable in that it contributed to the creation of a European political structure based primarily upon independent nation-states and in doing so was to mark a significant stage in the demise of the Holy Roman Empire, and of the political influence of the Roman Catholic Church. The Treaty confirmed the previously agreed Peace of Augsburg 1555, so granting the right of religious tolerance for protestant groups - including Lutherans and the Reformed Church of Calvin.

The first six months of the conference were taken up with arguments about seating arrangements and various diplomatic procedures, as the conference made grindingly slow progress - with this large body of people relentlessly consuming food and other resources required by a local population almost all of whom were experiencing shortages and some even suffering famine.

Even after the treaty had been agreed in 1648, France and Spain continued at war, but internal problems affecting each country became a significant factor in forcing them to a settlement and to sign the Peace of the Pyrenees treaty in 1659. In the lead up to this treaty France, with Cardinal Mazarin taking the lead, had been arranging a clever strategy of alliance with England and of neutralizing the position of Germany and the Austrian branch of the Empire. Catholic France's alliance with Protestant England extended to the high seas, making Spanish colonial trading vulnerable. The allies' power was emphasized with the overwhelming French defeat of Spain at the naval engagement called The Battle of the Dunes in 1658. An engagement that revealed rather than began the military decline of the once powerful Spain.

In Europe during this period there was an ascendancy in both the intellectual and cultural spheres; but here I am focusing on the politics of Western Europe and at that time it is the military that was to the fore. A military increasing in strength and efficiency as its standing armies grew in size and improved in organization. The French army increased in numbers from 70,000 in the late 1660s to 300,000 by the century's end.

A French claim to the throne of Spain was justified on the basis of Louis being married to Charles's sister Marie-Therese, even though she had on marriage renounced any right to the Spanish throne. A conditional dowry was never paid and so, for Louis, a claim for the throne of Spain remained. Louis and his advisers adopted a piecemeal strategy of advancing their designs on Spanish territory by a series of alliances with larger European states, buying support from smaller independent provinces and pursuing a more general diplomatic policy of reducing Spanish influence. Then in 1667 the French army attacked the Netherlands, occupying a large swath of territory during the initial stages of its advance. This was too much for other nations and England, the United Provinces, and Sweden, formed an anti-French alliance, whilst the cautious and militarily weak Austrian Emperor Leopold endeavoured to mediate between the parties. The treaty of Aix-la-Chapelle brought a French withdrawal and a temporary peace. But conflict began again in 1672, this time by a French advance into Holland. The strong French army drove all before it in its advance until in desperation the Dutch broke down their sea dykes to cause extensive flooding, so making further French advance impossible. The French were forced to retreat and the military initiative passed to the Dutch and their new allies the Austrian Empire which had joined the unwieldy collection of states composing the Coalition of The Hague.

The conflict now spread, with the powerful French army achieving success on a number of fronts but with the Coalition forces holding together. A situation of stalemate was concluded in 1678-79 with the Treaty of Nijmegen. The French had gained some small territorial concessions but their broader designs on Spanish territory and in controlling the Dutch were now thwarted ambitions rather than a realistic consideration. A lesson had been learned by the English, Dutch, and others, that the most powerful military force in Europe had at least been contained by their unity.

Thwarted ambition generated dissatisfaction and the French, still confident in the power of their well-trained and experienced army, renewed their aggressive foreign policy, embarking on incursions into the Austrian Empire and across the western German border. Although national claims to their neighbour's territory had traditionally been justified by some quasi-legal claims based on uncertain historical associations, now we see more of a direct involvement of the French judiciary in producing legal rights to justify an expansionist foreign policy. Following a series of judicial decisions, based on contested aspects of the peace that had been drawn up at Westphalia, the French army was mobilized to annex small areas of territory (including the city of Strasburg) along their eastern border with the Hapsburg Empire. At the same time the French also provided diplomatic encouragement and financial support to the Turks and others hostile to the Empire on its eastern side. But the Empire still retained sufficient strength to defeat the eastern aggressors and join an anti-French alliance composed of both Protestant and Catholic states. The alliance contained the French, and military action was halted in 1684 with the signing of the treaty of Regensburg.

Such was the continuing fear of French military strength and its latent expansionist ambitions that what had been a somewhat ad hoc alliance formed into the League of Augsburg. It was composed of the Austrian Empire, the Dutch Republic, Spain, Sweden, and a number of smaller states. This was a grouping of states ostensibly building a defensive alliance but, when the Dutch King William of Orange became the King of England (as William III), the defensive League became an offensive Grand Alliance.

Even faced with this formidable opposition Louis and most of his ministers were confident in the superiority of their army and navy and so war began yet again. The Grand Alliance grouped their forces together and a series of bloody engagements were fought, both on land and at sea, over the next four years. Whilst not militarily defeated, the French could not sustain the cost of their large military force, and already weak morale at home due to famine following crop failure in a number of provinces; a difficult situation made even worse by disease, high unemployment, and inflation. But similar factors also caused the Grand Alliance to break up and in 1697 general war weariness as well as economic and political reality culminated in the two treaties of Rijswijk.

Peace would be short-lived and now diplomatic attention turned to the succession in Spain as Charles's life was obviously reaching its end.

In 1700 Charles named Philippe du d'Anjou (grandson of Louis XIV) as his heir to the Spanish throne and to all of its European and overseas territories. A gift that, after lengthy consideration of possible implications, was accepted by Louis who appeared to encourage Phillippe to rule Spain in Spanish rather than French interests. The other European states initially grudgingly accepted this succession but subsequent French military action against the Dutch, and their insistence on sharing the English trade with the Spanish colonies, caused the Grand Alliance to regroup.

Although England's King William III died in 1702 he had already forged a military alliance that would resist the French when war over the Spanish Succession began in 1701. The French experienced a series of military setbacks due to their having to face two formidable generals in the Duke of Marlborough and Prince Eugene of Savoy. War weariness had exhausted the French people's will to sustain military conflict and economic reality eroded their politicians' motivation to continue. But Louis refused the terms for peace originally on offer and the exhausted French army was once more expected to fight. The English army led by Marlborough made a decisive victory at Malplaquet, (incurring massive casualties, due partly to Marlborough's enthusiasm for full-frontal assaults) and the French were forced to come to terms with their enemies in a series of treaties negotiated in 1713-14, including those of Utrecht and Rastatt.

The French had suffered military defeat against the combined forces of England, the Empire, Sweden, the Dutch, and others, but the underlying strength of the French economy remained. Whilst the Dutch economy, weakened by the military expenditure and with an economic base reliant on the activity of a population of only two million people, struggled to keep a large well-equipped army in the field and did so to the detriment of maintaining the power of its navy.

A balance of military power and shared economic interests across much of Europe, allowed a period of peace, even if underlying territorial ambitions and historic discontents remained. The early years of the eighteenth century down to 1740 was a time of intense diplomatic manoeuvring and political re-alignments, with some relatively minor military action. Including Spain's unsuccessful attempt to assert territorial rights over northern Italian lands which were then being controlled by the Austrian Empire. With a Russian attempt at expansion south being checked by the Ottoman Empire, which also gained Hapsburg territory at the Treaty of Passarowitz as the outcome of successful resistance to Austrian aggression.

The brief period of relative peace in Western Europe came to an end in 1740 when the balance of power was shifting as the question of Austrian succession and of English violations of the terms agreed to in the treaty of Utrecht became significant factors in causing the uneasy balance maintaining a more general peace began to tip towards war.

Smuggling by English privateers backed by merchants attracted the close attention of Spanish naval patrols and English merchants, aware of the superior power of their official (Royal) navy, pressured an initially reluctant Prime Minister, Robert Walpole, to act in support of their interests. The amputation of the ear of a captured English seaman, Captain Jenkins, and a public outcry fuelled by the Captain's oath that he committed '…his soul to God and his cause to his country', gave the excuse for England to declare war on Spain. The fact that the cause of the Spanish aggression was the breaking by the English of an international agreement was overlooked; but then both sides had often breached the agreements in their aggressive competition for trade advantage in the West Indies. The 'War of Jenkins Ear' saw England at war with Spain and its erstwhile ally France. This was a war that involved territorial possessions in the Americas and it was in the West Indies that the power of the British navy (and allied privateers), by defeating their military escorts, prevented Spanish and French merchants from trading.

Meanwhile Prussia had invaded Silesia and the Austrian Empire, now ruled (from 1740) by the young Empress Marie Theresa, mobilized its forces and the Austro-Prussian War began; with France taking another opportunity to engage with its traditional Hapsburg enemy whilst it was also having to face an enemy to its east. England then invaded Spanish territory in Italy and yet again war was raging across Europe.

As usual, following a period involving considerable slaughter and also considerable expense, the parties negotiated for peace and the treaty of Aix-la-Chapelle 1748 saw the uneasy cessation of hostilities on the Continent. But the English continued to fight over territory in North America, and Austria was unhappy at the Prussian possession of Silesia. It was in the face of Prussian strength, its ally Austria's weakness, and the perception of a threat to its own claims to the Duchy of Hanover, that led the English government to purchase the service of 50,000 Russian soldiers to be deployed on the eastern Prussian border, ready to act if required. But these attempts to strengthen their positions failed when Russia gave its support to Austria and Fredrick of Prussia took pre-emptive action and, in 1756, invaded Saxony. This action marked the opening of the seven years war, a conflict involving a range of commercial as well as political disputes. The well-trained and highly disciplined Prussian army soon gained the upper hand, with a number of high profile victories that kept the Russian and Austrian forces apart. As the war developed, the overwhelming Russian victory at the battle of Kunersdorf was followed by a succession of Prussian military defeats, with complete defeat seeming to be the most likely outcome. But an exhausted Prussia was 'saved' by the death of the Russian Tsarina Elizabeth and with the mentally unstable Peter III, an admirer of Fredrick, becoming Tsar. Peter straight-away signed a unilateral peace agreement with Fredrick and even offered the Prussian King a loan of his army. But when, following Peter's assassination in 1762, his wife Catherine II (Catherine the Great) succeeded to the throne she withdrew Peter's offer of military support to Fredrick, although she did continue to observe the peace agreement.

French hostilities with England continued but this was a time when Britain was gaining in military power and was engaged in consolidating and extending its possessions in the Americas, India, and Africa. And, in developing plantation-based production, mineral and precious metal extraction, as well as trading and taxation systems that would allow these possessions to be efficiently exploited. In the face of British military superiority (especially at sea), and the relative weakness of France and more especially of Spain, caused the French to sue for peace in 1760; although it was to take until 1763 before a formal treaty (the Treaty of Paris) was agreed.

Now the major European powers were more and more turning their attention to overseas interests but here it was Britain that for the most part held the advantage. It controlled most of the eastern half of North America and Canada, although some concessions were made to France and Spain with the return to them of some West Indian Islands and the Philippines (to Spain) in the East Indies. But even in the 1760s the military and administrative costs of maintaining North American colonies caused Britain to, in 1764, introduce a number of measures to raise income. One of these was the Stamp Act of 1765 to which the various assemblies e.g. Pennsylvania and later New Jersey, Georgia, and Massachusetts (represented in England – and later France - by Benjamin Franklin) and the eight other colonies and their representative assemblies responded with angry resolutions as well as the boycotting of British goods and the more symbolic act of burning stamps. For ten years discontent with British colonial governance simmered on, with attempts by individuals such as Benjamin Franklin, the elder William Pitt, and the Earl of Chatham, to find room for compromise, until in 1776 the Continental Congress issued their Declaration of Independence; so founding the United States of America.

Just as in the previous two centuries, it does seem that the political manoeuvring, diplomatic machinations, and military adventures, characterizing relations between nation-states that had continued throughout the 17th and 18th centuries made a further contribution to the formation of today's nation-states and also reinforced the hegemonic terms for international relations that would endure. Terms based nakedly on self-interest (as perceived by ruling elites) progressed by diplomatic and economic means if possible but, too easily, by military aggression if necessary.

In relation to European politics.....during the early period of the

French revolution the National Assembly had voted in 1790 to renounce war. But this intention fell victim to Thermidorian internal reaction and the external hostility to the revolution of the Prussians, the Austrian Emperor, and the Papacy. When in 1792 the Emperor Leopold rejected French demands for him to end the alliance with Prussia the French declared war, with the claim that they were doing so in defence of a free people against an aggressive monarch, the King of Bohemia and Hungary (the Austrian Empire).

The early stages of the war went against France and saw Prussian and Austrian forces advancing. But the Battle at Valmy was a significant turning point, when a French army composed mainly of inexperienced recruits forced the Prussians into retreat. The French followed up victory at Valmy by pushing the Prussians back and taking control of strategically and economically important territory, including the Netherlands and the area of the Middle Rhine. At this point the French policy changed from self-defence (defence of the revolution) to a commitment to support '....all peoples that wished to recover their liberty'. Thus justifying their own territorial expansion and laying down a challenge to kings and aristocracies; and consequently to the rulers of most European states.

Seemingly in defence of its revolutionary foreign policy France declared war against England in early 1793. Then, in rapid succession, Spain, Denmark, Sweden, a number of Italian states and the Ottoman Empire, joined England, the Prussians and the Austrian Empire to oppose France. The conflict went badly for a beleaguered France and even though they rescinded their externally directed revolutionary ambitions their offers to negotiate a peace were rejected.

This rejection led France to organize almost all of its resources into the service of the military as the Convention effectively mobilized for all-out defence of the revolution. This fostering of a national resolve to defend their freedoms and ideals generated a new wave of focused determination which, coupled with the extending supply-line difficulties of the invaders, saw the French pushing the Coalition forces into retreat. During this favourable reversal of French fortunes a young artillery officer named Napoleon Bonaparte distinguished himself during the final stages of the Battle for Toulon. The balance of military advantage turned from defence to offence as the French chased the armies of the Coalition ranged against them back into their own countries. Peace negotiations were re-opened and the Peace of Basle and the Treaty of The Hague were agreed in 1795, bringing at least a partial halt to hostilities on the European mainland.

Probably the most significant gain for the French, other than a clear demonstration of their strength to the rest of Europe, was gaining the Austrian controlled part of the Netherlands; a territory that was brought within the Republic. With the coming to power of a new French government 'The Directorate' in 1795, political changes reinforced a more general dilution of the national mood of revolutionary fervour. This more conservative government set about a process of negotiating short-term compromise and longer-term peace with its antagonistic European neighbours. But a peace that was initially to be facilitated by force or the threat of it. A French plan involved two of its armies advancing in a pincer movement towards Vienna. Bonaparte, now in command of a smaller army, was charged with the capture of Lombardy. French intention was to use this region as a negotiating counter during the expected comprehensive peace settlement, so allowing a political balance in Europe that, due to its reflecting the underlying military reality, would lead to a period of peaceful co-existence.

Paradoxically, the Directorate's plan for peace was thwarted when the increasing military success of Bonaparte in 1796/97 gave him the political power to advance his own ambitions for France (and himself). When peace was agreed with Austria in the Treaty of Campo Formio it was a peace that reflected Bonaparte's own intentions rather than those of the French government; with the Austrians ceding territory along the Rhine as well as formally accepting the annexation of the Netherlands and the French retention of Lombardy. Now Bonaparte embarked on an imaginative (some might say 'romantic', others 'foolish') strategy of throwing the Turks out of Egypt and in the same act disrupting the main English communication link to the east.

In Bonaparte's absence The Peace of Campo Formio was proving to be an uneasy one, with a general suspicion of French intentions being exacerbated by the French behaviour in the satellite republics being run by its military commanders. Starting in 1798 a second Coalition was formed that included England, Russia, Austria, Sardinia and Naples. The early military momentum was with the Coalition partners whose forces pushed the French back towards France. But Bonaparte, returning from his unsuccessful adventures in Egypt, saw the French re-group and quickly secure the military initiative.

Bonaparte seized control of France in November 1799 and straightaway began to organize his plans for military conquest. Early victories in Northern Italy and the obvious superiority of the French military led to a Treaty of Luneville (1801) in which the Terms of the Treaty of Campo Formio were confirmed. Peace with England was secured in the Treaty of Amiens, with England making a series of territorial concessions involving Egypt, Malta, and the acceptance of those previously made in the Treaty of Luneville. To the detriment of its economic prosperity, England continued to be denied access to Continental trade which included access to the Baltic timber and the Dalmatian oak preferred for its shipbuilding industry. Britain, so reliant on exports, initially experienced a period of difficult trading conditions as stocks of manufactured goods built up in its warehouses, unemployment increased, and with it unrest in the towns and cities; and with the national debt rising quite dramatically. Britain continued to sustain its military threat to France, and did gradually improve its economic position. An improvement due partly to the smuggling of its goods to Continental countries, but more so to the increase in trade with regions outside of the Continental System.

By now France was the most powerful country in Europe; as to her revolutionary credentials, these had been significantly diluted as a putative people's revolution had given way to a process of middle-class political ascendancy. Whilst Bonaparte was content to allow this process at home his acceptance was conditional on support for his wider personal and territorial ambitions. He provoked the Coalition members into a war that was to last for four years, four years that saw the now Emperor Napoleon's armies gain a string of military victories over Prussia and Austria at – Ulm, Austerlitz, Jena, and Auerstadt – and over the Russia at Eylau and Friedland; leading to Napoleon being described by the German philosopher Hegel as '….the spirit of the future..'. Against England he continued to use exclusion from trade with the continent as the main means of at least containing its economic prosperity. His 'Continental System' linked the military land war to a comprehensive trade war that had impacted most heavily on the enemy across the Channel.

Spain was the first country to effectively resist French control with a nationalistic uprising that would sap resources and tie down some of Napoleon's best soldiers for six years. It was through a Spain in revolt that England would launch its own attack on the French when Sir Arthur Wellesley (later Duke of Wellington) led an army that advanced into the Spanish part of the Iberian Peninsula from its base in Portugal. The defeat of the French in battles during the Iberian campaign encouraged the Austrians to initiate their own war of national liberation. But lacking the intervention of the English, this rebellion was short-lived with the Emperor's army soundly defeating the Austrians at Wargram. To the north the Prussians were going through a process of social reconstruction that included rebuilding the army that Napoleon had already defeated so decisively. Mutual mistrust led to an end of the French alliance with Russia in 1812 causing an over-confident Napoleon to embark on an ill-conceived attempt to defeat the Russians. Of the 500,000 elite soldiers of the French Grand Army that entered Russia only 100,000 were to struggle back, the defeated remnants of a once great force. Defeated by a combination of Russian resistance, disease, hunger, and the freezing conditions of the vast plains (steppes) of Eastern Europe.[17]

But the French regrouped, re-built their army and, even in the face of the advancing Russian forces, and a declaration of war by Prussia,

---

[17] John J.Mearsheimer (2001, p59) has it that Napoleon had 674,000 '….troops at his disposal for the Russian campaign', with 470,000 of these perishing in Russia, another 100,000 taken prisoner, with just 93,000 struggling back.

they resisted the peace conditions on offer. It would be a series of military setbacks during 1813, culminating in the Battle of Leipzig ('Battle of the Nations'), that would highlight the changing balance of military power and open the way for the invasion of France itself. So, with the English poised ready to advance from the Spanish border and the Prussians and Russians advancing from the north east, the embattled Napoleon fought a militarily astute rear-guard action but one that could not long resist the powerful alliance of forces ranged against him.

The glorious revolution stood bowed when on 1st April 1814 the Prussian King Frederick and the Russian Emperor Alexander reached Paris. Napoleon was forced to abdicate and was exiled to the island of Elba. Even his escape a year later and the brief attempt to regain power was crushed on the battlefield of Waterloo. And so, one more soldier with ambitions of empire was consigned to history. Thousands dead, vast swathes of land laid waste, towns and villages pillaged, some territories gained for one country soon passed to others, the potential for creating wealth of thousands of young men held moribund within the long-years of military service. From this tawdry series of military misadventures engaged in by most European states arose a selection of national myths, supporting inflated ideas of national superiority with which we continue to deceive ourselves.

The sad end to revolutionary hopes was not solely the fault of Napoleon; he was but a catalyst operating within a complex political context founded on the short-term nationalistic intentions of emerging centralized nation-states controlled by ruling elites set on ensuring that the national interests they promoted closely reflected their personal ambitions and the shared economic interests of sections of the upper classes.

Of some additional interest is the economist Adam Smith's outline of national debt and the cost of war in accumulating this: 'In Great Britain.......the reduction of public debt in time of peace has never borne any proportion to its accumulation in time of war. It was in the war which began in 1668, and was concluded by the treaty of Ryswick, in 1697, that the foundation of the present enormous debt of

Great Britain was first laid.' ('Wealth of Nations', 1776, pp 927-929) Immauel Kant ('Speculative Beginning of Human History', 1786) had also highlighted the costly business of preparing for war; 'One must understand that the greatest evil that can oppress civilized peoples derive from wars, not, indeed, so much from actual present or past wars, as from the never-ending and constantly increasing arming for future wars.'

Following the Napoleonic wars (1815) the British government decreased the overall tax on the rich as well as easing the system of payment of dividends (and yet were faced with a national debt rising to a massive £848 million by the War's end), whilst heavily increasing taxes on basic goods such as soap. With the Corn Laws increasing the price of bread, to the benefit of larger landowners, but impacting disproportionately on the poorer sections. The mass of the population faced increase taxes, a succession of poor harvests, and rising rural unemployment due to mechanization. Unemployment was further exacerbated by the addition to the potential workforce of 300,000 ex soldiers and sailors demobilized at the War's end.

Nelson,[18] Wellington, and some other senior officers, were showered with state-provided financial rewards and exuberant praise, whereas most of those in the ranks were simply cast aside - to become retrospective heroes in due course when the British state required a convenient trope for recruiting the masses to support future wars. A passionately told, flag-wrapped, drum and bugle sounding, narrative of British heroes of a series of bloody conflicts as somehow representing some sense of 'genetic' British bravery expressed from Agincourt through to the Napoleonic Wars, used to fuel the propaganda for recruitment for the Boer War, and even more so with WWI.

At the beginning of the century Europe had experienced the military expression of rival national factions in Britain, Russia,

---

[18] Nelson was a gifted and determined self-publicist - even to the extent of himself having pamphlets, in which his 'character and exploits' were dramatically depicted and lauded, printed and distributed throughout Britain.

Prussia, and Austria, faced with the territorial ambitions of Napoleon Bonaparte. The bloody and destructive outcomes for the participating nations had been played out at the battles of: Marengo (1800), Trafalgar (1805), Ulm (1805), Austerlitz (1805), Jena (1806), Eylau (1807), Friedland (1807), Wargram (1809), Borodino (1812) and the drawn out Peninsular Wars (1808-1813). Then a pause for Napoleon's resignation, later escape from open imprisonment on Elba, and his return for a series of relatively minor engagements leading to the French defeat by the British and Prussian armies at the Battle of Waterloo in 1815. The Vienna Settlement of 1815 resulted in an uneasy peace, one bristling with inter-nation suspicions, and with nations each still seeking to advance their own interests during a time when 1.5 million men formed the standing armies of France, Britain, Russia, Prussia/Germany and the Hapsburg Empire.

Russia was the first to let discontent with the European status quo show as it translated its long held ambitions (or rather the ambition of Tsar Nicolas I and the coterie of aristocratic and military self-interest that surrounded him) for control in the Balkans into warfare. It found an excuse to provoke the Turks when the Ottoman-Turkish Empire granted France religious (Catholic) concessions in Palestine. In July 1853 Russia advanced into the Danubian principalities of Walachia and Moldavia; in response the Turks declared war. They were anticipating support (even if somewhat reluctant) from Britain and France, assuming that they would want to protect their own economic interests in the Middle-East. The French military leaders were still harbouring a collective resentment of the Russians who, aided by the winter weather, had earlier in the century transformed defeat by the French at Borodino into victory as what remained of the Grand Armée of 500,000 men had made an inglorious retreat back to France. England and France did join the conflict by late spring 1854, reinforced the following year by troops from the Kingdom of Sardinia whose leaders were expecting to gain British and French support to drive the Austrians from northern Italy.

The Crimean War highlighted Russia's military weakness, a result of its relative lack of military industrialization. Even if, in the lead-up to conflict, Russia was dedicating four-fifths of state revenue to the military it was a military trained and equipped to fight eighteenth-century battles. A military soldiered mainly by serfs, many having been reluctantly wrenched from the their homeland and officered by privileged and mostly militarily unproven sons of the upper classes; often distracted by the appeal of impressive uniforms and being lionized within a vibrant social scene (depicted in Tolstoy's 'War and Peace', a novel set earlier in the century). The Russian assault was starved of supplies as its horse-drawn wagon trains became bogged down in the muddy terrain that stretched from Moscow to the battle front. Whereas forces that the French/British alliance had mobilized to stop Russian expansion benefitted from trained standing armies, modern weapons, railways to transport men and supplies, and experienced officers trained to approach war in a more strategic way; such as disrupting Russian supply lines by naval blockade in the Black Sea. The firepower of modern steel-barrelled artillery laid down a marker for military conflict for the next 100 years as the weakness of cavalry and massed infantry, as well as traditional fortifications, were exposed to the relentless destruction of accurate cannonade.

Innovations such as the use of the electric telegraph enabled the co-ordination of forces. An innovation noted by American observers who had travelled to the Crimea and which would contribute to how their own civil war (of 1861-65) would be fought. By the War's end 480,000 (possible as many as a million) Russians had died, many from dysentery, cholera, and infected wounds, and 500 million roubles had been spent; France lost 100,000 men and Britain 25,000, with disease taking a heavy toll. The populations of all of the combatant nations paid the financial cost in rising taxes and in generally higher food prices. This was perhaps the first 'media' war, with the dispatches of journalists such as the London Times reporter William Howard Russell becoming available to the British public within hours of actions and the photographs taken by Roger Fenton providing an immediacy of images illustrating life at the front.

The Treaty of Paris signed by the combatants in March 1856 was pretty much a humiliation for a financially exhausted Russia and a further step towards the dismantling of the Ottoman, and the remnants of the Hapsburg, empires. Other outcomes were to make a united Germany certain and a united Italy more likely. The continued repression of the nationalistic ambitions of ethnic groups within the central European part of the Empire contributed to tensions that would in turn make a significant contribution to the more immediate causes of the First World War. Indeed, adding to disparate narratives of ethnic and nationalistic tensions that continue in places like Chechnya today.

When Alexander II became Tsar in 1856 he took the lessons from the humiliation in the Crimea to be that: industrialization should proceed at a pace, serfdom brought to an end, and the military modernized.

A German State was established in 1871 with a Kaiser as Head of State; the head of a nation industrializing at a rapid pace and fiercely proud of its (Prussian) military tradition; a new nation led by an elite group grounded in an ideology of warfare. One feature of the new Germany that would haunt relations between it and France well into the next century was the annexation by the new Germany of the French territory of Alsace-Lorraine.

In Europe by 1860 there were 2.25 million men under arms, with Britain alone spending £15.6 million per year on the military. The nineteenth-century saw the beginnings of national expenditure being systematically allotted to fund the military, primarily from taxation and government borrowing. Now the world was set on a future of what would be in effect institutionalized, whole nation warfare. The assumed normality of conflict as a central aspect of international relations based upon each of the more powerful nations progressing their leading elite's perception of self-interest, at pretty much any cost to others. Morality was only introduced, and then loudly, to assess the actions of other nations rather than the actions of those doing the assessing; invoked when it suited, ignored when deemed necessary.

This institutionalization of conflict included: large standing armies, a significant proportion of a nation's financial wealth being spent on weaponry, and a populist narrative of jingoistic nationalism being promoted by governments, national religions, various militaristic cadet groups, and most of the increasing more available national mass media. The foundations of the 20th/21st centuries 'war industry' had been laid.

Many of Europe's politicians and much of the mass media mendaciously endeavoured to foster nationalistic collective identities formed out of the bundle of ragbag ideas, half-truths, imaginative historical narratives and mostly miss-constructed outlines of shared heritage. The central institutions of the state were aided by the mainstream media in fostering a spurious set of shared interests in some 'imagined community' as noted by Benedict Anderson (1983). Drawing all classes and other social groupings into a belief that they shared some 'common interest', detailed knowledge of which was being held by wise…. politicians, industrialists, church, and military leadership. A toxic mix of disparate national loyalties, expressed in jingoism, national chauvinism, and in times of crisis providing an international setting characterized by crude media propaganda and heightened forms of antagonistic xenophobia.

In the U.S., lines of implacable disagreement between some northern and southern states had been emerging for some time and came to a head with the election in 1860, of a more socially liberal Republican President, Abraham Lincoln (although he was against whites marrying blacks). In February 1861, seven southern states ceded from the Union (later to be joined by four more), with Jefferson Davis becoming President of the Confederate States of America. The primary issue seemed to have been over the institution of slavery, but some have argued that the need for workers (so freed slaves) to drive industrial development in the northern cities was an underlying motive of the industrialist elite pressing for action. Most southern political leaders considered that the real issue was the right of individual states to make their own laws. The first military clash came in April when the Confederate General Beauregard ordered his troops to fire on the Union soldiers in Fort Sumter; more a symbolic act of intention than an act of war, with the only casualty being a horse.

The outcome of the war was pretty much predetermined, the unknowns were how long would it last and how much it would cost in lives and money. The southern alliance could not come close to matching the north in terms of industrial resources and available manpower. The north's population being 20,000,000 - plus 800,000 immigrants between 1861-65 - whilst the south had a population of 6,000,000 and negligible immigration. The Union army 1,000,000, the Confederate army with 464,000 at the start of the war (falling to about 150,000 by the war's end)……..in 1860 the north had 110,000 manufacturing establishments, the south 18,000. The south could find no European allies who might have been able to assist either diplomatically or with breaking the north's blockade of southern ports. The main export income for the south came from cotton, but the blockade of southern ports – the north had a far superior navy with about 90 warships at the start of the conflict and 1040 at its end, compared to the Southern State's 14 seaworthy ships at the start and no more than about 100 at its end - significantly reduced exports from the south limited the income available to pay the costs of sustaining a war. The north, along with all of its other advantages, was aided by thousands of black slaves who fled from southern plantations, some to act as guides for Union troops, others to fight in northern regiments. By the end of the war 180,000 black soldiers were serving in Union regiments.

In Robert E. Lee and Patrick R Cleburne the south had two militarily gifted generals but realistically their only achievable aim could have been to make the war so difficult for the north that they would have negotiated a settlement that at least went some way to protect the interests of southern business people and the plantation aristocracy. As with most civil wars, this was a nasty, bloody, affair, with 359,000 Union and 258,000 Confederate soldiers having to die (about one third in battle, two-thirds from disease) and swathes of the southern territory laid waste before General Lee accepted the inevitable when he surrendered to General Ulysses Grant at Appomattox on the 9th April 1865.

Mechanized warfare had provided the material means for a series of senseless engagements of the type that would later characterize the European theatre in the First World War. With most engagements having indefinite military outcomes apart that is, from the slaughter of thousands of young men as they marched into a hailstorm of bullets and the thunderous roar of cannonades.

The historian Howard Giles noted that:

'Most battles quickly degenerated into murderous firefights at close range, each side blazing away until one or the other withdrew. Even later in the war when tactics had been refined and the spade took over as the main "weapon" as the armies dug in, generals often needlessly threw away the lives of their men in massed attacks......As such, most actions rarely seemed to achieve more than another pile of bodies. Even when a decisive victory was achieved, the enemy nearly always managed to limp away to fight another day. Inevitably, it became a dreadful war of attrition.' (Giles, 2003)

The soldiers' experience being brought vividly to life in Stephen Crane's novel The 'Red Badge of Courage': 'The battle was like the grinding of an immense and terrible machine....' '....men, punched by bullets, fell in grotesque agonies. The regiment left a coherent trail of bodies...... They accepted the pelting of the bullets with bowed and weary heads.' (Crane, 1895)

'*Four score and seven years ago our fathers brought forth on this continent, a new nation, conceived in Liberty, and dedicated to the proposition that all men are created equal.*'

These are the opening words of the Address delivered by President Lincoln on the Battlefield of Gettysburg, Pennsylvania, on 19th February 1863 – apart from the obvious omission of women, the proposition, as embodied in the American Constitution, also excluded Native American Indians. And, as the Supreme Court had ruled in 1857 (see above), black slaves were 'property' rather than citizens and they too were in effect excluded from the Address. The Gettysburg Address cleverly (it was a skill-fully 'crafted' rally cry) echoed the words in the second sentence of the American 'Declaration of

Independence': 'We hold these truths to be self-evident, that all men are created equal, that they are endowed by their Creator with certain unalienable Rights, that among these are Life, Liberty and the pursuit of Happiness'.

This is just the sort of Americanese, writ large, of exaggerated but brilliant humanitarian ideals that owes more to the free-flying imagination of single-minded politicians, unbridled by any sense of moderation, as shaped by the cynical art of the speechwriter, than to the reality of human social relationships within the context being described. Wonderful, inspiring phrases, if only those who produced them and those that cheered them could live up to these ideals!

A telling positive correlation can be made between the rising tide of death in the war and the rising profits of the financiers, bankers, and munitions companies, who between them produced the finance, munitions, and other materials necessary for the continuation of warfare and for the commission gained for arranging the government loans to pay for these. As the old socialist soar goes 'War is extremely horrible but it is also extremely profitable!'

With this civil war we can more easily begin to identify those who benefit markedly from preparing for and indulging in the activity of modern warfare. During the conflict millions of rounds of ammunition was used, tens of thousands of tons of pig-ion, coal, and steel, hundreds of thousands of rifles, thousands of artillery pieces, a range of food and animal feed, blankets, medical supplies, uniforms, barracks, tents, railway engines and carriages, wagons, horses - bankers negotiated government loans, traders arranged imported war-goods - many of the workers in munitions factories, those making uniforms, boot-makers, and those making other war materials were on overtime etc. etc. Massive profits were made during this war.......a message not lost on arms manufacturers, suppliers, and investors for the future.

In the late nineteenth century the US, along with most of the governments of Europe, spent a massive amount on building their military capability. Military planning became a central feature of government, the art of diplomacy ostensibly intended to avoid war continued to be no more than a means deployed to prevaricate, to persuade allies to a cause, to mislead (by direct threats or by identifying common enemies), and to negotiate time for further military preparation. Economic industrialization had been accompanied by the industrialization of the military, with military expenditure being in effect an important economic stimulus. A Keynesian 'demand-led' approach, if a means to this that he would not generally have approved of. A similar economic stimulus could have been made if instead of being spent on military preparedness, the same level of investment had been made in building schools, hospitals, libraries, scientific research centres, improved social services and similar non-military infrastructure. The claim that we need a strong military to protect our civil life is undermined by any rational consideration and will be considered in the concluding chapter below.

Companies such as Nobles, Armstrong, Krupps, Smith and Wesson, Tzhmash, Mauser, Daher, and many others, supplied ever-improved (in killing 'efficiency') munitions. The killing power of rifles, machine-guns, and artillery was undergoing continuous development, (steel cannons were produced with a range of up to 5,000 metres). And in the later part of the nineteenth-century hundreds of new warships were eased down slipways of Europe, the US, and Japan; bristling with cannons, and some with armour plating up to 24 inches thick.

Between 1874-96 the leading European nations increased military spending by 50% and between 1880-1914 military spending by France increased by 100%, of Britain and Russia by 200%, and Germany by 400%. Throughout the history of organized human conflict there had always been some competition between combatants involving weaponry and tactics, but by the end of the nineteenth-century leading nations were engaged in a veritable arms 'race' that continues down to today. If any weapon was possible (however horrific its effect), be it machine gun, armour-piercing shell, poison gas, chemical weapon, most 'civilized' nations felt they could not be without it. Vast resources were from now on to be diverted to supply the means to kill and maim, and so the means of gaining massive profits for the arms and finance industries; recourse to war had become 'inevitable'.

Apart from the human carnage and wasted material resources resulting from civil and international conflicts there was also the evil inflicted due to the civil powers pursuing their colonizing ambitions and trading interests. In Britain there was some condemnation by representatives of the middle and working classes of the brutality, corruption, and avarice that was a central feature of colonization but there was also many prepared to defend (indeed glorify) colonialism; or more selfishly just wanting their representatives to challenge for a greater share of the plunder gained from the possession of colonized lands, for themselves.

The wish to create spheres of influence, or even more directly control empires, has been an almost defining feature of civil life…. just a few examples would be the violent formation of the Akkadian, Assyrian, and Mycenaean, empires - the Phoenician colonization of north Africa - the periods of Pharonic control of Nubia - the geographically extensive Macedonian Empire brought together by Alexander - the equally extensive Roman Empire - Scandinavian peoples attempts to colonize areas of the north Atlantic and Great Britain during the 'Viking' period – the Aztec and Inca control of much of central and south of South America - The Qin Empire of China – the extensive Mongol empire across Eurasia and China - the Muslim empire of Mogul India – and Saladin's Arab empire in the Mediterranean region - the Ashanti and Zulu empires in Africa - and the Polynesian and Maori in the south Pacific. Just a few more notable examples of humankind's elite-driven propensity to seek to acquire the territorial resources, stored wealth, and even the enslavement, of others.

In more recent times it has been European countries seeking to colonize distant lands long-occupied by other, less economically developed, peoples. This began as early as the fifthteenth century, with Spanish and Portuguese exploits in the Americas displacing or controlling the local ruling groups, looting the gold and silver and, along with the British, French and Dutch, establishing plantations. Enslaving, murdering, forcing religious conversion, and the relentless economic exploitation of native peoples in the process of extracting wealth from their lands. Wealth mainly in the form of very cheap labour (slavery), precious metals, gemstones, valued raw materials, and agricultural produce including sugar, then later on cotton, tobacco, opium, and meat, being the primary goods.

It was in 1498 that the 'Cape of Good Hope' (southern tip of Africa) was first rounded by the Portuguese (if Africa had been circumnavigated long before). During the sixteenth and seventeenth centuries the Portuguese and to a limited extent the Spanish, then later the Dutch and the British, used this as a route to the east and each successively established regular trading links with regions of the Middle and Far East. Trading initially in the much valued, and so very profitable spices such as: clove, cinnamon, cardamom, nutmeg, ginger, turmeric, and pepper; this last being used to mask the smell and taste of decomposing meat; a fairly common condition of this food.

From the early seventeenth-century the Dutch had sought to challenge the Portuguese and Spanish dominance of Far Eastern trade. An ambition made easier when, in 1616, the Dutchman Willem Schouten also found the route round the Cape. Soon the English would also be using this route (a route, 'rutters', which the Portuguese and Spanish had endeavoured to keep secret) and both nations then competed with the Portuguese and Spanish as well as each other for the lucrative trade in the east, trade that now included cotton, porcelain, precious metals, and other commodities valued on European markets, in addition to the trade in spices.

The Dutch brought a Protestant thoroughness to their methods of drawing wealth from their mercantile activities in the east. Illustrated in the progress of the Dutch East Indian Company (VOC – Vernige Oost-indische Compagnie), a joint-stock entity receiving its charter from the States-General (parliament) in 1602. A charter that provided for a monopoly of navigation rights east of the Cape of Good Hope (and west through the straights of Magellen). The company was run by 17 directors (Heren Zeventien or Gentlemen XVII) a group that would only meet a couple of times a year, to pour over balance sheets, and to consider the risks of its various enterprises in relation to potential profits. Although more modest versions of this type of joint-stock company had been established in Northern Italy, the VOC was an innovative extension of this basic arrangement with a specific purpose of accruing personal wealth. This purpose was successful to the extent that this would make the Dutch East India Company the largest enterprise in Europe by the end of the seventeenth-century. Its charter gave it the right to make (and the freedom to break) treaties with native leaders, to build forts and to appoint local governors, who in turn could oversee imposed systems of 'justice'. In effect, the right to use force to further its own financial interests and even, if necessary, to wage war and occupy foreign territory!

The VOC established its first base in Bantam, Java, in 1607 before re-locating to Djakarta (re-named Batavia) from where it endeavoured, with a relentless determination fuelled by avarice, to control both local trade and the trade back to Europe – trade extending to Ceylon, China, Formosa and Japan. Just one incident to illustrate the Company's methods was action taken in 1621 by Jan Peterszoon Coen the ruthless Governor General who did more than any other single individual to establish, mainly by force of arms, - wielded against both other European traders and indigenous peoples - Dutch control of the Far East. When the people of Great Banda (now part of Indonesia) resisted the Company's attempt to control production and trade in the most valuable spice of nutmeg (in effect to control the world's supply), Coen had 2,500 of its inhabitants massacred and 800 others transported to Batavia.

The Dutch also used Batavia as a base from which to explore the Southern Ocean. In the 1640s Able Tasman was dispatched to seek the great land to the south that had been noted by ships that had strayed off the routes to the east. He succeeded in this task– sailing round Australia 'discovering' Tasmania, New Zealand, and the Islands of Fiji and Tonga. Naming what we now know as Tasmania as Van

Diemen's Land after the Dutch Governor-general who had ordered Tasman south. In Tasman's assessment the prospects for wealth so far south did not look promising so the Dutch lost interest in the southern lands.

The Europeans enabling the Dutch occupation in the Far East were a collection of merchants, plantation owners, administrators, soldiers, sailors, and some protestant clergymen. A significant proportion of each occupational group were freebooters, fortune hunters, and thieves. Life in these colonies was often hard (with the constant danger of disease) but, if fortunate, the potential rewards were great. Rewards that could more successfully be extracted by a ruthless approach to advancing their own as well as the Company's interests. According to one historian quoted by Mike Dash '…The Company as a body was avaricious, and its employees were often demoralized by its institutionalized greed….every able-bodied man from the Councillor [Governor-general] of the Indies down to the simple solider considered it an absolute must to care for himself first.' (Dash 2002, 'Batavia's Graveyard').

If they managed to survive the often harsh conditions these individuals could hope to return home in one of the many *retourchips* that carried trade goods and supplies between Europe and the Dutch possessions in the east. Towards the end of the seventeenth-century (at the peak of its 'success') the Company had 10,000 soldiers under arms, along with 150 merchant ships and 40 warships to protect them. Each returning ship would have a cargo on which profits of up to 1,000% were being made.

Throughout the eighteenth-century the Company increasingly faced direct competition from the British whose navy had become the most powerful in the world. From the middle of the seventeenth-century England's parliament had introduced a series of Navigation Acts which permitted only English ships to carry any trade goods landed in any territory controlled by the English Crown; Acts specifically aimed to inhibit the Dutch. Serious financial problems and a wave of corruption scandals led to the Company ceasing to trade in 1798, with the Dutch Government taking possession of the

Company's overseas territories. In 1814 Britain captured the small Dutch colony (established in 1652) at the Cape of Good Hope; a strategically important stopping place on the route east. By which time the power-balance in the Far East had shifted decisively to favour the British. In 1800 European nations and their overseas possessions amounted to 55% of the Earth's land surface. This would grow to 67% by the last quarter of the century. It has been estimated that between 1820 and 1920 55,000,000 Europeans migrated overseas, 'pushed' by such factors as unemployment, religious persecution, poverty, and 'pulled' by the prospect of economic prosperity and the excitement of opportunities available in these economically underexploited regions.

The progress of European industrialization, with its increasing need for raw material for its factories and new markets for its manufactured goods, provided additional incentives to establish links with lands from India and further east to China. By the nineteenth century European countries had already seen the potential of taking seeds or cuttings of valued plants from one region of the world to take advantage of suitable climates, soils, and cheap available labour, in another. Obvious examples being tea from China to India and Ceylon, cocoa and coffee from South America to various parts of Africa, rubber from Brazil to Malaya, the chichona tree (source of quinine which could be extracted from the bark) from South America to Java, and tobacco from the Americas to Africa.

During the eighteenth and nineteenth centuries Britain's most important overseas colony was the sub-continent of India. As with the Dutch and the Dutch East India Company in the Far East, so too did Britain allow its elite-perceived interests in India to be progressed via a chartered joint-stock company; in this case the English East India Company (EEIC) initially named 'The Company of Merchants of London trading into the East Indies'. The EEIC had received its first Royal Charter in December 1600 from Queen Elizabeth I with a further Royal charter granted in 1609 extending the company's monopoly of Indian and South-East Asian Trade. A further charter was issued in 1656 by the Lord Protector (Oliver Cromwell) in which the company was given '…the authority to hold, fortify, and settle overseas territory'. The highest body in the EEIC was the General Court, composed of all the investors, but this body had little to do with the day-to-day running of the Company and available evidence suggests that the maximization of profits was the sole motivation for these 'gentleman'. The executive body was the Court of Committee, composed of 24 Directors elected by the General Court and headed by a Governor and a Deputy Governor.

The EEIC applied the same motivation, and used similar methods, as the Dutch EIC to set about drawing wealth from the Far East. From early in the 17th century the Company's main rivals were the Portuguese, French and Dutch with a plethora of other 'East India' companies being spawned in Europe, including:

Swedish East India Company
Danish East India Company
French East India Company

And the Imperial or Ostend Company charted in Vienna. A company given protection by the Hapsburg Empire under the Treaty of Utrecht (an 'East Indies' company in all but name).

James Lancaster was given command of the first EEIC fleet to reach its far eastern destination in 1602 with the lead ship, the Red Dragon, armed with 38 cannon; so prepared as much for conflict as for trade and as such a clear symbol of the methods to be used by the Company. A letter, ostensibly from Queen Elizabeth (in fact drafted by the merchants themselves), notes the aims of the company to be 'trade and friendship' but the subsequent operation of the company suggests that the emphasis was significantly more on trade than on friendship, with the latter being dependent on the extent to which native peoples (or their rulers) were prepared to collude in their own exploitation. Lancaster was able to negotiate the establishment of a 'factory' in the port of Bantum in Java. This provided a strategically well-placed base from which to trade directly with Chinese merchants when they made their annual visit to the port with a large fleet of junks laden with silks, porcelain, and other high value goods.

By the application of a clever strategy of playing local and regional native interests against each other, and if this failed having recourse to the ruthless use of military force, the Company gradually extended its control over the sub-continent. A significant stage in this expansion followed the Battle of Plassy in 1757 which gave the Company control of Bengal. The main sources of wealth were land taxes, customs revenue, and trade. Company profits from revenue collection alone had reached £7.5m by 1765. At the end of the eighteenth century India was contributing £500,000 annually to the British Treasury, and the trading monopoly with China returned £3m per year in tea duties alone.

The behaviour of two of the Company's principle employees, Robert Clive and Warren Hastings, illustrate the way in which the Company pursued its interests. Clive seems to have been dedicated to the ruthless accumulation of personal wealth and glory, and although initially Hastings showed some sympathy with the Indian people (he felt that they should administer their own country) he also ensured that he was able to amass a large personal fortune (£175,000, equivalent to many millions today) by the time he retired in 1785. Following the battle of Gheriah in 1756, in which European forces had overwhelming manpower and weaponry advantages, the usual practice of plundering a captured city or town took place, with soldiers taking a share based on rank. Clive's share as a Lieutenant Colonel was £5,000. Felipe Fernadez-Armesto noted the 'great man' Clive, as: '......great in this case as, at least in greed and grasp and grip.' (Fernadez-Armesto, 1995 p365)

Most employees of the company took their lead from the stockholders and used the advantages employment with the Company allowed to gain wealth by means that were occasionally legitimate (within the context of their employment) but were more often based on corrupt practices. Along with the process of wealth extraction undertaken by the company so also the corrupt administration of its employees gave no benefit to the mass of Indian people.

The historian Thomas Pakenham asked the pertinent question: 'Was it constitutional for a consortium of London businessmen to govern overseas territories, construct forts, dispense justice, raise revenues, coin money, wage war [engage in drug dealing!] and yet be outside direct control of parliament and answerable only to and indirectly (through the royal charter) to the crown?' (Pakenham, 1991, p169)

And the historian John Keay noted that: 'Imperial conceit would demand a glorious pedigree for 'our Indian Empire' but the plight of India's indigenous peoples in the eighteenth century scarcely affords it.' (Keay, 1993, p292)

It wasn't only the indigenous people of India and south-east Asia that were exploited by the EEIC, it was a company that also profited from the use of and the trade in slaves; mainly from Indonesia and West Africa.

By the end of the eighteenth century the Company's behaviour included breaking treaties, wholesale corruption, and excessive cruelty - exposed by, or rather brought to the attention of, a select committee of parliament - became too much even for the British Government; and the India Act (1785) and the India Charter (1793) introduced more state control, giving the British Crown the power to appoint the Governor General and a Board of Control (six Commissioners – including a British Secretary of State and the Chancellor of the Exchequer) whose remit was to control and direct the Company. At the same time as a 'sweetener' to the Company, and to send a conciliatory message to other joint-stock companies, the Government made a significant reduction in the duties on tea, so offering the prospect of a useful increase in the profits to be made from the China tea trade. According to Keay (ibid,1993) 'In return for surrendering administrative independence in India the Company was rewarded with the most important commercial opportunity in its history.'

By 1817 Britain was effectively in control of all of the sub-continent, apart from the fractious tribesman in the North West frontier, and those of the Sindh province, who would only be subdued by 1842. The British Indian Army had 120,000 troops (mostly Indian 'Sepoys') led by British officers, plus 3,000 mercenary Ghurkhas, to control around 300 million Indians. According to one historian '........the British waged more or less continuous war against the Indian people' (Britannica 1974 Vol. 4, page 891). A prolonged campaign to conquer Afghanistan had ended in a humiliating defeat for the British. But India served as a secure base from which to enable further British expansion in Java, Borneo, Sumatra, Sri Lanka (Ceylon), Burma, and China.

Trade with China not only involved tea, silks and porcelain, (and the 'dumping' of cheap European textiles) but also the narcotic 'opium'. A drug that sends those taking it into a euphoric state where cares are diminished and a sense of well-being attained. This as but a transitory state, the maintenance of which comes at a cost, personal and for society, as the pleasant pastime activity becomes an addiction and the occasional escape from everyday reality becomes a narrow world-view in which the addict can focus only on seeking the pleasurable escapes. For the addict, the 'fixes', that had initially brought pleasure would now only bring relief; and this the transitory relief of the temporarily satiated addict. Few addicts have any ability to contribute usefully to society.

As the heavy use of opium spread from the trading centres, the Chinese Government noted with alarm the detrimental impact it was having on whole communities (and also the increasing drain from China of silver used, along with tea, to pay for the drug) and so it decided to ban the drug's import. China moved to make the trade illegal from 1796, but in response the British East India Company (EEIC) turned to smuggling. Possibly as much as 5000 cases of the drug a year were smuggled into China up to 1830 when the Company progressively increased this highly profitable activity to up to 40,000 cases per year. In 1839 the Chinese authorities confiscated 20,000 cases of the drug in Canton and expelled British merchants from the City. The British Government reacted by coming to the merchants' aid and in effect going to war ('The Opium War') with a trading partner. Amongst other acts of aggression it sent an armed fleet up the Yangese River to attack Nanking. The military strength of the British forced the Chinese to capitulate and pay an indemnity of 21 million silver dollars, open up five 'Treaty' ports, sign the 'Treaty of Nanking' which leased Hong Kong to Britain, and also having to make other concessions to ease trading conditions. Perhaps worst of all (because the most humiliating), the Chinese were forced to accept the continuance of the opium trade - which reached 100,000 cases per year by the 1870s.

British control of India (still dominated by the EEIC) continued to be based on the unprincipled but clever playing off of one native interest (elite group) against another, and the use of military force when required. All the while extracting as much wealth as possible by such measures as the land tax – Pakenham (1991, p169) noted that: '.....the Company's men lived by the ledger and ruled by the quill.' Or rather, they meticulously recorded their legalized pillaging in this way.

Native troops (Sepoys) serving in the Company's Bengal Army had some awareness of the central role they played in maintaining the Company's position. In the year 1857, a combination of factors including a peasant rebellion against the hated land tax, and a simmering if general dislike of the Company in groups whose families had had land confiscated during protests earlier in the nineteenth-century, contributed to offer an opportunity for rebellion within the British Army. An army whose native members were confronted with an ultimatum to agree to serve overseas (General Enlistment Act 1856); in effect to contribute to the force for consolidating British colonial interests further east. But it was the infamous introduction of new Lee-Enfield rifles, whose cartridges were believed to be coated in cow-grease (risking religious pollution for the Hindu troops), that set the uprising in motion. Conflict spread throughout much of the army and the opportunistic Mughal Emperor, Bahadur Shah (along with some other dispossessed local rulers), gave his support and so helped to provide a legitimizing focus for the Sepoys and other groups rising against the British.

The rebellion was termed a 'mutiny' by British officialdom, partly at least in order to justify the harsh treatment of sections of the army (including rebellious soldiers being fired from cannon). It failed due to a significant extent to British support from the Punjabi Sikhs. But the cost to the British included the loss of income from the land tax, the disruption of the opium trade, and a more general reduction in economic activity. For the native peoples there was the cost of casualties, with 40,000 people dying in the siege of Delhi alone. Two key outcomes were the ending of the centuries long Mughal Empire in India and the final end of the East Indian Company. In future British India would be controlled from the India Office in London, a control locally exercised by a Viceroy appointed by the Crown and based in Delhi.

The colonial powers acted in ways that were based on exploitation, were often cruel, and were throughout oppressive. We might accept that the indigenous elite groups displaced by the major powers had mostly taken a similar self-interested approach to their own governing and their passing was rarely mourned by the indigenous populations. This hardly justifies the ways in which the European colonizers behaved but it should make us aware that, in relation to good and evil - it is perhaps not 'who' rules but rather 'how' people are ruled that matters; or rather the system of governance, as we would now suggest.

By the end of the eighteenth century, the British had established the occupation of Australia, Tasmania, New Zealand, and the western Pacific islands of Fiji, Tonga and those of the Gilbert Island chain. Whilst other European nations laid claim to New Caledonia, the Marquesas, and Tahiti (French), and Mariana (German).

At 1900 pretty much the whole of the Far East was either directly controlled or under the indirect influence of European Powers, if a few areas that did not offer much potential for exploitation were relatively unaffected. Globally, any piece of accessible land, whether island or a continental landmass, was likely to be brought under the 'protection' of some colonizing industrialized nation.

One of these, Japan, started on the road to industrialization later than had most European nations. Following the civil war in 1868, the restoration of the Emperor and the ending of feudalism, astute Japanese businessmen and others of the ruling groups advanced the development of a financial system that was tailored to finance the process of industrialization. As this progressed, and with it the capacity to wage war, the Japanese looked to create their own mini empire. Expanding first to neighbouring islands of Ryukyu, Bonin, and Kuril, going on to force China to cede interests in Taiwan and southern Manchuria. Then, early in the twentieth century (1904-5), Japan defeated Russia and was able to gain control of Liatung, and part of the large island of Sakhalin.

South America was to experience a different type of control by European (and later the US) powers after its first European colonizers, Spain and Portugal, had become fatally weakened. Firstly, by their inability to support colonies at a distance when the Iberian Peninsula was being occupied by the French from 1807-14. Then secondly, by the disruption caused during the drawn-out period of the Peninsular Wars as Napoleon's army fought an increasingly rearguard action against Wellington's forces and Spanish guerrillas; along with the generally debilitated condition of once powerful nations in economic decline.

The South American colonies were rarely governed wisely by Spanish and Portuguese administrators, merchants, and many others, most greedy for silver and gold, along with a Catholic Church greedy for converts as well as at least a share of the loot. The disruption in the European home nations allowed the colonized, especially Creole elites, an opportunity to be free of the colonizers. Nationalist movements made progress in some countries, and civil conflicts, at times breaking out into war in others, showed not just the weakness of the colonizing powers but also the fact of bitter rivalries between competing elite groups contesting for control within countries across the continent. The main division was Creole against those of the merchant class and descendants of the administrators loyal to Spain or Portugal. These groups came together on occasions when their combined strength was required to put down more popular uprisings or slave revolts (as in Cuba and Mexico).

During the period of the wars of independence, or of internal national conflict, the military came to the fore and gained a level of power that would be retained following independence. In many of the newly independent countries 'independence' meant only that colonization had been replaced by indigenous military dictatorships supported by powerful large landowners. By the time in 1825 that Bolivia was declared a Republic the whole of Spanish South America had freed itself of direct colonial control; at least politically rather than economically. The disruption of this period in the first quarter of the century left a legacy of armed rebel bands and gangs of bandits roaming the countryside and living off the land right up to 1850s. Most countries of Spanish South America experienced prolonged political turmoil.

In Paraguay, whether due to President Lopez's wish to fulfil territorial ambitions or to pre-empt Argentina and Brazil's claims on Paraguayan territory, Lopez recklessly declared war, initially on Brazil then on Argentina. Brazil, Argentina and also Uruguay, formed a 'triple-alliance' and a bloody war - lasting from 1864 -1867 (some would say 1870) ensued, a war that ended with the killing of President Lopez and in humiliating defeat for Paraguay. Some historians have suggested that Britain was involved on the triple-alliance side. There is no clear evidence to support this claim, but there is some circumstantial evidence in that Britain did offer local diplomatic support and the outcome fortuitously generously benefitted Britain's commercial interests in the region. Not least British banks, including Baring Brothers and Rothschild's, who made loans available (if at very high interest rates) to enable the nations of the triple alliance to progress the war.

The years of war saw the armed conflict become genocidal (the Paysandú massacre coming at the war's end) as the three invading nations ruthlessly put the population of Paraguay to the sword - almost 50% of Paraguay's people fled the county. The Triple Alliance set up a puppet government in Montevideo that progressively rolled-back the social and economic progress that had been made by the Francia and Lopez regimes. The country was ransacked, and the victors adjusted their own borders to encompass some extensive and juicy bits of Paraguan territory. But the victor-nations ended the war deep in hock to British bankers. And the future of Paraguay was then to follow the same model of development as pertained across most of the rest of the sub-continent; one focused on serving the investment and trading interests of Europe and the US, along with its own Hacienda, Estancia, Plantation, Rancho....estate-based indigenous aristocracy, most of whom had descended from European, forbears.

Some countries fragmented, as pockets of nationalism emerged and demanded their own independence. And although in places peasants were mobilized to fight outside of the cities in countries such as Mexico, Guatemala, Peru, and Bolivia, most Indian communities continued their lives relatively unaffected by the political upheavals. But when the interests of merchants, financiers, miners, and big farmers, came up against the interest of Indians it was invariably the former that got their way. According to Tulio Halperin Donghi (1993 p100): '....whether directed at the Church or at Indian communities, the dissolution of collective ownership was a goal of most "progressive" governments of the period'.

This conflict of interests became increasingly apparent in the latter half of the century when big landowners used clever lawyers to wrest land traditionally held in common by villagers from them; not dissimilar to the various types of enclosures of common land that had been taking place in Britain and across Europe, and the taking of common lands from the native peoples of North America.

By the time the political landscape of South American nationhood was settling down the military had a significant degree of influence, even when not in direct control. The cost of supporting standing armies placed a heavy burden on national budgets, for some countries this amounted to nearly 50% of total government income. It was this situation of some economic instability overseen by politically weak governments that the next wave of 'colonizers' would take advantage of. These European 'colonizers', were wiser than those being displaced and measured success in terms of economic profit rather than more simply in controlling vast swaths of land. European nations were also dissuaded from obvious political interference in South America when, in 1823, in a speech made to Congress and the House of Representatives, US President James Munroe warned European nations against attempting any direct colonization in South America *'In the discussions to which this interest has given rise and in the arrangements by which they may terminate the occasion has been judged proper for asserting, as a principle in which the rights and interests of the United States are involved that the American continents, by the free and independent condition which they have assumed and maintain, are henceforth not to be considered as subjects for future colonization by any European powers.'*

In setting out this US Government perspective Munroe was motivated by the fact that the US was looking to extend its own influence in the area; influence extending to both the annexation of territory and the advance of its political and trading interests.

The US did not become a significant threat to Britain's global economic dominance until the 1850s; and then mainly only in Central America and some of the Caribbean Islands. In countries such as Mexico, Brazil, and Argentina, British businessmen and the agents of mainly British companies gave support to this or that elite group's attempt to maintain or gain power. Throughout the nineteenth-century the imports of British manufactured goods rose. Here, as had previously been the case in India, the import of cheaply made British cotton goods resulted in the decimation of the indigenous textile industry.

As well as being able to profit by developing the local economies – mining, extraction of oil and hardwoods, construction, utilities, railways, and in a range of other capital projects - British businessmen, and to a lesser extent those from Germany and France, developed an export trade back to Europe in beef, mutton (refrigerated shipping from1883), wheat, sugar, maize, hardwoods, and coffee, as large swaths of rain forest and pampas was turned into grazing lands or for the cultivation of crops. Although British merchants and manufacturers had established themselves across the continent during the first half of the century the more significant capital investment was made from the 1850s, and between 1870 and 1913 British investment rose from £85m to £757m, and 50% of the shipping (by tonnage) using the ports of Argentina and Brazil was controlled by British companies. British banks were predominant by the 1860s. On very rare occasions the British did resort to 'gunboat diplomacy' to advance its interests... joining forces with France in the 1850s to blockade Rio de la Plata. And Italy and Germany joining forces to blockade Venezuela at the end of the century; initially with US collusion if later, partly in response to public opinion, the US came to oppose this action.

Filipe Fernandez-Armesto notes that the British businessman Weetman Pearson (later Lord Cowdray) '...was said to have looted more from Mexico than any man since Cortes'.

As the century progressed it was the US to the north that brought aspects of both classic forms of colonization – control of land and economic dominance – together as it progressed the consolidation of its own borders. A process that in the first half of the nineteenth century had included the Louisiana Settlement, Britain and Russia giving up claims to territory in the North West (Oregon), and Spain abandoning its claim to Florida; then the US annexing Texas in 1836 and further Mexican territory in 1846-48.

During the eighteenth-century the British Government became increasingly interested in the southern continent, and in the 1770s the government sent Captain James Cook on the first of a series of voyages, during which he carried out meticulous charting operations. Actual occupation began in 1788 when a fleet of 11 ships reached Botany Bay carrying about 1000 people – 570 male convicts, 160 female convicts, and 250 free citizens. A second fleet arrived in 1790, with a settlement being established in Sydney Cove. Exploration of this vast new territory and its progressive settlement went hand in hand throughout the nineteenth century. Notable expeditions being those undertaken in 1790s by George Bass and Mathew Flinders, the latter changing the name of the continent from New Holland to Australia in 1817; a move that signified the shift in the balance of naval power between the two European nations. By early in the nineteenth-century the coastline of the southern continent had been charted and the early settlers were learning to cope with the often harsh environment, with a steady stream of convict and voluntary settlers continuing to arrive.

From the very first contact the relationship between settlers and indigenous peoples, 'Aborigines', was antagonistic. By the time that the European colonists first landed aboriginal people had occupied the continent for over 40,000 years, an occupation begun by people migrating from southern Indonesia and spreading out across the vast continent.

These were a people that would develop a rather special world-view, one that integrated the living and the dead in a way that reflected the ways in which the land and its animal life supported their own existence – they saw living interconnections, real and imagined merged together, densely intertwined within all aspects of their environments. There was a general belief that their ancestors were created out of the water, sky, and animals, during a 'dream time' when the natural world was infused with an animalistic spirituality. On death the ancestors had been absorbed into rivers, rocks, and other natural features, so assuming an enduring spiritual presence in the landscapes. When contact was first made with Europeans some Aboriginal groups considered them to be the returning spirits of their Aboriginal ancestors.

It is difficult to obtain exact figures but very rough estimates suggest that the continent was occupied by possibly over 1,000,000 Aboriginal peoples at the time of initial colonization, divided into possibly 500 distinct tribal groups. There was an element of inter-group conflict (especially apparent with the Maoris of New Zealand), over hunting lands and other resources, but the cost of losing menfolk in conflict would have such an impact on small groups occupying mostly quite hostile environments (as in Australia itself) that negotiations and compromise, or the acceptance of another group's superiority, would probably have been the more usual ways of containing conflict.

These technologically primitive but culturally rich peoples, with little sense of ownership and of regular industry, would suffer a similar fate to indigenous people elsewhere in the world when advancing 'industrial civilization' sailed or marched over their horizons.

The systemic racism that was a contributory factor in making the ill-treatment more acceptable to the perpetrators was signalled by Britain declaring the whole continent 'Terra Nullius' – basically indicating that it was a land uninhabited by human beings and therefore not 'owned'. The 'non-human' inhabitants were treated inhumanly from the very beginning. Treatment illustrated by the reprisal inflicted for a minor insult to Britain, when the commander of the first fleet to arrive to establish the penal colony at Sydney Cove and the first British Governor of New South Wales, Arthur Phillip decided in response to some perceived insult to randomly select ten Aborigine men and to have them beheaded in public.

The coveting of land that sustained the Aboriginal peoples, along with the underlying racism of the European mindset towards native peoples, were the two main factors that set the background context within which the colonizers approached their relationship to the indigenous peoples of Australia, Tasmania, New Zealand, and other islands of the region.

In places Aboriginals fought back…… notably at Parramatta, Pinjarra, and Battle Hill, among others, following leaders such as Pemulwuy, Calyute and Yegan. A mostly untold history of colonization would be of resistance, of those that refused to bow. But the technological advantages, the ability to provision larger numbers of fighters, plus their ruthlessness, easily favoured the Europeans. In Australia the notorious Native Police forces (often using Aboriginal trackers to track Aborigines) engaged in massacres, and some farmers ventured out on murderous punitive expeditions in response to the theft of stock; often taken by a people whose own means of subsistence was being stolen from them by those now seeking their extermination.

In 1824 settlers were given official permission to shoot Aboriginals. During a time when in Britain childhood was being created with factory laws, some general education, and the idea of 'play''……aboriginal children were being forced into labour.

Aboriginal women were routinely raped by Europeans and, along with their men-folk, were often poisoned, tortured, or shot. Europeans hunted aboriginals simply for sport and at times settler groups also engaged in the wholesale slaughter of men, women, and children.

In Queensland alone, between 1824 and 1898, 10,000 Aborigines were murdered, both casually and systematically; perhaps not surprising when the language infusing the discourse used in the anti-aboriginal propaganda included descriptive concepts such as 'wild animals', 'nuisance', 'thieves', 'vermin', 'primitive' (meant as an insult), and suggested that they were 'fair game'. A report by a Royal Commission, tasked to consider the situation, noted that: 'The treatment of Cape York people was a shame to our common humanity'. During the hundred years from 1788-1888 it is thought that the Aboriginal population of Australia was reduced from about 1,000,000 to 100,000.

The island of Tasmania stands out in the bleak legacy of genocides carried out by 'civil' peoples with the original 6,000 natives being completely wiped out by the end of the nineteenth-century – they were in effect hunted out.

The Maoris of New Zealand, having a significant militaristic element to their own culture, took longer to subdue but this was effectively completed by the end of the mid century Maori wars. A population of over 150,000 in 1800 being reduced to 42,000 by 1893; if this conflict was more of a 'draw' between the Maoris and the British. Most of the violence involved land disputes – as settlers endeavoured to transfer ownership from native peoples to themselves (to transform the status of land from being a common resource to a privately owned commodity), using a legal framework designed by the British and so favouring the settlers. Along with the actual violence used on the native peoples of Australia, Tasmania, and New Zealand, settlers also brought diseases such as small pox and venereal disease. Every possible degradation, humiliation, and cruelty was inflicted on these peoples by their 'civilized' colonizers.

Elsewhere, the increasing needs of capitalist economic development required new sources of raw materials and expanding markets for manufactured goods. This, allied to the acquisitive characteristics of the merchant and of the imperialist nation state, was to bring the vast continent of Africa into the sphere of expanding European civil life. A continent whose interior territory was pretty much unknown to outsiders until the nineteenth-century. The northern coastal regions had been involved with the development of civil life from its efflorescence in the Mediterranean region circa 2000 years BCE and in Egypt from even earlier as one of the civilizations contributing to knowledge of astronomy, mathematics, medicine, trade, architecture, religion, agriculture, the arts and to the administration of civil life. It is possible that as early as 600 BCE a Phoenician ship, at the request of the Egyptian King Necho, undertook the approx. 17,000 mile circumnavigation of the continent (as recorded by the Greek Historian Herodotus). And around 460 BCE a fleet under the command of the Phoenician, Henno the Navigator, set off west from Carthage with the intention of repeating this 'mythical' feat. Henno sailed down the west coast at least as far as the Senegal River and then ventured some way up the river into the interior. He returned with colourful stories describing exotic animals such as crocodile and hippopotami, and bringing back the skins of three female apes (probably gorillas). From early on Arab caravans had trekked deep into the Saharan and sub-Saharan regions engaging in trade, in precious metals, manufactured goods, salt, and in slaves.

Portuguese sailors voyaged south in the 14th and 15th centuries, establishing trading forts in the more hospitable locations along the western coast, with again the main trade being in slaves. Sub-Saharan Africa of this time had already seen quite significant development in civil societies, going back perhaps as early as 3,000 BCE with the Kerma settlements in the region that became known as Nubia and certainly with the later Napatan settlement in the same region about 500 BCE. More recent and more substantial civil settlements included a Mali Empire begun perhaps as early as the first millennium CE but certainly consolidated by around 1230 CE when the Malinke people organized themselves to repel the encroachment of a southern aggressor

(Soninki) from Ghana on the River Niger. The Mali Empire was a civilization whose prosperity was closely connected to the River Niger and its hinterland; the fertility of which was released due to a significant contribution of slave labour working on the land. It also benefited from a monopoly control of gold-fields and salt-mines, both of which provided valuable products with which to trade with their northern neighbours. The ability to organize an effective civil administration enabled the efficient collection of taxes – tax on all trade into and out of the vast region over which the Malinki came to rule. A rule to which the many subject tribal groups paid annual tribute in such goods as rice, millet, and weapons. Contact with northern Muslims led to the Mali upper classes adopting Islam as their preferred religion and there is a record of one king of Mali, Mansa Musa, undertaking a pilgrimage to Mecca (Haji) in 1324 with a vast caravan of 60,000 people. He is reputed to have had 500 slaves, each carrying a solid gold bar weighing four pounds. Musa's entourage distributed gold in exchange for hospitality as they travelled north to Timbuktu, east to Cairo, then on to Mecca. At its civil peak towards the end of the fourteenth-century, the Mali Empire had an administration based on provincial governorships with local mayors controlling the larger towns and cities and a huge standing army ready to move swiftly to put down any attempt at rebellion. It also developed its own distinctive art forms and had a level of scholarship admired by counterparts of the Southern European universities with whom there was contact.

In the east of the continent, with its heartland nestled within the highlands of Ethiopia, the Kingdom of Axum enjoyed a thousand-year ascendancy. Emerging in the 3rd century BCE, it exerted a significant regional influence extending at times as far north as the southern Mediterranean shore. Its Emperor converted to Christianity in the 4th century BCE, thus establishing a firm cultural link to the Middle East and to southern Europe. A period of relative isolation set in during the rise of Islam, when the Empire was surrounded by generally hostile neighbours, and it never regained is central role in east African trade. A further factor in the Empire's demise involved climate change and the erosion of much of its most fertile soils. As the shrinking Empire reduced to the status of a modest kingdom, dynasties came and went until the restoration of the Solomonic Dynasty in 1270 (Emperor Yekuno Amlak who claimed direct descent from Solomon and the Queen of Sheba) establishing a line of dynastic decent that would last until 1974 when Haile Selassie died. The 17/18th centuries were ones of relative isolation and general decline, with the remains of the Empire separating into fractious regional power-bases. In 1855 Tewodros II (Ras Kassa) seized power and set about bringing unity to what had become a disintegrating state and introduce some aspects of modern civil society. Although mainly an agrarian economy, if one characterized by extensive trading links to the north and east, the Ethiopian Empire had institutions of administration and culture that would fairly be describe as civil. It developed its own Ethiopic syllabary from roots in the Southern Arabian alphabet.

In the mid 1440s King Mutota of the Mwene Mutapa (or Monomatapas) had established a kingdom extending across the vast Rhodesian Plateau and east into what is today's Mozambique. Although a largely agrarian region, there was a variety of small-scale economic activity, including iron-working and textile production. These commodities, as well as gold and cooper, and slaves, were the basic trade-goods exchanged with Arab and Swahili merchants based in the cities.

A situation only reversed when a confederation of the Shona people gradually formed the Rozwi Empire. An empire that was to oversee a period of prosperity until conflict with Europeans expanding from the south in the mid-nineteenth century symbolically brought an end to indigenous rule when, exhibiting his usual self-effacing modesty, Cecil Rhodes had the country named after himself! As he noted in his book 'Confession of Faith':

"We know the size of the world we know the total extent. Africa is still lying ready for us it is our duty to take it. It is our duty to seize every opportunity of acquiring more territory and we should keep this one idea steadily before our eyes that more territory simply means more of the Anglo-Saxon race, more of the best the most human most honourable race the world possesses."

We can see, writ large in Rhodes's revealing comment, both the racism that reflected the mindset of many Europeans of the time and also the underlying personal greed that used assumed racial superiority as a justification for the aggressive approach taken to pursue the accumulation of wealth. We can also note the use of the proactive word 'duty', suggesting a moral weakness, a dereliction of duty, if the spread of Rhodes's version of some fictional 'Anglo-Saxon race' isn't undertaken.

The power relations between colonizers and indigenous peoples can be seen in the battle of Omdurman (Sudan) in 1898, when the poorly armed Mahdists chanted 'There is one God and Mohammad is his Prophet', as they advanced towards the British artillery, only to fall victim to the relentless logic of forces clashing in the context of asymmetric military technology between each side. When the smoke had cleared by late morning on the 2nd September the already swelling bodies of 10,800 dead Mahdist soldiers were strewn across the sun-burnt plain, and witnesses spoke of the pitiful cries of some of the 16,000 wounded piercing the air. The British commander, Lord Kitchener, could show his Christian sensibility with the self-satisfied expression 'I thank the Lord of Hosts for giving us victory as such little cost'. Attributing the low casualty rate, 48 dead and 382 wounded soldiers on the British side, to the intervention of a Christian God rather than to the superiority of the Martini-Henri and Lee-Metford repeating rifles, the rapid fire of the Maxim machine guns, and the merciless destruction wrought by the field-artillery, all combined in sending wave after wave of blistering fusillades of lead against a Mahdist army armed mostly with swords and single-shot rifles. The 'victor' at Omdurman would just two decades later experience a casualty rate of over 1,000,000 killed in another military action in the face of the truly 'godless' bloody reality of advancing military technology – as they too were sent off to war in 1914 blessed by Christian clergymen to fight German soldiers similarly blessed!

So this brief overview of civil life in sub-Saharan Africa, up to the time of colonization by the leading European powers, shows an aptitude to develop a level of civil life that the economic resources and the social conditions of the time could sustain. A level of civil life that colonizers and covetous adventurers such as Rhodes tried to deny. Even if within the indigenous civil life this aptitude was just as mired in the evils of self-consciousness – at the 'tribal' level the waging of war and widespread involvement in the institution of slavery - as was the civil life in the northern hemisphere. Empires such as those of the Ashanti, Yoruba, and Dahomey, gained a significant proportion of their wealth from the slave trade and in turn used some of this to purchase arms from the Portuguese, the Dutch, and later on the English. Arms used to engage in conflict with their neighbours. The historians Jane Burbank and Fredrick Cooper suggest that the military peoples of: 'Ashanti, Dahomey, Oyo, Benin, produced... efficient slave trading mechanisms.' (Burbank and Cooper, 2010, p179) A 'commodity' gained in warring or by more specific raiding to the south seeking captives.

The cruelty of the Zulus under their leader Shaka is well-attested too. The Zulus (not showing such a level of civil development as the empires that had developed elsewhere in Africa) rose in 1816, from a relatively small clan (like the Matabele, the Zulus were also a confederacy of widely dispersed Bantu peoples) able to field about 350 warriors, to become, by the 1850s, a nation able to field a ferocious and well-trained army 50,000 strong, one armed with the short stabbing assegai so effective in hand-to-hand combat. They were a people who gloried in violence and who allowed themselves to be led by a militaristic elite that had little respect for the cultures and lives of other tribal groups.

What even this brief account of civil Africa does is clearly contradict any claim of little pre-colonial civil development beyond Carthage and Egypt. We can note that for at least four millennia, the African continent had been developing its own versions of civil life, if also versions that included quite wide-spread civil and tribal strife.

In the sixteenth century the Dutch showed interest in the east coast of Africa and began to displace the Portuguese as the main traders; building trading forts at favourable places along the coast, The Dutch also established a stopover for the 'retourschips' (the East Indies bound 'return ships') for replenishing water and other stores on the long journey to the East Indies - at the Cape of Good Hope. Building a fort there and establishing the basis of a colony in the 1650s. At around the same time the British were showing an interest in the west coast, an interest that, prior to its being brought to an end within the British Empire, had focused on supplying the slave trade. Little was then known in Europe about sub-Saharan Africa beyond the more accessible coastal regions. The penetration into the interior of the 'dark continent' was pursued, mainly by tracing the source of the major rivers - a means of travelling inland made much easier with the invention of steam-powered gunboats and the discovery that quinine could cure, or at least alleviate, the symptoms of malaria; the death rates of Europeans fell by 80% following the widespread use of quinine.

From about the 1850s European interest in the continent increased to become what has been described as a 'scramble for Africa' (repeated by Thomas Pakenham 1919, in the title of his substantial book 'The Scramble for Africa'). A scramble characterized by the leading European powers competing with each other to grab or at least control as much territory as possible. The evils that resulted in this approach can be seen at their worst in the way that King Leopold II of Belgium took part in the scramble with some self-seeking enthusiasm. Leopold seemed to have been a man whose thoughts were focused on his own ego to the extent of it displacing any sense of humanity. This narrowing of interest led him to seek aggrandizement for his relatively modest European kingdom and the accumulation of as much personal wealth as possible. From his gaining the throne in 1865 he travelled widely in the Middle and Far East and took an interest in territories that might offer the potential to become colonies of Belgium. Leopold read with increasing interest about what was happening in Africa. Including his learning about the journey of the British Lieutenant Verney Cameron, the explorer who took three difficult years to cross Africa from east to west. A journey that he wrote up in letters home and in articles sent back to The Times newspaper in London (read each day by Leopold). Cameron suggested that the land presented a veritable honey-pot of wealth in minerals and precious metals just waiting for the brave investor. Leopold offered, via the Royal Geographic Society of London, to pay the expenses incurred by Cameron and in 1876 he gathered members of the Society, some explorers, and other interested parties, at a conference in Brussels. This conference on Central Africa was ostensibly a scientific debate framed in the language of informed geographers but in fact, as subsequent developments revealed, it was but another step in advancing Leopold's personal ambitions.

The 'opening up', or rather the mapping and assessment of the potential of the central and south areas of the continent, was continued at a pace. Henry Morten Stanley, whose already harsh treatment of tribal groups had preceded his setting off, in 1876, to repeat Cameron's earlier journey crossing the continent from east to west. Stanley himself had boasted of his party having in 1875 killed 33 and wounded over 100 Bumbireh tribesmen that he felt had insulted him. An incident that took place on his return from a trip which included the circumnavigation of Lake Victoria. A trip during which he met King Mtesea, the cruel Kabaka of Buganda, who was reputed to have had 30 of his full and half brothers murdered when he acceded to the throne.

It was in June 1877 that King Leopold heard the news of Stanley's successful crossing of Africa, during which he had confirmed the extent of the River Congo and also that it wound its way into the heart of a sprawling treasure-trove of potential wealth.

Media distortion (and Stanley's shameless approach to self-publicity, aided by the public's propensity to 'hero worship') and the highly selective reporting of Stanley's travels in Africa led to his being feted when he returned to England in January 1878. But his attempts to garner business and political interest in significantly increasing the British presence in central Africa were generally unsuccessful. Frustrated with Britain's lack of interest in taking up the opportunities offered in the Congo, and having completed a book on his journey through the heart of the 'Dark Continent', Stanley travelled, by invitation, to Brussels to meet King Leopold. The outcome of this meeting being that by late 1878 Stanley and Leopold arranged to work together to advance their shared interest in the Congo, or rather Stanley agreed to work for the King for the next five years. The mindset of covetousness invoked fears of being pre-empted by others and so Stanley agreed to the King's request to keep their plans as secret as possible. He returned to the Congo in Feb 1879 and began to establish the first few of an intended chain of trading stations – a task involving driving a path into dense jungle and dynamiting through rocky obstacles along the way.

But by now Britain was also taking a closer interest in Central and West Africa, and the French were consolidating their own interests in the north-west of the continent, each signing treaties with a number of local kings. Treaties that gave the French significant trading rights in exchange for offers of protection for compliant tribal groups. The French presence in the Niger Delta included a gunboat, the Voltigeur. This, in addition to protecting French local interests, was able to allow passage further afield and so to extend its influence by signing treaties with some local kings and chieftains at some distance from the coast.

The successful advance of French control caused increasing concern to Britain, its reaction being to step up its own activities along the west coast, especially in the Niger region. It had been influential in the region for some time and the number of British traders increased steadily. Most of these being middlemen working for the North Africa Company (NAC), a trading group specifically established to take full advantage of any opportunity to gain profit, mainly to be made in the lucrative palm oil trade. The NAC was a company run and owned by a group of aggressive and greedy stakeholders whose local agents had been active mainly in areas accessible to the River Niger, and so areas where they could gain some level of protection and threaten the locals with gunboats. A threat made actual during a number of punitive expeditions that left whole villages destroyed and the inhabitants - men, women, and children - dead or mutilated.

Whilst generally given a friendly reception, the British representative, Edward Hewett, ('Her Majesty's Consul for the Bights of Benin and Biafra') encountered a less than enthusiastic response from some native leaders with one chief, King Ja-Ja of Opobo, in particular, being a man who had a shrewd understanding of trade and of the value of the resources under his control. Especially of his local monopoly in the palm oil trade, to maintain which he was prepared to use violence against any individual or group who threatened this. Hewett's response to opposition from leaders such as Ja-Ja was to use their obstructive approach as justification for Britain adopting even more aggressive methods. Hewett deployed gunboats to shell villages and towns, and machine guns (Maxim guns) against the civilian populations of any of the settlements that were deemed to be unfriendly to Britain; or rather the economic interests of British traders, meaning in effect the NAC. During the early years of the 1880s the British and French competed to gain influence and control in West Africa. At about this time the Germans also began to take a closer interest in the region and, through surreptitious and clever diplomacy, they were able to take control of Cameroon in the name of the Kaiser.

The generally fairly chaotic competition for large parts of Africa was seen by the stronger European powers (encouraged by national politicians who were in turn pressured by leaders of industry and trade, as well as jingoistic elements in their populations) to be an impediment to progressing their economic interests and so their representatives were brought together for the Berlin Conference which began in autumn 1884. The venue was the German Chancellor Otto Von Bismarck's impressive Berlin residence with representatives of 14 European governments attending, plus observers from the US. The outcome of the Conference was the division by European powers of vast regions of Africa, and included a statement of the principles that should guide their commercial and civilizing activities.

Article 11 of 'The General Act of Berlin' Feb.26th 1885

'The Signatory Powers exercising sovereign rights or authority in African territories will continue to watch over the preservation of the

native populations and to supervise the improvement of the conditions of their moral and material well-being. They will, in particular, endeavour to secure the complete suppression of slavery in all its forms and of the slave trade by land and sea'.

For mendacious statements this is about as misleading as they come - in terms of slavery alone, the actual changes would be made in who were to be the slave owners, along with the expansion of those enslaved to the whole population in territories such as the 'Free Congo'!

Article 11 continues: *'They will protect and favour, without distinction of nationality or of religion, the religious, scientific or charitable institutions and undertakings created and organized by the nationals of the other Signatory Powers and of States, Members of the League of Nations, which may adhere to the present Convention, which aim at leading the natives in the path of progress and civilization. Scientific missions, their property and their collections, shall likewise be the objects of special solicitude.'*

The subsequent action of the signatory powers highlights Article 11 as representing the very highest level of diplomatic hypocrisy. The primary aim of the Berlin Conference was, in effect, to legalize the crimes against humanity that the theft of African territory represented. An international attempt at legitimizing a theft, and the means used to carry it out, that had already taken place.

At this time all of Africa excluding Ethiopia, Liberia, and nominally at least Egypt, was under the control of European nation-states or, in the case of the Congo Free State the personal control of King Leopold II (it would later on be controlled by Belgium). Germany controlled Togo, Cameroon, Tanganyika, and South-west Africa – Portugal: Mozambique and Angola – Spain: a region on the North-east coast and Spanish Morocco – Italy: Libya and Italian Somaliland – France: most of West Africa and northern central region (including the vast French Equatorial Africa) French Somalia, and most of the north of the continent (Algeria, Morocco, Tunisia) – Britain: Kenya, Sudan, Nigeria, Gold Coast, Uganda, British Somaliland, Nyasaland, Northern and Southern Rhodesia, Bechuanaland, and The Union of South Africa

The Berlin conference, and subsequent negotiations, agreed borders on the basis of carving up the land in line with their own economic interests balanced against what they could get away with – the traditional lands and the interests of native peoples were in effect ignored; arrangements that have contributed to the exacerbation of tribally-based conflicts into post colonial times. The long and continuing tradition of including high-flying humanitarian phrases in treaty documents was clearly apparent in Article 11 of the Berlin Treaty, but its irrelevance to actual behaviour was no more clearly illustrated than in the Belgium King's personal fiefdom of the Congo.

The tasty joint of the whole continent had been set before the Conference and was now being nicely carved up; the spoils of determinedly acquisitive aggression. It had already been lightly seasoned with some initial contacts, making natives peoples fully aware of the intentions and the potential power of the would-be colonists, and was ready to be devoured by the predatory nation-states of Europe. Commerce, Christianity, and Western civilization - were to be gifted to Africans' in exchange for the more nourishing fare of vast wealth for the Europeans.

In the Congo the King, through his agents in the 'International Association' on the ground, set out to squeeze his 'share' (share being in practice as much as possible) of this wealth by in effect enslaving all of the native people living within the 1½ million square miles of territory under his 'protection'. Leopold made a fortune from selling land and mineral concessions to a number of European-based companies. But it was the forced labour of the Congolese native peoples where we see the expression of the most terrible of evils. The population was forced to kill enormous numbers of elephants (for their ivory tusks), and to build the infrastructure including roads, railroads, a network of trading posts, homesteads, and other buildings that would enable Leopold's agents and those of the private companies, to more efficiently extract the resources that they garnered - or rather the booty that they were looting - from the land and its peoples.

The native chiefs had generally used their traditional power (backed by customs and laws) to accrue relatively modest wealth and advantages for themselves and their family members but Leopold's agents took this exploitation to a considerably higher level. Whole villages were burnt to the ground if the natives were not malleable enough to conform to the demands of capitalist production, and resource extraction. A people whose lives had been framed within the patterns of day-light and night-dark and in the rhythm of the seasons, were expected to adapt to the iron discipline of regular, measured, time and of quantified production. Wives were taken hostage and sexually and physically abused until their husbands had returned with sufficient wild rubber.

Think of any possible abuse that can be inflicted on a people and it happened in Leopold's Congo. Men such as E.D.Morel and Roger Casement reacted with horror at what they saw and endeavoured to bring the situation to the attention of the western world. Casement's Report of 1904 estimated 3 million people starved, shot, tortured to death……in sum 'murdered'. But later, better informed, reports estimate the figure to have been about 10 million.

The extent of the crimes (of enslavement, torture, mass murder…. in effect genocide) being perpetrated on behalf of Leopold became both an international embarrassment to the government of Belgium as well as prompting moral outrage in some European countries. In Nov. 1907, Belgium's parliament voted to annex the territory, and the Congo became a colony controlled by the State rather than one owned by the monarch.

For the sake of gaining a more balanced perspective it should be kept in mind that – although in the longer term, given the mindset of ruling elites in Europe western, colonialism was probably inevitable - the process of colonization was to some extent facilitated by the willingness of elites of favoured tribal groups in most African territories to form alliances with the potential colonizers. What were initially mostly more equal voluntary alliances became much less equal forced allegiances as the presence of the colonizing nations became more entrenched.

A much less known (in the West) colonization was that undertaken by Russia in Asia. For centuries Russia had extended a fairly loose type of control over its neighbouring lands, a control extending at times as far east as the border with China. But during the nineteenth century there appears to have been an intention to match Western European countries and to impose a more formal system of control, allied to this was the wish to gain a warm-water seaport facing the Pacific; this would be Vladivostok (meaning 'to rule', 'or ruler of the east'). Siberia, the Caucasus, and large parts of central Asia were taken over and wealth gained, mainly via a poorly administered system of taxation (more akin to tribute) and control of trade. Especially the trade in furs and timber along with, if opportunity allowed, the looting of valuables from occupied lands. The low density of indigenous population levels made it difficult to organize much resistance to Russian expansion. Expansion which would only be halted due to its rubbing up against the Far-Eastern interests of other, more powerful, industrializing states.

Russia sent military forces, and in their wake settlers, to gain and colonize Siberia and lands further east to China; with some Russian businessmen even casting acquisitive eyes over this border. The emancipation of Russian serfs in 1861 had perversely made many of them more vulnerable to exploitation and led to large numbers of peasants migrating east. As in the US, if on a much smaller scale, colonial eastwards expansion from Russia and Ukraine also displaced indigenous peoples.

Following the completion of the trans-Siberian railway, a significant increase in trade in manufactured goods went eastwards and a range of raw materials returned westward. The momentum of Russian expansion was thwarted by other industrialized countries such as Britain in Southern Central Asia and China. With its potential control over Northern China and the Korean Peninsula being curtailed by its defeat by Japan in the Russo-Japanese war of 1905.

Far to the west of Europe the colonization of North America continued at a pace throughout the nineteenth-century. In 1803 the US paid $11,250,000 and cancelled nearly $4m of debt for 828,000 square miles, a wide swath of land running through the centre of the North American continent. This, the Louisiana Purchase, in effect what was already a colony being sold on to other colonists, opened up the central area of North America to the settlers from Europe who would travel in a steady stream of wagon trains (and later in the century the railroads) west across the Mississippi. The Purchase covered a large area in the centre of the continent, including the whole of what became Iowa, Arkansas, Nebraska, Missouri, Kansas, Oklahoma, North and South Dakota, most of the area that was to become Louisiana, and Minnesota, and parts of what would become Montana, Wyoming, Texas, Colorado, and North and South Dakota.

The main outcome of war with Britain in 1812 was the European state giving up its claim to land south of the 45 (degrees) parallel and to Oregon territory. It was during this period that the cartoon version of 'Uncle Sam', and the tune that was to become the national anthem 'The Star Spangled Banner', along with colourful emblematic images of America, began to take shape. Florida was gained from Spain in 1819 and most of Texas from Mexico in 1836; with the US/Mexican war of 1846-48 resulting in the US annexing large parts of the south west.

These conflicts contributed to the creation of a vast new country; one whose national flag flew over the homelands of people whose ancestors had drawn sustenance directly from the land, who had for eons been able to watch red-skied sunsets draw in over rolling prairies across which contented herds of buffalo grazed, and over tree covered hunting grounds as the Sun set on distant horizons. Diverse groups of native peoples who had developed rich and complex cultural legacies unaware of the dark clouds of humanity drifting across the Atlantic to engulf and then destroy their traditional ways of life.

The US government adopted a particular model that was applied to ensure the transfer of land occupied by native peoples to white settlers and to corporate bodies. A model of relentless occupation based on signing treaties to cover an area of territory in which the rights of each party were outlined and then the US either directly finding an excuse to break the treaty or in their coming to the 'defence' of settlers, miners, hunters, and other groups who had themselves broken treaty conditions. The US army killing or forcibly – and in as much as treaties voluntarily entered into are legal documents, illegally - removing vast numbers of native Indians from their traditional homelands, was the central mechanism by which settlers gained land as civilization marched west.

The killing included planned starvation and infection by European disease. Diseases of smallpox, cholera, tuberculosis, sometimes inadvertently spread but at other times actually used as a killing tool; on occasion presents of small-pox infected blankets were knowingly given to natives. In places forced migration and actual massacres were justified on the basis of aggressive actions by Indians responding to their ill-treatment. But this was not just some economically motivated action, although this was invariably the main driver. The Indians were set up as part of the frontier culture of the newly emerging US nation. Painters then photographers, newspapers and magazines, without much sense of obligation to offer the truth and a bit later the cinema industry, as well as the populist narratives echoed by local and national politicians, all contributed to framing the image of the American Indian as an impediment to progress itself. The characterization of Indians as lacking intelligence, unreliable, violent, promiscuous, heathen, uncultured, and when possible as 'inhuman'. Similar to attempts made to characterize black Africans, Australian aborigines and indeed, native peoples whenever they were encountered by 'civil' peoples, so seeking to endorse and justify their persecution. Those who killed Indians and stole their lands were projected as heroic, god-fearing Christians, bravely engaging in furthering the interests of the US.

All cultures are prone to mythologizing their past, and to inventing national heroes, but the mass culture of the USA, using the newly emerging mass media and communication systems, attained a new level of meta-fictional invention. This mythologizing was economically underpinned by the idea of 'products', the commodification of mythology. It has created marketable products - films, TV shows, magazines, clothes, toys, guns, games, etc.- from mythologies linked to a purposefully imagined history. Not least, when western movie scripts made their contribution to the mythology of 'winning the west', as if it were a deserved prize rather than having been the home-lands of many collectivities of native peoples from time immemorial.

In the late 1860s, when the persecution of Native American Indian peoples was at its height, General Carleton, at the time engaged in a campaign to clear the south west for settlers, ordered that: 'There is to be no council held with the Indians, nor any talks. The men are to be slain whenever and wherever they can be found.'

Whilst the threat or use of military force was the most commonly used means of clearing territory of indigenous peoples, the systematic and cynical killing of the buffalo was just as effective in terms of genocidal outcomes. The buffalo represented 'life' for many of the plains Indians, such as the tribes of the Arapaho and Cheyenne, and those of the Sioux Nation. Buffalo were a productive source of images and colourful narratives that were indelibly imprinted into native cultures. They had for centuries provided the tribes with food, fabrics, tools (bone), decorations (bodily adornments), and the hunting stories which had enriched the cultural imagination for generation following generation; tales told, and hunting scenarios re-enacted, in vibrant dances in the musty glow of smoky campfires.

Between 1870 and 1880 about 15 million buffalo were systematically slain by hunters. William Cody, as 'Buffalo Bill' the national hero, was in reality a brilliant self-publicist who became famous on the strength of an ability to shoot a rifle at generally placid animals whose bodies made a large enough target. He had the entrepreneurial foresight to put a fictionalized idea of the 'winning of the west' into a circus-like stage show with which he toured the US and Europe. General Sheridan, tasked with clearing the Great Plains of Indians, suggested that the extermination of the buffalo was a prerequisite to obtaining peace and to advancing civilization. There was the implicit promotion of an idea that the relatively newly created nation of the United States had some assumed (or rather invented) god-given right, to control the continent from the Atlantic to the Pacific coasts.

Taken on its own, the idea of the US state having some divine permission to expand its borders seems just stupid – and could be used by any covetous nation wishing to encroach upon neighbouring territory – but when we realize that the idea of some 'Manifold Destiny', (first used in an article in the July-August 1845 edition of the 'Democratic Review') is of the type of mendacious invention used historically by those who intend on justifying actions that just laws would not allow. Seeking to draw some spurious authority by inventing a link to some or other god's will. Some attempt to link the obviously unacceptable to some higher authority. In the context of the US state marching west seeming to absolve the actor (thief) from the action (theft).

Key Indian wars took place between 1865-90: with the Red River wars in the south east of 1865-85, the Apaches campaigns of 1865-1886, the campaigns in the North West in 1865-1890 and the Sioux campaign 1865 -1890. During this 25 year period the Fourteenth Amendment was added to the US constitution, an amendment that gave equal rights to all citizens of the United States apart, that is, from Native American Indians and slaves. By the last decade of the century Indian resistance was all but ended, and with the corralling of remaining groups onto impoverished reservations whole ways of living disappeared. The now yellowed paper treaties and the faded records of disingenuous speeches made by white leaders are but remnants of the institutional bad faith, avarice, and greed of US politicians - operating in the interests of cattle-ranchers, prospectors, land speculators, financiers, traders, and settlers - who were influential in setting the direction of the country for the next 150 years.

Rarely was the process of overrunning North America simply one of an evil colonizer using superior technology and a more murderous, acquisitive, national temperament to take control of lands occupied by peaceful native groups living some idyllically peaceful lives – tribes (as most groups living in proximity during our self-conscious stage of human evolution) had at times fought each other, with themselves forming alliances to more successfully wage inter-tribal war.[19] These more local conflicts did have a generally limited impact on the people and even less impact upon the land itself but they count as evil and would have continued even if the white man had not arrived. Indeed, even during the persecution of tribes some Native Americans worked for and with the persecutors (at times taking an active part in the killing) usually against their own traditional enemies – such is the moral complexity characterized by observing the range of behaviours arising from human thinking at the level of self- consciousness.

The approach to colonialism taken on the ground by individual Europeans, private corporations, and the agents of national governments, were each but local adaptations of a more general approach taken across in the world as the blight of self-conscious civilization encompassed almost all its peoples. An approach formulated from a collective mindset that assumed the 'foreign' as but a potential source of wealth; and for nation-states some dubious international prestige and a contribution to national identity. An approach given determinate authority by uneven levels of technological development. Crudely summed in the pithy phrase of Hilare Belloc: 'Whatever happens we have the Maxim gun and they have not'.

But colonization was not simply the replacement of ideal lives lived by peaceful peoples by the aggressive perpetrators of gross exploitation. Colonization was generally evil in intent and practice, but it often replaced, or colluded in 'partnership' with, local elites - kings, princes, tribal chiefs, favoured families, dominant castes, and other elite ruling groups - who had themselves exercised power over tribes and ethnic groups in conflict with their neighbours. What colonization did was to 'industrialize', and increasingly globalize (de-

---

[19] Jake Page, p62, 2003....refers to a massacre of 500 native American people buried in a mass grave very roughly 1,000 CE..... he suggests tribal conflict.

localize), the exploitation; expanding the types of evil inflicted, and of significantly increasing its quantified level of expression. Economic and actual colonization displaced numerous types of centuries-old adaptations to a range of natural environments.......by peoples' conscious of intimate links to the seasons and to the fauna, flora, and the natural features of the land. Indigenous peoples displaced by a civilization determined on a relatively more recent type of adaptation to the environment based on using up, control, domination, and of the commodification, of almost all aspects of the natural environment. An adaptation of mass manufacturing, of the exchange of goods between people involving some abstract value measured by money. Money representing alienated value (alienated from the fundamental relationships of exchange that non-monetary systems were based upon) and as such can be accumulated and its power to control deployed.

Western influence went further than disruption in the economic and cultural spheres, it also included the idea of nation-statehood; spreading the potential for the same mindless nationalism that usually accompanies the socio/political construct of nation-hood. The synthetic creation of nation-hood during colonial times has enlarged the potential for conflict inherent in the false aura of power, usually comingled with some sense of some past injustice or an imagined national destiny. In the Middle-East, Far-East, Africa, and South American, nation-states were initially created to suit strategies of global-politics by powers pursuing economic and imperial ambitions, rather than in the interests of the indigenous populations. Borders were drawn on behalf of the colonial powers by agents lacking much if any understanding of tribal occupation and traditional patterns of land use; so seeding future generations of disputes.

Colonization was a key element in determining the pattern of global politics from the late nineteenth-century onwards. The experience of colonization gave further advantage to the already advantaged members of the elite groups in the leading European nation states, the US, and later on Japan.

International politics was characterized by a group of leading industrialized nation states that had throughout the century worked to increasingly (US, England, Russia, Japan, and France), or newly (Germany and Italy), unite, often diverse, peoples under one flag by artfully creating a national 'ego-identity'. That conceptual core entity of nationhood whose particular form is elusive and liable to change, but which can operate as a powerful force… something that can have a determinant hold on populations. One that can drive a nation to engage in terrible conflict. A force that can be manipulated by leaders to justify exploitation and gross inequality of its own citizens and well as those who live elsewhere. An entity – nation-hood - made up of the imaginatively constructed content of a collective consciousness constituted by ideas of shared history, shared language, shared economic interests, if possible a shared religion, set within a geographic boundary. With a similarly simplistic sensitivity to ego-centric national slights as do touchy ego-centric individuals.

Many civil nation-states now had standing armies, and most were able to introduce conscription when required. States whose economic development had provided the incentive to reach out and project their power to South America, Africa, and throughout the Middle and Far East. Nation-states armed by an industry in the hands of individuals prepared to let business interests overcome any moral qualms that they might have felt. This encouraged by politicians inveigled into the national egoism as part of their mindset. Nation-states looked suspiciously at each other's actions as they determinedly sought to advance their elite-group's perception of its own interests. Aggressive economic measures, the threat of military action, and at times actual conflict, were regular features of international relations. The greed-based scramble for overseas dominions encouraged international relations to be more about competition than co-operation.

Peaceful periods were exceptions and war, in defence of some elusive but conceptually powerful entity called the 'national-interest', was easily turned to. National-interest being a concept that epitomizes the successful process of solidifying the world geographically into historically synthetic entities called nations. When the idea of some national interest could be successfully appealed to, without more than some superficial examination of just what this can actually mean, it was deployed in a discourse to justify gross economic exploitation, killing and maiming, and to the spending of vast amounts of money on the military.

The legacy of exploitation-based colonialism became entrenched across the world – primarily a legacy of slave-enhanced economic regimes in the Americas and various types of often equally oppressive colonial regimes in Africa, and the Middle and Far East. The leading colonial powers at this time were Britain and France. By 1900 Britain's overseas investment amounted to over 160% of its internally generated annual national income, France 120%, and Germany 40% of theirs (each returning approx 5% per annum). The institutionalization of various processes of economic extraction that survived the abolition of slavery; and indeed would to a significant extent survive post colonialism itself from the 1950s. A relentless form of economic exploitation and hegemonic dictatorial political control infused with racism, as Western nations often claimed to be driven by a missionary intent of bringing the benefits of enlightened civilization to the 'backward' peoples of the world.

In terms of more obvious evils: millions of people died of famines in India (8.5 million in the years 1866, 1879, 1897, 1900), China (20m during the period of the T'ai-ip'ing Rebellion 1850-73) and between 9-13 million (1876-79), Brazil 500,000 (1877-1878), and 1 million had perished in Ireland in the 1850s and another million in Ethiopia 1888/9. These being just some of the more noted. Each of these being caused, or significantly exacerbated, by the action of, usually foreign, governments.

Mechanized, or rather industrialized,[20] warfare was developed, producing the slaughter of millions of mostly young men but also of civilians. An outcome becoming ever-more obvious from the Napoleonic campaigns towards the beginning of the century, then

---

[20] 'Mechanized' being a concept missing the point of the profit motive driving powerful individuals to favour conflict and the development of ever-more 'superior' weaponry.

during the Crimean War in 1850s and the US Civil War in the 1860s. The wars of independence such as the series of Italian wars in 1849, 1859, and 1866, and that of Cuba 1895-8. And in the conflicts suppressing the peoples of the many nations being ruled over by empire-building invaders such as the long drawn out US/Apaches campaign and the Anglo/Zulu (1879) and Anglo/Sino wars (the 'Opium Wars - 1856-60). With nearly 300 wars recorded for the nineteenth century, 70 of these being in the last decade; reflecting the increasingly bitter colonial experience and the more conflictual wider international context.

The primary beneficiaries of the preparation and expression of industrialized warfare were private companies such as Krupp (Germany), Armstrong (Britain), Creouset (France), Nobel (Norway), Smith and Wesson (US). Since the first appearance of civil life we can identify competition between groups in the development of more powerful weapons – stone to bronze, bronze to iron, iron to steel, foot-soldier to horse/camel/elephant rider, spear to short stabbing sword, crossbow to longbow, longbow to musket, musket to repeating rifles, maxim gun, and cannon, shells to conventional missiles, and these to hypersonic missiles etc. - was a defining feature of developing civil life. But the industrialized acceleration of this competition, and the related resource implications, began to see government financing, and international relationships, determined on the basis of superior weaponry. A danger being that a country would see its own superiority, its military preparedness, as but a temporary ascendancy …... another pressure to take pre-emptive action (the 'Trap' noted by Thucydides circa 443 BCE). In countries such as Russia, Germany, France, Austria, Ottoman-Turkey, and Britain, military planning was increasingly influencing political decision-making.

Chapter 4 The Modern Period: industrialized warfare

For some of the nations involved in the later nineteenth century wave of industrial development – nations such as the US, Germany, Japan, Italy, and Russia - the division of interests in the world were regarded as unfair and unjustified. This was not such an issue (for capitalists) in the US and Russia, where extensive land-masses offered opportunities for expansion and their geographic proximity to more remote areas of the world (especially China for Russia and South America for the US) also offered opportunities for investment and trade. For Japan, its relative isolation from most industrial nations (and a more insular national mindset) meant that competition with European nations for markets and raw materials was not too much of an issue; if it would become so in the first half of the 20th century.

But for Italy, and even more so for Germany, the lack of colonial opportunities - unsatisfied even by the 'gift' of relatively small regions in North Africa for Italy and Cameroon and parts of West Africa for Germany - and the historical antipathy between these and some of their European neighbours (France, Russia, and Britain) contributed to the resentment of their own ruling elites.

Germany, partly due to the relative lack of much pre-unification integration of industry and finance, progressed the process of industrialization later than its major western European neighbours. But once began, and with the benefit of unification (taking place between 1866-71 out of the German Confederation), it experienced the quite rapid expansion of its industries. In the 1880s Germany's economy was performing at about 35-50% of Britain's, on most accepted measures of industrialization such as: iron/steel production, use of power, share of world manufactures, etc. Then progressively up to around 1910, it reached similar levels and by some measures exceeded that of Britain; including in the percentage of world manufacturing with output 14.8% Germany to 13.6% Britain by 1913. During this thirty year period (1880-1910) the population of Germany increased from 48m to 67m, and the country had advanced to become the leading industrial power in Europe. Its leaders tended to interpret (and in most cases this was a fair assessment) any diplomatic initiative taken by its European neighbours as a potential threat, or at least as an attempt to reinforce existing unfairness.

If one man can be said to have guided Germany's industrial development in it would have been Otto von Bismarck (a Prussian), a clever if devious politician. Bismarck was a pragmatic individual and, following the significant part he played in achieving German unification under Hohenzollern rule, he used his diplomatic skills to maintain fairly good relations with most other European nations. His Triple Alliance of 1882 helping to control antagonism between Austria and Italy.

The strong influence of Prussian militarism tended towards the build-up of the German military. From about 1898 (Bismarck had been dismissed in 1890) the country embarked on the modernization and serious expansion of its navy; a project overseen by Admiral Alfred von Tirpitz the 'Father of the German navy'. Between 1874-1896 German military expenditure increased by about 50% (as did that of most other European nations), and its GNP was also increasing. It was during the next nearly two decades (to 1914) that military spending would increase significantly beyond the rise in GNP. Between 1880-1914 German military expenditure increased by 400%, compared with Britain and Russia 200%, and France 100%. A national mood was being fostered in all of these countries of admiration for the military and suspicion of the motives of other nations.

An indirect outcome of the nineteenth century consolidation of old and the formation of new nation-states was the uneasy inclusion of minority group within some of these – Irish (Fenians), Basque (Carlists), Spain (Catalans), France (Bretons), Belgium (Flemish), and some of the German speaking minorities of the Russian controlled

Baltic provinces, There were Polish speaking minorities in eastern Germany, and a mix of 'misplaced' peoples, principally: Kosovans, Serbs, Bosnians, Albanians, in the Balkans, and to the south-east Armenians, and the Kurds in Ottoman Turkey, Syria and Iraq. These had a geographic location connected with their minority status; so a sense of identity connected to place that would later provide a focus for campaigning for autonomy and experiencing conflict with others. Other, more dispersed minority groups included Gypsies (Sinta and Romany) and Jews. The former seem to have been prepared to find subsistence, to exist as a group, within the interstices of civil life – to live on the social and economic margins of any national society; earning a living by adapting their traditional occupations to changing economic circumstances – their collective identity being reinforced by their excluding otherness. For Jews, in some places complete assimilation or fairly close social integration was possible, in others they were reluctantly tolerated, whilst in a few they were actively persecuted. But in most of Europe they were treated as social inferiors and the butt of insults, pictured as caricatures of themselves, and blamed for all manner of economic ills. During the nineteenth century 'pogroms' had been carried out, the most well-known of which were the three pogroms (in effect massacres) that took place in Odessa 1821, 1849, 1859.

In the Far East at this time, Japanese interests, more specifically its wish to control Manchuria and Korea, were aggressively pursued when Japan declared war on China in 1894. A war that had been fermenting for some time, with the main disagreement being over Korea, at that time an autonomous state, nominally a co-protectorate of the Japanese and the Chinese but in fact more closely linked to China. In the background there was also Japanese suspicion of Russian intentions over northern China and the Korean Peninsula. A rebellion – the Tonghak Rebellion – was used by the Japanese as an excuse to declare war on China.

The Japanese won a decisive victory, with significant battles taking place around Seoul and Pyongyang, and surprising defeats of the

Chinese navy. The naval Battle of the Yalu was both a humiliation for the Chinese and a landmark in naval warfare; being one of the first naval battles in which ironclad ships and torpedoes were used. When they reached Lushun (Port Arthur) the Japanese found evidence that Japanese prisoners had been murdered and their bodies mutilated, with Japanese reaction being to slaughter almost all of the inhabitants of the port.

The Treaty of Shimonoseki (April. 1895) gave Japan control of Taiwan, part of the Pescadores (Peny Hu) Islands, and the strategically placed Liaodong Peninsular (sometimes called the 'Regent's Sword'); Korea becoming in effect a Japanese protectorate. But perhaps the most humiliating and economically damaging aspect of the settlement was the large Chinese indemnity payment, equivalent to about 150m US dollars.

European powers - as if a pack of jackals circling as they prepare to attack an already wounded beast - sought to take advantage of the Qing dynasty's weakness in order to gain more trading opportunities for themselves. In 1897 Germany annexed large parts of Shantang province. In 1898 Britain annexed the Wei-hai-wei Peninsula and gained control of the 'New Territories'. The Russians moved into the Liatung Peninsula which also allowed them control of the port of Lushun. Even the French were active, annexing the region of Kuang-chou-wan and symbolically gaining a stronger hold in the area of Indochina that would see both them and the US suffer military humiliation in the Vietnam War in the second half of the twentieth century. The increasing global ambitions of the US led them to also declare an interest in China towards the end of the nineteenth century.

China's reaction to these encroachments was a degree of internal dissatisfaction from students and others and a call for faster modernisation of its industry and its military. A nationalistic backlash was targeted at European interests, among the victims of which were Christian missionaries with about 30,000 Chinese Christian converts being killed, mostly by marauding mobs. The mobs were composed of members of the new anti-western 'Boxer' ('Righteous and Harmonious Fists') movement; a secret society into which members were initiated in a series of rituals and with certain physical exercises ('callisthenics') that they believed would give them protection against bullets. European punitive attempts to defeat the movement in fact contributed to its spreading, and by 1900 the Boxers controlled large areas of China, including Peking where they besieged the European compound (Legation Quarter) home to foreign diplomats and businessmen. The western powers (and Britain's Japanese ally) saw in the Boxers a significant threat to their financial (trading) interests so they put aside their own differences and in August 1900 an 'expeditionary' force (Austria-Hungary, Russian, British, French, Italian, American, but the majority of the 20,000 - some sources note 45,000 - troops were Japanese) marched on Peking (Beijing). This force destroyed many villages on their way to Peking as they waged war on the local population, and then on arrival proceeded to sack and loot the City (stealing a number of important Chinese historical artefacts), with thousands of Chinese civilians being killed. The subsequently signed Xinchou Treaty (its international status was in fact more protocol than treaty) was felt as a complete humiliation by the Chinese and one of a number of unequal treaties, with China having to pay a large sum in indemnity to each of the European nations and to agree to having European troops based in Peking. Taken overall, the impact of this period of turmoil was to significantly weaken the power of the Chinese government over some of the provinces and creating social and political conditions that would contribute to the revolution that took place in 1911. A revolution led by Sun Yet-sen who had founded a republican movement, which would later become the Kuomintang; taking power when it deposed the boy Emperor.

Late dynastic China was hardly a country that could be respected for its social and economic conditions, but during the final years of the nineteenth century we can see a clear example of opportunistic bullying of one nation by a group of others, as China fell victim to the trading and territorial ambitions of militarily more powerful nations. An alliance of industrialised nations combining to open up China to their trade as naked economic ambitions were being played out in the Far East.

Japan-Russian competition over Korea and Manchuria came to a head in February 1904 when the Japanese destroyed a Russian navel squadron moored in Port Arthur. In response Russia declared war on Japan. Given that Russia was an ally of France and Japan an ally of Britain this could have further tested the Anglo-French alliance, but a sense of greater common interests (the background reality of increasing German power) allowed the conflict to remain localised to the Far East. Indeed the French and British responded to this potential clash of strategic political interests by resolving some of their own colonial disagreements. The Japanese reinforced its land forces and Russia endeavoured to reinforce its Far Eastern army. Then, following a number of smaller clashes, a Russian force of 330,000 men fought a Japanese force of 270,000 men at Mukden over two weeks in early 1905. Casualties were high, with 90,000 Russians and 70,000 Japanese being killed.

Japanese success in this conflict was due partly to their own military skills and their modern equipment but also due to the significant logistical problems facing a Russia with its undoubted military might based mostly in the west and a lack of the means to easily deploy a sufficient amount of troops and equipment to the Far East. The extension of the Tran-Siberian railway (1901-04), through Manchuria to the Russian Port of Vladivostok, was built with agreement from China and but on completion there was insufficient rolling stock for substantial supplies to reach the Far Eastern army. The lumbering Baltic Fleet did eventually arrive in the region, only to be defeated by the Japanese in the Battle of Tsushima Strait (May 27th 1905).

An offer of mediation by US President Theodore Roosevelt was accepted and the subsequent Treaty of Portsmouth (Sept. 1905) settled control of Manchuria in favour of China with Japanese control of Korea being accepted. Russian expansionist moves to advance its ambitions in the Far East had been halted and the humiliation of this conflict contributed to the fermenting anti-tsarist/revolutionary activity in its major cities. Relatively few Russians cared about a war being waged 7,500 miles from St. Petersburg but many were incensed by the military humiliation.

As the new century began the nation that had been the midwife to the industrial revolution, and which had accumulated the largest Empire, was paying the price of colonization. Britain was at odds with the settlers of Dutch origin who resisted British control in South Africa. Where, since Britain had displaced the Dutch from the Cape in 1806, it had served them as a key provisioning point on the long journey to more important imperial interests in India and the Far East. A hardy collection of mainly Dutch and some British settlers enabled the spread of settlements northwards. When, from 1833, Britain ended slavery in its colonies (even if it would introduce racial segregation in South Africa in 1828) Dutch farmers, the Afrikaners (Boers), wanting more freedom from British control, a freedom that included the right to keep slaves, embarked on the 'Great Trek' taking them further into the heart of southern Africa. Fighting Zulus (of the Nguni tribe) along the way, as they ruthlessly occupied native lands. These 'Voortrekkers' founded the political entities of the Orange Free State (OFS) and the Transvaal. Given that the whole colony was a cost to the British exchequer, British interest in the colony was low and initially it accepted the establishment of the Afrikaans Republics to the north.

The British view changed markedly when the discovery in the late 1860s of commercially viable deposits of gold and diamonds significantly altered the financial prospects for the colony. The productive diamond mines at Kimberly were within the OFS, a region that was annexed by Britain in 1871, with the State's government reluctantly having to accept £90,000 in compensation. The labour intensive activity of mining, along with shortages of white workers, led to a high level of native employment. Although having to live away from their families, and being paid less than white workers, they were able to earn sufficient to purchase modern rifles and gain a certain status within their home communities.

The 1870s and 80s had seen the rise of a number of mining magnates working for companies such as De-Beers and Wernher, Beit, & Co. One of these magnates being Cecil Rhodes (others were Alfred Beit and Julius Wernher) who by 1890 had already made a personal fortune and was a rising politician. Rhodes allied a sharp business brain and a generally acute political understand to overarching personal ambition. A combination of factors that led him, in 1890, to organize (he did not actually take part) a second Great Trek, one intent on extending white occupation even further north into Mashonaland. This trek was much more an invading force made up of a ragbag collection of white adventurers, prospectors, tradesmen (bakers, butchers, engineers) some wanting to settle, most seeking an easy fortune… unlike the Boer trek which had been undertaken by a more homogenous group of farmers along with wives and children – seeking land and freedom.

The adventure was successful due to a mix of clever negotiations, and lies about their intentions told to local tribes led by the dominant King Lobengula of the Ndebele. This new country that Rhodes had established in the name of Britain he modestly named 'Rhodesia'. Soon after this Rhodes was persuaded by Dr Jameson, the administrator of Rhodesia, to fund an expeditionary force to attack the Ndebele and gain Matabeleland. The militaristic socialization of the Ndebele culture was their downfall. The impis of young men had been sating their bloodlust (a key aspect of gaining status within their tribal groups) by raiding into the lands of more peaceful peoples north of the Zambezi. But they came to view their main enemy as being land-hungry white men and were eager to test themselves and their protective 'magic' against this threat.

The incident that was to precipitate the defeat of the Ndebele occurred when a Shona raiding party from Mashonaland (part of Rhodesia) crossed the border into Matabeleland and stole some Ndebele cattle. They were chased back into Mashonaland by a large group of Ndebele - who still had the right, at least theoretically, to punish this type of lawbreaking - and the Shona group was caught and then massacred within sight of the town of Fort Victoria. This act in itself caused a wave of shock to run through the white community…..a shock made worse when the excited Ndebele then killed or carried off a number of black servants from white homes, and also stole some white-owned livestock.

This raid into Mashonaland formed the basis of a stream of propaganda casting the Ndebele as a threat that was linked to unfounded ambitions attributed to Lobengula. This manufactured threat of a 'native uprising' caused Sir Henry Lock, the British High Commissioner in the Cape (misled by the propaganda and by the duplicity of Rhodes) to prepare an official British force to be used to punish Ndebele aggression.

But by the time this force mobilized and had reached Lubengula's capital of Bulawayo Jameson's force had already invaded (Oct. 1893) Matabeleland and, armed with superior weapons, had defeated the foolishly 'brave' Ndebele impis. It had then moved on to occupy a Bulawayo from which Lubengula and most of its population had fled. A few weeks later the King, by then convinced of the comprehensive defeat inflicted on his people, committed suicide. It had cost Rhodes the lives of 50 of his men and just £50,000 to double the size of Rhodesia.

The history of more or less British controlled South Africa from this time was characterized by a white population for the most part prospering in a social structure that was designed to significantly favour whites; being 'fearful' of a black population outnumbering them by about 10 to 1. An imbalance of economic advantages to whites, with the potential political strength of blacks being contained by a social milieu that fostered ideas of racial superiority, with a clever manipulation of antagonisms between black (then later also 'coloured') groups, along with oppressive laws applied with determination and when required the use of force. On the streets the 'jambok' was liberally wielded to encourage compliance and to discourage protest.

In Rhodesia, the victorious Company (Rhodes's chartered British South Africa Company) interpreted international law to mean that it now 'owned' the whole of the conquered lands over which Lobengula had ruled as king. Jameson's men set about extracting their personal due (under the Victoria agreement), many taking 6,000 acre landholdings incorporating the most fertile faming land. The Ndebele (when not warriors were farmers and herders) were in effect dispossessed of their most valued properties; their land and cattle. Estimates suggest about 300,000 head of Ndebele cattle were taken possession of by the Company, rustled by whites raiding from the Transvaal, or stolen by traditional enemies such as the Shona. The Ndebele had lost their status as proud warriors and to a significant degree their ability to maintain themselves and their families. They were forced to labour for the white-man, a role that would be the fate of most blacks in Southern Africa for the next 100 years, during which justifiable resentment bubbled under the surface. The Shona, although freed from the power of the Ndebele, also felt the pressures of the white government. In particular a 'hut tax' was introduced and some of their own prize cattle taken by the company on the crude pretext that they might just have been some of those stolen from the Ndebele.

In the last decade of the century Rhodes and representatives of other business interests were pressuring Britain to extend its control in SA but of more significance to Britain was the threat of the rising European power of a Germany engaged in extending its influence to the north west of Britain's South African colony.

The antagonism between Britain and the Boers had festered. The former being uneasy about the rising strength of the Boers and frustrated at their unwillingness to become part of the British Empire. The latter, united by their religion, ethnic identity (including a shared Dutch language) and recent shared pioneering community history. This, along with a fiercely independent collective temperament contributed to their being unwilling to give up their independence. The British High Commission and The Colonial Office (especially Joeseph Chamberlain) were continually being badgered, mislead and lied to, by Rhodes as he pursued his long-term ambition of a Federation of the whole of South Africa under British rule (and Rhodes's control). Other SA business men were concerned about Boer control over some trade routes, along with their also wanting easier access to the increasing mineral wealth (gold and precious stones) of the Boer Republics.

Towards the century's end tensions increased, with British public opinion being fed exaggerated information on how British immigrants

(Uitlanders) within the Boer republics were being badly treated.

An attempt at negotiations on areas of disagreement was started in May 1899, with Sir Alfred Milner (British High Commissioner) leading for the British and Paul Kruger leading for the Boers. These negotiations soon stalled, not least due to the Boers being sensitive to the British Government's attempt of stir up British public opinion against them; framing the dispute as both the victimization of British citizens (the Uitlanders) and a challenge to the imperial right of Britain to rule southern Africa. The obduracy of the Boers, as perceived by the British cabinet, some newspapers, and a section of the British population, gave the British government an excuse to begin sending troop reinforcements to the Cape; most of the first 10,000 coming from India.

The British High Commission, Rhodes, and most of the powerful British business and financial interests in SA, wanted to ensure British domination over the Boers. The British military establishment wanted war, not least as an opportunity to keep the army on its mettle but also to avenge the earlier military humiliation suffered at the hands of the Boers. This, along with a jingoistic mood of the British population, (stirred by much of the right-wing press) combined to pressure the British Government towards decisive action. The Liberal and Labour parties, and a significant proportion of the population, shared the view that the Government's actions in SA amounted to imperial bullying and argued that conflict could and should be avoided.

But by early autumn the Boer leadership felt that war was inevitable and when they learned that a second wave of 47,000 troops were to follow the first 10,000 they decided to act. The war began on 12th October when a large well-armed Boer force advanced into northern Natal and by early 1900, following a series of successful skirmishes, the Boers, led by Louis Botha and Jan Smuts, laid siege to the British garrison towns of Mafekin, Kimberly, and Ladysmith. A Christian god was called upon to bless and protect the Boers as they set out to invade Natal just as the same Christian god was called upon to bless and protect the British troops that departed from Southampton in order to progress the war.

As reinforcements arrived to strengthen the British side, the tide of war steadily flowed against the Boers. By mid 1900 the British had relieved the besieged garrisons and had occupied the Boer capital of Pretoria. At the Battle of Bergendal on 27th August the Boers suffered a significant defeat; with Kruger fleeing to Portuguese controlled Mozambique. For this and his other military actions in South Africa Lord Roberts, in charge of the British force, was awarded a gift of £100,000 and raised in social prestige with his promotion to an earldom.

In the face of the obvious strength of their enemy in conventional warfare the Boers changed tactics, avoiding mass battles and turning instead to guerrilla 'hit and run' warfare. This phase of the conflict illustrates how a determined force adopting tactics of harassment could, with some measure of success, hold off a significantly superior military force. British frustration at being unable to make significant military progress led to Lord Kitchener (Chief of Staff) ordering the adoption of a brutal 'scorched earth' policy. This meant that whilst the Boer men-folk were away fighting, their homes and crops would be destroyed, their animals killed and their families - the elderly, the wives and the children along with servants and their families - turned out to survive as best they could in the inhospitable veldt. Later on, displaced families were increasingly confined in concentration camps – an inglorious act of revenge. It was in these camps that most of the Afrikaans civilians died. The camps were overcrowded, disease-ridden, enclosures populated with semi-starving victims, able to access only very limited medical aid. The plight of the Boer women and children was brought to the public's attention by Emily Hobhouse when she highlighted the high mortality rate among civilian Boers. In a somewhat shamefaced response to public outrage in both Britain and mainland Europe the government set up a 'Ladies Commission' headed by Dame Millicent Fawcett. Her report on the situation was a systematic outline confirming Hobhouses's accusations. The Fawcett Report recorded in some detail the grim conditions that pertained in the camps. At their peak they held 111,619 whites, and 43,780 'coloured' people, imprisoned in unsanitary, disease-ridden conditions.

British military strength gradually wore down the Boers and towards the end of the conflict about 5,000 Boers were in fact fighting on the British side. Peace was agreed, by Great Britain on one side and the South African Republic (Transvaal) and The Orange Free State on the other, at Vereeniging at the end of May 1902; with a Treaty being signed later on in Pretoria (the 'Treaty of Vereeniging'). This settlement still left blacks without a vote in the two republics, unlike the by then franchised blacks in Cape Colony. After a period of British military rule, both of the Boer republics were granted conditional self-government as colonies of Great Britain; with South Africa being united into one country in 1910.

The Anglo/Boer war cost Britain 22,000 lives, £200 million, and a large measure of international humiliation. On the Boer side 7,000 fighting men were lost, 28,000 women and children died in the concentration camps, and 14,000 native South Africans also died. In historical terms just another small war but its significance lay in its being an imperial war fought at the century's beginning by the nation that led the world into the industrial revolution at the start of the previous century. A war, the worst aspect of which was that it was a conflict fought primarily to advance the business interests of a small clique of men, and to defend the 'national ego' of Britain. The background to the war illustrates layers of evil being expressed during the nineteenth century as the British fought the Boers who held their lands owing to their killing and taking land from the Zulus who had in turn taken the land from and killed other less aggressive native peoples.

In the British tradition of rewarding its military leaders, Kitchener was given the then small fortune of £50,000 (most of which he used to buy shares in South African gold mining) and made a viscount for his part in the war. On the other hand when, at the war's end, the ordinary troops returned to Britain many encountered unemployment and poverty, if somewhat alleviated by demeaning charitable support.

The early years of the twentieth century would see a significant amount of industrial resources being directed to an arms race between the leading European nations, swelling the material means for the great evil that would find expression in WW1. 'The War to Defend Civilization' were the words that would be stamped on the British campaign medals, but it would be a war that in defending civilization did in fact leave vast swaths of territory across which the battles were fought as but wastelands of cratered mud, strewn with unexploded ordinance (one in every three shells failed to explode) and dotted with the skeletal remnants of scorched trees. Invariably, the war also left despair all across the continent in the millions of homes grieving sons that had died.

So how could the civil nations of Europe have gotten to the point of throwing themselves at each other at such great material and human cost? War – a time when the best of civil life is put to one side and the historically ever-present evil underbelly of civil life is exposed to unleash itself in an inhuman (but paradoxically all too human) paroxysm of violence.

Seeking for the more fundamental causes of a single historical conflict such as WW1 would takes us into the biological constitution, the underlying psychological characteristics (certainly of the leading individuals), the effect of collective behaviours (tainted by the phenomenon of in-group/out-group antagonisms as a source of separation), and a range of economic, historical, and social factors that would have developed in complex systems of interaction operating over long periods of time. I will come back to these potentially causative factors in the Conclusion, but for now I am only going to offer a fairly superficial (this does not mean untrue) level of analysis. One that echoes most standard 'histories' covering the period from the end of the nineteenth century up to the outbreak of war.

If we wish to identify a more fundamental cause of war, lying in the depths of humankind's collective psyche, then we will need to step back and gain a more evolutionary perspective……war is a primary characteristic of the 'self-conscious' stage of humankind's evolutionary development (as is evil itself) and creating the conditions that foster progress to the next stage (I term 'world-consciousness' - and a post warfare world) continues as a possible future. If one dependent on our species being able to design out conflict from international relations; with peace rather than war as a default mode for disagreements unresolved by diplomacy, and a willingness of nation-states to accept decisions on any issue made by a legitimate international body. More than this, the very idea of nation-states should be under scrutiny and we should be asking......can we advance civil organization beyond the 'othering' tendency inherent in the notion of nation states?

By 1900 the economically developed nations had industrialized the means of warfare including: conscript armies, officer training in military colleges, and the actions required to turn a nation's peacetime economy into a wartime economy. The basic element for the national mobilization for total warfare had taken place; military preparedness changed from being seen as a burden on the taxpayers, so one on which expenses were to be kept to a minimum to, by the end of the century, armed forces being accepted as necessary to protect trading interests and to enhance national pride.

The 'Concert of Europe', was a regulatory system established in the nineteenth century that pertained from 1815-1848 and then from 1871-1914. Initially known as the Vienna Settlement, this was a series of treaties that would reinforce the position of the five 'Great Powers' - Britain, France, Germany, Russia, and Austria. Allowing a certain level of security and independence and was intended to reduce the potential for their fighting each other. This 'Concert' formed the basic political framework for much of Europe in the nineteenth century. As the century progressed there was at least some acceptance of the value of diplomacy for sharing national perspectives on issues and as a process of identifying and negotiating the means of resolving these.

A cynic might suggest that the underlying rationale of holding this agreement together was at least the perception by the leading nations of a rough balance of military power, so encouraging them to accept a more certain if uneasy peace over the uncertain outcomes of war. But militarism was perhaps the most prominent feature of the industrially developed nations during the last quarter of the nineteenth and early years of the twentieth centuries. An incessant determination to develop and deploy ever more powerful weaponry saw soldiers by 1900 armed with modern bolt-action/magazine-fed rifles (Lea Enfield and Mauzers) able to kill at 1400 meters, and infantry with steel field-guns able to fire shells up to 5,000 metres, along with machine guns, dynamite, and barbed wire.

These developments on their own making the close-range battles characteristic of earlier nineteenth century wars no longer viable, now the military advantage shifted towards the well-prepared defender. Navies were becoming equipped with enormous Dreadnought battleships (first built 1905) protected by armour plating from 4-24 inches thick and able to fire shells of up to 12 inch calibre (they would be even bigger later in WWI). Driving these behemoth's through the seas were the considerably more efficient rotary turbine engines. Their being preferred to the up/down motion of reciprocating engines which were less suitable for moving heavy loads at higher speeds. Rotary engines, increasingly powered by oil instead of coal, were able to power the heavy Dreadnoughts through the water at speeds up to 21 knots. Wireless telegraphy, introduced from 1900, made for a significant improvement in communication between ships at sea and their shore bases. The industrially developed nation-states of Europe were in a position to organise, militarily, politically, economically, and now also socially, for total war.

Military expenses of the 'Great Powers' (Russia, Britain, France, Germany Austria-Hungary, Italy) rose from £132m in 1880 to £205m in 1900 and to £397m on the eve of WWI ('The Times Atlas of the World' 1978, p250 cited in E.Hobsbawm, 1987, p350). A rise whose material presence can be seen in the building of warships.

The number of battleships launched annually between 1900-1914 being:

Britain:	49-1900	to	64-1914
Germany:	14-1900	to	40-1914
Russia:	16-1900	to	23-1914
France:	23-1900	to	28-1914
Austria-Hungary:	6-1900	to	16-1914

In recognition of a bristling military and the increasing risk of war, the first Hague Peace Conference (1898) was called to '…..consider disarmament and to promote judicial arbitration of international disputes'. The Second Hague Peace Conference 1907 '…..drafted rules to limit the horrors of modern warfare' (Best et al 2004).

But the role of governments was perceived by themselves to be primarily in protecting trade, generally irrespective of the interests of those being traded with. A clear example (noted above) being the British Governments willingness to defend its merchants 'rights' to trade opium to the Chinese from 1839. When a reluctant Lord Melbourne (British P.M.) allowed himself to be, in effect, blackmailed by Captain Charles Elliot (British trade supervisor at Guangzhou) and supported by the lobbying of British big businessmen, into paying the then vast sum of £2m as compensation to British drug dealers whose goods (1700 tons of opium) had been confiscated by a Chinese Government concerned about the debilitating effect the drug trade was having on the increasing number of Chinese people smoking opium. The British then sent a naval force to China to enforce its request for reimbursing the funds paid to the 'respectable' British drug runners. The outcome being China having to agree to humiliating treaty terms, which included it being forced to open up to foreign traders, including those trading in opium. And the British invasion of Egypt in 1882 seems to have been due to the Egyptian Government's threat to refuse payments for British holders of Egyptian Government Bonds - in which Prime Minster Gladstone was himself an investor. Just two examples of the many times that Britain, similar to other western European nations, and the US used, or threatened to use, military action to open markets or to otherwise protect the interests of wealthy investors.

As the First World War approached, the ruling elites in the opposing nations mobilized a patriotic propaganda campaign - one redolent with flags, military show, Royal families re-presented as kindly hallowed national parent-figures, shared romanticized histories, and various other ways cleverly deployed to manipulate a population towards a sense of shared national identity and a generalised suspicion of the 'other' (the foreigner). In sum: a mendacious preparedness for yet another unnecessary war.

The hate-filled ramparts formed by xenophobic national mythologies were artfully constructed; if mostly produced by an informal collusion involving politicians, the populist mass media, as well as schools, the churches, and even some trades union leaders. It was against these patriotic ramparts that the emerging if tentative links of international working-class solidarity were torn apart, never to be effectively rebuilt and developed into what might have been. This informal conspiracy of patriotic propagandizing was offered to largely receptive audiences within the populations of European nations. As C.A.Bayly (2004, p280) rightly pointed out: 'In fact nationalism and patriotism also drew on more profound desires and aspirations, outside the purview of the state, which had in earlier times often been attached to family, clan or religious groups'.

I would add 'tribe' 'club' and 'class' to this list - indeed any of the many identity-based groupings characterised by in-group solidarity and out-group antipathy.

The frayed threads of working class internationalism would be at least partially reconnected after the war, indeed there was a Third International. But the impact of the primacy given to nationalism over internationalism during the war had eroded global working class solidarity, and had undermined the aspiration for any significant global organization of workers. When the threads were picked up again in the 1920s it would be under the guidance of the Soviet Union and so became an internationalism tainted by direct association with a type of dictatorial elite-based communism.

The political context for war.

In July 1908 a group of disaffected young Ottoman army officers based in the garrison at Thessaloniki rebelled. Amongst these officers was Mustapha Kemal, a future leader of what was to become the Turkish Republic. One of the reforms that these 'Young Turks' campaigned for was to allow more autonomy for all national groups within the Ottoman Empire. Taking advantage of the disruption in the south-east of the Empire a number of these national groups took action – Cretans sought union with Greece - Bulgaria proclaimed independence – Austria-Hungary annexed Bosnia-Hercegovina causing the Serbs (supported by Russia) to reacted angrily. German pressure forced Russia to accept the annexation and in turn the Serbs had, if very reluctantly, to yield to the new political reality. These regional upheavals – in effect leaving the 1878 Treaty of Berlin in tatters - in the context of already heightened level of tension across Europe, would bring the whole continent to the brink of war.

A period of uneasy peace with occasional outbreaks of guerrilla activity was maintained up to 1912. In the two years leading up to the First World War, Turkey (regions of Thrace and Macedonia) was attacked, initially by Montenegrin troops who were within days joined by troops from Greece, Serbia and Bulgaria; driving the Turks out of Albania, Macedonia and Kosovo; which then declared themselves independent. But then Bulgaria was attacked by its former ally Serbia, supported by Greece and Romania; with Serbia then moving to occupy Kosovo and Macedonia. These conflicts, in the First Balkan War, were characterised by revenge killing, widespread rape, and the process that came to be termed 'ethnic cleansing', as different ethnic groups fought to avenge what were perceived as past injustices or to obtain more territory. Inter-group hatred, suspicion, and fear, was fermented by those seeking political control and/or economic advance.

But behind these regional tensions were the Great Powers operating in support of this or that favoured Balkan client state; adopted mostly in line with wider European alliances. This period of conflict substantially brought an end to the Ottoman rule in Europe. The two most significant outbursts of conflict were temporarily controlled by the Treaty of London (Dec.1912) and then the Treaty of Bucharest (Aug. 1913), but the level of inter-ethnic tension, with no real attempts by leaders to resolve divisive issues, was palpable. Written histories assessing the political relationship between ethnic groups in the region at the time use phrases such as 'tinderbox' 'explosive cocktail' 'hotbed of tensions'… I will add another 'a heated cauldron of ethnic-based nationalist discontents'...... to capture a sense of the pent up hatred that would be released and expressed in the descent into civil madness that would take place from 1914.

Between 1912-13 the Balkan Albanians had sided with the Turks and fought with them against the Serbs. But the Serbs proved to be the superior force managing to expel the Turks and, as the Turkish army retreated from Kosovo, the advancing Serbs massacred about 25,000 Albanians.

The Armenian peoples of the region abutting eastern Turkey have a history interlinked with the history of civil life in the Middle-East. Their lands were criss-crossed by trade routes between Eastern Europe and the Middle East. As long as 3000 years ago they have been identified as traders and agriculturalists. In response to the Seljuk Turk (Sunni Muslims) invasions in the eleventh century many Armenians fled to settle in southern Turkey and it was here that the Ruberian Dynasty established their new kingdom, with its capital in Tarsus. During this period (1078-1375) Armenian art and literature flourished. Throughout the time of the Crusades Christian Armenians had supported the European Crusaders in their campaigns against the Moslems. The break-up of the Cilician Kingdom saw the first significant Diaspora of Armenians when, following Tamberlaine's invasion of Cilicia, 30,000 of the wealthiest Armenians fled to Cyprus. By the nineteenth century most Armenians were living within the Ottoman Empire with the majority Christians among them being subject to the Moslem dhimmi system that allowed non-Moslems to practice their faiths but having fewer political and civil rights; including the right to bear arms or even to ride horses. The Armenians as Christians, and more so as Christians strategically positioned in relation to the politically unsettled Southern European region, enjoyed some support from France, Great Britain, and Russia, who all supported the Armenian campaign for political reform.

The Ottoman Empire had made some concessions in 1839. A move that only encouraged calls, in the 1860s and 1870s, for further reforms and for action to be taken against Kurdish and Circassian tribesmen who had repeatedly attacked Armenian villages; committing numerous acts of looting, rape, and murder. Following the 1877-1878 Russo-Turkish war the Russians agreed to withdraw from Ottoman lands gained during the conflict on condition that the persecution of the Armenians ceased and civic reforms were enacted. It was during these treaty negotiations that the Armenians began to campaign for the status of an autonomous region within the Ottoman Empire.

The uneasy relationship between Armenians and Ottoman Turks increased once the 'Treaty of Berlin' had been agreed, with the ruling Sultan Abdul Hamid II endeavouring to obstruct the implementation of reforms set out in Article 61 of the Treaty. In 1890 Hamid II created the para-military unit 'Hamidge', composed mostly of Kurds. And between 1894-96 this unit engaged in the officially sanctioned persecution of Armenians. Persecution to the extent of looting property, murder, and on occasion rape – it has been estimated that as many as 300,000 Armenians were killed in what became known as the Hamidian massacres. Although the Great Powers, previously supporters of the Armenians, were well aware of what was going on (western newspapers carried headlines calling Hamid 'The Bloody Sultan' and 'The Great Assassin') they now decided that their political interests would be best served by non-intervention.

Yet another massacre took place following an unsuccessful attempt to launch a counter revolution in 1909 when the Armenians were taken to have sided with those wishing to overthrow the regime set up during the 1908 Young Turk revolution. Reprisals against the Armenians saw up to 30,000 being killed in what became known as the Adana Massacre. These events did little to suppress the aspirations of the Armenians and a group in the north rose in rebellion; requiring the deployment of 20,000 Ottoman troops to regain control.

The first Balkan war in 1912 had changed the map of the region. Greece, Bulgaria, Montenegro and Serbia had all gained land and most of this at the expense of Ottoman Turkey, and of the Albanians who had just established their own state. 'The Congress of Ambassadors' held in London had resulted in the Balkan nations reluctant recognition of the newly established Albanian state but their own gains from the Congress led to what was in effect the partition of the Albanian peoples. About half of Albanians lived within the new Albania and the other half lived in lands now controlled by other Balkan states. States that, whilst pleased to gain the land, did not want the Albanians.

From 1912-15 Serbia, Montenegro, and Greece, in effect, carried out policies that would amount to 'ethnic cleansing'. The Serbian and Montenegrin armies burnt villages, chased thousands of inhabitants from their farms, villages, and towns, imprisoned many in concentration camps and, in October 1912 the Serbs killed 5,000 Albanians at Pristine. As the Albanians were expelled the Montenegrin and Serbian settlers were moved in to occupy the 'cleansed' farmlands and villages. A steady 'tit for tat 'of genocidal activity – in fact political policy – would continue with periods of more or less violence up to the outbreak of WW2. To be ferociously reignited in the final decades of the twentieth century.

The Balkan region of south-eastern Europe was further unsettled following two local wars; the first involving Serbia, Bulgaria and Greece – the Balkan League - combining to drive the Ottoman Turks out of south Europe and the second, an unhappy Bulgaria at war with its two former allies to progress its demand for more territory. Few if any of the leading nations of this region – Serbia, Bulgaria, Greece, Albania, Croatia, Montenegro, Macedonia, Romania, Slovenia (and indeed the Ottoman Turks) - were at ease with the then existing territorial arrangements. It is hardly an understatement to suggest that for the leaders (and much of the populations) of these groups, the Balkans seethed with ethnicity-based territorial discontent.

It was a matter of when rather than if discontent would be expressed in more extensive armed conflict, and the when turned out to be triggered by the assassination on 28th July 1914 of the heir to the Habsburg crown Archduke Franz Ferdinand (and his wife) by a couple of young Serbian nationalists. Franz Ferdinand had been dispatched to assist in the negotiation of a peace that would allow for the Slavic peoples on the southern part of the region to have greater political voice, especially in Serbia itself. Considered in the wider political context of mutual distrust, of nations bristling with modern armaments, led by politicians operating at the nation equivalent level of 'self-consciousness' (so imbued with national egoism – linked within tropes redolent of suspicion, competition, and conflict), a relatively trivial act of some sort was almost bound to trigger warfare.

Following the assassination (and encouraged by Germany) Austria then declared war on Serbia and began shelling Belgrade; such was the ethnic diversity of the Austria-Hungarian Empire that the mobilization orders had to be issued in twenty different languages. Russia mobilized its army to support Serbia then, on 1st August Germany declared war on Russia, The conflict spread when, on 3rd August Germany declared war on France and informed Belgium that it would have to accept invasion as part of Germany's strategy to attack the French. Great Britain then declared war on Germany and Austro-Hungary, claiming to defend, as newspapers put it, 'little Belgium' from German aggression. So it took but a week or so to launch a war that had been fomenting for at least ten years, but the context for which had been created in the nationalism, industrialism, military technological development, and a competitive capitalist economic system developing in the second half of the nineteenth century.

The ethnic divisions between and within nations in the Balkans (south east Europe) continues to be the most obvious way of framing the causes underlying the series of bloody, if regionally contained, Balkan wars. But there were more 'banal' reasons for WW1 related to the intentions of the Great Powers (Austria, Russia, Germany, France, Britain, and Italy) to advance their own strategic trading interests. This, along with the belief of some of the leading military high command that modern supply systems, military tactics (e.g. Germany's Schlieffen Plan), and modern weaponry, would allow short sharp wars favouring those sufficiently bold to commit adequate resources and to strike first.

Nation-statehood was not of course a requirement for conflict between peoples but it is a powerful form for marking out ('constructing') the type of collective identities that facilitate the mobilization of populations for war. There is the underlying identity difference of 'them and us' that a range of research has suggested that simply identifying a difference between groups can in itself foster inter-group pre-conditions for conflict. Whilst nation state-hood itself is not the only cause of inter-group conflict but it does provide yet another factor (along with religion, ethnicity, tribe, caste, class, etc) that allows the form of differentiation inherent in collective identities and can foster the perception of a group's 'imagined' shared interests. The resources available to nation-states can facilitate warfare in ways that would be quite difficult for small groups for whom conflict tends to be limited in casualties and geographically localised. A.C.Grayling in his book of popular philosophy 'The Meaning of Things' (2001 page 78), wrote about nationalism: *'The idea of nationalism turns on that of 'nation'. The word is meaningless: all 'nations' are mongrel, a mixture of so many immigrations and mixings of peoples over time that the idea of ethnicity is largely comical except in places where the boast has to be either that the community there remained so remote and disengaged, or so conquered, for the greater part of history, that it succeeded in keeping its gene pool 'pure' (a cynic might say 'inbred')………….Nations are artificial constructs, their boundaries drawn in the blood of past years…..'*

Eric Hobsbawm (1987, p105) commented in the national mood at the time (1890-1914): 'Political life thus found itself increasingly ritualized and filled with symbols and publicity appeals, both overt and subliminal. As the ancient ways - mainly religious - of ensuring subordination, obedience and loyalty were eroded, the now patent need for something to replace them was met by the *invention* of tradition, using both old and tried evokers of emotion such as crown and military glory and, …………., new ones such as empire and colonial conquest.'

On the whole a successful strategy, one expressed in patriotic enthusiasm when a generation of young men from different nations were so easily persuaded to kill and maim each other by politicians (backed by industrialists and some influential newspaper proprietors) at the start of the First World War, was to show. Due to industrialized nations being able to deploy massive financial, administrative, and propaganda resources to justify conflict, the outcomes, apart from a divided world, has been mass killing of soldiers and civilians; if, in terms of numbers, the latter has been more significant in the twentieth century.

If avoidable killing is evil then it was evil indeed that was the redolent characteristic reflected in events that took place from 1914 across what would soon become the tree denuded, shell cratered landscapes strewn with glinting threads of barbed wire, and the stench-ridden, rat-infested, and more often water-logged, trenches. Landscapes torn by the ear splitting noise of cannonade, the phosphorous flash of bursting shells, the zinging sniper's bullet, a steady stream of lead pouring from machine guns, the poison gas-induced choking as the delicate lining of gasping lungs were perforated, the pitiful cries of wounded and dying men.... the very wretchedness of warfare. All contributing to inducing the collective fear that must have gripped the bellies of thousands of soldiers in the eerily quiet moments leading up to the eruptions of live conflict. With images of home forming in their minds as they unready, hoped to live, but necessarily prepared to die.

A multiplicity of more significant and less significant decisions brought the military forces of Axis ('Central Powers') and Allied ('Entente Powers') nations together, each bristling with newly produced weaponry.

Europe's 'civilized' countries, collectively hypnotized with their gaze fixed on their nationalistic aims, were prepared to aggressively advance or aggressively defend the ambitions of their military/political leadership. But to note that they must have been collectively hypnotised, is to deny the element of human agency that would have been an active presence throughout the whole decision-making processes leading to conflict.

From 28th July 1914 the spark that began the process of actual warfare had been struck. What might be judged as a certain level of rational endeavour had long been building – the clanking choreography of military preparation, generals and government ministers considering numerous 'what if' scenarios, planning according to knowledge of the potential enemy's military strengths and according to suspicion infused interpretations of the enemy's intentions.

The recruitment and mobilization of hundreds of thousands of young men and the rain of propaganda directed towards populations in order to persuade them of the justification of war was but the culmination of such preparations.

The events that were to be played out on the world's oceans and on the death-blasted fields, heaths, and woodland landscapes across Europe, can surely only be defined as irrationality in its most distilled form. Not just the irrationality of this or that ill-thought out choice, of this or that stupid action, but four years of collective irrationality bordering on the profound, teetering on the incomprehensible to anyone who approaches the world with a humanistic sense of values.

What could justify millions of young men that historical circumstances, economic greed, and political limitations, had caused to form up on two opposed sides whose artillery then engaged in hurling thousands[21] of tons of shells whistling across the divide.

These massive bombardments then being followed by wave after wave of troops, tramping resignedly towards defenders, to meet, then pour tons and tons of bullets, grenades, and at times clouds of poison gas, onto each other. If we add the relentless toll taken by diseases of the trenches we have a death-toll of 10 million.

The suicidal stupidity of Passendale, the heroic stupidity of Gallipoli, the string of murderous confrontations along the eastern front. One can call up a gallery of images symbolising the depressing folly of war – the central weakness of the self-consciousness level of human thinking: selfishness (individual and group), narrowness of focus, the tendency to irrationality (misjudging outcomes and refusing to calculate/assess longer-term interests), the cognitively soothing

---

[21] At start of the war the French alone had a stock of 5,000,000 artillery shells, by 1916 they were using this amount of shells every month, and by 1918 it reached 10,000,000 per month.

decisions to decide on a course of action; action itself eases cognitive dissonance for individuals, groups and governments, on any issue. The various forms of human thinking focused on but narrowly elitist conceptions of self-interests.

The war at sea also developed, with the German and British fleets manoeuvring around each other, engaging at times – as ponderous Dreadnought battleships hurled 12 inch calibre shells, each weighing half a ton, across miles of water, most landing in the sea (as with most loosed munitions, an expensive waste, if a satisfactory outcome). But with those relatively few, but still too many, finding their intended targets tangling, melting, and distorting metal. Killing and mutilating soft-fleshed bodies, a torrid scene engulfed in red-hot fire until the wounded ship slid, hissing streams of steam, beneath the surface of the sea; to leak extended wisps of thick black oil down to today.

A new type of sea warfare was introduced during WW1, with the submarine. Submarines had been deployed to a minimal extent as far back as the US Civil War. But WW1 saw the submarine become an effective weapon when deployed against both military and merchant naval targets – extending warfare to beneath the oceans. In a little known novel 'The Undying Fire', published in 1931, H.G. Wells wrote a section based on submarine warfare, describing outcomes and lucidly suggesting some underlying threads/sinews making up the nationalist structures that lead to man taking up arms against man.

I think it is worth quoting this at length:

Wells takes up his story… *"Take some poor German boy with an ordinary sort of intelligence, and ordinary human disposition to kindliness, and some gallantry, who becomes finally a sailor in one of these craft. Consider his case and what we do to him. You will find in him a sample of what we are doing for mankind. As a child he is ingenuous, teachable, plastic. He is also egotistical, greedy, and suspicious. He is easily led and easily frightened. He likes making things if he knows how to make them; he is capable of affection and capable of resentment. He is a sheet of white paper upon which anything may be written. His parents teach him, his companions, his school. Do they teach him anything of the great history of mankind?*

Do they teach him of his blood brotherhood with all men? Do they tell him anything of discovery, of exploration, of human effort and achievement? No. They teach him that he belongs to a blonde and wonderful race, the only race that matters on this planet. …..And these teachers incite him to suspicion and hatred and contempt of all other races. They fill his mind with fears and hostilities. Everything German they tell him is good and splendid. Everything not German is dangerous and wicked.

The boy grows up a mental cripple; his capacity for devotion and self-sacrifice is run into a mould of fanatical loyalty for the Kaiser and hatred for foreign things. Comes this war, and the youngster is only too eager to give himself where he is most needed. He is told that the submarine war is the sure way of striking the enemies of his country a conclusive blow.

Let me go on with the story of the youngster……Comes a day when he realises the reality of the work he is doing for his kind. He stands by one of the guns of the submarine in an attack upon some wretched ocean tramp. He realises that the war he wages is no heroic attack on pride or pre-dominance, but a mere murdering of traffic. He sees the little ship shelled, the luckless men killed and wounded, no tyrants of the seas but sailor-men like himself; he sees their boats smashed to pieces……… These little black things, he realises incredulously, that struggle and disappear amidst the wreckage are the heads of men brothers to himself……For hundreds of thousands of men who have come into the war expecting bright and romantic and tremendous experiences their first killing must have been a hideous disillusionment. For none so much as the men of submarines. All that sense of being right and fine that carries men into battle, that caries most of us through the world, must have vanished completely at this first vision of reality. Our man must have asked himself, 'What am I doing?'

In the night he must have lain awake and stared at that question in horrible doubt……..We scold too much at the German submarine crews in this country. Most of us in their places would be impelled to go on as they go on. The work they do has been reached step by step, logically, inevitably, because our world has been content to drift along on false premises and haphazard assumptions and nationality and race and the order of things. These things have happened because the technical education of men has been better than their historical and social education. Once men have lost touch with, or failed to apprehend that idea of a single human community.'

Wells goes on to give a report of two actual U-Boat sailors who died in a Harwich hospital following their being captured after their craft was hit by a mine, whose fate was similar, if their end was no less uncomfortable, than many of fellow submariners.

"Think of those poor creatures dying in the hospital. They were worn out by fits of coughing and haemorrhage, but there must have been moments of exhausted quiet before the end, when our youngster lay and stared at the bleak walls of the ward and thought; when he asked himself, 'What have I been doing? What have I done? What has this world done for me? It has made me a murderer. It has tortured me and wasted me……. And I meant well by it……

So it was with the German youngster who dreamt dreams, who had ambitions, who wished to serve and do brave and honourable things, died.

I have quoted Wells at length because his outline seems to capture key aspects of the intermixing of the individual, the national, and some of the psychological processes involved in warfare. As Wells suggests: '*Most of us in their places would be impelled to go on as they go on*'.

The use of the submarine in conflict was specifically banned by both the Hague convention and by international law, so both Germany and Britain defied agreements that they had cynically signed up too; cynically, not least, because they had been undertaking research into submarine warfare years before the war began.

Once the land-war had been launched the German plan was for a rapid advance through then neutral Belgium, to sweep into Northern France (as per General Alfred von Schlieffen's plan). By the sixth week of the war the Germans were held by the French and the residue of Belgium forces about 20-30 miles from Paris. Then British mobilisation steadily reinforced the Allies and within a few months lines of fortifications had been drawn up from Flanders in the northwest, to the Swiss border in the south, and the 'Western Front' was established as delimiting the relatively narrow strip of countryside that, as the war continued, provided the landscapes for the slaughter and crippling of millions of young men. The gory scenes played out here and with equal ferocity on the eastern front were choreographed by an unimaginative, uncaring, military leadership (generals – supported by equally uncaring politicians) whose approach to war, for the most part, expressed the retention of a mindset of glamourous cavalry officers schooled in the battlefield strategies of the nineteenth century who could only adapt to industrial warfare by marching droves of young men into the fire of cannonades and machine guns over and over again.

The young men, drawn by the siren sound of marching bands towards what they were led to believe (on both sides) would be a short war, were for the most part neither more nor less brave than their enemy. They were stirred to volunteer or accept conscription by the mass media, politicians, and sections of populations excited with a patriotic fervour that was pervading the lands. Many European communists, socialists and some social democratic politicians despaired at how easily class consciousness and international solidarity between working people could be swept aside. In Germany, Rosa Luxemburg eloquently expressed her anguish at seeing nationalism given priority over the working class solidarity that she and socialist colleagues had determinedly endeavoured to foster.

European nations beguiled by propaganda and fired by a type of optimistic patriotism assuming their forces as being superior to the enemy's, felt the war would be settled in their favour by Christmas 1914. Across the continent local dignitaries including magistrates, teachers, churchmen, and elected representatives, all contributed to an up-swell of community mood impacting on thousands of young men driven by mixtures of patriotic enthusiasm, goading and guilt, to join-up. At a national level, the elite groups of politicians, businessmen, newspaper owners and journalists, novelists and populist philosophers, all contributed to creating the national mind-set that underpinned the drive towards war. Newspapers outlined gory details of 'enemy atrocities', most of which never actually occurred and those that did have some element of truth were embroidered by the excited imagination of editorial writer's intent on influencing public mood and to impressing their war-mongering proprietors.

Leading politicians and bellicose sections of the media contributed in their own ways to a narrative presenting their own nation as victim of the 'other's' aggression – of the need for a war for national survival against unprovoked, and so unjustified, aggression. No balanced historical context, no reasoned admission of perhaps at least some justification for Germany's action.

There were some dissenting voices, mainly on the political left, and the elements of the organised working class (T.U.s), not taken in by the misleading press (the duplicity of which they and their members would have gained direct experience of during recent industrial disputes) and holding to a more internationalist perspective. Peace rallies were organised in London, Paris, and Berlin. But once the conflict had broken out, such was the pressure of a jingoistic national mood that most leaders from these groups swung from opposition to support for the war – German Social Democrats, British Labour Party and the British T.U.C., as well as many French and Russian socialists, anarchists and syndicalists, deciding to go with the populist flow.

Any remaining voices of reason (urging restraint and negotiation) were drowned out by the rising tide of war-willingness. In Britain whole battalions were formed by volunteers from the same districts, brothers, cousins and friends that had grown up together, these were the 'Pals' battalions; Liverpool alone formed four Pals battalions. Biographic information notes the excitement felt by thousands of young men heading to the front. 'Your country needs YOU' was for some a stirring call to arms, but the generally grim conditions of working class life in all European nations must also have made the chance of regular army pay and all found conditions, along with the imagined image of returning as a hero, quite attractive.

The reality intruded on the imagined glory when the Pals regiments first saw action in the Battle of the Somme. Where an ineffective Allied bombardment of German positions left the enemy relatively unscathed and when the Allied soldiers were ordered to advance into waves of withering machine-gun fire wholesale slaughter ensued. With many of the battalions losing over half their numbers. When the news got back to Britain whole towns and cities went into mourning as the doleful tolling of church bells signalled the stark, fatal, reality of warfare.

At some point after the war began the balance of power shifted from politicians to the military – by 1916 Germany was in effect, led by the bellicose Generals Ludendorff and Hindenburg, France by Marshal Joffre, Britain by Lord Kitchener (Secretary of State for War) and Russia by a militarily wholly incompetent Tsar – In Austria, the Reichsrat was dissolved in early 1916 and for the remainder of the war the military took the lead.

One million soldiers (young boys and men) died and four million were wounded in some ferocious engagements (including the Marne and at Gallipoli) during the first year of the war. Then, from 1915, the land-war settled into ritualised periods of sniper action, artillery bombardment, and bored troops hunkered down in winding rows of cold, wet, rat infested trenches. With 'advances' being ordered when supplies (of men, munitions, food, medical equipment as well as shrouds and coffins) had been rebuilt to a sufficient level to allow an attack to be launched. Then, following hours during which the artillery sent tons and tons of shells whistling towards at the enemy defences, wave after wave of troops were ordered to advance through the smoky no-man's-land. To march in undulating lines across swaths of tree-denuded wastelands bridging the distance between the opposing combatants' lines. This last walk, this tramp towards summary execution for many of these young men, was across muddy, crater-pocked terrains, threaded with a matrix of glinting barbed-wire that by the end of each day's battle would be draped with stiffening, blood-drained, corpses from which had flown the memories of home – of mothers, lovers, and children – along with but glimpsed outlines of future lives never to be lived.

As suggested by Roger Osborne (2007, p423): 'War became a living nightmare of murderous industrial force inflicting anonymous carnage on millions of human lives'

Yes, within most of the World's nations lives could meanwhile be lived in relatively untrammelled circumstances, untouched by the War, and still to a significant extent matched to the changing seasons. But in the warring nations the change from the occasional young man leaving a rural region for adventure in a national army would become from 1914 a stream of young men conscripted or volunteered off to war never to return, their blood seemingly spilled to nourish the production of stone-cold war memorials that were later to spread across the country like mushrooms fruiting in woodland glades during the crisp autumnal days that these men would never again see. A vibrant body of clear-eyed young men replaced, in market towns and outlying villages, by a series of inert obelisks on which is recorded each man's premature non-existence in parallel lists of neatly chiselled names.

The rise in populations of most European countries had made millions of young men available for military service and the easy acceptance of the legitimacy of state power allowed conscription, with the propaganda machine of a popular press persuading many to march with the drum-beat towards their deaths and the killing of their own kind i.e. other young human-beings. The seeming inevitable pull for young men of the imagined 'fields of glory' that lay in distant lands or in defending one's nation, one's own people, drew them towards the battlefields of Europe. Glorious fields that today present as the neatly tended setting for the rows of thousands upon thousands of pale-aged white tablets etched with names and dates identifying just how young they were; around which grow the enduring red-flowered poppies that poignantly symbolise the red blood drained of so many young men so long ago. Fields redolent with glory only in its bitterly heroic form of glorious futility.

In the five month-long battle of Verdun, during which 23 million shells were fired, over 300,000 men were killed (of the 700,000 casualties) during the relentless German assault on the French held fortress of Verdun - in the four month battle of the Somme 1,300,000 men in total (both sides) being wounded, posted missing, or killed (the British and Commonwealth forces lost 20,000 men killed and 40,000 wounded on the first day of this battle -1st July 1916). And in a 10 day period in the lead-up to the first big 'push' that began the third battle of the strategically situated city of Ypres the Allies fired 4,250,00 shells from 3,000 cannon.

It has been estimated that 300 million artillery shells were fired during the war – one in three failing to explode, with most of these 'duds' still not having been recovered.

The dead toll is long, with:

1.8m German military killed

1.7m Russian military killed

1.4m French military killed

1.3m Austro-Hungarian military killed

740,000 British military killed (plus about 220,000 troops from the Commonwealth)

615,000 Italian military killed

116,000 US military killed

Estimated 10m fatalities and another 22m wounded, many of these to die from their wounds within a few years of the War's ending.

Just as many civilians (10m) were killed during this conflict as were members of the military.

A new technological feature of warfare used during this conflict was the use of the airplanes. Pre-Socratic Greeks had imagined flight (the legend of Icarus and Deadelus) - an 11th century monk, Eilmer of Malmesbury, is said to have built the first 'glider' – Leonardo de Vinci designed a man-powered aircraft – in the eighteenth century two Frenchmen pioneered balloon flight. The science of aerodynamics was initiated by Sir George Cayley as he identified the forces operating to lift a bird into fight – power, uplift, and drag –; from 1803 he built and flew fixed-winged model aircraft. The German Count Ferdinand von Zeppelin had launched a rigid 'airship' in 1900, and by 1914 Germany had eight of these in operation; although they were difficult to control, especially in poor weather conditions.

In one of its pre-WWI conflicts, the Italian military had dropped grenades from airplanes onto civilians in Libya, indicating who would be the primary targets of future aerial warfare. During the First World War it was the French in 1914 that first used airplanes (and indeed airships) to bomb civilians in German towns. By the end of the war the strategy of targeting civilian populations was being used by both sides, each of which had by then developed large-load carrying airplanes, capable of long-range flights, that were specifically designed as a weapon with which to kill and terrorise civilians.

In the WWI battlefields airplanes were at first used more for reconnaissance missions over enemy lines. Only later becoming machines for direct killing, including the dropping of munitions on trenches and for the aerial 'dog-fights' that created the first dare-devil pilots in the German 'Ace' Manfred Von Richthofan (the 'Red Baron') and the French 'Ace'. Rene Fronk, each being credited with shooting down about 80 enemy airplanes. The Canadian Billy Bishop (the 'Lone Wolf'), and the English Major Edward 'Mick' Mannock, were also credited with a high number of 'kills'. Aerial warfare, an innovation in WW1, was to become a significant element of warfare for the rest of the century as it spread conflagration from the battlefields to the towns and cities – a development seeing its horrific nadir in the bombing of places such as London, Coventry, Dresden, Hamburg, Hiroshima and Nagasaki, and across Cambodia during the Vietnam war - by when civilians had become in effect, taken for granted 'legitimate' targets of warfare.

The industrial processes applied to the manufacture of weaponry continued, with the invention of the armoured 'tank'. Similar to airplanes, this was another weapon made possible mainly by the previous twenty year development of the internal combustion engine. But, although they made a considerable contribution to the financial cost of the war, they contributed little to deciding the outcome - being unreliable and slow – of battles.

The introduction of 'gases' caused considerable alarm and in some battles thousands of gas shells were used. The use of poison gas was due partly to the frustration of generals at the stalemate of trench warfare[22]. When released, clouds of gas could kill men taking cover from bullets as it drifted over the sandbagged, redoubts and salients, and seeped along the trenches. Unlike artillery, machine guns, and rifles, it did not have solid metallic velocity that could take it straight to the heart of the enemy – instead its effectiveness as a weapon was dependant on wind direction and on occasion it would be blown back onto the lines of those who released it.

One example being the British release of chlorine gas during an engagement at Loos in September 1915, the wind changed and the returning gas caused 2000 British casualties. In battles such as that of Ypres in April 1915 the Germans released clouds of yellow-greenish chlorine gas towards the opposing force and, such was the fear and confusion created as the gas wafted toward the French lines, that the French and the Algerian troops alongside them fled, allowing the Germans to move easily forward to occupy the vacated positions.

On both sides scientists increasingly played a central role in the war, and most were as nationalistic as the masses – Scientists in each of the leading nations were conducting research into the use of various chemical gases.

For Jon Ager (2012, p116): 'In general, however, the Great War was seen as a catastrophe for Western civilization, and some, citing gas and other technologies, blamed science for contributing to the horrific character of modern industrial warfare.'

Scientists operating as the handmaidens of the military-industrial complex is probably a central factor in undermining any claims to both ethical neutrality and scientific objectivity – especially if, that is, we step back from the immediacy of the research situation to encompass the subjectivity of research directed decision-making.

As the war progressed, even more lethal gases such as phosgene

---

[22] The French first used 'tear gas' grenades to delay rather than kill the advancing Germans in Aug 1914 and the Germans initially used a similar non-lethal gas. Poisonous chlorine gas was first used by the Germans against Russian troops and then soon used by British and French.

and mustard gas (Yperite) were brought into use.

For Tim Cook; 'Soldiers exposed to lethal doses of lung gasses like chlorine and phosgene died badly on the Western Front. The afflicted flopped and writhed in agony, coughing up green bile from ashen faces as ravaged lungs struggled for breath before suffocation or heart failure ended their misery' (Cook – 'Journal of Military History', vol. 73 nos. 2 April 2009 672-673)

The Germans first used the more lethal mustard gas against the Russians at Riga in September 1917, delivered by means of artillery shells. By the war's end the Germans had used 68,000 tons of gas, the French 36,000 tons, the British 25,000 tons and if the war had continued beyond 1918 then each side had been planning a significant increase in gas usage…of between 30-50% of all artillery shells. About 100,000 soldiers were killed by gas (including 56,000 Russians, 8,000 French, 8,000 British, 9,000 Germans, 4,500 Italians, 3,000 Austro-Hungary, 1,450 US) and over 1,000,000 were injured. Victims of gas attacks who survived the war were usually quite painfully crippled with 'burnt out' lungs leaving an inability to breath properly and for many permanent blindness. To be injured with gas would be to suffer permanent disablement and for many a painful death in the months or years following the war's end.

Two of the leading researchers developing poisonous gas for warfare were the Frenchman Francois Grignad and the German Fritz Haber, both Nobel prize-winning chemists. In Germany the industrial production was undertaken, by workers employed by companies such as BASF, Hoechst, Bayer (these combined in 1925 to become IG Farben). With the Allies being supplied by companies such as the US Du Pont and the Dow Chemical Company, and the French Hercules Power Company. The US had a specific military unit, the Chemical Warfare Service, to oversee the production of chemical weaponry, much of which was developed by the up to 1200 chemists working at the American University Experimental Station in Washington D.C. In Britain gas production was overseen by the National Research Council.

The shear futility of trench warfare gradually eroded any

confidence that soldiers had in their generals, but an attitude of deference instilled into working-class boys growing up in class-conscious European states, mostly held the line on discipline; by men exhibiting a passive, almost bovine, willingness to advance when ordered.

By 1916 it was becoming clear just how costly was the toll of the conflict being accounted in human lives lost. The futility of the task was seeping into the consciousness and conversation of the troops. Many of the individuals who refused to fight on, or were caught attempting to desert (some as young as 16), faced a summary tribunal followed for most by the firing squad – even if they were clearly suffering from accumulative fear or shell-shock – they were sacrificed due partly to the instinctive dislike of any challenge to military discipline but also as a warning to their fellows.

Most foot-soldiers grumbled amongst themselves and endeavoured to keep their heads down and focus on personal survival. But at times such as: April 1917 when, following a disastrous action killing 250,000 French and Algerians, almost half of the French army (68 divisions) refused to advance. Possibly as many as 100,000 British soldiers rebelled at Staples. In August 1917 a rebellion by German sailors at Wilhelmshaven sparked a series of similar acts.[23] These and other acts of disobedience were mostly overcome by a mixture of relatively minor concessions and blunt brutality, along with the imprisonment or execution of those identified as leaders. Newspapers conspired to keep their readers ignorant of such outbreaks of the humanitarian expression of man's common sense.

Populations in the conflict nations were by 1917 becoming increasingly disillusioned with the war – the shortages, for many the hunger, and for almost all a growing awareness of the stark reality of war made obvious by the continuous stream of returning coffins containing the curdled human cream of a nation's future.

In France, along with mutinies in the army, there was public unrest

---

[23] Sailors in Kiel, refused to set sail to face near-certain defeat at the hands of the British navy.

including strikes, bread riots, and a series of protests at the many shortages and at the runway inflation that had seen prices rise by 80% in little more than three years. Dissatisfaction with the war had been building throughout 1916 and in Russia it came to a head with a rising in February1917 in the City of Petrograd. Across Russia most cities saw bitter anger expressed at the war, and at the appalling living conditions that many people were experiencing. Nicholas II (Tsar) and his group of mostly arrogant aristocratic advisors were aware that their position was becoming untenable. The Tsar had only ever shown but little concern for the well-being of the overwhelming mass of Russian people and so could expect little sympathy from them; he abdicated in early March.

By 1917 the industrial strength of the US (approx. 2½ times that of Germany) was being mobilised in the war effort and shiploads more food, along with an enormous amount of military hardware and thousands of troops, began to cross the Atlantic to replenish, and then increase, the strength of the forces facing the Germans; 800,000 men by October 1917 and about 2,000,000 by the war's end. Actual military defeat happened swiftly as the Central Powers in effect collapsed in the Balkans, Palestine, Syria, and were in retreat along the Western Front.

This war was not some international conflict that had an inevitability due to 'human nature', nor was it the outcome of one side's wish to dominate the other; clearly inappropriate are the simplistic narratives of heroes and villains, good and evil. This war was more the outcome of: the fatal expression of a burgeoning military machine, the draw that battle has for many young men, a series of diplomatic miscalculations and indeed some crude mistakes, along with the tacit encouragement of financiers and business men with fortunes to make. Prominent agents being politicians with their level of consciousness firmly fixed in the self-conscious mode; attempting to assess national interests in terms of short-term economic prospects and territorial control (determined mainly by elite group interests), and the dumb sensitivities of national egoism. And these set in a wider chronological context of the global ambitions of Germany, France, and Britain. All elements of the perverse logic of war, whose operation relies on the thought patterns identified with the hegemonic utilisation of military threat, economic inducements, and political posturing.

What took these nations to war were the relatively small number of elite groups whose members occupied a range of key decision-making positions in each nation – although significant proportions of the masses of each county should bear some greater or lesser degree of responsibility, even accepting that their understanding of issues had been shaped by carefully deployed propaganda.

The war came to an end in November 1918 – as Germany succumbed to a crumbling political situation in Berlin and Vienna, and the High Command's final acceptance of the inevitability of defeat due to the overwhelming military odds that US intervention had realised.

The Paris Peace Conference began in January 1919 with a formal peace treaty being signed by the allies and Germany in June 1919 (the 'Treaty of Versailles'). Then between 1919-23 additional treaties were signed by the Allies and Austria, Hungary, Bulgaria and Turkey. The Treaty of Versailles could have been designed with the foresight to offer a peace with at least some honour for the defeated but instead it imposed conditions intended to humiliate Germany and her allies – a Germany that had not in fact surrendered but had 'concluded an armistice' (a distinction that Adolf Hitler would later take advantage of).

Post war negotiations also brought modern Poland, Czechoslovakia, and the pre-Yugoslavian 'Kingdom of Serbs, Croats, and Slovenes' into existence. In addition, by including territories that were formally part of Germany in the settlement, the Allies made another contribution to its sense of injustice and its motivation for the invasion of Poland in 1939 that would trigger British entry into WWII.

The war has cost the Allies 57 billion dollars (at 1913 prices) and the Central Powers 24.7 billion dollars, and it is in this difference that victories are almost always decisive in industrialised warfare – it is economic advantage (which in turn relates directly to the industrial capacity of any nation), not any measure of the relative bravery of each nation's soldiers that decided the outcome of the first (and indeed the second) twentieth-century world war. Military deeds only provided the narratives of self-sacrifice, heroism, and national pride that allowed an illusionary gloss (of assumed military skills) to be attached to such grisly enterprises – perhaps a type of defence mechanism of a national consciousness realised to manage the ultimate human stupidity that is warfare.

The distraction of the First World War had been taken as an opportunity by the Turks to progress their ambitions for direct control of the fertile highlands of central and eastern Anatolia; the traditional homeland of the Armenians. This action was a specific policy decided on to cleanse the Ottoman Empire of Armenians in a process known as Turkification. It is important to note that this action – what became a genocide killing over 1.5m men, women, and children – was official Ottoman 'Young Turk' Government policy.

In the period leading up to WW1 the Armenians had been very much second-class citizens, with a range of legal restrictions and special taxes being imposed specifically on them. In 1915 the Turkish government, in effect, declared war on the Armenians – the second twentieth 20th century government led genocide (after German action in Namibia) - an action that would later be replicated as official government policy in other countries including: Stalinist Russia, Nazi Germany, Maoist China, Pol Pot's Cambodia, and General Suharto in Indonesia and East Timor.

This action set in train a period of the relentless persecution of Armenians, that would only come to an end when, in 1923, the Ottoman Empire ceased to exist and the Republic of Turkey was established. The Turkish government instigated the demobilization of Armenian units that had been part of the Ottoman army; they were then reformed as unarmed 'labour battalions' as a prelude to these 4,000 men being murdered.

It is important to highlight that this period of genocide was a premeditated strategy adopted by a government that was endeavouring to modernise - to become more 'civil' in a western

European sense. During the course of the war the thundering throb emanating from the smoke-swept battlefields of Europe were used to cover the cries of a number of Balkan minority groups being subjected to killing or being displaced by their neighbours while much of civil humanity was looking elsewhere. Such is the complexity of conflict zones that there were also times and places when Armenians killed many unarmed Moslem Turks, if on nothing like the same scale as Armenians casualties.

I have touched on just some examples of inter-ethnic conflict in the Balkan region during the first half of the twentieth century; I would note that every massacre-rape-displacement attributed by one side or the other is either vociferously denied or just as vociferously defended on the grounds of justifiable revenge for outrages against them (or mostly their long dead ancestors). But three things are clear: a) The inter-ethnic violence has been going on at least throughout the 19th and 20th centuries - b) That atrocities (crimes against humanity) were committed by individuals from all of the predominant ethnic groups; but importantly, not by all members of each group - c) That no amount of violence had resolved the underlying issues for the longer-term. The collective memories of each group is only of the injustices and atrocities that they have suffered in the land they shared - I might have added a forth point to the more local ones already noted - d) That prominent European powers, and the US, Russia, and China, from 1945, have played a disgraceful part in supporting groups who were clearly engaging in the murder and the displacement of men, women, and children. As recently as the 1990s most of the mainstream media were complicit in ignoring evidence, or promoting evidence that was obviously fabricated, in justifying military action to encourage the groups favoured by NATO – the most notorious being the excuse found for the bombing of the Serbs in 1999, killing over 500 civilians in an action that had not been approved by the UN Security Council; the first such non-approved NATO military action.

Paddy Ashdown – (a UN representative to the Balkans in the 1990s) ex-SBS officer and then ex-leader of the UK's Liberal-Democratic political party, said on a BBC Radio 4 programme

(2/4/2010) "I saw Bosniacs drive out Croats, Croats drive out Serbs, and Serbs drive out Bosniacs – and what I saw brought tears to my eyes"

During this period of conflict an elderly Serbian peasant is credited with having pithily observed that these warring groups were: "The same piece of shit divided by the cartwheel of history."

In the history of the Balkans we can see a number of factors contributing to suspicion and fear of neighbours – historical separation mainly due to differences in: religion, culture, mating arrangements, as well as in places separation by difficult to negotiate local terrain, all reinforced throughout the years as grounds for inter-group suspicion and fear become ever more polarized and group identity became evermore entrenched. Difference is reinforced when historically rooted animosities seep into each new generation, with children being socialized into the powerful narratives of past injustices (along with a collusive collective amnesia of the murderous acts of its own people); with ambitious leaders seeking possible opportunities for future retribution. But the basis of these differences are socially constructed, they are but relational differences which overlie the underlying commonality of being human. If taken together they have led to the coalescence into the most powerful basis for inter human conflict. Social psychologists such as Henri Tajfel and John Turner (1979 – Social Identity Theory) have offered theoretical frameworks within which to understand the power of group membership and others such as Muzafer Sherif (1950s and 60s) have offered experimental evidence which suggests just how powerful simply being in one group rather than another can have in how any individual sees his own group (emphasising the positive and minimising the negative characteristics), and how he perceives another group (minimising the positives and maximising the negatives, stereotyping..... to prejudice). If Tajfal and Turner were pioneers on group-related identity and solidarity their findings have been supported by a range of subsequent studies. It is this instinctive 'tendency' towards solidarity in mere group difference that is exacerbated by the interweaving of the differential embroidery of religion, ethnicity, and nationality. If we can also add the individual motivation of the covetousness of a neighbour's material goods (historically in the Balkans primarily land) and the political ambitions of leadership, then out of this toxic mix - of difference, material greed, and ambition - invariable comes fractured communities and inter-group conflict.

Nationalism (and in the Balkans religion) shows itself as a projection of the in-group/out-group dichotomy writ large. With a complex framework of structural factors formed from, history and culture, to which clings accretions of narratives fostering national self-esteem, collectively acknowledged grandiose images, and the various means that an organised society can deploy to promote elite-group self-interests and to make these appear to be the self-interests of all citizens.

The 'civil' world that emerged from the First World War had seen the demise of dictatorial European monarchies and, while constitutional monarchies were retained in some countries (including Britain, Greece, Holland, Sweden, and also with China and Japan's emperors) and more dictatorial monarchs in some others (mainly central and south-eastern Europe) the mythical idea of some supreme being entitled to rule due to some special state of grace passed into history – and so a 5,000 year long feature of civil life had undergone significant change. Although the need for populations to want to believe that some humans, simply by right of birth, had a set of special qualities and the willingness of some individuals themselves to collude in this pretence, and so to accept the financial and social privileges and nationalistic 'civil worship' on offer, was to continue to show some support for supreme unelected leadership during the rest of the twentieth century and beyond.

Between the two World Wars Russia became an insular society as the originally felt commitment to world revolution – 'workers of the world uniting' - became subsumed within the nation's attempt to consolidate its economic and military power in the content of running an industrially backward country that had suffered heavily in the war. Having to make progress in a world where it faced extensive trade boycotts and open hostility from abroad, especially from countries such as Germany, England, France, US, and Japan etc. Britain, France and the US sent troops to attack Russia even after the League of Nations had been established. According to Winston Churchill (then British Minister of War) the intention was to strangle a communist Russia at its birth. A great deal was made in the western mass media of the murder of the Romanov Royal family by the Bolsheviks but very little was made about this privileged family's taken for granted self-indulgence and indifference to the suffering of countless numbers of Russian peasants.

More positively, some leading politicians such as Woodrow Wilson, Jan Smuts, and Roger Cecil, did come to advocate the setting up of some sort of international body to facilitate negotiations between nations in dispute. One of Wilson's 14 points that had been offered to the 1918 peace negotiations was the setting up of a 'League of Nations'. An organization that the US itself was not to join because Congress refused to ratify the treaty of Versailles which had contained the provision for setting up the League.

As long ago as 1784 Immanuel Kant had written: *'The greatest problem for the human species, whose solution nature compels it to seek, is to achieve a universal* **civil society** *administered in accord with the right. ....Thus must there be a society in which one will find the highest possible degree of freedom under external laws combined with irresistible power i.e. a perfectly rightful civil constitution, whose attainment is the supreme task nature has set for the human species;.....etc'* (Fifth Thesis of essay 'Idea for a Universal history with a Cosmopolitan Intent') and *'The problem of establishing a perfect civil constitution depends on the problem of law-governed* **external relations among nations** *and cannot be solved unless the latter is'* (Sixth Thesis)

He urged nations: '..........to leave the lawless state of savagery and enter into a federation of peoples. In such a league, every nation, even the smallest, can expect to have security and rights, not by virtue of its own might or its declarations of what is right, but from this great federation of peoples alone form a united might, and from decisions made by the united will in accord with laws.'

(Kant then notes that similar ideas had already been suggested by Abbe St. Pierre and J.J.Rousseau)

It was to take more than a hundred years of continuing conflictual international relations before Kant's prescient (but in fact common sense) suggestion was taken up; probably the most moral concept, 'universal peace', being relevant to the morality of human relationships.

It had taken the terror of WW1 to make leaders (especially Woodrow Wilson) see the need for some supra-national body, with the moral authority and some practical powers, to settle disputes between nations. No member nation was expected to cede sovereignty but all were expected to respond positively to the majority will of the League and, more specifically, seek to avoid war. The League of Nations (LoN) was established in 1919 based in Geneva (in politically neutral Switzerland) and incorporated in the Versailles Conference 1919 Treaty with Germany.

The Assembly of the League, supported by a secretariat, had permanent representatives from the principle allied powers with a rotating membership of representatives drawn from the other nations. The League also worked in conjunction with an international Court of Justice based in The Hague (Netherlands). The primary remit being that: 'Any threat of war is a matter of concern for the whole League and the League shall take any action that may safeguard peace.'

The wider mission of the League was to promote international co-operation and to ensure that nations did not resort to war as a means of settling disputes. At this time another international organization which was affiliated to the League was also formed: 'The International Labour Organization' (ILO). The charter under which the ILO was to operate included measures intended to ensure that workers in all nations that were members of the League had certain basic rights and working conditions and that women and children would be protected; plus the 'free association of workers' was to be a basic right. It was felt that the application of these universal conditions would result in similar costs of employing workers and so would, by reducing labour-cost competition, also contribute to peaceful coexistence between nations.

The Assembly of the LoN had recourse to three central 'sanctions':

1   It could call upon nation-states in dispute to discuss this in a reasonable manner (within the Assembly).
2   If in the collective view of the Assembly one nation could be identified as the 'offender' then it could be called upon to desist from any aggressive or otherwise provocative action.
3   If the view (expressed as a 'ruling') of the League was ignored then it could order economic sanctions to be imposed, even including trade isolation if necessary. In addition, sanctions could be enforced by military action.

Article 8 of the Covenant of the League of Nations: '....committed the signatories to the lowest level of armament consistent with national security and the fulfilment of international obligations'.

Apart from having to deal with the daunting task of managing the national self-interests of its members, the League was weakened by the fact that the US refused to join, Germany was not allowed to join[24] as was not considered to be a member of the International Community, and nor was a Bolshevik-led Russia. So three of the most powerful nations in the world - who had significant potential for conflicts arising from internal 'nationalist' problems, territorial

---

[24] It did join in 1926 only after it signed the Locarno Treaty and so formally accepting the Versailles settlement – Hitler withdrew Germany from the LoN in 1933.

disputes with neighbouring states, or potential conflicts that could arise from their trading ambitions – were not members.

The LoNs had a mixture of successes and failures, with the balance being significantly towards the latter; this being the cause of its being overall judged an over-optimistic failure:

Some successes:

Aland Islands –	1921 dispute between Sweden and Finland,…both sides accepted the Leagues suggested compromise.
Upper Silesia –	1921 dispute between Germany and Poland…both sides accepted the League's suggested compromise.
Turkey –	1923 the League was unable to prevent a war but it was able to intervene to ease the humanitarian crises involving 1,400,000 refugees, mostly women and children.
–	Prevention of war between Turkey and Iraq in 1925/26, and between Poland and Lithuania 1929
–	When Greece invaded Bulgaria in 1925 Bulgaria appealed to the League and Greece was ordered to withdraw and also pay a fine - Greece accepted the ruling and withdrew.

Some failures:

Italy 1919 –	Dispute between Italy and Yugoslavia - The League did try to intervene but to little effect.
Teschen 1919 –	Dispute between Poland and Czechoslovakia over control of the coal-bearing land around the town of Teschen – The League's suggested compromise was rejected by both countries and the dispute continued until WWII
Vilna 1920 –	Dispute between Lithuania and Poland – Lithuania appealed to the League but Poland refused to consider losing control of Vilna

- The Polish invasion of land controlled by Russia in 1920 – no

intervention by the League and in 1921 Russia, accepting the reality on the ground, conceded to Poland's demands and signed the Treaty of Riga. At a stroke doubling the size of Poland, but creating an enduring source of bitterness.
- When Britain, the US and France continued to send troops to fight in Russia – even after the setting up of the League – The League took no action even though two of its leading members were involved as aggressors on foreign soil.
- When Italy and Greece were in dispute over part of Albania the League actually took the side of Italy, the aggressor.
- Following Germany's default on a payment of the unrealistically heavy war reparations, France and Belgium invaded Germany's most important industrial region of the Ruhr – thus making it even more difficult for Germany to pay reparations – here were two of the Leagues' leading members in direct contravention of the League's rules. The League took no action – and its credibility suffered accordingly.
- In 1931 Japan invaded the Chinese province of Manchuria – China appealed to the League under Article 11 of the League's Charter – after some equivocation and a delayed report that on balance judged Japan to be in the wrong, the League ruled in China's favour.....the Japanese response being simply to resign its membership of the League.
- In 1935 Mussolini's sent 400,000 Italian troops into Ethiopia in direct contravention of the League's rules and although the League's Assembly did condemn the invasion some of its leading members (including Britain and Frances) offered tacit support to Italy, again undermining the League's credibility.

According to Micheline R.Ishay (2004): 'The League's and the ILO's efforts to counter conflict between nations and ease economic inequality, feeble from the outset, would quickly collapse under the pressure of nationalism and war – and the absence of the US .....weakened the organization's credibility.'

During the Second World War the Assembly did not meet and in 1946 its work was superseded by the establishment of the United Nations.

The position of the League had been fatally undermined by the unwillingness of nation-states to accede to its authority – as the memories of the First World War faded the self-interests of nation-states once again came increasingly to determine international relations. Never very strong in practice, the League was at least a glimpse of an idea of what might be possible….the collectivisation of international security. It was bold if timely in its establishment and ambitious in its aims, but sadly if predictably, disappointing in its implementation.

Although the League of Nations was but a failed attempt at international co-operation it was a sign that nation-states were, at least in theory, prepared to accept some higher (transnational) 'morality-based' authority. It did establish some important actions – child labour, rights of women, anti-drug smuggling – that moved these issues onto the international agenda. In a more practical way the League's humanitarian work included some work in developing countries to improve agriculture (in seeds, clean water, tools, and scientific advice) as well as medical care.

The story of the League of Nations shows the fairly obvious point that the extent to which it would be successful would be the extent to which it included all of the world's nations as members and the extent to which each of these was committed to peaceful co-existence. Fundamentally, the willingness of nations to cede sovereignty over the right to unilaterally engage in armed conflict.

The 1928 'International Treaty for the Renunciation of War as an Instrument of National Policy' (the Kellogg-Briand Pact) was signed by sixty-five nation states, but it was more aspirational than realistic given the cynical underlying motives and perspectives of the leading nations involved.

Even these tentative signs of possible international movement towards co-operation and security were relegated to the blurred background of international relations when economic depression engulfed the world in the 1930s. The structural means of co-ordinating international action to ease the financial crisis was disregarded as each nation focused more on its own internal problems.

Within but twenty years of the First World War (the 'war to end wars') ending, another major bout of the expression of evil was to begin. History shows that the roots of organized warfare are embedded within the very structure of civil humankind - as individuals, groups, and nations. This being primarily due to individuals and leaders interpreting reality on the level of self-consciousness so translating a narrow interpretation of national self-interests in international affairs. As I did with the first World War above, I will also just follow a fairly conventional historical analysis of the causative progression towards WWII. This, analytically superficial but descriptively useful, approach will focus on an admixture of national aspirations and social relations, as well as international economic and political factors.

If we accept that decisions taken by a Nazi-led Germany during the later 1930s made war inevitable given the then nationalist dynamics of international affairs, we can begin to trace some origins of these decisions to the settlement made at Versailles in 1919. Whereas Germany had in November 1918 signed an armistice to end hostilities, the outcome of the conference was to present them with a series of conditions that amounted to more of a humiliating defeat.

Amongst the more contentious of the conditions set out in the Versailles Treaty were: loss of territory, including Alsace Lorraine to France; recognition of the independence of Austria; the re-constitution of Poland, with the German city of Danzig and north-western Prussia isolated along a narrow corridor through Polish territory; the loss of German colonies and other overseas interests. In addition, German negotiators also had to accept de-militarization of German lands west of the Rhine, an army limited to 100,000 men, a very small navy, and no air-force.

Germany was to make repatriation payments (Article 231 - the contentious 'war-guilt' clause) set provisionally at 20,000 million gold marks then finally, in April 1921, raised to 132,000 million gold marks, to be paid to the 'victors'. This was a figure set by the Allied Reparation Commission calculated on the basis of Germany paying the cost of the war in terms of the loss and damage estimated to have been suffered by the Allies. These, and a number of other conditions, were felt by the Germans (and to some extent viewed by the US Congress which refused to ratify the final Treaty) to amount to a punitive treaty; their being more about punishment and revenge rather than a justifiable settlement. The conditions of the Treaty gave substance to a simmering criticism by conservative elements of the Weimar government focused on the accusation that the German Army did not lose WW1 on the battlefield but that the war was lost by weak politicians at the Château of Versailles. This was but one of Hitler's claims as he espoused a narrative for the rise of a third Reich. Another more enduring theme was of Germany greatness being undermined but sections of its own population – primarily Jewish people, but also communists, trade unionists, gypsies (sinta), and those who they judged to be mentally and physically disabled. Seeking to promote some imagined 'Aryan' racial purity.

It would be the SS led by Himmler that would take the primary role in prosecuting Hitler's (Aryan) racial policy. As the 1930s progressed the Nazis flooded the country with anti-Semitic propaganda. Jews were purged from occupations in the civil service, and progressively from the legal and educational systems and most other professions. In September 1935 the Nürberg Act removed civil rights from Jews, banned Jew/non-Jew marriage, and would lead to the widespread confiscation of Jewish property. For the next couple of years the government had to balance its wish to persecute Jews with risking economic instability if leading Jewish businessmen decided to move abroad. But by the late 1930s the balance was shifting towards the former and when on 7th November 1938, a 17 year old Jew shot dead a relatively low grade diplomat serving at the Paris embassy, the Nazi's reaction was fierce. The government used the killing as an excuse to orchestrate a new wave of anti-Jewish persecution and on the 9th November Jewish individuals and families were attacked in the street, Jewish property ransacked and set on fire; with many synagogues also being destroyed. By the end of this 'Kristallnacht' (night of broken glass, aptly named given that an estimated four million marks worth of glass was smashed) 20,000 Jews had been arrested and up to 400 killed. Jews and many active anti-Nazis had to look on while their property was looted or destroyed. But the individual persecution and daily experience of petty humiliation that Jews were subjected to was probably a more vindictive expression of the regime's anti-Semitism.

Now the SS moved more determinedly to corral German Jews into restricted areas ('ghettos') of cities. An approach that would be replicated from the late 1930s as Germany invaded one country after another. Himmler and Heydrick were responsible for setting up four special units of the Einsatzgruppen whose role was initially to follow the army into Poland and round up Jews into the ghettos. But later on their more direct part in the killing began when the army invaded Russia and these units were then ordered to closely follow the advancing front and kill all Jews and Soviet political commissars as they hunted them out. It was estimated that in the City of Kiel alone over 33,000 (mostly Jews) were victims of the Einsatzgruppen. The pressure to increase the killing rate led to mobile gas trucks (made by a Berlin company) being introduced and these accommodated the gassing of 20 or 30 individuals at a time. Such was the orgy of blood curdling murder that when the head of Einsatzgruppe Unit D, Otto Ohlendorf, was interviewed after the war he spoke of the 'great ordeal' suffered by his men, with a German military doctor noting the '...immense psychological injuries and damage to their health...' (Shirer, 1973, p960). By 1945 these units had been involved in the murder of 1,400,000 individuals.

The concentration of Jews in city-centre ghettoes would facilitate the plan to transport them – men, women, children, babies - to the concentration camps and so to slavery or death. For Himmler's deputy, Reinhard Heydrich (Head of the SS's Secret Service SD that would become the feared 'GESTAPO' - Geheime Staatspolizei) this procession toward death was his undertaking 'house cleansing'; for Hitler and the leading Nazis it was the 'final solution'. The primary scene for this 'solution' would be the network of concentration (death) camps erected across Germany, Austria, and Poland. In places whose names have become synonymous with evil: Buchenwald, Sachsenhausen, Dachau,

Ravensbrueck (a camp specifically for women), then later Auschwitz (where as many as 2 million Jews were slaughtered), Treblinka and Belsen in Poland, and Mauthausen with its numerous sub-camps and Lochau in Austria, being the more notorious.

Britain had pioneered the use of such (extra-legal) concentration camps during the Boer war, which had caused horrible suffering and death for thousands of Boer families. The western nations had themselves supported anti Bolshevik White Russians who had carried out a pogrom killing 100,000 Jews in the 1920s. But however merciless these precursors in evil they were not on the same vast scale of the pogrom run by the SS's Deaths-Head Brigade; a group of blindly loyal Nazi misfits and killers (as well as many of the ordinary but obedient) who were proud of the skull-and-crossbones insignia on their Unit's badge. This was a system organized by administrators proud of the efficient operation of the evil processes they facilitated.

The first camp, at Dachau, had been up and running since as early as 1933 and by the year's end held more than 30,000 detainees. This would be the model for the later death camps that would initially kill 100,000 people taken from mental hospitals before moving on to 'process' about 6 million mainly Jewish victims but also many, communists, socialists, Slavs, pacifists, religious resisters to the Nazis (in particular the Christian 'Confessional Church'), the disabled, homosexuals, gypsies, and any others judged by the Gestapo as anti-social. Tens of thousands of Russian prisoners of war would also be exterminated by the end of WWII.

Such was Hitler's commitment to his delusional racial purity ambitions that the pogrom to annihilate the Jewish people of Germany and German-occupied Europe was carried out in spite of its diverting significant resources in order to progress this policy. The transportation required rolling stock and engines that could have been used to transport war materials, and at times these movements clogged the railway system. The killing involved the 'loss' of thousands of skilled and professional Jewish and other workers, and the means to progress the overall exercise diverted thousands of troops that might have made a useful contribution to the war effort.

Of wider interest, it was also the case that 400,000 German citizens, categorized by the Nazi's as 'mentally unfit', that had been murdered prior to the start of WWII, were excluded from charges at the post war Nuremberg trials, as this was deemed as possible interference in the internal affairs of a nation. This decision conveniently meant that it also reduced a possible defence of those appearing before the international court that would involve comparing Nazi treatment of those categorized as mentally unfit with how badly these had also been treated in the victor countries; something the latter wanted to avoid.

By the end of 1941 almost the entire Jewish population of mainland Europe was in countries directly occupied, or at least indirectly controlled, by the Nazis. The extent to which the nominal rulers of these co-operated in Hitler's 'final solution' varied. Vichy France, Poland, Romania, the Netherlands, and Austria, were amongst those prepared to cooperate in the deportation of their Jewish citizens to the labour or death camps. Romanian troops themselves actually conducted a massacre of 60,000 Jews in Odessa in Oct 1941. Bulgaria, and to some extent Italy, lacked much enthusiasm for helping the Nazis in this task, and Denmark stood out as an example of what passive non-cooperation could achieve. Most Danish people refused to assist with rounding up and transporting Jews, and many found quite imaginative ways to frustrate the SS. In all, just 116 Danish Jews were victims of the Nazi terror out of a Jewish population of 7,380. But we need also to bear in mind that many individuals in all of these European countries, including Germany itself, risked their own lives to hide Jewish neighbours, help Jews escape the country, or otherwise frustrate the Nazi progrom.

I wish to pause to draw attention to an aspect of my writing style.

Throughout the above section, I have been describing individual Nazis using derogatory psychological traits including: murderous, delusional, thugs. I have used these to make the outline more conventional, perhaps even a bit more engaging. They add some sense of personal drama to the text.

I think this is acceptable but I want to highlight the misleading nature of this style - one common with many history books. I am profoundly sure that if we are determined to minimize the expression of evil in the world, we should not view evil as being embodied in this or that particular individual (or indeed country). This form of demonology is too easy and seems to absolve society from investigating the wider elements that foster evil behaviour. It is the behaviours and the social (including historic) conditions they are set in that we should judge as evil, not the individual - this does not in any way absolve individuals from responsibility for their actions; individuals can still be judged as culpable. But as behaviour operates in a social context analysis can more coherently incorporate social as well as individual psychological factors into any consideration.

A more useful investigation into an evil act - such as the killing of 6m Jews and those in other groups - would take us, yes into attempting to gain an understanding of the immediate perpetrators of the killings, the leading Nazis, camp guards, heads of companies supplying the killing equipment, etc. But we must also consider the socialization processes they had been subjected too, seeking to identify the possible sources of traits (primary motivational factors) that would be expressed in the decision-making processes leading to the killing. This aspect of our investigation would identify the nexus of social structures that might contribute to providing the conditions from which evil behaviours could be expressed. I note 'could be' not 'would be' - in terms of individual socialization - because we can only seek to identify conditions of possibility not ones of determination.

To the extent that the generation born from the start of the century to the 1920s shared the experience of growing up in a Germany beset by economic problems, as an international pariah state, and a nation harbouring a sense of being humiliated by the settlement of Versailles, we can see at least some factors that might explain what we might term the 'Nazi mentality'. This is a crude categorization for individuals whose own reaction to the interactive and interconnected processes of growing up in post war Germany made them psychologically vulnerable to the persuasive analysis Hitler offered of the nation's problems and his proscription for making Germany 'great again'.

For many, Germany during the 1920s could seem like a nation in crisis and it is the case that some people are more prone than others to turn to political extremes, to convincing religious or political saviours, when their experience is of continuing uncertainty, resentment, and material deprivation. History suggests that such conditions of political and economic crisis offer fertile ground for religious or political extremes, and Hitler and the National Socialists were well-positioned to take advantage of this.

A genuine, cause-seeking, analysis would involve a detailed study of individual Nazis and their supporters, seeking some common intermix of individual psychology and familial and social experience. The philosopher Hannah Arendt, an observer at the Nuremburg trials, noted how ordinary the Nazi defendants looked - she used the phrase 'the banality of evil' to described her feelings on seeing a succession of very ordinary men shuffling into the dock to face their accusers.

Identifying the social/psychological conditions within which innocent newborns become transformed into adult agents of evil should be a primary concern. But to seek to trace the necessary deep-rooted analysis of the sources of evil that encompass social structures, as well as individual and social psychology, might possibly reveal that the Nazi regime operated through but a more extreme version of similar national social structures (and within international relationships) that still pertain in the world today. When we are facing the probability of a third world war and millions upon millions of human-beings being singed off the face of the Earth in a cataclysmic thermo-nuclear holocaust.

This might be the consequential conclusion to the many within and between nation conflicts obvious in a world of hegemonic nation-states bristling with weaponry; with a politically influential 'war-industry' programmed (indeed seeking) to have them used. A world controlled by groups of individual men and women who promote national interests as expressed in a language redolent with concepts such as suspicion, duplicity, conflict, threat, and aggression. Narratives of competition spun by politicians who are but another branch of the same interdependent elite-group system in which another, the industrial-financial-military-media nexus, repeatedly polishes and rehearses the virtual scenarios replicating how to use their awesomely lethal weaponry. Weaponry provided by an amoral industry whose profits depend on the uses of weapons (their products) and/or the development of evermore sophisticated means of destruction and killing - in essence, the same conflictual determinants/conditions pertain today to those that led to WWI and WWII.

A principle theme of this book is based upon the idea that we can trace the origins of the 'conflictual' social structures back to our hominoid evolutionary stage and so we can identify the fundamental psychological characteristic (mode of consciousness) that has continued to operate throughout all of civil life down to today.

In evolutionary terms, what mode of consciousness would we be identifying? I have throughout this text been suggesting the level of 'self-consciousness'. A broad but identifiable level - in terms of information processing capacity and other primary psychological characteristics - of the evolution of consciousness characterized by any individual who identifies with influence groups such as my family, my tribe, my interest group, my class, my nation, and similar accidental and limited in-group/out-group determinations. I won't develop this more theoretical theme any further here and will return to a more extensive consideration in the concluding chapter. But if we are determined on the eradication, of even just the grossest expressions of evil such as perpetrated by the Nazis during WWII, then we will need to eschew the narratives of demonology and face the implications of the 'my's' inherent in self- consciousness and the social structures that have been constructed - nationally and internationally - by people operating within the morally limited parameters that are a primary characteristic of this level of consciousness.

The majority of Germans did not vote for the Nazi Party in 1933. We might blame the German people for passive obedience, for not actively fighting and taking up armed or even passive, resistance. But if we sincerely reflect on how we ourselves might have behaved if subjected to similar socialization and in similar political circumstances could we say that, even if we felt bitterly opposed to the Nazis, would we have done more than resign ourselves to the political circumstances, got on with our daily lives, and hoped for the best?

Some Germans were pacifists and refused conscription into the army; some did join protest or more active urban guerrilla groups (many paying for this with their lives), but after the war little was said about these brave individuals. This because the international narrative was intent on heaping blame on (demonizing) the German people; most of whom were themselves terrorized by the Nazi regime. How else could allied actions such as the militarily unnecessary slaughter of thousands of men, women, children and babies, in the blanket bombing creating the firestorms that engulfed residential areas of cities such as Berlin, Hamburg, Cologne and Dresden (100,000 civilians killed in Dresden alone - compared to 13,000 in London's Blitz) have been justified. With such mass bombing of civilians being pointedly excluded from the charges facing the Nazis at Nuremberg due to the allies also being guilty of such a terrible 'war crime'. These trials were a public reinforcement of an Allied conspiracy to blame a nation for the war and for the holocaust, rather than being but one necessary aspect of a more extended process intended to understand the wider context for the war's origins.

If the 'final solution' was the means of Hitler progressing his program of a genetically inaccurate and ethnically distorted conception of 'Aryan purity', it would be by invading neighbouring countries that he would gain the *Lebensraum* ('living space') he was seeking for a new Greater Germany. The staged expansionist program that he would progress was not just for territory but also for access to the materials that could underpin military strength and so the means to sustain warfare. Alsace-Lorraine held the iron and steel, Rumania the oil, Poland the coal, and Czechoslovakia the armaments industry; all materials required for the fulfilment of Hitler's military ambitions. By

1938 the German army, navy, and its air-force, were considered, at least by Hitler, to be ready for action.

The German forces had already gained some real-life military experience with its support of General Francisco Franco, leader of Spain's military rebels (the fascist Falange) in his successful attempt (1936-1939) to overthrow the elected republican government. Although German military support never reached the level provided by the fascist Italian government dominated by Benito Mussolini, Germany did send a significant amount of men and materials. Early on both governments gave official recognition to the right-wing Spanish rebels. The historian J.A.S. Grenville noted that at the opening of hostilities in late 1936 the republican government and the fascist rebels each had access to comparable military assets but for Grenville (2005, p217) 'What decisively tipped the balance was the help Hitler and Mussolini gave to Franco...' and this help was especially decisive in the early stages of the war; the two countries taken together carried out well over 5,000 air-raids. Whilst the Italians provided over 70,000 men (mostly from the Italian fascist militia) and large amounts of military equipment, the German contribution was about 16,000 men, including military advisers, technicians, and instructors, and somewhat less equipment. The actual fighting by the German contingent was primarily undertaken by its Condor Legion. This notorious military unit, commanded by General Hugo von Sperrle, included tank and anti-tank companies, at least two battle cruisers (the Deutschland and the Admiral Scheer) and 8 squadrons of airplanes (about 100 planes – Heinkel 51 and Messerschmidt 109 fighters and Junkers 52 bombers). It would be the bombers that would cause so much destruction during the siege of Madrid, with at least 1,400 civilians being killed. In the Basque town of Guernica, at about 5 pm on market day 26th April 1937, wave after wave of German bombers flown by German pilots, systematically destroyed the town centre. With groups of busy fighter planes machine gunning civilians trying flee the bombs. An event that was graphically immortalized in Picasso's mural-sized painting.

Possibly as many as three quarters of a million people died in the bitterly fought Spanish Civil War. A significant number of anti-fascist Germans travelled to Spain independently to join with individuals from many other nations in the pro-government International Brigade, or fought in other pro-republican units - about 2,000 of these anti-fascist German volunteers died during the conflict. But in terms of outcomes, it was the support for the Spanish fascists by the fascist leaders of Italy and Germany that made a difference.

In relation to the German preparation for its own military ambitions the Spanish experience was noted by Herman Goring (head of the Luftwaffe), as being a useful training ground for its military. He singled out the destruction of Guernica as being especially useful as a testing ground.

As the bitterly fought war progressed the major western powers looked on, assuming neutrality, but prepared to see democracy crushed and indeed to turn a 'blind eye' to the supply of strategically important military and other goods to the fascists – Indeed, Italian bombers flew on gasoline drilled in Texas.

Apart from their shared military ambitions and fascist political views (oh, and massive sense of self-destiny), their involvement in the Spanish Civil War further cemented the relationship between Mussolini and Hitler. Their two regimes formed an anti-Comintern Rome-Berlin pact (Axis) in November 1936. An agreement that Japan would join the following year. A Japan that was itself building a formidable military force and which had colonized Korea and Taiwan and, in 1931, had invaded Manchuria and controlled large parts of Northern China. The Seiyukai Party government (supported by large landlords and big business) that displaced the government of the Minsei Party (drawing support from intellectuals and urban workers) came to power in December 1931. But despite a failed military coup attempted by a group of nationalist officers in 1936, the 1930s saw the military high command take increasingly tighter control of the country, and by the second half of the decade it was considering further expansion into British, Dutch, and French, colonies in S.E. Asia; and even the US colony in the Philippines.

The increasing militarization of the world expressed itself in the

Far East during 1937-8 with the Sino-Japanese War. This war was but another outburst of active conflict during a period of simmering aggression between the two nations. The ambitions of Japanese high command was a primary reason for its elevating a minor skirmish over a misinterpretation of an incident that happened at Lugouqiao near Beijing in July 1937 into war. With the military, in effect, overruling diplomatic efforts to find a peaceful resolution. Japanese troops advanced further into China, meeting weak resistance from a Chinese army unprepared, poorly led, and ill-equipped to face them. But further south in the region around Shanghai, Chinese elite troops were better able to defend themselves and in turn launch a strategic counter attack aimed at encircling the Japanese held area of the region.[25]

A battle for the city of Shanghai ensued, with the Chinese taking significant casualties (possibly as many as 270,000). After three months of conflict Japanese reinforcements landed to the south of the city made the Chinese defensive positions vulnerable and by mid December the Japanese were in control of the City.

Then followed the Japanese advance on the city of Nanking and the events known as the 'Rape of Nanking' – so named owing to possibly as many as 20,000 Chinese women being raped by the Japanese occupying troops – along with this atrocity it has been estimated that 200,000 civilians (possible many more) were systematically massacred, essentially an orgy of killing.

Coming back to Europe....by late 1937 Hitler felt that his internal control over the German people and his re-armament programme had reached levels that would enable him to move on to the next stage of his plan for Germany. He was also reassured by lack of any significant international re-action to his and Mussolini's intervention in the Spanish Civil War, the impotence of the League of Nations in relation to the Italian invasion of Abyssinia in spring 1936, and similar lack of response to Germany's March 1936 re-occupation and militarization

---

[25] An air-borne attack on Japanese naval ships went wrong, with bombs being dropped on the international settlement of the City, causing up to 3,000 casualties.

of the Rhineland (in direct contravention of the Versailles Treaty). Hitler and his close Nazi colleagues judged that the complex and somewhat diplomatically muddled state of European politics, especially the extent of mutual distrust between nations, offered international conditions conducive for action.

Once Hitler felt that the absorption of Austria into a greater Germany had been settled he began planning for a move against Czechoslovakia; the decision to invade being made as early as April 1938. Then followed a period of intense international diplomacy, led by Britain and France; but pointedly excluding Russia and indeed Czechoslovakia itself. These attempts at diplomacy culminated in September in a conference in Munich, which also involved Mussolini, during which the Sudetenland region, with its largely ethnic German population, was offered to Hitler in exchange for peace. Neville Chamberlin, Britain's Prime Minister, returned home from the final meeting in Munich famously brandishing a piece of paper signed by Hitler below his written commitment to settle all future Anglo-German differences by diplomatic means.

Hitler had to consider a number of potential difficulties as he prepared his next move: he could not be sure how Britain and France would respond to an invasion of Czechoslovakia, his high command suggested that they might not have the military resources to guarantee a success, and there were also signs that a growing proportion of Germans were becoming concerned about provoking a wider European war.

In accord with the Munich agreement, German forces had moved into the Sudetenland in early October. Thus separating this region from a Czech state that was struggling with its own internal political disagreements. Hitler was ready to take advantage of the growing rift between the Slovaks and Czechs (including Slovak pressure for an independent state) the main cause of making the country difficult to govern. The loss of the Sudeten region meant the dramatic reduction of the key resources - coal, chemicals, lignite, timber, and iron and steel - that had made the nation economically viable. Two Czech presidents - up to 5th Oct was Beneš and then Dr Emil Hácha - were vilified in a series of Hitler's speeches, and in direct talks Hácha was being bullied into accepting German control. Even with this pressure - including the threat from Hitler to 'annihilate' his country - the Czech President (accompanied by his Foreign Minister Chvalkovsky) still refused to surrender his country to the Nazis. But the threats from Hitler were relentless, and were at times expressed in ways verging on the hysterical, culminating in Goring's threat to bomb Prague. In March 1939 the German army crossed the border and within a few days Hitler was taking the salute of a parade of German soldiers marching through the streets of Prague; in the same week Germany had also regained control of Memel in Lithuania.

By spring 1939 the diplomatic deception and hegemonic belligerence shown by the Nazis over Austria and Czechoslovakia had at last made the British and French accept that Hitler could not be diplomatically appeased and that more decisive action would be necessary. On 31st May they formed an agreement that they would come to the aid of Rumania or Poland if these were attacked. Grenville (2005, p233) pointed out the irony in Britain offering support to the Polish Dictatorship that it had denied to the Czechoslovakian Democracy.[26]

As an Axis/Allies polarity begun to take more obvious shape Germany formed a 'Pact of Steel' with Italy, committing the country to follow Germany into warfare; an Italy that had recently (May 1939) invaded Abyssinia and occupied parts of Albania, but was militarily unprepared, and had a population generally lacking much enthusiasm, for a wider industrialized war.

Hitler now turned his attention to the east and Poland. By now German re-armament had advanced at a remarkable rate - in 1930 the country had no combat ready air-planes and an army of less than the 100,000 allowed under the terms of the Versailles Treaty. But by the

---

[26] Such is the complexity (and moral vacuity) of international relationships biased towards the narrow pursuit of national elite-group interests, that at this time, Britain was actually encouraging German military support for the Finns in their border conflict with Russia.

end of 1939 it had over 8,000 combat ready fighters and bombers, an army of 1,000,000 men; a mix of conscript and professional soldiers - now with mainly Nazi supporting generals at its head. An army quite well equipped with modern Panzer tank and anti-tank groups, along with other highly mobile armoured units, and a navy being steadily strengthened, with one battle-cruiser following another as they eased their way down slipways into the cold gray water of the Baltic Sea. Ready to supplement this military capacity were the nearly 8 million (end 1938) members of the Hitler Youth movement - 14-18 year old youths who had been subjected to years of Nazi indoctrination and who had all been expected to take an oath of allegiance committing them to sacrifice their own lives for their Führer, Adolf Hitler. Reluctant parents were warned that if they did not co-operate in the enrolment of their children into the Nazi youth movement they risked having them taken into the care of the state.

The ease with which he had gained Austria and Czechoslovakia reinforced Hitler's confidence in his assessment of likely international reaction. After a period of his trade-mark disingenuous diplomacy Hitler offered the Polish government a deal that involved their agreeing to join the anti-Comintern Pact (along with Germany, Italy and Japan), the return of the free City of Danzig to the Germans, and ceding of a broad corridor through Polish territory in order to allow more easy access to East Prussia. In January 1939 Hitler added the bonus of a promise of some Czech (Teschen) and some Soviet Ukraine territory that Poland had an historic interest in. Hitler felt that the Polish dictatorship also shared his anti-Semitism and anti-communism, so might concede to his demands, along with a mutually beneficial security arrangement. But the Polish government (with their foreign secretary - Colonel Josef Beck - leading the negotiations) was determined against conceding to Hitler's demands, its members had more confidence in the capacity of the Polish army than its subsequent performance would justify.

Aware of British and French diplomatic attempts to form a pact with Russia, Germany offered them a more attractive deal and, in August 1939, the German and Russian foreign secretaries agreed a non-aggression pact (the Ribbentrop/Molotov Pact). Part of which was a secret arrangement that included the Soviets being offered the Baltic States and the parts of Poland that they coveted. Hitler considered that the formation of the pact with Russia would deter Britain and France from going to war in support of Polish independence. Behind all the negotiating too-ing and frow-ing during 1939 it seems that Hitler was already determined on the invasion of Poland and, if necessary, of testing his Reich army in the heat of wider warfare. As early as April 1939 he had issued just five copies of the top secret document code-named the 'White Case', in which the 1st of September was set for the invasion date and noted the task of the German armed forces to be: '.......to destroy the Polish armed forces. To this end a surprise attack is to be aimed at and prepared for.'

By August it was clear that Hitler would not gain his aims involving Poland without military action. He was still of the view that Britain and France would be reluctant of going to war over Poland. He used national radio to accuse Poland of provocative border activities that were in fact actions undertaken by SS soldiers wearing Polish army uniforms. So, using this 'provocation' as an excuse, the German army mobilized and in the early hours of 1st September, with the support of air-power, the first of 50 divisions of the Germany army were ordered to cross the Polish border. By the end of the month the mechanized German army had in effect rolled over the poorly equipped Polish defenders and was in control of Warsaw. Then, from 17th September, the Red Army would be attacking Poland's eastern border. By 1945 at least 5.7 million Poles would have been killed, with 3 million of these being Jews.

At the end of August Britain had signed an Anglo/Polish alliance committing Britain to come to its aid in the event of a German invasion. The British government followed through on this commitment, and on 3rd September the German government was informed that the two countries were now at war. France soon followed with a similar declaration.

So, within but 20 years (two decades) of the end of the 'war to end war' the hellish terrain of another world-wide conflict lay open to the immediate future. And why would this not be a reasonable expectation given that the same fractured international political system, with essentially the same structural dynamics prioritizing national (elite-determined) interests, continued to be the predominant mode of global governance. World leaders - leading mostly voluntarily dumb and obedient populations to a considerable extent propagandized into adhering to a form of nationalism determined by elite interests - traced a public narrative of peaceful intentions that in limed reality overlay a hard-edged practice of political hegemony and of preparing for and pursuing competition and on occasion conflict.

As Britain and France stood back waiting to see Germany's next move, control over timing as well as military momentum was with Hitler; if in early 1940 the actual balance of military capacity in Europe favoured Britain and France. The two allied nations having 151 divisions facing Germany's 135 divisions, with France alone having access to 3,254 tanks to Germany's 2,439. Whilst Germany had marginally more aircraft, Britain would soon address this difference. Viewing war as his and Germany's destiny seemed to have been a deep-rooted motivational factor for Hitler. But in the early stages of the war he also retained a pragmatic sense of strategy and his next move was taken to ensure access to Swedish iron-ore. In April the German army attacked lightly defended Denmark then crossed the Baltic to invade Norway. Here the resistance, reinforced with British troops and supported by its navy, was the first real test of the German forces. The German casualties reached 5,000 men and its navy received a serious mauling. But Hitler's main military aim had been achieved and, in addition, Norwegian Fiords would provide suitable bases for the growing German submarine fleet, allowing easier access to the North Atlantic and to the trans-Atlantic convoys of material that Britain's war effort would depend upon.

With the Scandinavian campaign judged a success Hitler was ready to move on to further advance, and from the 10th May 1940 (the same day that Winston Churchill had replaced Chamberlin as prime minister of Britain) the German army began its now well-practiced form of mobile warfare known as 'Blitzkrieg' as it crossed into the Netherlands. The Dutch and Belgium army divisions were easily overwhelmed by the advancing German troops. Next would be France and, strategically at that time, the German military leadership was superior to that of both of the main Allies. Its Panzer tanks, and other mobile armoured units, with air-craft in support, proved effective in outflanking the French and British forces. The defenders were divided (in the Ardennes) and in retreat. The allied armies' were soon in a slow, ordered, retreat west that increasingly became a rout; leaving most of their heavy armour behind as they fled.

Within six weeks of crossing the Dutch border German officers were standing on the tops of the cliffs of Normandy surveying the coast of a Britain now isolated across the Channel, and jackbooted troops were strutting along the Avenue de Champs-Elysees in the centre of Paris. It was a Britain that, although retaining some pride from the rescue of over 338,000 British (BEF), and some French, troops from the port of Dunkirk, was being run by a government with a coalition War Cabinet composed of five members (the Conservatives Churchill, Chamberlin, Halifax, and Labour's Clement Atlee and Arthur Greenwood) gravely considering the alternatives of pressing for peace with Hitler or standing alone against him. Halifax, as Foreign Secretary, reluctantly favoured negotiating with the Germans, and in July Hitler was publically calling for Britain to make peace. But Churchill, supported by Atlee and Greenwood, was determined to resist and felt the British people were with him.

Hitler did have plans for the invasion of Britain but the outcome of the aerial engagements together known as the 'The Battle of Britain', in May/June 1940, suggested to the German high command that massive resources would be need to be deployed if a successful campaign was to be progressed. By October Hitler had decided to put his invasion plans on hold and instead turned his attention towards the east. Here lay the vast expanse of the Soviet territories and as much 'Lebensraum' as even he could wish for. In addition, his army (the Wehrmacht) had proved its ability to sweep all before it when engaged in land-based warfare, so why would it not be easy enough to repeat this against what Hitler's intelligence services were telling him were, the Soviet Union's poorly equipped Red Army.

By spring 1941 the Germans were effectively in control of most of western and central Europe. This control had been extended to Hungry, Rumania, and Bulgaria, and, following the invasion of Yugoslavia and Greece (including Crete), German military occupation reach south to the Mediterranean.

Stalin and Molotov considered that the Germans were militarily stretched just to maintain control of the land they had occupied and that Hitler continued to be distracted by preparation for the invasion of Britain. This misled them into adopting a more aggressive strategy, as Stalin sought control of the Baltic States and eastern parts of the Balkans. Up to spring 1941 Stalin and Hitler engaged in a diplomatic relationship based on mutual flattery, with German expansion in Europe being coded by them as a series of justified 'defensive measures'. But Hitler progressively lost patience with Russian military activities, especially its occupation of Lithuania on the Prussian border, and in the background was his long-term aim of turning on the communist Soviet Union. Ambition and impatience (and months of secret military planning) came together and, in the early hours of 22nd June 'Operation Barbarossa' was launched.

The army that rumbled across the Russian border on that morning was the largest military force that had ever been assembled - 3.5 million men in 190 divisions, 3,600 tanks, and 2,700 airplanes, with a vast supply system ready to enable the advance to maintain its momentum. Hitler's strategy, based on the highly mobile panzer tank-led Blitzkrieg, involved the army advancing on three separate fronts, each aiming to destroy the Red Army forces prior to the wider occupation of Russian territory. Such was his dislike of communism that Hitler directed his generals to ignore the 'normal' conventions of warfare - in particular the Hague Convention - German officers were directed to be brutal and ruthless and not to let any misplaced 'gentlemanly ideology' inhibit their fighting spirit. Of 5 million Russian soldiers taken prisoner during the whole campaign (to 1945) 3 million died and many of these had been brutally shot down when trying to surrender.

By early autumn each of the three German fighting groups had advanced deep into Russian territory, with Leningrad in the north, Moscow in the centre, and Kiev in the south, each under threat. Massive casualties suffered by the Red Army were of little concern to Stalin and most Soviet generals and, in terms of a wider strategy; the retreat had made a useful contribution to absorbing the German momentum. The 60,000 German casualties within the first six weeks (announced in German newspapers) did have a significant impact on public morale in Germany.

Hitler's invasion plans were deficient, due in part to the poor quality of intelligence reports in their gross underestimation of Russian military resources; the estimate was for about 5,000 tanks when the actual number was 20,000. Hitler also believed that Stalin and the Bolshevik regime had but a tenuous hold on the country and so could not withstand the pressure of a successful invasion. But, as autumn drew on, the Germans faced two key factors which first slowed then halted their advance. These were the steady reinforcement of Russian positions and the beginning of the Russian winter weather; the same two factors that had made such a crucial difference to Napoleon's 'Grand Army' in 1812. The rains began in October, turning unpaved roads into muddy tracks and so conditions unsuitable for mechanized units. The temperature dropped to well below zero, causing fuel and water to freeze; with frosts so hard that even just starting tanks and other vehicles became a problem. The freezing cold and blizzard conditions impacted on troop morale, and frostbite would kill 112,000 German soldiers by the campaign's end.

By late 1941, the Germans, their Axis partners, and in the north the Finns, had advanced on all three fronts, with Leningrad almost surrounded in the north and the central army group less than 40 miles (fighting in the forests abutting the western suburbs) from central Moscow. But the Russians had been gradually building their military capacity; consolidating their forces in preparation for a counterattack on the Moscow front. It was a counteroffensive led by General Georgi Zhukov, with 100 Red Army divisions trained and equipped to fight in cold weather at his disposal, being launched along a 200 mile long front. The German resistance was determined, but their supply lines were over-extended and they were steadily pushed back, losing 200,000 men killed and as many as 700,000 wounded. In addition to the actual losses, this action was a bitter blow for Hitler and the German High Command as, for the first time, an army of the Third Reich had suffered a significant setback on the battlefield. The strategy of Blitzkrieg and the notion of an invincible Wehrmacht had been shown to be at least an exaggeration.

In the north, the Germans and Finns had been more successful, with the City of Leningrad being almost completely surrounded by September; so began a siege that was to last for 872 days. A period during which 641,000 civilians died from disease, starvation, or from exposure to the bitterly cold winters of 1941, 42, and 43. The 200,000 Red Army defenders held out against 750,000 soldiers of the German and Finnish forces until June 1944 when the siege was lifted.

During 1940/41 Hitler's action against Britain had continued but with little significant impact. On balance, even the mass bombing of British cities (the 'Blitz') had little impact on industrial output, and in general made the population more determined to resist. Up to about early 1942 the German navy was unable to sink a sufficient amount of British shipping to make supplies an issue. Indeed in most naval engagements with the British - the flagship German battleships Admiral Graff Spee sunk in 1939 the Bismarck sunk in 1941 and with the Tirpitz badly damaged in 1944 – the German navy suffered the heavier losses. Until the British were able to devise ways of dealing with them, the 200 odd German 'U-boat' submarines active in the Atlantic would pose the most serious threat; sinking 1,664 mainly merchant ships in 1942 alone.

Throughout 1941, Hitler and Ribbentrop had been urging the Japanese leaders to launch an attack on Allied interests in South East Asia. The Germans considered that a threat to US and British interests in the Far East would divert US resources away from supporting Britain; the lease-led scheme, and food and fuel supplies sent across the Atlantic, were providing a lifeline in supporting Britain's and later

Russia's resistance. Japan had for at least a decade been frustrated, mainly by the US and Britain, in its attempt to gain access to south Asian raw materials and markets for its manufactured goods. By October 1941 the new government, led by General Töjö Hideki, felt it had no alternative but to go to war. Hitler's success in Europe, based on fast moving mechanized forces, encouraged the Japanese government to think that they could replicate this success in the Far East.

On the 7th December the Japanese air-force attacked the important US naval base at Pearl Harbour (in Hawaii). Within days of the first attack Japanese bombers had also attacked the US Cavite naval base in the Philippines and a number of important US airfields, also in the Philippines (including Clark and Iba airfields). Taken together, these raids inflicted considerable damage to US warships and their air-force, with about half of the US aircraft capability being put out of action.

What has been typically presented by US and western media and most historians as a 'surprise attack' (by the 'typically' cruel and devious Japanese) is misleading; true in terms of day and place but quite predictable given the way in which a militarized Japan was being treated. In fact, prior to the Pearl Habour action, Henry Stimson, the US Secretary for War, aware of the economic and diplomatic pressure they were putting on Japan (specifically in relation to its occupation of China and the economic blockade), noted in his diary that they, the US, should be seeking a way to manoeuvre Japan into firing the first shot.

The week following the attack on Pearl Harbour saw extensive Japanese military action elsewhere in the region. On 8th December the Japanese were bombing Hong Kong, which surrendered to a land force on 25th. On 9th December Bangkok in Thailand had fallen; enabling the rear-guard protection of Japanese forces as these moved down the Malaya peninsula, taking Singapore at its southern tip in early February. It was at Singapore that the British suffered the humiliation of having 90,000 troops surrender to a smaller Japanese force. On 10th December the Japanese landed at Luzon in the Philippines and had taken Manila by the 2nd January 1942. With its modern navy, supported by a range of air cover, and a familiarity with the waters of the South China Sea and the western Pacific, the Japanese invasion fleet easily beat off an Allied attempt to intercept it in the Battle of the Java Sea on February 27th.

By March 1942, the Japanese were occupying or otherwise in control of an extensive region. One extending from Burma and Sumatra in the west to the Marshall Islands in the east - south as far as the Solomon Islands and north to part of the large Sakhalin Island and northern Manchuria. Within but five months the Japanese had erupted out of their homeland and inflicted military defeats on the US, China, Britain, and on other Europeans nations that had been in possession of colonies in south-east Asia. In doing so they gained access to sources of the valuable industrial materials they had been seeking.

To the west, more German military resources had to be deployed to assist the generally militarily inept Italian land forces in southern Europe and North Africa. The Italian government had declared war on Britain and France in May 1940. With Mussolini intent on emulating Hitler's success in both gaining territory, as well as military glory. The Italian people mostly lacked much enthusiasm for war and the military hierarchy cautioned on the lack of preparedness for progressing any lengthy campaign. Italian forces did initially defeat the British forces in Somaliland and occupied most of East Africa. But an attempt to invade Greece ended in humiliating defeat at the hands of brave and tenacious Greek resistance fighters.

The main theatre of war for the Italians was North Africa. Where they began their campaign in early September 1940, using their base in occupied Libya from which to launch an invasion of Egypt. Here the poor quality of the Italian military leadership was clearly exposed as their troops were fairly easily defeated by British and Australian defenders, with 130,000 being taken prisoner. Mussolini had depleted his supreme command of some of the more able officers and promoted a number of inexperienced officers. Men whose loyalty to Il Duce was the primary qualification for their gaining a high command.

In February 1941 the German General Erwin Rommel, with two divisions of German troops (soon be known as the Afrika Korps) and two divisions of Italian troops, landed at Tripoli (Libya). From where they regrouped and, with fast-moving mechanized divisions in the vanguard, they pushed eastwards. Rommel's advance made swift progress, pushing the British and Dominion forces back as far as Tobruk. But here he was unable to dislodge the 14,000 Australian (9th Division) defenders; losing momentum, due in part to his supply-lines becoming overstretched. Tobruk being a strategically important port that could have been a key supply base for the Axis forces; without it supply was from Tripoli 1500 km behind their lines. The British made two unsuccessful attempts to lift the siege but they were at least able to supply and reinforce Tobruk from the sea. After the initial attempt to capture the town had been beaten off most of the Australians were replaced by British and Polish troops as the port settled into a siege that would last for 241 days, until November 1941.

In addition to supporting the Italian ambitions in North Africa, Hitler had his own more strategic motives for German involvement. If the Suez Canal could be taken then British access to the Far East would be disrupted and from Egypt the Germans could work their way north-east to take control of vital Middle-East oilfields.

After a lull in the fighting, during which the Allied army re-grouped before launching a well-supplied counteroffensive (Nov. 1941 - Operation Crusader - which also lifted the siege of Tobruk). Then, following a series of fiercely fought tank battles, the outnumbered (in tanks) Axis force was pushed west as far as El Aghelia by the year's end. Here, the Axis force rested, re-grouped were resupplied and, by early January 1942, Rommel was again ready to launch his force eastward. This time he did manage to capture Tobruk (gaining a useful amount of military supplies and taking 35,000 prisoners), taking Benghazi by end January, and reaching Alexandra (Gazala) by early February. Within but six weeks of the start of Rommel's offensive the Allied forces were desperately trying to hold a defensive position at el Alamein within 50 miles of the outskirts of Alexandra. The first battle of el-Alamein (1-27 July) halted Rommel's advance, partly due to his troops being exhausted. Now the soldiers of both armies were at a stand-off, with their supplies running low and, apart from occasional skirmishes and some probing, the next four months was a period of rebuilding military capacity.

In the spring it had seemed that Hitler's ambition to gain control of the Suez Canal would be achieved within weeks. But Rommel's force had been depleted by the withdrawal of some troops back to Europe and, due partly to effective British naval action against German shipping, his reserves of fuel and ammunition were low. The allied leadership was aware of the implications of losing control of the canal and northern Egypt so sent sufficient reinforcements to allow the Allied forces to prepare for a counteroffensive. By this time very few Axis supply ships – carrying tanks, fuel, and ammunition - were able to avoid the attention of British warships.

In contrast to Rommel's force being poorly re-supplied at the time that fighting restarted, the newly appointed commander of the 8th Army, General Bernard Montgomery, was in a much better position. He had almost six times as many tanks (1230 to 210), nearly three times the number of troops (230,000 to 80,000), as well as overwhelming air superiority, than Rommel. And, due to ill-health, Rommel at this time was recuperating in Austria.

The fighting started again in October (the Allies Operation 'Torch') and it was the 2nd Battle of el Alamein (23 Oct - 4 Nov.) that began to turn the tide of the campaign decisively in favour of the Allies. Their tanks and other armoured units broke through the Axis lines and Rommel (who had been ordered to return to Africa), running short of fuel and ammunition, planned for an ordered retreat that would allow him to preserve his force for a later offensive. But Hitler ordered him to hold the line; a militarily inept order that resulted in avoidable losses. When even Hitler saw this was a mistake, the delayed retreat was less well-ordered than it might have been. A retreat that forced Rommel all the way back to the Libya's western border with Tunisia.

Meanwhile, more British and US forces had been gathered in Gibraltar in preparation for an invasion (a wider, strategic, element of Operation 'Torch') to the west of Tripoli. In overall command was the

US General Dwight D. Eisenhower. In November 1942 this invasion fleet cruised east into the Mediterranean and landed troops in a number of locations in Algeria and Morocco. This region of North Africa was controlled by France and although the invasion force initially encountered some resistance from troops still loyal to the Vichy regime this was soon overcome. After re-grouping and consolidating their position, the allied troops advanced eastwards towards Rommel's force.

Now trapped between two armies, and with the Allies having superiority in air and naval support, defeat for the Axis force was now a matter of when rather than if; and the when was completed, after much hard fighting, in May 1943. Rommel had by then resigned his command and on the Axis surrender 250,000 German and Italian soldiers were taken prisoner. The North African campaign had tied down 1,000,000 Allied service personal and their support (often under fire) had been a massive logistical operation, but now these experienced military units and the supply line organization could be directed towards southern Europe.

Nationalism can be one of a number of primary factors that foster the expression of evil; elements of this include the construction of some national mythology claiming estimable characteristics for one's own nation, and assigning derogatory characteristics to others. It's interesting to consider the veracity of one of the latter that emerged on the Allied side during the war, and that endured well beyond it.

Italian servicemen have often been subject to superficial assessment as to their fighting ability but, in addition to poor quality leadership and poor training, they also, during most WWII engagements with the allies were armed with markedly inferior weaponry. Even so, there were many examples of Italian bravery and of their fighting skills. Probably the most well-known being the soldiers that were sent to fight with the Germans on the eastern front. Here the mountain troops of the three Alpina divisions (Tridentina, Julia, Cuneense) stand out, especially for their role in the bitterly fought Battle of Stalingrad. Two whole divisions (Julia and Cuneense) were destroyed, and the third badly mauled, as they fought a determined rear-guard action against a much larger Russian force. Following a number of fiercely fought engagements in Northern Africa, both the British commander General Alexander and the German commander General Rommel praised the fighting qualities of Italian soldiers. National identity does not define degree of bravery, but self-serving nationalist mythologies do. The potential coward and the potential hero lies within each of us, if mostly we just share a self-protective ordinariness - 19th and 20th century industrial wars have invariably been won by the best equipped, largest forces; bravery and cowardice can be features of both the 'victors' and of the 'defeated' equally.

In North Africa it was the ability to reinforce and sustain an army i.e. 'logistics' that made a fundamental difference to the outcome, not any asymmetric indicator of bravery between combatants. And it was the ability of the Allies to supply and reinforce their North African forces that progressively wore down the Axis army.

When the Africa campaign was over, and with the Allies holding the naval superiority across the Mediterranean, military planning turned attention to Italy with its access to southern Germany. The Italian campaign began with the invasion of the large island of Sicily. A seaborne landing saw the first units, of what would be a force of nearly half a million men, landed on the island. The bulk of this force was made up of the British 8th Army under General Montgomery's command, and the US 7th Army under the command of Maj. Gen. George S. Patton. The German defences were relatively weak, with the main resistance coming from panzer tank units. Once he could assess his military vulnerability the German commander, Field Marshall Albert Kesselring, decided to evacuate his surviving force back to the Italian mainland.

By now the Italian government had lost confidence in Mussolini and at the end of the month he was forced to resign, with the King appointing Marshall Pietro Badoglio as the new head of government. By early April the Allies followed close behind the German withdrawal, crossing the Straits of Messina to establish a bridgehead on the 'toe' of southern Italy. The state of the roads and stiff German resistance made progress difficult. But a second landing further north at Salerno stretched the defenders resources and Naples was taken by the 1st October. Further reinforcements came with another landing on the south-eastern coast that advanced north, capturing Brindisi within two weeks. The Italian King and his government fled south to the safety of Allied hands and then on 29th September Italy surrendered and itself declared war on Germany. Now the German strategy in Italy was to do as much as possible to defend Germany's southern flank. Given this, Kesselring determined on a strategy of military deployment that would make the Allied advance as costly as possibly. A key aspect of this was a defensive line - the Gustav Line - with Monte Cassino at its south-western end. Initially this line of defence held the allied advance and it took a number of combined assaults by the attacking forces to enable a break-through, allowing Rome to be taken by 5th June.

This advance had left the town of Monte Cassino as a smoking monument to the destructive power of the shelling and mass bombing the town had endured. Continued Allied progress was hard-fought, as the German troops put up stiff resistance, buying time for another line of defence to be established across the Italian peninsular - the Gothic Line - just to the south of La Spezia crossing the Apennine mountain range to the Adriatic coast north of Ravenna in the east. Due partly to continuing well organized resistance and the loss of troops redeployed to the newly opened western front in France, the US and British forces made only slow progress. From August the Allies did launch a number of, mostly localized, offensives including the 8th Army's Operation 'Olive' on the Adriatic side of the line on 25th of the month. On the western side, a mainly US force broke through to the City of Bologna, with Forli, Ravenna, San Marino and Rimini, being under Allied control by early November - The Allied force facing the Germans was composed of units of Indian, Canadian, Greek, and New Zealand troops, along with the US, British, and a Free Italian unit. Now the winter set in and this, along with the mountainous terrain, halted any significant further Allied progress. It would be after a spring offensive mounted the following year that the Germans and remnants of Fascist Italy's forces (RSI) finally surrendered on 2nd May.

During this period, Italian Partisans had been harrying the German communication lines and the on the 27th April they captured Mussolini and some fellow fascists as they fled north. Il Duce and his fascist companions were shot by firing squad two days later with his body being hung upside down from a lamppost in the Piazza Loreto in the centre of Milan; an ignominious end to a vainglorious man.

On the Russian front, the government had the ability to mobilize far more military manpower than German military strategists had planned for and its expanding Red Army was being supplied by an effective armaments industry, mostly located to the east of the Urals. At the Tehran Conference of late November 1943, Stalin, Churchill, and Roosevelt, had agreed a broad coordinated strategy, intent on defeating the Nazis. Two key aspects of this being that the Russians would aim to push the Germans back from the east and that the US and Britain (and some 'Free' units of nationals from occupied countries) would plan for a landing in France during 1944, so pushing against the Germans from the west.

The German offensive on Kursk in summer 1943 was the last offensive on a similar scale to those of 1940 and 1942 - and here they were fought to a standstill, losing a large amount of men and equipment. The tide of war in Eastern Europe was turning and from January 1944 the Red Army slowly began to take the overall military initiative. The Germans and their Allies initially proved resilient and for the first half of 1944 they managed some successful localized counter-offensives. But only in a few places did these actions temporarily delay the Red Army's progressive advance west. When the western allies landed on French beaches in June 1944, some German divisions were transferred from the eastern front to reinforce their western forces. A change that really only accelerated the inevitable as Russian forces gained momentum on a broad front - they reached Warsaw by January 1945, occupied the Baltic States, reached Budapest by February, Vienna by March, and in early April were pouring into Konigsberg in East Prussia.

Throughout the early months of 1944, the Allies had been building troop numbers and stores of military equipment in locations across southern England - this was facilitated by the Allied navy having gained the ability to significantly reduce the effectiveness of what had been a serious U-Boat threat to Atlantic supply convoys. On 6th June 1944 an Allied army embarked on the task of opening a western front on the mainland of Europe in 'Operation Overlord'. This force was composed of British, US, Canadian, and the 'free' units of countries occupied by the Nazis; French, Polish, Norwegian, Czech, and others. The initial landing, of about 175,000 troops, took place on five beaches along the Normandy Coast. Once the beach-heads had been established, and the port of Cherbourg (and later the large port of Antwerp) captured, 1.5 million men and millions of tons of military equipment would follow within a short time. Before the war's end 3 million Allied military personal would be deployed to the western front. US General Eisenhower was in overall command, with Britain's General Montgomery as operational commander. Operation Overlord was, taken overall, a text book invasion - the defenders were unsure where the landings would take place so had to spread their resources to cover most of the north-west coast of France. Heavy Allied bombing degraded German transport and supply lines, with fighter aircraft ensuring air superiority for the invading force. In addition, from 1943, the Allies had had access to a stream of intelligence reports based on code machines (British 'Ultra', was especially useful in 'listening in' to U-Boat and command communications, and the US had their own 'Magic' code breaker), and code breaking experts who been able to break the en-coded forms of German communications. This allowed the Allied High Command reasonably accurate information of German troop deployments. Even so, the coastal defences, organized by the now Field Marshall Rommel, provided a major challenge to the invading forces.

The first six weeks following the initial landing saw hard fighting along the new front. With a decisive breakthrough coming in late July early August when the US army reached Avranches. The Free French were allowed the honour of advancing into Paris on 25th August. A series of German counterattacks failed to hold the progressive, if uneven, advance of the main British force to the north and the US forces through the centre and to the south. In October, the Germans had to surrender a large number of troops and an amount of war materials at Aachen.

As the winter approached the pace of advance slowed and on 16th December the Germans launched a massive surprise counter offensive. Hitler's plan was to force a way through the allied lines, intending to capture the extensive port facilities of Antwerp. Gaining this would enable the Germans to cut the main supply route for the allies and so reduce their capacity to advance, allowing time for the German forces to regroup. The two factors of surprise, and low cloud forcing USAF and RAF planes to remain on the ground, assisted the large highly mobile force that the Germans had mustered. Following a two hour bombardment with heavy artillery, units of tanks and armoured vehicles led the assault, against the US front line. During the first two days of fierce fighting the Germans advanced, gaining a 60 mile 'bulge' in the Allied front. But the Allies had taken up fairly strong defensive positions and, having been fighting for months, were psychologically prepared to absorb the German onslaught. After the first two days the cloud base lifted allowing the Allies to exploit their air superiority. Another critical factor in halting the German offensive was their running out of the fuel vital to maintain their mechanized momentum; a shortage due in part to allied bombing of the German supply lines. This offensive in the Ardennes, the 'Battle of the Bulge' (as it became known), was to be the final action in which any German advance would be made and from now they would be fighting whilst in continuous retreat. The action had cost the Germans 100,000 men killed or wounded and the loss of a massive amount of material, including many panzer tanks being abandoned as they run out of fuel; experienced troops and munitions that they were unable to replace. This action also resulted in 81,000 US soldiers being killed. From early 1945 the Allied advance was renewed and the last major military objective, the River Rhine, was reached by April 1945, with the first crossing being made at the Remagen (Ludendorff) Bridge in March.

The Allies now knew that they were approaching the final stages of the war, and the US/British forces advancing steadily from the west and the Russians from the east, were each determined to overrun as much territory as possible. This, in order to strengthen their position for what they knew would be difficult negotiations, on borders and political influence, once the war had ended.

Since the initial landings in June 1944 there had been a sense of urgency on the allied side as intelligence suggested the possibility of the Germans having the capacity to develop an 'Atomic bomb'. In 1938 the German physicists, Otto Hahn and Fritz Strassmann, had discovered that the bombardment of uranium with neutrons caused the uranium atoms to split, and that a product of this 'nuclear fission' being the release of energy - it would be the release of this energy in an uncontrolled chain reaction that would provide the enormous destructive power of the Atomic Bomb. There was also the more immediate concern with the introduction of the pilotless V1 then V2 rockets, carrying high explosive cargos, mainly targeting London from early June 1944 to end of March 1945. These were the first long-range guided ballistic missiles, capable of speeds over 3,000 miles per hr, carrying 2,000lbs of high explosives; on impact they would cause a huge blast-wave capable of destroying whole rows of London's tightly packed terraced houses. A new weapon had been introduced into the world's military killing capability. One with implications for future weapon delivery systems.

At the end of April Red Army soldiers were fighting on the outskirts of Berlin and by 2nd May the City, now mostly reduced to rubble by Russian shelling and allied blanket bombing, was surrounded. By which time Adolf Hitler and his (then wife) Eva Braun had committed suicide (as had Goebbels and Himmler) and it was left to the German Chief-of-Staff, General Alfred Jodl, to sign the document of unconditional surrender and so both symbolically and actually bring an end to the Third Reich. When the fighting in Europe ceased Russian forces had met their western Allies just east of the River Elbe.

The series of conferences involving the leaders and foreign

secretaries of the three leading Allied countries (United States, Britain, and the Soviet Union) held at Tehran, Yalta, and Potsdam, saw each party endeavouring to persuade, cajole, or bully, the others into a post-war redrawing of national borders, and to define areas of control and influence, in line with the leaders' perspective of their own national interests. Little interest was taken of the views of the mass of people whose political future was being negotiated. Soon after the war's end the outcome of the conferences was seen to impact adversely on the people of the Baltic States and on those of Greece and Italy, and with a significant portion of the world's nations being divided into two antagonistic political and military groupings.

In the south-east Asian theatre of conflict the Japanese expansionist strategy had been contained by a combination of national forces, but predominantly with the US taking the lead. The Allied command began to formulate a plan to roll back the Japanese occupation of islands in the western Pacific and South China Sea (island by island); beginning with the Solomon Islands the Bismarck Archipelago, and the large island of New Guinea.

The initiative on where to begin was taken out of US hands when, in early July 1942, the Japanese occupied the island of Guadalcanal at the southern end of the Solomons where they soon began to construct what would have been a strategically important air-base. The US response was to land the 1st Marine Corps on the island. The Japanese resistance was determined and over the next few weeks each side sent reinforcements. In late August the Japanese launched an attack on the marine's beach-head and so began a period of intense fighting. Initially, each side was able to deploy about an equivalent number of troops (roughly 22,000 each).

At sea, in a series of minor engagements the Imperial navy lost more ships that the US navy. Then, in the Battle of Tassafaronga, the Japanese suffered very heavy losses, including eight destroyers sunk. The US naval superiority in the region resulted in Japan not being able to land significant reinforcements of men and materials on Guadalcanal. Only 4,000 of the 12,500 Japanese troops sent were actually landed. Whereas the US was able to land a substantially greater number of troops to reinforce their units. By January 1943 the Allies had double the number of troops than the Japanese and, accepting the reality on the ground, the remaining Japanese force evacuated the island. By this time a force of US and Australians had also staged and consolidated landings on the east coast of Papua (the eastern side of the strategically important New Guinea). These two successful engagements secured the Allied supply lines from Australia and New Zealand.

By mid 1942, the Allies had moved on to open a new front on the Aleutian Island group located about 1,500 miles to the north-east of Japan; on the southern limits of the Bering Sea. On gaining the islands by late spring 1943, the US was able to construct air-bases that enabled bombers to reach targets in Japanese occupied islands in the Kuril chain further south; lying between the Aleutians and mainland Japan.

During the summer the US had continued to advance through the Solomon Islands, often meeting fierce resistance as they progressed. The Japanese fought hard over the island of Vela Lavella but by October they were facing defeat and so evacuated their surviving force from the island. Defending the Solomon Islands had cost the Japanese 10,000 killed with the US losing 1,150 men. The US moved on to the large island of New Britain with the town of Talasea being taken by March 1944. During this period there had been a number of intense naval engagements in the area and although both sides suffered losses the numerical balance favoured the Allies. At this stage of the war the Allies could more easily replace their lost shipping than could the Japanese.

From now the Japanese high command accepted that they would be waging a defensive war and so adopted a broad strategy of strengthening their strategic positions and counterattacking when opportunity allowed. From late 1943 to spring 1944 they endeavoured to reinforce their bases in a line running from western New Guinea to the Caroline Island chain about 1000 miles to the north east. The US command were now aware of the military limitations of the Japanese and were more confident in the fighting abilities of their own navy, air-force, and marine units, in the tropical conditions they were encountering.

Invasion of the Gilbert Islands began in late November 1943 and by Feb 1944 the Allies were attacking the Marshall Islands and bombing air-bases on the Caroline Islands. The impact of the latter being the destruction of 200 air-craft, an outcome that in effect nullified the strategic value of these islands to the Japanese. The next objective would be the strategically important island chain of the Marianas, beyond which would be mainland Japan with little but sea between them. Keenly aware of the need to retain the Marianas, the Japanese poured reinforcements into the area. They now had over 1000 land-based aircraft, with another 450 based on nine aircraft carriers, and all of this within a theatre of conflict taking in the Marianas, the Carolines, and western New Guinea. The US offensive began in June, involving 500 ships and over 125,000 troops. They landed two marine divisions on Saipan Island (Marianas) on the 15th, a force facing 30,000 Japanese defenders determined to resist. The US force was able to significantly reinforce its marine units and by mid July, after very heavy fighting, Japanese resistance had been overcome.

From the 19th June a significant naval engagement had began between the Japanese Combined Fleet and the larger US 5th Fleet, in what became known as the Battle of the Philippine Sea. An engagement in which the Japanese lost 400 planes and 2 air-craft carriers (the US lost 130 planes). Taking the Marianas had cost the US force 4,750 men killed but the Japanese lost 46,000 killed or taken prisoner. From the Marianas, the long range B-29 Super-fortress bombers could strike at the Japanese homeland. Such was the seriousness of these defeats that the Japanese cabinet led by Admiral Töjö resigned, to be replaced by a new government led by General Koiso Kuniaki.

On July 27th/28th the US high command, including General MacArthur and Admiral Nimitz, met with President Roosevelt in Honolulu to consider their position. The most significant outcome being that they decided that the next major US objective would be to expel the Japanese from the Philippine Islands; so, edging steadily closer to Japan proper.

The US chose the relatively small Philippine island of Leyte to begin this new campaign and on the 20th October they landed four divisions, in support of which they had also deployed a large surface fleet (under the command of Nimitz) to the area. As expected, the Japanese defenders had established strong defensive positions and the fighting across the island was fierce. At the time of this land-based conflict there was also an intense navel engagement, the 'Battle of Leyte Gulf'. The outcome of this being a massive defeat for the Japanese Imperial navy, establishing dominance for the US that would be maintained throughout the rest of the war.

Leyte was taken by December1944 and by early January 1945 the US forces had taken the neighbouring island of Mindoro and had landed marines on the west coast of the most important Philippine island of Luzan. Once again, the Japanese troops put up stiff resistance but the capital, Manila, fell to the US force on 3d March. The US takeover of the Philippines was aided by an indigenous resistance movement that had been harassing the Japanese. The loss of the Philippines was a significant blow to the Japanese, a loss compounded in July when a mainly Australian force landed on the large island of Borneo that, working its way south, was able to cut off Japanese access to the very important oil-fields on the southern tip of the island.

It was during the Battle of Leyte Gulf that the Japanese launched their first concerted 'Kamikaze' mission undertaken by the newly formed 'Special Attack Unit'. The first attack using planes to be flown on purpose into military targets had been against an Australian ship (NMSA 'Australia') when 30 sailors had been killed. From October 1944 there would be over 2,500 planes piloted to destruction on these suicide mission. The (Kamikaze -'divine wind') pilots were between the ages of 19-23, most of whom had volunteered to die on behalf of the 'divine' emperor, but many others had come under significant pressure to volunteer. The use of these types of weaponry - similar suicide weapons - included speed boats, gliders, and even submarines, all laden with high explosives. The most extreme form that these suicide missions took was the use of the then heaviest battleship in the world armed with the largest guns ever mounted on a warship. This, the flagship 'Yamato', set off in early April 1944, on a suicide mission to Okinawa with only sufficient fuel for the outward journey. Its orders were to run aground on the island and then keep fighting until destroyed. But the US was able to detect the ship on route and it was sunk on 7th April by carrier-based air-craft before it reached Okinawa, with the loss of almost all of the crew. This desperate act reflected the desperation of the Japanese high command, most of whom had by now realized the parlous situation their country was in.

Up to the spring 1943 the British led forces to the west had made little progress against the Japanese in Burma. Then, in May, they reorganized their Far East command structure, with vice Admiral Louis Mountbatten being appointed supreme commander of the British and Dominion force in south-east Asia. The most significant set-back suffered by the Japanese in this theatre of conflict was the outcome of their attempt to invade north-east India; began in March 1944 and named 'Operation U-Go'. Here a series of connected engagements have been recorded as the Battle of Imphal and the Battle of Kohima. The Allied forces had the advantage in terms of air-support and tank numbers and, following a period of at times heavy fighting, by July the Japanese (commanded by Lieutenant General Kawabe) were forced to withdraw. They had lost 30,500 men killed (many by starvation and disease) and 30,000 wounded. In addition to their suffering the biggest defeat in the war up to this time, these engagements also significantly reduced their ability to defend their occupation of Burma.

In an offensive the following year a force composed of Chinese, US, and British Commonwealth soldiers, led by General Slim, advanced south from northern Burma. Crossing the Irrawaddy River, these units made steady progress against the Japanese. They attacked the strategically important town of Meiktila (a centre of Japanese communications), overcoming the defenders by 3rd March 1945. Mandalay was taken by the 13th as this disparate military force advanced towards Rangoon. There was a short pause in the fighting due to seasonal rain, with the Allies able to benefit from their more secure supply lines. As the rains eased in late April the Allied advance began again, with Rangoon being taken by an Indian division on 1st. May. At this time the Allies had been advancing on three broad fronts. There were the British and Commonwealth (Indian and African) force on the western flank/side. In the centre there was the X-Force led by US General Joseph S. Stilwell (Chief-of-Staff to the Chinese nationalist Army). Due to disagreements with Chiang, Stilwell was recalled in October 1944, to be replaced by Lieutenant General Daniel Sultan. Sultan's force was mainly composed of US troops, supplemented with three Chinese Nationalist divisions (trained and equipped by the US) and a unit, 'Merrill's Marauders', trained by the British (on the model of General Orde Wingate's 'Chindits') in jungle fighting techniques. This group advanced south through the centre of the country with its main objective being to gain control of the strategically important Burma Road. Then, following pressure from the US, the Chinese Nationalist leader Chiang Kai-Shek had reluctantly agreed to deploy a substantial proportion of his Yunnan Army group (15 divisions of 175,000 men) to the Burma campaign. This, the Y-Force, advanced south on the eastern flank of Sultan's central force. During what had overall been a four month retreat south the two Japanese armies involved had suffered heavy casualties, each losing over 30% of their fighting strength. These losses would be compounded with another 10,000 troops killed as the fighting continued into June and early July, by when the Japanese were confined to the Tenasserim province on the eastern coastal strip at the northern end of the Malay Peninsula.

The dropping of the Atomic bombs on Hiroshima and Nagasaki and the surrender that followed would make the final stages of the Burma campaign a mopping up operation rather than seeing any further significant military action.

In the main theatre of the far-eastern war the US, at the same time as it was consolidating its hold on the Philippines, had advanced north to the island of Iwo-Jima. Here the 20,000 Japanese defenders, commanded by Lieutenant General Kuribayashi Tadamichi were well-dug in and prepared to offer strong resistance to an attempted invasion. An invasion that began on 19th February 1945 with the landing of US marines. The island was overrun by mid March, following fighting during which 6,000 marines were killed, and at sea some US ships were lost to Kamikaze missions.

It was about this time that the US high command took a decision to bomb Japan into submission. In order to progress this they increased the intensity of the air-raid missions from bases in the Marianas, and began to use napalm fire-bombs alongside the high explosives and switch to night-time raids in order to accentuate the terror.

The next island target, and on one plan the last prior to an invasion of the Japanese homeland, would be Okinawa. This, the largest of the Ryukyu Island chain is located just 350 miles from Japan. After taking a couple of the small outlying islands in late March, the marines invaded the main island on the 1st April. This was a major action, with 60,000 marines taking part in the initial landing. It would take nearly four months of gruelling fighting to take Okinawa; with 12,000 US and 100,000 Japanese troops killed.

Now air bases in Okinawa could add to the capability of the US to reach Japanese cities. One of the most deadly raids targeted Tokyo on the night of 10th/11th March when a quarter of the City's (primarily wooden) housing was destroyed, with 80,000 civilians killed and about 1,000,000 made homeless. This short period of the intentional mass bombing of civilian populations saw similarly destructive air-raids on 60 other cities and large towns - including Osaka, Kobe, Nagoya, Yokohama, and Toyoma. In effect the ordinary Japanese people were specifically targeted to be murdered and terrorized as they paid the price of having an increasingly militarized leadership. One whose rise to power was in large part due to the unfair economic treatment of Japan by western colonial powers in the 1930s.

Given the parlous state of Japan in June/July - with a beaten military, and a land of smashed and smoking cities- it was clear that surrender was the only reasonable option. But the decision taken at

Potsdam for unconditional surrender caused consternation within the Japanese leadership; with some of the senior military still seeking to prolong the conflict rather than surrender; others arguing for surrender, and the rest being undecided. It was this time of Japanese vacillation and US determination to finish the war that sealed the fate of the people of Hiroshima and Nagasaki. It was two 'Atomic devises' released (ignited 1,000ft) above these two cities by the crews of B-29s based on the Marianas that would bring a hellish end to Japanese resistance.

This war had seen a culturally obedient nation led to destruction by a deluded military in the service of some fantastical view of the Emperor's divinity. But, as with Germany, the Allied nations (official and populist) post-war demonization of the Japanese nation was an attempt to erase the bravery of many Japanese people who had opposed the war. The main organized opposition to Japanese militarism, the Trades Unions and the Communist Party, had been suppressed in the lead up to conflict but their ex-members (those not in prison) were amongst those who were prepared to offer some, if mainly passive, resistance. Resistance that took the form of such activities as strikes (over 400 in 1943 alone), industrial sabotage (especially noted for aircraft manufacturing), and mass absenteeism. In terms of specific organizations, there was the 'Japanese People's Anti-War League' formed in 1942, and even within the military there was the 'League to Raise the Consciousness of Japanese Troops' founded 1939. Diary entries and letters home from troops (especially those conscripted - the 'tokkatai') offer more evidence of opposition to war. A significant number of Japanese Buddhists, perhaps unsurprisingly given its (humanistic) ethical stance, also opposed the war. As we saw with Germany, the Allied propaganda sought to frame the Japanese as being a nation of 'evil villains', and so deserving of the blanket bombing and other indignities that its ordinary people were subjected too.

In the greater Balkan region of Europe, similar to what happened in the First World War, conflict was used to cover an opportunity for some groups to progress their own ethnic-based agendas; primarily in terms of seeking revenge for real and assumed past atrocities, or to progress nationalistic aims, at times with the active collusion of the Nazis.

One more notorious action was that undertaken by groups of Albanians who had sided with the Axis countries. Supported by Germany and Italy, they themselves turned into the perpetrators of genocide in order to progress the aim of a greater Albania. Between 1941-43, a Kosovan-Albanian 'police force' (the Vulnetara) established by the Germans progressed the 'cleansing' of the region of Serbs, Jews, Gypsies, in fact any non-Albanians were liable to be interned, deported, or murdered. Then in April 1944 an Albanian Waffen SS unit – the 21st Waffen SS Mountain Division (Skanderberg Division), mostly composed of Albanian Moslems and some Albanian Roman Catholics; an unruly bunch of misfits, criminals and ultra-nationalists. Within a few months about half had deserted, reducing the force from just over 6,000 to about 3,500. This unit made its own merciless contribution to the ethnic cleansing and genocide of Serbian Orthodox Christian, Jewish, and Gypsy peoples living in Kosovo. One incident in particular illustrates their approach – On 28th July 1944 a unit of the Skanderberg Division arrived at the 1000 year old village of Velika, situated at the bottom of a steep-sided valley. They then proceeded to loot the village (including the churches), set fire to about 300 homes and massacred 428 Serbian villagers, 120 of whom were children. In 1947 one of the Unit's commanders, August Schmidthuber, was put before a tribunal on the charge of participating in a range of atrocities including the massacre and deportation of civilians – he was found guilty and executed. Nearly 500,000 Serbs died in WWII and after the War President Tito expelled 175,000 Moslems from Yugoslavia to Turkey. As parts of Kosovo were 'cleansed' of Serbs Albanians settlers moved in just as Serbs had previously moved into Albanian lands – same ambitions, same techniques, same levels of cruelty, similar results.

If it was not for the vast resources of the US – initially made available via lend-lease prior to their committing even greater resources (men and materials) to the actual fighting – then it is doubtful that the war could have been 'won' by the allies (that's not to say that it could have been won by the Axis powers). More probably, if Russia had not been able to defend a sufficiency of it resource-rich regions from the Germans, some negotiated stalemate in Europe would have been a more likely outcome, leaving Germany in control of substantial parts of northern, central and Western Europe.

In 1940 Germany, Japan, and Italy, were producing $7.75 billions worth of arms compared to the $10 billion of the USSR, Britain and the US – by 1943 the figs were $18.3 and $62.5 respectively. During the 1944 D-Day landings Germany could draw on 320 aircraft to face 12,837 aircraft of the Allies.

It is overwhelming the case that financial power, applied to the operation of economies on war footings, has won conventional (non-guerrilla) wars in the 19th and 20th centuries and not some mystical national spirit – many individual Germans, Japanese and Italians were as brave and others as cowardly as many British, Americans, Russians, and their allies.

In relation to evil, bravery as an attribute might just make the killing, the expression of evil, worse just take the 'brave' crews of the German Luftwaffe and British Bomber Command. Yes, young men knowingly risking their lives each time they set off on a mission. Young men hailed by their own side as brave, be-medalled if they live or die. And yet these missions would flatten city streets and kill hundreds, possibly thousands, of old men, women, children, and babies - what price bravery, paid for in a currency of burnt and twisted flesh? In most conflicts, it has been the ability to reinforce and sustain an army i.e. 'logistics' that made a fundamental difference to the outcome, not any asymmetric indicator of bravery between combatants.

So what were the wider outcomes of this, the second 20th century, World War?

The war was fought at a terrible cost in lives and widespread human dislocation and misery, along with extensive environmental damage;

with the economic costs being debilitating for all of the European countries involved. The economic costs bordered on the catastrophic for countries such as France, Britain, the USSR, and of course Germany, Italy, and Japan. This was a war fought until 'unconditional surrender', as a strategic aim of the allies, had been achieved and as such the economies that fought each other mobilized for a total-war approach and in the process most had exhausted themselves economically. Populations, especially those of Germany and Russia, had to manage on meagre living conditions, as shortages, rationing, loss of citizen's rights (including freedom of expression, of association, of movement, and for most 'aliens' even liberty), and for some the effects of mass bombing, had to be stoically borne as 'manpower' and material resources were diverted to the business of war – a business that in its progressing many private companies made fortunes. Propaganda, disinformation, and censorship, played their respective roles as they were artfully brought to bear on populations in order to progress the anti-democratic art of manipulating public opinion – an art that would now come of age in the science of psychology - along with more practical tactics of persuasion gleaned from the blossoming advertising industry.

Statistical 'cost' of WWII.

Killed - 85 million - four times as many as WWI (including 35 million Russians - 13m soldiers and 23m civilians – and 5.7m European Jews)

Refugees - 23 million

British civilians killed by German bombing 50,000

German civilians killed by Allied bombing 600,000

Japanese civilians killed by allied bombing 900,000

Total of 100 million soldiers mobilized, 20 million killed, as were over 50 million civilians.

Main combatants had: 286,000 tanks – 557,000 combat aircraft - 11,000 naval vessels –

40 million rifles.......a massive waste of technological resources. In terms of today's money, trillions and trillions of dollars (equivalent to 10 years of total world production capacity)

Massive and wide-ranging environment degradation - from the

production and use of the millions of tons of bombs, artillery shells, bullets, miles and miles of steel amour, millions of engines, etc. etc. and even today, the thousands of wrecked shipping rusting on our ocean floors continuing to leak heavily polluting diesel fuel into the seas.

The immeasurable streams of tears and the intensity of heartache and despair that produced them - tears of mothers, fathers, grandparents, brothers, sisters, wives and girlfriends - the children whose fathers never came home and the children never born because of this.

Most tellingly.......... the practices and prejudices of international politics had not been changed - national interest (as defined by ruling elites) continued to determine a narrow range of priorities - and the institutions put in place to contain the potential failings in nation to nation disagreements had lacked the means to enforce even pre-agreed principles.

Chapter 5 'Post-World War II: the institutionalization of international hegemony'

On 2nd September 1945, on the upper deck of the USS Battleship Missouri (at anchor in Tokyo Bay) the Japanese Foreign Minister, Mamoru Shigemitsu, signed 'By Command and on behalf of the Emperor of Japan and the Japanese Government', the Instrument of Surrender of the Japanese Empire; and so, once the document had also been co-signed by representatives of each of the Allied nations, the twentieth century's second world war was officially brought to an end.

Amongst the final acts of Allied military aggression had been the 'rising' of an artificial sun about 2,000 feet above a hospital in the centre of the Japanese city of Hiroshima, and another of similar size above the city of Nagasaki. A crude (insensitive) message was written by US sailors on the side of the solar 'Atomic' bomb (equivalent to 12,500 tons of TNT) dropped on Hiroshima offering "Greetings to the Emperor from the men of the *Indianapolis*" - the name of the ship that transported the bomb to the Marianas Islands for loading onto the Boeing B29 Superfortress bomber the 'Enola Gay'. The intended greetings did not reach the Emperor, indeed he – Michinomiya Hirohito - survived the war to be reinstated, with the agreement of the US, as Emperor and went on to live a long and very privileged life. But the people of Hiroshima and Nagasaki, the civilians, did receive the full impact of the callously flippant message ..... with about 150,000 of them - non-combatant men, women, children, and babies - being burnt off the face of the earth in the immediate blasts and about 110,000 dying with a few months from radiation sickness or other injuries. Relatively modest numbers in the context of WWII's total, but the manner of the deaths of citizens of the two Japanese cities indicated a qualitatively different weapon had been introduced to the business of war making.

This final florescence of killing, as these people's lives were singed from the face of the earth, was but a small part of those 55 million killed, 30 million of whom were civilians (plus up to 28million more as a result of conflict-related famine and disease), over the five year period of international conflict between 1939 and 1945.

Just over 25 years earlier the world-wide shock at the relentless orgy of killing seen in WW1 had made populations and leading politicians realize the need for some institutional forum for settling international disputes - so that WWI would be the 'war to end all wars' - and so, in 1920, establishing The League of Nations. An institution that fell apart with the League's specifically being unable to prevent conflicts in Manchuria and Abyssinia, and more generally in what had repeatedly been its inability to enforce its collective will on nation-states determined on aggression. The ineffectiveness of the League, rooted in the unwillingness of nation states to cede sovereignty on the issues involving between-nation disagreements, became obvious with its inability to deter the aggressive actions of the axis powers during the mid-late 1930s. By the end of the decade the world was at war once again; a period of conflict that would end with an even greater death toll than the earlier war.

In relation to the future of humanity, the one chink of light revealing a possibly different framework for international politics than had pertained up to WWII was engendered by a post WWII manifestation of the recognition of the need for some institutional forum established to maintain peace between nation states. A need that would come to be embodied in the United Nations. During the war meetings had been taking place involving Allied leaders and their foreign secretaries. Initially in London on New Year's Day 1942, when a 'Declaration of the United Nations' was signed by 22 countries - the last, being the Moscow conference in October 1943 that produced the 'Moscow Declaration' which, in its fourth paragraph, identified the need for a post-war organization with similar aims to those of the League of Nations.

In order to progress the aims of the Moscow Declaration a conference was set up at Dumbarton Oaks, Washington, from 21st Aug. - 7th Oct. 1944 with the aim of designing just such an international organization.

The final draft document agreed by the Dumbarton Oaks Conference contained 12 chapters (four of these noted below) on the constitution of an international body intended to serve as a forum to maintain peace between nation-states. The first two chapters set out the aims and principles, the third the basic condition of membership, the fourth sets out its organizational structure, with the rest offering more guidance on administrative arrangements.

PROPOSALS FOR THE ESTABLISHMENT OF A GENERAL INTERNATIONAL ORGANIZATION [1]

There should be established an international organization under the title of The United Nations, the Charter of which should contain provisions necessary to give effect to the proposals which follow.

CHAPTER I. PURPOSES

The purposes of the Organization should be:
1. *To maintain international peace and security; and to that end to take effective collective measures for the prevention and removal of threats to the peace and the suppression of acts of aggression or other breaches of the peace, and to bring about by peaceful means adjustment or settlement of international disputes which may lead to a breach of the peace;*
2. *To develop friendly relations among nations and to take other appropriate measures to strengthen universal peace;*
3. *To achieve international cooperation in the solution of international economic, social and other humanitarian problems; and*
4. *To afford a centre for harmonizing the actions of nations in the*

achievement of these common ends.

CHAPTER II. PRINCIPLES

In pursuit of the purposes mentioned in Chapter I the Organization and its members should act in accordance with the following principles:

1. *The Organization is based on the principle of the sovereign equality of all peace-loving states.*
2. *All members of the Organization undertake, in order to ensure to all of them the rights and benefits resulting from membership in the Organization, to fulfil the obligations assumed by them in accordance with the Charter.*
3. *All members of the Organization shall settle their disputes by peaceful means in such a manner that international peace and security are not endangered.*
4. *All members of the Organization shall refrain in their international relations from the threat or use of force in any manner inconsistent with the purposes of the Organization.*
5. *All members of the Organization shall give every assistance to the Organization in any action undertaken by it in accordance with the provisions of the Charter.*
6. *All members of the Organization shall refrain from giving assistance to any state against which preventive or enforcement action is being undertaken by the Organization.*

The Organization should ensure that states not members of the Organization act in accordance with these principles so far as may be necessary for the maintenance of international peace and security.

CHAPTER III. MEMBERSHIP

1. *Membership of the Organization should be open to all peace-loving states.*

CHAPTER IV. PRINCIPAL ORGANS

1. The Organization should have as its principle organs:
   a) A General Assembly;
   b) A Security Council;
   c) An international court of justice; and
   d) A Secretariat.
2. The Organization should have such subsidiary agencies as may be found necessary

The final conference arranged to draw up a founding charter was convened in San Francisco on 25th April 1945 and by 25th June, following complex negotiations between the main parties, a final document was produced - 850 delegates, 3,500 support staff, along with 2,500 media representatives - at that time this was probably the largest international conference in the history of humankind. The final document was signed by representatives of 50 nations on 26th June 1945 (the UN would have 194 member-states by 2022).

In terms of governance, the main body was the General Assembly composed of representatives of all member states, each with an equally weighted vote. But with an additional Security Council that would have five permanent members (four initially, but Nationalist China soon after, to be replaced by communist China in the 70s) - France, United Kingdom, United States, Russian Federation (initially USSR) - and ten others, elected by the General Assembly to each serve for a two year term on the Council. The Security Council takes a leading role in deciding upon actions to be taken and it also makes recommendations on who will take on the role of General-Secretary of the UN. Only the five permanent members of the Security Council would have the right of veto on any proposal to come before it, the non-permanent members would not.

President Roosevelt endeavoured to focus the attention of the delegates on the overriding necessity of nations combining to act in the interests of the aims of the Charter rather than in their own narrow national interest with this warning that........ 'If we fail to use it," he concluded, "we shall betray all those who have died so that we might meet here in freedom and safety to create it. If we seek to use it selfishly - for the advantage of any one nation or any small group of nations — we shall be equally guilty of that betrayal."

This was a warning of some particular relevance given the experience of the earlier attempt, in the League of Nations, to institutionalize the political means to achieve peaceful co-existence between nations. An institution whose failure had been primarily due to nations not being prepared to subsume national interest within a wider commitment to prioritize international peace over self-interest. The fact that it was a US President offering this warning was of special relevance given that the US, intent on an isolationist foreign policy, had refused to join the League of Nations - even though it had been an American president, in Woodrow Wilson, that had been instrumental in setting it up.

The subsequent history of the UN saw nations (especially the US) for the most part failing to respond to Roosevelt's warning and the pernicious fault-lines of short-sighted nationalism would once again repeatedly inhibit the cause of world peace. Since WWII there have been over 100 wars and these have seen over 50 million people killed, many more injured, and millions made homeless.

Chris Harman offers a corscurating summary of the initial permanent members of the Security Council, summed up as: '.....between them they dominated, oppressed and exploited the rest of the world' suggesting that: 'The rulers of each needed a sense of international harmony as a cover for consolidating structures of control.' (Harman, 2002, pp543/4)

Simplistic certainly, harsh possibly, but any assessment of the work of the UN could only sensibly conclude that it has failed its main peace-keeping mission. In a world rife with injustice and with millions living in abject poverty, associated organizations such as UNICEF, UNESCO, UNEF, WHO, and the International Court of Justice set up in the Hague, have made at least some more positive contributions to world governance. And subsequent amendments to the original charter have enlarged and so developed the aspirational fundamentals of the UN. Most obviously with the adoption: in 1948, of the Universal Declaration of Human Rights, UN Convention on the Prevention and Punishment of the Crime of Genocide (1948), the Declaration of the Rights of the Child (1959), Declaration on the Rights of Disabled Persons (1975), and the UN Convention on the Elimination of all Forms of Discrimination Against Women (1979).

Into Harman's suggested disingenuous facade of international harmony has been the seeping of more positive human values expressed in a range of additional amendments and the Charter can now can serve as the foundations for a renewal of the UN's constituting aims.

The preamble of the Declaration of Human Rights runs:

'Whereas recognition of the inherent dignity and of the equal and inalienable rights of all members of the human family is the foundation of freedom, justice and peace in the world,

Whereas disregard and contempt for human rights have resulted in barbarous acts which have outraged the conscience of mankind, and the advent of a world in which human beings shall enjoy freedom of speech and belief and freedom from fear and want has been proclaimed as the highest aspiration of the common people,

Whereas it is essential, if man [sic] is not to be compelled to have recourse, as a last resort, to rebellion against tyranny and oppression, that human rights should be protected by the rule of law,

Whereas it is essential to promote the development of friendly relations between nations,

Whereas the peoples of the United Nations have in the Charter reaffirmed their faith in fundamental human rights, in the dignity and worth of the human person and in the equal rights of men and women and have determined to promote social progress and better standards of life in larger freedom,

Whereas Member States have pledged themselves to achieve, in co-operation with the United Nations, the promotion of universal respect for and observance of human rights and fundamental freedoms,

Whereas a common understanding of these rights and freedoms is of the greatest importance for the full realization of this pledge,

Now, Therefore THE GENERAL ASSEMBLY proclaims THIS UNIVERSAL DECLARATION OF HUMAN RIGHTS as a common standard of achievement for all peoples and all nations, to the end that every individual and every organ of society, keeping this Declaration constantly in mind, shall strive by teaching and education to promote respect for these rights and freedoms and by progressive measures, national and international, to secure their universal and effective recognition and observance, both among the peoples of Member States themselves and among the peoples of territories under their jurisdiction.

Followed by the Articles:

Article 1.
All human beings are born free and equal in dignity and rights. They are endowed with reason and conscience and should act towards one another in a spirit of brotherhood.

Article 2.
Everyone is entitled to all the rights and freedoms set forth in this Declaration, without distinction of any kind, such as race, colour, sex, language, religion, political or other opinion, national or social origin, property, birth or other status. Furthermore, no distinction

shall be made on the basis of the political, jurisdictional or international status of the country or territory to which a person belongs, whether it be independent, trust, non-self-governing or under any other limitation of sovereignty.

Article 3.
Everyone has the right to life, liberty and security of person.

Article 4.
No one shall be held in slavery or servitude; slavery and the slave trade shall be prohibited in all their forms.'

Then follows 26 Articles setting out different aspects of human rights.

Taken overall, the initial Charter and its subsequent amendments represent the enlightened expression of how human beings should live together on this one World that we share - it echoes insights that have been expressed in religions at their human best. If a number of these have exhibited an intolerance of homosexuality, a tolerance of slavery, and some consider women to be inferior to men. But all of them do show an awareness of some basic requirements for a civilized life. For Micheline R. Ishay, all of the world's major religions advocate: '..... protection for the poor, the disabled, the sick, and the powerless, praise good and impartial rulings, encourage some forms of social and economic justice, condemn arbitrary killing, offer moral prescriptions for wartime, and so forth.' (Ishay, 2004, p60).

Similar types of moral prescription can be seen in legal injunctions from the early time of civil life; when people living in towns and in cities, so not closely linked by family or tribal-like groupings, understood the need for some mutually satisfactory guidance to facilitate community life; and this embodied in formal 'codes'.

One such early legalistic code was that of King Ur-Nammu. From references to this code, as noted in later texts, we do know that it attempted to address corruption as well as excusing widows and orphans from paying taxes. The code also imposed some limits on the power of the priesthood and of wealthy landowners. At least three notable legal codes were drawn up in the name of kings during the second millennium BCE with another, the Jewish Torah, being composed between 900 - 300 BCE.

As early as the fifth century BCE philosophers such as Plato, Aristotle, and a bit later Cicero, were offering more theoretical justifications for individual human rights. During the mediaeval period it was civil traditions and the religions that served to provide guidance to believers - Christianity, Islam, Confucianism, Hinduism, Shintoism, Buddhism, and Judaism. Then, from the period of the Enlightenment we see a progressive secularization of the debate on political systems and human rights. With insights being offered by individuals such as Hugo Grotius, Abbe Saint-Pierre, John Locke, and Immanuel Kant. Grotius advocated religious tolerance, Saint-Pierre proposed a supra European body to arbitrate between states in dispute, Locke argued for individual human rights, and Kant noted the need for a world-wide federation of nation-states.

See especially Kant's essay 'Idea for a Universal History' (1784) where he advocates *'.....a federation of peoples in which every state, even the smallest, could expect to derive its security and rights not from its own power or its own legal judgement, but solely from this great federation, from a united power and the law-governed decision of a united will.'*

Enlightenment ideas on human rights realized a conception of humankind as an entity that transcended nation state-hood. A conception that can be seen in the American Declaration of Independence (*'We hold these truths to be self-evident, that all men are created equal, that they are endowed by their Creator with certain unalienable Rights, that among these are Life, Liberty and the pursuit of Happiness'* .....even accepting that its *'all men are created equal'* excluded slaves, native peoples, and women) and in the ideas that motivated many in the French revolution (Liberty, Equality, Fraternity) and it was these that formed the basis for the debates (and demands) on governance and human rights into the nineteenth century.

The post-war foundation of the United Nations laid the institutional framework and offered the inspirational language of universal peace and co-operation between nations and for human rights - it represented an institutional authority and a diplomatic framework for world conscious values to be expressed. For the globalization of peace and for the protection of individual rights........a framework encompassing institutions that would reflect civilization at its very best. Politicians had once again risen to reflect the will of the World's people....of nations exhausted by conflict.... for peace.

But international politics during the following 75 years since the founding of the UN has hardly fulfilled its aims and principles.......at best the UN does still retain a residual potential for providing the political means for constructing global peace and a world within which human rights are respected (and protected) but....but....but this institution, or rather the behaviour of its members, would need to undergo radical reform. Not least, national sovereignty will, to some agreed extent, have to be ceded to this higher (trans-national) level of governance. Given just how much national sovereignty has been ceded to provide the economic and trading conditions required by private finance and multi-national corporations in the past two centuries, then the idea of conceding the right to go to war, within an international legal system (an international forum) in which all nations are equal before it, would seem to be more of a sensible development of governance than a threat to national wellbeing.

To place the creation of the UN in the context of my description of evolution: The broad developmental categorization of this species capacity being: non-conscious - conscious - self conscious, with 'world-conscious' as being predicated as the one yet to be fulfilled. There being no clear boundary between each category and some features of the next stage of evolutionary development can be identified in its precursor stage. I would suggest that institutions such as the UN or at least its underlying aims and principles represent insights (glimmers) into the patterning of information that will characterize the next identifiable stage of evolutionary development – 'world-consciousness' – and could provide an alternative (evolutionary mode) to the extinction of the human species.

Soon after the end of WWII a number of other international institutions, apart from the UN, had been set up. In global finance there were the organizational outcomes of the Bretton Woods conference – embodied in financial institutions such as: the World Bank and the International Monetary Fund (IMF). And, in terms of trade, the General Agreement on Tariffs and Trade (GATT), would provide a framework for trade in goods and services between nations. An agreement that would subsequently be renegotiated in a series of 'rounds', beginning with the Annecy round in 1949 and concluding with the protracted final 'Uruguay round' lasting from 1986-1994 when a new framework for trade - the World Trade Organization (WTO) - would subsume the GATT arrangements within a wider set of agreements expanded to include some financial services, intellectual property rights, and agriculture. The inclusion of agriculture has caused considerable controversy due to these measures introducing liberalizing requirements that clearly favoured the economically developed over economically developing nations - currently 161 countries are included in the WTO, with up to 20 more currently progressing the negotiation process for entry.

The two most powerful post-war nations, the United States and the Soviet Union; wartime allies but now each manoeuvring to advance what each viewed as its own interests were developing an intensity of animosity that would (in the 'Cold War') be the most significant internation relationship during the next three decades. It has even been suggested that the decision to explode the two atomic devices over Hiroshima and Nagasaki was to some extent influenced by the wish to show the Soviets just how militarily powerful the US had become.

Although counted as a victor of the war, Russia's people had fared badly, with 8.6 million military and possibly as many as 17 million civilians killed, compared with Britain's 330,000 military and 62,000 civilians and the US's 300,000 military and minimal number of civilians killed. Russia's industrial base had been degraded and its agriculture badly disrupted and left disorganized.

In the early post-war years Stalin's political attention was focused on gaining control over internal regions (e.g. Ukraine[27], Chetna) and on countries neighbouring the northern and western borders of the USSR. As well as the continuing repression of any hint of internal dissent; with many of those surviving the firing squad being consigned to face the harsh conditions in the Siberian gulags. Russia's western cities had been ravaged (none more so than Stalingrad), and its industrial base was shattered. The post-war Soviet focus was on economic recovery and in trying to construct a communist 'buffer zone' between it and the West. Russia did progressively withdraw its occupation forces from each of the eastern European states that it had controlled at the war's end, but only when it considered that it would be leaving behind communist governments loyal to the Soviet Union.

In 1946 the lines of territorial division in Europe between 'communist' east and 'capitalist' west were becoming clear, leading Winston Churchill, in a speech made in the US, to note that from the Baltic in the north to the Adriatic in the south '...an iron curtain had descended on the continent.' And whilst the post-war division of Europe created two ideologically opposed blocs, it also demarcated each bloc's agreed areas of interest and so offered an, if uneasy, mutually accepted status quo.

By 1948 the Russians felt that insufficient pressure was being put on Germany in relation to the payment of war reparations that had been agreed at Potsdam. They also objected to plans for the three 'western zones' to unify and the intention to introduce a new, common, currency for these. The military vulnerability of Berlin seemed to offer the Russians a situation where the advantage lay with them and one where diplomatic pressure could be supported by action on the ground. At the time (early 1948), Western-controlled Berlin was being supplied along two railway lines, one highway, and three air 'corridors'

---

[27] The Ukraine had been subjected to widespread famine in 1930s as an actual policy aim for Stalin as he sought to punish the republic's pressure for independence - Ukraine was in effect sealed off, unable to import food, and with its own harvest exported to Russia or stored in guarded granaries. The people of Ukraine starved, with an estimate 25% of the population (7 million people, 3 million of them children) starving to death.

- a steady flow of people and supplies passed along these routes. The Russians began their action by attempting to disrupt these supply-lines using more bureaucratic measures. Including delays caused by lengthy customs inspections and by temporary closing of rail-lines for 'technical' reasons. Given no helpful response from the US and Britain to address their grievances, on 24th June the Russians closed the supply lines, imposing a land-based blockade on the City. The western allies considered possible courses of action. Launching a war was one option but even the generally gung-ho American military accepted this was unrealistic given the location of Berlin and the strength of the Red Army.

The US and Britain decided to face down the Russians by using air-corridors that the Russians had allowed them to continue in use to keep the Western-controlled zones supplied; shooting down aircraft would certainly have raised the level of the dispute. Surprisingly, throughout the period of the airlift the Russians even maintained their air-traffic control service to guide US/British pilots. The airlift saw a continuous stream of transport aircraft taking tons and tons of goods to the 2.25 million citizens of a beleaguered Berlin. Over the period of the airlift (June 1948 to May 1949) 2.3 million tons of food alone had been flown in, at a cost to the west of $224 million. Stalin was faced with the likelihood that the air-lift would continue and that there would be no significant concessions made to address the issues of concern, so he gave the order to reopen the land links between the west and the City. The Berlin airlift was over, but the episode was determinedly interpreted for the western public as an example of naked Russian aggression and it fed into the international polarization of two 'camps', east and west, communist and capitalist (both categorizing descriptors being inaccurate). No sense of a balanced two-side assessment was offered by either side, each only interpreted motivation and events to suit themselves; a significant and systemic issue with international politics more generally.

The Berlin incident fed into the western suspicion of Russian intentions and ensured that a new western military organization, NATO, would come into being; which it did on 4th April 1949. The eastern countries, led by Russia set up their own military grouping in 1955, with the Warsaw Pact. Now ideological differences had been accentuated by military solidification and the two groups, each brisling with modern weaponry, were eyeing each other with deep suspicion fed by an underlying ideological animosity.

Spending on armaments of each of the superpowers was pretty much matched over the 22 post war years 1948-70 - at about $11 billion each in 1948, rising to about $74 billion by 1970. Politicians, encouraged by the military industry (the armed service, the arms industry and mostly jingoistic mass media), of each superpower then expressed their animosity towards each other by engaging in proxy wars, with their taking opposing sides in a number of international disputes (primarily in Africa and the Middle East).

Superpower animosity would be at its most obvious in Korea. The fairly immediate background to the Korean War was the commitment made by the war-time allies at the Cairo Conference in 1943 to a unified, independent Korea, a political status that both communist and nationalist Koreans had been seeking for decades. Following the Japanese surrender in 1945 the US had asked that they continue their occupation of the Peninsula in order to deter aggression from communist and nationalist guerrilla forces in the north. The Americans began to move their own troops into the South from Sept 1945, whilst the Russians were offering military training to the Northern forces - and support for the newly established 'Korean People's Republic' (KPR 6th. Sept 1945). Kim Il Sung led the Communist Party and he would become the first President of North Korea and, from the end of the war, would incrementally establish one of the most repressive regimes (a dynasty - himself, son, grandson) the world has seen.

The Americans would encounter similar problems in establishing a legitimate government in South Korea as they would later on encounter in South Vietnam. That of finding leaders who were capable of administering the country, were not corrupt, and who enjoyed the confidence as well as support of the citizens. They had to resign themselves to a leader, in the virulent anti-communist Dr. Syngman

Rhee who did not sufficiently meet any of their initial requirements and who would run what Paul Kennedy (1989, p493) termed '....an unsavoury and repressive regime....'. Attempts by the UN to arrange elections that would hopefully fulfil the commitment made at the Cairo Conference were rejected by a North, suspicious that there would be widespread vote-rigging in the more populous South. A suspicion subsequently justified during the election that led to Rhee becoming the President.

Kim II Sung took a reckless gamble when he launched an invasion south across the 38th parallel on 26th June 1950, assessing that, such was the political dissatisfaction in the south (where there was increasing left-wing activity) and along with a popular will for a united, independent Korea, that unification would be welcomed by most of the population.

Diplomatically, the US sought a UN mandate for its involvement and, given their influence within the General Assembly, they were able to gain the necessary two-thirds majority. As at that time Communist China had no place on the Security Council, and Russia had made the mistake of refusing to attend the session, no veto was invoked. This UN approval enabled the US to claim an international mandate for their action.

The willingness of North Korean leaders to bear massive casualties, along with Chinese reinforcements, allowed them to gradually push back the southern ground troops. The determined northern advance was to reach as far as 80 miles south of the 38th parallel before US General Ridgeway was able to establish a new defensive front.

From as early as December 1950 tentative negotiations aiming to bring the war to an end had been taking place but, partly due to the difficulties the US/South Korean side had on agreeing conditions for a ceasefire, but perhaps more so to the obdurate intransigence of Syngman Rhee, no early agreement could be made. Negotiations taking a more reasonable approach did at last begin in July 1951. But it took until July 1953 before an armistice was signed, bringing a cessation to hostilities, with a four-mile wide demilitarized zone being established across the Korean Peninsula.

When the war ended Korea - with possibly as many as 4 million people being killed, 2 million of these being civilians - was divided at just about the same 38th Parallel that that had marked the division between the two countries at the start of the conflict three years earlier. With one country (the North) now being run by a cruel, repressive dictatorship, the other (the South) being run by a cruel, repressive dictatorship. The South only gained some limited democratic rights by the 1990s - the North none at all as at 2023.

The wartime allies in the east and west became increasingly polarized by the ideological differences of their leaderships and suspicions over each other's territorial ambitions. This polarity, and its underlying tensions, served the interests of ideologues on each side. Especially in the US, where determined groups within the ruling military, business, and political elites sought to progress their perception of their own personal interests by characterizing (at times caricaturing) communism as an 'evil', and in not fitting some mythical concept of what constitutes 'America'. To frame it as a political ideology that was determined on international expansion, so to presenting some unspecified threat to American wellbeing.

The Soviet Union and much of central Europe had emerged from the World War II with manufacturing capacity and much of its heavy industry devastated; running at production rates much reduced on pre-war levels. Swathes of farmland had been laid waste and farming communities fractured by the tide of warfare. Although difficult to measure accurately, it seems that farming output had been reduced to about 75% of its 1939 level. Overall, the dislocation and devastation of war had left the whole region in a parless state, a condition that required firm central government coordination, and it was regimes of this type that took control. Clearly forms of communism were already in place as the dominant political system in the Soviet Union and in counties such as Yugoslavia, Poland, Hungry, Bulgaria, Rumania, Czechoslovakia, and others, where the anti-Nazi resistance activities of communists had given them a patriotic credibility that other political groupings lacked. By 1946 communist governments were taking a lead in rebuilding and developing both industry and agriculture, with private business playing a minor role. One that would be further reduced as communist governments adopted ever more detailed centralized planning of their economies.

At the War's end a number of south-east Asian countries that had been occupied by the Japanese especially Vietnam (French), Indonesia (Dutch), Burma (British), refused to accept the return of the colonial powers. An India within the British Empire had a strong and growing independence movement, with leaders intent on self-determination as being the basis of future governance. Across colonial Africa, the early gathering of what the British prime minister Harold Macmillan would later (1960) note as a 'wind of change blowing through the continent of Africa', was developing as more majority black populations in the colonies claimed the right to rule themselves.

In endeavouring to find a 'third way' to approach international relations, a number of prominent leaders of the developing countries formed their own 'non-aligned' grouping. Leaders such as Josip Tito (Yugoslavia), Jawaharlal Nehru (India), Achmed Sukarno (Indonesia), Gamal Abdul Nasser (Egypt), Kwame Nkrumah (Ghana), formed in 1953/4 an initially fairly loose grouping of the 'non-aligned' countries linked to their membership of the UN. The constitutional structure for the organization was formalized, in terms of agreed principles and conditions of membership, during the 1955 Bandung Conference, hosted by Sukarno. At this conference ten 'principles' were formulated and agreed, with the first principle noting respect for human rights and support for the UN charter setting the tone for those that followed. The non-aligned movement was founded in Belgrade (Yugoslavia) in 1961 and by 2012 the organization had 120 member countries representing 55% of the world's population. Although internationally non-aligned these, and other developing countries, saw in the eastern block a series of economic models that offered alternative ways of progressing industrial development to the western dominated capitalism that had mostly ill-served them in the past.

Many of these economically developing countries would be used as an ideological battleground on which the cold war would be played out by proxy. A cold war that 'officially' began in 1947 with the US declaring its intention to use political and economic means to contain 'all manifestations of communist expansion'; and this however obviously indigenous (Cuba, Vietnam, Greece, and Angola), or democratic (France, Italy, Greece, and Tanzania) the campaign for a communist government might be. The US determinedly refused to consider that communist allegiance might, for most, be more the frustrated political expression of pent up outrage at often centuries-long exploitation, rather than a more fundamental commitment to an ideology.

Just at the time when most of the world's peoples were exhausted by the ravages of warfare the world's leaders opted to return international relations to the same competitive and conflictual basis that had pertained for centuries - just when the world was desperate for visionary leaders prepared to design a system that would transcend national self-interest they would instead only have leaders who would in the UN create an enlarged and improved version of the League of Nation but a new organization that retained the same enduring fault-line of allowing primacy to national sovereignty. And so the conditions for pursuing 'national interest' generated by and aligned with elite-group interests. A few hundred political leaders, if supported and encouraged by thousands more in big business, finance, media owners, senior military, and some more ambitious politicians. These, the ruling elites of the major powers, were determined to progress the same strategic approach to international politics that had resulted in two world wars during the twentieth century and from 1945 would see over 100 'smaller' wars - and an air of threatening hegemonic tensions throughout the world. We should also acknowledge that in all countries, if more so in democracies, the people also bear some responsibility for their leaders' actions.

The threat of, or actual, conflict primarily serves the interests of the industrial – military - financial - political - media complex (to broaden former US President Eisenhower's elite power-grouping). In that such tensions help to control populations, and for these to accept vast amounts of spending on armaments, and even military action to ensure countries comply with the economic interests of the dominant (capitalist or communist) ideologues. And, as ever, conflict and profit are positively correlated; the greater the extent of the former the higher the amount of the latter.

There is a veritable 'industry' of interests ever-seeking to profit from conflict (see Naomi Klein 2007, 'The Shock Doctrine' on this), and a critical shortcoming of most popular mass media is that it is representatives of these groupings (industrialists, academics, media, politicians) who are called upon to interpret the news events - they contribute to, indeed that they often create. An interpretation of a world where 'competition and conflict' 'them and us' are the assumed normality and in doing so they accentuate the relatively superficial (the symptoms), so smothering any attempt to analyze the underlying causes of conflict. Purposely failing to expose the political, financial, industrial, interests (economic greed, economic and social inequality, short-term perceptions, and invariably ignorance) the root of which this or that conflict are the symptom of - the actual lived condition of peoples. The combined influence of the media, arms industry lobbyists, prejudiced academics, and ambitious politicians ever-prepared to use fear and othering to advance their careers, the creation of a fetid global milieu rank with suspicion and uncertainty. A world of international instability, a world inexorably grinding towards a major conflagration that would likely involve thermonuclear weapons systems.

Given its economic power and military range, the US would have been able to deploy more positive influence on the process of post-war international relations but unfortunately the Truman Doctrine gave rise to motivational-diplomatic-political structures that increased the potential for conflict and as Osborne (2006, p460) noted that the US: '.........government confused what was good for America [and what] was good for the world.' I think Osborne was being somewhat generous; I would go further and suggest the US government disingenuously assumed that what was good for its ruling elite groups was good for all US citizens as well as for the rest of the world.

The events of the crisis over Berlin and the Korean War were interpreted by both of the sides of the Cold War in line with their own ideological perspective (serving as explanatory frameworks) placing them seriously at odds with each other. Leaders of the US, and their western acolytes, were guided by a conviction that there was a red menace progressively taking control of south eastern Asia; and during the 1950s they failed to distinguish between Russian and Chinese intentions.

They interpreted the strength of the communist-led (but most quite politically mixed) insurgencies in Indo-China, Malaya, Indonesia, and the Philippines (and indeed the growing strength of the communists in Japan) as but further evidence of the red menace rather than the expression of peoples' frustrated with oppressive foreign occupation and the indifference of the indigenous political elites to their plight. The US Sec. of State Dean Acheson and Sec. of Defence George Marshall had argued for a more sophisticated (nuanced) political approach and for the US to promote more politically progressive movements in Europe, South-east Asia, and elsewhere; and indeed as had President Truman during the Korean War. But they had to contend with the belligerent tone of right-wing politicians in Washington - most being as much concerned about trades unionism and the promotion of social democratic ideas in America, as of any communist advance overseas. Any moderates also had to contend with a predominately right-leaning US mass media.

So, the major powers had together fostered an international political context redolent with mutual suspicion, allied to the threat of military aggression. With each of the great powers determined to pursue their national interest as this was perceived through the ideological perspective of the elite ruling groups in each country. The population of each nation were fed a veritable stream of anti the other side propaganda. In practice, we see the formation of two 'blocks', one led by the US and the other by the Soviet Union. Politicians (and their spokespeople) for each of these power-blocks interpreting any action of the other as direct aggression, or at least indirect manoeuvring in a greater power game, and claiming its own actions as but defensive reactions to aggression by the other side. Words like freedom, democracy, defence, justice, truth..... were left as but hollow conceptual husks as any original (authentic) meaning was winnowed out of them in the duplicitous explanatory narratives concocted by diplomats at the behest of their political 'masters'.

George Orwell's 'Newspeak', seems to be an appropriate descriptor for the ways in which language as explanatory narrative has been misused by mendacious politicians and diplomats.

The US government was able to use its anti-Soviet propaganda (as assisted by a mostly willing mass media) as an excuse to undertake a domestic purge against communism, or indeed pretty much against any even modest left of right-wing political or big business views. To present any, even quite modest, political view in support of collective provision of services and of economic equality as pro communist. A propaganda campaign that managed, at least for politically naive citizens, to equate communism with being 'un American'. Although there had never been any serious debate on just what being American means in terms of political/cultural substance much beyond streams of flowery rhetoric wrapped in a flag, to the background rhythm of an anthem. Or the repeated biased interpretation of a constitution initially designed by an economically and socially privileged group of individuals (men) for political conditions applying over 200 years ago.

Greece had been the first inter-national stage on which the east/west animosity would be as played out, with initially Britain then the US (following the Truman, in effect anti-communist, doctrine of 1947) pouring in massive amounts of military aid to support a royalist party in the EDES with communist bloc countries to the north-east (Albania, Bulgaria, Yugoslavia - only later on did Russia get more involved) supporting the Greek communist party EAM-ELAS; many members of both of these now opposing groups had fought determinedly, at times together, against Nazi occupation during the war. Following a bitter civil war lasting until 1949 the communists were defeated. By the war's end possibly as many as 80,000 Greeks had been killed and another 500,000 displaced from their homes.

Then, as now, the ability to express their power was of central importance to the world's more powerful nations. The war had ended with the US showing its military power in the Atom bombs exploded over two Japanese cities and in Sept, 1949 a US spy plane flying along the coast of Siberia detected a level of atmospheric radiation that indicated a recent nuclear explosion - radiation that had been released by a Soviet nuclear test held on 19th August in the USSR province of Kazakhstan. Within four years both the US and the Soviet Union had the Hydrogen bomb (about 100 times more explosive power than the atomic bombs used in Japan) and the nuclear arms race was joined. Leaders of each of the ex-allies had become implacable enemies, with the US spending 20% of its GNP on the military and the Soviet Union spending 40% of its (much smaller) GNP.

From 1951 Britain, led by a prime minister in Winston Churchill ever concerned about Britain's status on the world stage, set the nation on the road to develop its own independent nuclear bomb. By 1952 Britain had the Atom bomb, and by 1957 the Hydrogen bomb; although it had to purchase Polaris missiles from the US in order to obtain an effective delivery system. Not to be outdone, the French considered that they should also have a similar independent ability to deploy nuclear weapons and President De Gaulle's (a man with a sense of national grandeur to at least match Churchill's) government determined to join the 'nuclear club' - by 1960 the French had become full members.

It wasn't long before communist China had developed its bomb, with the first test explosion taking place in 1966 - since then Israel (secretly and illegally), India, Pakistan, and North Korea, now complete the list of nations that are known to have nuclear weapons and they too can deploy these fearsome weapons - South Africa and Ukraine are unusual in they it did have nuclear weapons but have since dismantled their nuclear capability and have signed the Nuclear Non-Proliferation Treaty.

There are currently estimated to be about 4,000 thermo-nuclear warheads actively deployed and another 10,000 known to be available - and bear in mind that each one of the 4,000 can alone totally destroy a city the size of London, Jakarta, Beijing, Moscow, New York, or Tehran, and make the land for at least a 50 mile radius effectively uninhabitable. Even a relatively small modern warhead, such as those carried on Britain's ageing submarine-based Trident missile system, would, if detonated 2,500 metres above a city, kill, maim, or otherwise seriously injure, all living creatures and destroy all buildings, within about 14 km from the initial blast. Such an explosion would produce a massively destructive fireball, the intensity of which could blind anyone observing the event from as far away as 80 km.

Some of the delivery systems now deployed can fire dozens of these warheads - indeed a US Minute-man III missile can deliver 12 warheads, each with a power of up 475 Kilotons; the bomb dropped on Hiroshima in 1945 was about 15 Kilotons. Today's nuclear weapons are of such awesome destructive power that using them would truly be an evil act whether in a first strike or in retaliation, nothing could morally justify their use and clearly the humanitarian solution to this precarious state of affairs depends upon the willingness of all nations to forgo this weaponry.

And bear in mind that those politicians, and probably their close family members, who give the order for nuclear weapons to be released will be safely bunkered deep and comfortably underground. If only to emerge, months later, into a post apocalyptic wasteland to reflect on their handiwork.

Its elite sourced antipathy towards anything remotely socialist extended to the US's increasing involvement in the internal politics of the economically developing countries, with a perspective narrowly focused on its own political interests.

For US diplomat George F. Keegan

"In the face of this situation [the assumed threat of communist advance] we would be better off to dispense now with a number of concepts which have underlined our thinking with regard to the Far East. We should dispense with the aspiration to 'be liked' or to be regarded as the repository of a high-minded international altruism. We should stop putting ourselves in the position of being our brothers'

keeper and refrain from offering moral and ideological advice. We should cease to talk about vague — and for the Far East — unreal objectives such as human rights, the raising of the living standards, and democratization. The day is not far off when we are going to have to deal in straight power concepts. The less we are hampered by idealistic slogans, the better."

The sentiment expressed in Kennan's comments are not dissimilar to those noted in a directive issued by Adolf Hitler to his military leaders in relation to his 1941 intended invasion of Russia:
"The war in Russia cannot be fought in a knightly fashion. The struggle is one of ideologies and racial differences and will have to be waged with unprecedented, unmerciful, and unrelenting hardness. All officers will have to get rid of any old-fashioned ideas they may have........."

And both seem motivated by an arrogant sense of military power.

If an antagonistic relationship defined US/Soviet interaction during the decades following WWII then, such was the influence of each of these 'superpowers' that the wider context for international politics became one characterized by polarization between western democracy and eastern communist competition.

The US/Soviet antagonism came to a dramatic crisis in 1962 over a situation played out on the Caribbean Island of Cuba, just 90 miles from mainland America. The US had long sought to control the politics of Central America and of some of the larger Caribbean Islands, including Cuba, where highly profitable US investments (especially in the sugar and construction industries) had been made. If we believe that nations have the right to self-determination then the US Central Intelligence Agency (C.I.A) can be viewed as a 'virus' infecting the politics of nation statehood; a body determined (at almost any cost) to maintain right-wing regimes; ideally at least nominally democratic ones, but more-often quite murderous military dictatorships would do.

Cuba by the 1950s had become a popular holiday destination for

US tourists - especially those keen on gambling in the casinos (then illegal in most US states) and employing the services of the many drug dealers and prostitutes vying for trade in Havana. Much of this 'leisure' industry had been taken over by the US-based Mafia crime syndicate. Although the Mafia (Costra Nostra) had initially moved into Cuba during the 1930s it would be with the Batista regime in the 1950s that they would enjoy the most conducive political conditions for their range of nefarious operations - gambling, prostitution, drug-running (Cuba was an important link in the transport of heroin from mainland South America to the US), and money laundering. In addition to these, what might be considered to be more traditional Mafia criminal activities, they also undertook to 'pacify' workers organizations by the threat or use of violence against any radical trades unionists in urban areas and similar for peasants organizations in rural locations. The Mafia in Cuba operated as a large, multi-interest corporation - owning banks, construction businesses, as well as hotels, night-clubs and casinos. In December 1946 the Hotel Nacional in Havana was the venue for a notorious Mafia conference at which Mafia bosses ('Godfathers' and their acolytes) from across the US, as well as those based in Cuba, met to discuss their wide-ranging business arrangements. After a hard day of discussion; the attendees were entertained by the famous US singer Frank Sinatra, specially flown in for the occasion.

President Batista and senior army officers were generously rewarded by what was in effect their criminal partnership with the Mafia. With many Cuban and US businessmen, as well as large land owners, also benefiting from the Mafia's insidious presence on the island. Meanwhile the masses remained poor. A poverty that provided fertile conditions for the revolutionary activities that would begin in earnest with the landing of the motorboat 'Granma' in December 1956. The overloaded and leaky Granma provided the means for Fidel Castro and his group of 82 would-be revolutionaries to reach the Island and then set off to gain the relative security of the Sierra Maestra mountain range. In fact only 12 revolutionaries managed to reach the mountains, the rest were killed or captured during engagements with Cuban government forces initially alerted to the landing by a helicopter pilot and then later betrayed by a guide.

It would take until New Years Day in 1959 for Castro and his victorious revolutionary army to march into Havana. This military success was due to steadily increasing support from the Cuban masses and also to Castro being able to recruit and deploy a determined force of fighters against a poorly led, mostly demoralized, government army.

Initially, the new Cuban government's relationship with the US was tentatively friendly. But even as the government introduced quite modest agrarian reforms and rent-controls the relationship soon deteriorated. This in turn drove a leadership including Fidel and Raul Castro, Ernesto 'Che' Guevara, and Camilo Cienfuegos, individuals determined to end US domination of the Cuban economy, into taking more radical measures; nationalizing large industries, and banks, and introducing more significant land reforms. The US increased its economic sanctions until it had imposed what was in effect a crippling economic blockade on the Island. Thousands of the rich, the criminal, and members of the middle classes, fled to US. The majority settling in Florida, with a small group of these plotting evermore ingenious ways to bring down the revolutionary government.

The mass of the Cubans remaining on the Island seem to accept the conditions, and a system of food rationing that at least provided the basic material conditions for life. I think the sense that all lived under the same conditions, that deprivation was shared, allowed a solidarity, if little real enthusiasm, in support of the government. A support further solidified with the abortive 'Bay of Pigs' landing (fiasco), when CIA trained and supplied Cuban expats failed in an attempted invasion of the Island.

Economically, the Soviet Union stepped in and offered the Cubans a new market for their basic exports, especially the vitally important sugar crop. This was a politically satisfying international relationship for the Soviets who had, since the war, been mostly having to defend its position and influence in Europe in the face of Western pressure. Facing such actions as the strategic deployment of NATO forces, provocatively including the positioning of US nuclear missiles in Turkey, close to its border with the Soviet Union.

Soviet conventional military activities on Cuba had been going on for some time until on 16th October 1962 when a US U2 'spy-plane' on a routine high-altitude flight over the Island, returned to its base with photographs clearly indicating the construction of missile silos. The temperature of international tension soared and President J.F. Kennedy engaged in a series of intensive discussions with a small group of close advisers (the Executive Committee of the National Security Council - ExComm). Out of which came the decision to give Khrushchev a deadline of 29th Oct to begin removing the missiles from Cuba, with the threat of a US military invasion if the Soviets refused to cooperate.

No doubt the provocation of NATO missile sites in Europe gave the Russians a sense of entitlement for their setting up similar missile sites on Cuba. However, the US claimed that NATO's European missile deployment was a defensive measure intended to contain Soviet expansionism, whereas nuclear missiles on Cuba would be an offensive act - even then glossing over the US supported attempt to invade Cuba and the various (some quite comical) CIA plans to assassinate Castro.

On the 28th October Khrushchev informed the US that the removal of the missiles would begin immediately and supply ships already at sea would turn back, this on condition that the US gives a commitment not to support another invasion of Cuba. For two weeks the world had teetered on the brink of possible nuclear war over the siting of 42 medium range and 24 intermediate range missiles in a context of the US having 25,000 nuclear weapons and the Soviets about half this number. Militarily, the siting of these missiles would have made little difference to the outcome of a nuclear exchange between these two superpowers, but America's national ego would not allow missiles being positioned so close to mainland USA. If anything, it was John Kennedy's more judicious approach, and his resisting the more hawkish advice to straight-away bomb Cuba, that gave Khrushchev time to consider the sombre implications of continuing with the plan to deploy the missiles.

Another US president, at another time, might take a different, more belligerent approach and another Russian (or a Chinese) president might not care about the implications! Such is the simple dynamics that could lead to millions of deaths - are national egos (and quite personal judgements) worth this? Do we need a respected international body that could apply balance and fairness to judge (intervene - and hold the parties apart for a period of more reflective consideration) situations of international tensions? It would seem sensible (in a desperately 'sensible' sense) to have some international mediation arrangement (or failing successful mediation - a body empowered to give binding direction to all parties involved) to serve as a forum charged to mitigate the potentially oh so destructive heat of immediacy, and national egoism, egged on by hawkish military advisors, involved in these situations. The most significant barriers to achieving this are:

Firstly, the need to cede national sovereignty in the area of international disagreements, secondly, the make-up of a mediation body that would have the respect required and, thirdly, what would be its 'terms of reference.'

Here lies the nub of legitimacy, authority, and the effectiveness, of the United Nations itself as a body.

As European states with overseas colonies were endeavouring to recover from the war-time depredations and were focusing on political manoeuvring over the future of the continent they also had to address the groundswell of the peoples of the colonial countries demanding national self-determination.

For Britain, the most significant colonial issue would be the independence of India, considered to be the 'Jewel in the Crown' of the British Empire. A possessive phrase highlighting a 200 hundred year long process of Britain's drawing massive wealth from the people and lands of the sub-continent. The active campaign for self-rule gained an organizational focus in 1919 when the Indian National Congress political party, led by the England-educated lawyer

Mohandas (Mahatma) Gandhi, began a strategy of non-violent non-cooperation with the British rule. Ironically, Congress had been formed in 1885 by a British civil servant, Allan Octavia Hume, with the aim of its serving as a manageable forum within which leading members of the Indian educated elite groups could express any dissatisfaction they had with the ways in which the British were ruling the country. Britain also wanted to offer a means by which they could devolve local and regional government to more western educated Indians in order to both, ease the administrative burdens on Britain, and also to channel, and so control, the political aspirations of the more vociferous individuals amongst the Indians. But towards the century's end a number of prominent members based in the states of Maharashtra, Punjab, and Bengal – led by those such as Bal Gangadhur Tilak supported by Bipin Chandra Pal and Lala Lajpat Rai – aspired to more than just a subject role in governing their country and they began to demand self-rule. Although a proportion of Congress members were Muslims, a group of leading Muslim intellectuals, based in the Aligarh Muslim University (in today's Uttar Pradesh), felt that Muslims needed their own political organization and so in 1901 formed the All-India Muslim League (AIML). Although the League's initial focus was in promoting the educational prospects for young Moslems, it became increasingly involved with broader political issues. Just after the end of WWI an early leader of the League, Muhammad Ali Jinnah, endeavoured to form a Hindu-Muslim anti-British alliance, but this came to nothing and he withdrew from direct political involvement. During the inter-war years there was some degree of co-operation between the two organizations but outbreaks of inter-ethnic communal violence (in particular during 1922, which saw a succession of violent riots in major cities) were an ongoing source of political and community division. By the 1930s AIML, now led by Sri Muhammad Iqbal, began to demand a post-colonial two-nation settlement, even identifying regions of Northern India (Punjab, Sindh, Baluchistan, and the North-West Frontier province) that would be suitable for a new, Muslim, nation. But Congress remained implacably opposed to this.

The campaign for independence made significant progress during the Second World War, due partly to India having been taken into the war by Britain without its people being properly consulted. What had been a long-term aspiration began to be a more immediate prospect. Ali Jinnah had re-engaged with politics in time to join other leaders of the Muslim League (as AIML was re-named) and those of a Congress financed and influenced by a group composed of upper-class urbanites, owners of big businessmen, industrialists, and large rural landowners (collectively termed by Harman, 1999, p552 '….a coterie of Indian capitalists'), during a protracted period of negotiation; seeking to find a political solution for Indian self-rule. Britain had tried to contain the campaign for independence by a mixture of relatively minor political concessions and often harsh repression. But by 1945 the British Government had resigned itself to losing political control of its prized colony as it reluctantly accepted the reality of the conservative writer Edmund Burke's eighteenth century observation that however much you attempt to contain national aspirations that: 'The use of force is but temporary. It may subdue for a moment; but it does not remove the necessity of subduing again; and a nation is not governed, which is perpetually to be conquered.'

Attempts to leave behind a united India (population of 480 million, with 120m Muslims being the largest minority - plus 12m Christians) proved futile, with the Muslim League only being prepared to accept a version of unity with weak central control and a significant amount of power ceded to regions; thus allowing a strong voice for Muslims in those regions where they had a majority. Whereas Congress was only prepared to accept a unified India with a strong central government. This marked difference of view could not be resolved, and by 1946 it was clear that the most realistic option was a two-nation arrangement – a 'partition' of the sub-continent.

Mahatma Gandhi had been leading a series of actions in support of a non-violent campaign for independence and he consistently condemned the communal violence, as well as trying to persuade Hindus, Muslims, and Sikhs, to recognize a unity of religious faith underlying their particular forms of religious beliefs. For Gandhi: 'There are as many religions as there are men and women, but they are all rooted in God'.

In order to focus the attention of the two main Indian parties onto the self-rule negotiations - at a time of increasing and widespread communal violence – the British gave a deadline of August 1947 for withdrawal. Partition, when it came, would be in line with a plan drawn up by Lord Louis Mountbatten (the last Viceroy of India), creating a border between the two new nations based on a report issued under the Chairmanship of a London-based barrister, Cyril Radcliffe. A man with very little direct knowledge of the communities that he divided with his pen.

Partition took place on 14th August, with the creation of Pakistan and was completed on the following day with the creation of India - two nations born in bitter, bloody, communal violence; orgies of killing, rape and the destruction of homes; fairly termed massacres in some places. In Punjab alone possibly as many as 500,000 were killed and overall 14 million Hindu, Moslems, Sikhs and others, were displaced. The long sad shadow of religious division cast over Partition brought the animosity between these new-born nations to a new level. One that would soon see them at war over who would control the extensive fertile states of Kashmir and Jummu. Kashmir (70% Muslim) was one of the princely states that the British had allowed to choose which of the new nations they would join. The Sikh Maharaja of Kashmir, Hari Singh, vacillated over which nation to become part of but when Pathan tribesmen (said to be backed by Pakistan) invaded from the north, he called on the Indian government to come to his state's assistance.

As a condition of taking military action the Indian government insisted that Kashmir would have to cede its sovereignty to India, and this was agreed. The Pathan invaders were initially driven back by a combination of Indian and local Kashmiri defenders. But counter-attack by the tribesmen (increasingly supported by regular Pakistan forces), produced a stalemate of sorts, with military operations being launched when one side or the other felt that conditions were in its favour.

It took intervention by the UN in January 1949 to end immediate military hostilities, with Kashmir being divided one-third Pakistan and two-thirds India, to the satisfaction on neither side. The resultant dissatisfaction being a continuing focus of bitterness between the two nations. As but one further source of animosity that has seen region-based communal violence continuing down to today - the enmity between these countries over Kashmir now has the added danger of each possessing nuclear weaponry.

Britain, if viewing the whole process of decolonization in the Far-East somewhat resentfully, so undertaken somewhat grudgingly, did take an economically realistic approach rather than letting too great a sense of imperial grandeur influence its decision-making. Resigning itself to the reality of situations similar to those observed by Burke (above).

India was the first, if most significant, of Britain's colonies to achieve independence in the post-war period and soon it would be other far eastern territories that from 1942 had fallen to Japan. Britain's imperial prestige, and associated mythical invincibility, was undermined by the relative ease by which a British army of about 90,000 troops had been so easily overwhelmed by a smaller Japanese force when taking Singapore. A loss of invincibility underlined by the Japanese Navy's mauling of the Royal Navy's far eastern fleet, including the sinking of the battleship Prince of Wales and the aircraft carrier Hermes.

In 1948 it would be Ceylon, following a mostly peaceful campaign for self-government involving strikes (including quite lengthy general strikes in 1946 and 1947), demonstrations, and reasonably low-key negotiations, that would be next. The political party at the forefront of negotiations was the United National Party (UNP), founded by Don Stephen Senanayake when, in September 1946, he brought together three right-wing parties. At the 1947 election the UNP gained more seats (42 out of 95) than any of the other parties and put together a coalition that would form the first Ceylonese government after the hand-over of power. Ceylon was granted dominion status as a state within the British Commonwealth when it became the Dominion of

Ceylon at independence in February 1948; it would be 1972 before it would gain full independence as the Republic of Sri Lanka.

Burma also gained independence in 1948, adopting a constitutional model from the British that proved to be unsuitable for a mainly agrarian and poorly administered country. The first post-independence government was led by U Nu, with support from the army headed by General Ne Win, but its power was mostly restricted to larger urban centres, with communists groups (Red Flags and White Flags) controlling large areas of the countryside.

General Ne Win would take over from U Nu in 1960 and run the country as a one-party state for the following 26 years. The one party being the 'Burma Socialist Programme Party' which maintained a form of authoritarian government that had little in common with traditionally understood socialism and was one that achieved little economic benefit for most of Burma's people,

When the Japanese retreated from Indonesia in 1945 (having held out the promise of post-war independence) the Dutch endeavoured to re-occupy their former colony. But in August 1945, the Central Indonesian National Committee declared independence and elected Achmed Sukarno as the first president. The Dutch refused to recognize this move and sought to regain control of this mainly Muslim country made up of over 3,500 islands spread over 3,000 miles of ocean. Then followed a four year war between the belligerents before the Dutch finally accepted the reality on the ground and, on 27th December 1949 the Dutch Queen gave constitutional sanction to the transfer of sovereignty to the United States of Indonesia. This turned out to be an astute move by the Dutch in that it enabled the retention of their investments and also allowed them to receive a level of Marshall Aid from the US that would facilitate economic recovery in the Netherlands.

The new Indonesian government adopted a policy designed to maximize national self-sufficiency whilst attempting to follow a non-aligned strategy in its international relationships. An approach that appealed to a number of other newly independent nations. The constitutional arrangements established at independence broke down by 1958 when Sukarno, supported by the army if opposed by communists groups such as the PKI, introduced a more authoritarian approach to government - his 'guided democracy'. Sukarno's ambition to expand Indonesia into parts of neighbouring Malaysia were thwarted when a combined force of British, Australia, New Zealand and Malaysian troops moved to defend the country. An abortive military coup in 1965 (now officially blamed on communist insurgents) led to General Suharto becoming president, with hundreds of thousands of communists being massacred and ties being cut with the Soviet Union and China. With the US becoming the nation's main arms supplier and contributor of aid. Suharto was to rule (as military dictator leading a kleptocracy) for the next 31 years with his plan of 'New Order'. These were three decades of endemic corruption[28] and economic inefficiency, and although there was some economic growth there was little economic benefit for most of the population.

If the British and Dutch experienced serious difficulties with their colonial possessions it would be even more so for the French and their south-eastern Asia colonies. These were difficulties compounded by a post-war 'Free France', led by the belligerent and imperialistic General de Gaulle, being determined to regain its pre-war colonial possessions in Indo-China. When the Japanese left the ex-French protectorate of Cambodia King Norodom Sihanouk (scion of a royal line that had been involved in ruling Cambodia for centuries) tried to pre-empt French attempts to reclaim the country by proclaiming an independent status for Cambodia (as Kampuchea). In August 1945 Son Ngoc Thanh became prime minister of a new government. But the French returned in force later that year to re-impose colonial rule, albeit with a promise of a greater role in government for Cambodians. Sihanouk led a national independence movement during a protracted period of negotiations prior to an agreement on conditions for independence being finally reached, with the King declaring independence in October 1953.

---

[28] New Internationalist', April 2016 – estimates are of $35 billion being 'stolen' by the Suharto family during the General's period in office.

If parting with the resource rich (rubber, corn, rice, cotton, timber) Cambodia was difficult for the French then the military humiliation it received in trying to hold on to Vietnam would have a more lasting impact on its international status. The French had maintained a repressive colonial regime in Vietnam from 1874, (determinedly displacing traditional structures of governance) but were forced to depart by the Japanese during WWII. Following the Japanese surrender in 1945 the French returned, but it was a return to a Vietnam where an indigenous independence movement was becoming organized. This movement took two primary political forms. One being a Nationalist Party that modelled itself on the Chinese Republic (Kuomintang – Chinese Nationalist Party) which had run China from 1912 after displacing the Qing dynasty. The second indigenous political movement was the Communist Party of Indochina whose campaign would be led by the Party's founding father Ho Chi Ming on his return from exile in Hong Kong. The heavy-handed French crushed the rising Nationalist Party, leaving the main opposition as the communists who more easily adapted to the type of a clandestine (guerrilla) operations required to further the independence campaign. Indeed, Ho Chi Ming was to lead an insurrection with implications for world-wide power politics, and to influence sections of a generation of western youths, into the 1960s. The communists (Viet Minh) initially established their military headquarters in a cave-complex located in an isolated area of the north. The populist policies of the communists (especially plans for land reform), together with their military tenacity, along with wide-spread native hatred of the colonial power, enabled them to make steady progress against the French. A progress coming to a head at the battle of Dien Bien Phu (from March 13th to May 7th 1954) where the French were humiliated. The extent of the Viet Minh's military power came as a complete surprise to the commanders of the defending French 'Far East Expeditionary Corps', their being surrounded and battered into submission by the communist's heavy artillery. The defender's situation was hopeless and the inevitable surrender came on 7th April 1954. Ho Chi Ming initially attempted to make friendly contacts with the US (he had been supplying them with information about the Japanese during the war) but this was not reciprocated.

As regions of north Vietnam came under communist control, land reforms and price controls were introduced that were generally popular with the peasantry, but there was also a ruthless campaign of imprisonment and mass execution of those deemed to be members of the landlord or imperialist classes. Over a million refugees fled south.

An international conference held in Geneva, from April to June 1954, was set up to see if a final settlement on issues outstanding from the conflict in Korea could be agreed and also to seek arrangements for peace in Indochina. For Vietnam, a Geneva Accord divided the county into a North and South at the 17th parallel, and also agreed to an election to take place in 1956, with unification intended to follow. The US delegation, aware that their favoured political group would most likely lose a fair election, refused to accept the plans for a Vietnam-wide ballot. During this time the French were keen for the US to get directly (militarily) involved, an invitation resisted by an indecisive Eisenhower. As an alternative a process of sending US 'advisors' did begin, with their number growing steadily as the hold of the Republican government became increasingly weak. Starting with the government led by Ngo Dinh Diem, the south saw one corrupt and inefficient administration replaced by another, with the US endeavouring to prop up each failing regime until the task become hopeless when it would then try to influence the succession. Communist guerrillas in the south adopted a strategy of targeting government officials; with 4,000 being killed in 1961 alone.

In December 1960 the National Liberation Front was formed by individuals with a range of left wing political views but all were dedicated to the liberation of South Vietnam and the unification of the whole country. This grouping - its military wing being the Vietcong - was made up of ex-Viet Minh, plus a mixture of left-wing groups based in the south, with the communists paying a central role, if one initially exaggerated by those in the government seeking evermore US support.

From March 1965, the American advisors were joined by ground-troops, an escalation that aligned with what more reactionary (i.e. the majority - right-wing and the nominally 'liberal') US politicians viewed as an appropriate response in relation to the 'domino theory' (of one nation after another 'falling' to communism) and was precipitated by the Tonkin incident of the previous year when two US warships, cruising in international waters off Vietnam, were fired on by North Vietnamese coastal patrol boats.

Short-sighted ideological considerations, and no doubt confidence in its vastly superior military power, had drawn America into a war that would reveal the limits of naked force to overcome indigenous liberation movements. A war that would see social upheaval across the US as many young people reacted to the horrors of a televised war, the call-up; as well as the grim flow of flag-draped coffins returning to America. By the War's end US casualties would be nearly 60,000 killed and 150,000 wounded (disproportionately black soldiers).[29]

By comparison, at the War's end, one in seven Vietnamese people had been killed - 2 million of these being civilians (with another 2 million civilians being seriously injured), the majority as a result of the US bombing strategy. Atrocities were carried out by both sides but those committed by the Americans were overwhelmingly more destructive and murderous than those of the Vietnamese rebels. Especially the drenching of large swathes of the countryside with the highly toxic defoliate Agent Orange (400,000 tons - 5 million gallons - of Agent Orange mostly dropped on civilian areas, villages, hamlets, fields, etc.). US B52 bombers had obliterated villages and towns, as they dropped more bombs on Vietnam, and neighbouring Laos and Cambodia, than had been dropped on Europe during the whole of the second world war - the term 'carpet-bombing' expresses its coverage and the graphic images of bloody, twisted and burnt bodies of innocent children expressed its horror.

---

[29] With many sons of the rich US elites - including George W Bush, a future president - avoiding the draft by moving abroad or in Bush's case by joining the National Guard. Another future president, Donald Trump, conveniently being declared medically unfit due to a 'spur' on his foot, seemingly a condition that did not prevent his active engagement in a number of sports at that time, and one that seems not to have troubled him at any other time in his life.

Estimates of up to 3,000,000 deaths (800,000 children made orphans) during the time of US direct involvement in Vietnam alone. Even the CIA estimate deaths from US bombing just in the north was running at 30,000 per year by 1967 and bear in mind that the largest proportion of these were civilians. Thousands of square miles of fertile farmland in both north and south Vietnam, Laos and Cambodia, along with extensive rice paddy-fields, land drainage systems, thousands of hamlets, towns, and in northern cities whole residential neighbourhoods.........all destroyed by the ferocity of carpet bombing, from being drenched in poisonous chemicals, and by the behemoth that was the 'Rome Plough'; a massive tractor used to clear land of all vegetation, as well as churning through the miles of dikes that were of such vital importance to irrigation. Over 1,500,000 cattle, along with almost all the pigs and chickens being kept in the area devastated by US military action, being killed. Added to the immediate casualties of warfare there were thousands more wounded who died later on, and the thousands who would die of starvation in a once fertile land where food production had been decimated. All forces engaged in the war contributed to the destruction and killing but the US, because of its shear industrial military power, allied to a lack of concern for its victims, had cast a visitation of human and ecological catastrophe across Indo-China and left much of Vietnam a smoking, poisoned, waste-land, with much of its population battered, starving, and grieving.

Throughout this period the US mass media failed abysmally to report fairly, in anything even approaching a balanced way on the impact of US action. Or on the military setbacks, at least until the later stages of the war when these became impossible to deny. Even when the mass killing of civilians was reported it was invariably either the fault of the 'communists' or an unfortunate error caused by the 'fog' of war. When massacres by US or South Vietnamese Government, troops were exposed they were treated as an aberration involving 'brave soldiers/GIs under unbearable pressure'. The My Lai massacre fell into this latter category - with the blame eventually being pinned on a non-descript Lieutenant. The mass of the people of southern

Vietnam, and later those of Laos and Cambodia, were absolutely terrorized - for most US senior officers the victims became the enemy, so ceasing to count as human beings. We don't need to speculate on how the US 'free-press' would have reported if it had been the Soviet Union that had acted in similar ways because with Afghanistan during the 1980s, and the then Soviet invasion, we were able to see a very different US media approach. One where the Soviet Union was repeatedly condemned for killing civilians. The truth of any incident was not properly investigated, even just an accusation was sufficient to mobilize a press outraged at 'Soviet brutality'. A brutality that was an aspect of its involvement in Afghanistan, but which was at a level that would hardly be noticed in the normality of the killing inflicted on Indo-China by the army of south Vietnam, south Korean and other mercenaries, and by the US military.

In the Philippines, with the Japanese surrender in 1945 the remnants of their occupying army left the parts of the country that US and indigenous Philippino forces had not already re-gained. An agreement on self-rule drawn up before WWII, had been overwhelming passed by a Philippine Constitutional Convention held in 1934, and approved by F.D. Roosevelt in 1935. After the war it would be this agreement that would provide the constitutional basis for a fully independent Philippines from July 1946. A series of five more or less corrupt governments to 1965, with leaders more or less anointed by the US (the first, Manual Roxas, being enthusiastically supported by General McArthur) with an agreement on leasing over 20 military bases to the US. These governments were generally repressive and keenly anti-communist. 'Communist' being anyone determinedly against the impact of these authoritarian governments in thrall to big business, large land-owners, and foreign (read mainly US) investors.

Over the past 2500 years China has shown itself to be difficult to govern as a unified entity – this due to its tradition of war-lords ruling local fiefdoms, peasant's movements, invasions from the west, east, and north, and often intense rivalry between both religious and ethnic groups. The later continues today, with the Han making up 92% of the population and their encroachment on lands traditionally occupied by other groups - Zhuang in Guangxi, Miao in the south-west, Uighur Muslims in the north-west, the Hui Muslims, and of course the land of 4 million Tibetans.

With the rise to President in 2012 of Xi Jinping, we see a focus on a form of nationalism set in the context of renewal and a growing sense of a Chinese destiny involving a global scope; even the dynastic-period conception of China as being the centre of the civil world. A China ramping up claims to large areas of the western Pacific, not least with its declaration of an Air Defence Identification Zone (ADIZ) encompassing almost all of the East China Sea and further assertive naval manoeuvres around its offshore island claims. Drawing a reaction from the US and Japan making their opposition clear; refusing to accept the ADIZ, or to recognize the offshore island claims.

The process of de-colonization across the vast, tribally and ethnically variegated, continent of Africa has been a mostly painful experience for the mass of the people. Yes, it's fair to assume that most wanted self-determination, and freedom from more or less racist colonial masters, but almost all held high expectations of the black leaders who replaced them. More than they, their children, and now their grandchildren, have received, as the aspirations expressed at times of independence have faded to disillusionment (and at times and in places, fear) as the masses have been repeatedly let down by a series of post-independence rulers.

Whilst some political concessions had been made by the colonial powers prior to the Second World War, it was the wartime experience of many of the future leaders (often Western or USSR educated) that determined them on national self-determination. But even the concept of independence was problematic - independence 'from what' was clearly from direct control of the colonial powers, but freedom 'as what' was another consideration? Should the entities due to become independent merely follow the territorial patterning determined by colonial mapmakers? Where borders were more often the outcome of hegemonic power-politics, forming territorial tectonic plates where colonial powers had rubbed against each other at the edges of colonial competition over potentially exploitable regions. Outlining an imperialist matrix upon which the entrails of colonial exploitation had been fought over. Borders that made little geographical sense, many being ones that separated tribal and ethnic groupings and perhaps even worse, borders that included diverse peoples within artificial nations whose post-colonial control would be, often bitterly, contested.[30]* It would perhaps have been improbable to consider any real possibility of re-drawing borders (perhaps based on ethnicities and encompassing groups with some sense of shared territorial identity) - not least, there was no pre-colonial divisions that could be termed fixed borders which could have served as acceptable divisions by which to geographically define post-colonial nations. Other than perhaps the colonial powers mutually agreeing to diplomatically 'dissolve' colonial borders and just to leave Africans themselves to negotiate territorial divisions based upon their own understanding of pre-colonial conditions (at least as a starting point).

A movement had begun in the nineteenth century for an essentially African entity encompassing all peoples of the continent and those millions constituting the African Diaspora (especially those in the Americas). This movement, Pan-Africanism, highlighted sources of unity based on mutual interests; focusing on culture, governance, and a shared history of exploitation. Early in the twentieth century, the intellectual, W.E.B.DuBois, took the lead in promoting Pan-Africanism and between the two 20th century world wars men such as Marcus Garvy (founded the Universal Negro Improvement Association), and C.L.R Jones, brought enthusiasm and some organizational skills to what had become a cause. Pan-African conferences were held throughout the 1920s and during the heady pre-independence years from 1945 leaders such as Jomo Kenyatta, George

---

[30] Estimates suggest about 10,000 discrete territorial units were contained with the new nations - see Martin Shipway, 2008, p20.

Padmore, Seretse Khama, and especially Kwame Nkruma, promoted the idea. An idea that also reflected communist universalism, one that was attractive to a number of those leading the drive for independence. Pan-Africanism offered a self-determined route to transcending the artificial colonial division of the continent. Perhaps Pan-Africanism was just too idealistic, and the immense task of negotiating through all of the practical issues made it unviable at that time.

The more mundane drive for independence involved over 50 nation-states (each progressing its own timescale towards self-determination) and the idea of some greater Africa became but a small voice in the mix of hopes that would be over-ridden by the self-centred motivations of national African elites, and the continuing self-interest of the colonial powers. At least the 'spirit' of continental unity did re-emerge in the foundation of the Organization of African Unity in 1963 (OAU) [31] Modelled on the UN, it currently has 54 member nations. Its ambitious plan for 2013-2063, along with the interim steps towards this does make quite inspiring reading, if as yet (2023) there has been but little progress toward reaching some key objectives that should have been achieved six years ago.

The AU Commission Strategic Plan 2014-2017 included the objectives:
1. Human capacity development focusing on health, education, science, research,
3. technology and innovation;
2. Develop agriculture and agro-processing;
3. Inclusive economic development through industrialization, infrastructure development,
4. agriculture, and trade and investment;
5. Peace, stability and good governance;
6. Mainstreaming women and youth into all our activities;
7. Resource mobilization;

---

[31] Addis Abba has continued to be the location of its headquarters - in May 2001 the OAU became the African Union.

8. Building a people-centred Union through active communication and branding; and
9. Strengthening the institutional capacity of the Union and all its organs.

But having had chairpersons such as Thabo Mbeki (2002-2003), Muammar Gaddafi (2009-2010), and Robert Mugabwe (2015-2016), along with an, at best, varied record so far[32], does not allow for much confidence in the organization.

The visionary idea of a single united states of Africa has at best been diluted with the A.U. Up to now it has been a relatively ineffective forum within which self-important politicians offer high-flown narratives of hope to those millions living lives of desperate poverty and in fear of violence across this resource-rich and beautiful continent of stunning landscapes and wide horizons.

At the time when independence was achieved for most colonial nations a primary task for the new leaders (and their elite and/or military supporters) was to create a sense of nationhood for ethnic groups that did not have much geographically defined shared historic or cultural identities preceding the colonial experience. There was strong tribal and clan governance and rich cultural experience, but this was more physically (and psychologically) located in farmlands, pastures, deserts, savannah, and forests. Traditional local territories defined by tribally-based accommodations made between neighbouring groups since the earliest times of human occupation.

European nations had accrued their nationhood over centuries, even in America the nations of Canada and the US were established by peoples who not only broadly shared a continuity of history (connected to that of Europe), culture, and religion, but also a sense of 'pioneering purpose' that would hold them together in a federated

---

[32] There has been some progress in primary education and with the inclusion of women in government, but with nothing whatever being done to reduce economic inequality, which is not even in its objectives, or to raise living standards which is!

forms of nationhood. In Africa, many of the new constitutional arrangements were modelled on those of Europe, including military forces with an ethos of obedience to commanding officers inherited from the imperial powers. Nationalist ceremonies were invented, colourful flags produced, and western style national anthems composed and played on musical instruments imported from Europe. In places attempts (some more, most less, justified) were made to connect to some perceptions of glorious past African empires - Zimbabwe/Benin, Ghana/Ashanti, the short-lived Mali Federation combining the Sudanese Republic and Senegal in Mali, and KwaZulu-Natal/Zulu. In most of the new nations the deep-rooted indigenous fault-lines: of tribe, and the newer one of religion (primarily Christianity/Islam), the emerging one of class interests, and the personal ambitions of some in the leadership groups, would not be easily contained within a commonality of nationhood.

Tribal membership provides the colour for the ideas and normative values created from the meaning-laden palettes of shared culture, contiguous history, kinship relationships, and social expectations. Invariably, as the concept of membership becomes appropriate to describe any individual's connections to some circumscribed group there is the immediate (and decisive) creation of 'others', of the non-members of the home group. If this otherness involves just a few individuals on the fringes of the group (tribe) then they are just dismissed (even pitied) but if they are members of another identifiable group then more significant, rarely respectful and usually derogatory, judgments can be involved.

Tribe members are enclosed in emotionally satisfying meaning-networks, allowing the peace of mind most crave, within a framework offering deeply-rooted attachment to a territory and to the generations that have gone before and those that will come after. An emotionally sustaining, economically protective, 'shell' of belongingness within the potential chaos of existence which lies beyond the familiar; within the imagined threat of the unknown.

Commentators such as Bruce Rozenblit (2008) and Elizabeth Crouch Zelman (2015) highlight the wide-ranging impact of the 'us and them' polarity characteristic of tribalism and its manifestation even in civilized settings circa the twenty-first century. For Rozenblit (2008, p17): 'The behaviors that I assign to tribalism actually are a set of group-inspired behaviors that humans use to distinguish the in-group and the out-group, the "us" and "them". These behaviors had their roots in human society long before tribes actually existed and became more fully entrenched as formal tribes developed. They remain a major component of contemporary society.'

If post-war sub-Saharan Africa was subject to a degree of US/Soviet overt and covert involvement then their activities in the Middle East were much more obvious. Prior to more significant superpower involvement, most of the Middle East was more or less depending on the degree of assertiveness-rebelliousness-factiousness of local populations controlled by Britain and France. The broad outline for a post World War I Middle-East was planned, in secret, during negotiations between Britain and France. Planning that culminated in meetings held during December 1915 between a British delegation led by the politician Sir Marks Sykes and a French delegation led by the diplomat Francois Georges-Picot. Neither Sykes nor Picot had the detailed knowledge of the Middle-East that they pretended too and these negotiations, which took place mainly in London, did not involve any direct input from any legitimate Arab leaders. Following a series of factious meetings, the 'Sykes-Picot Agreement' was drawn up - an agreement that carved an imaginary 'line-in-the-sand' from Acre on the Mediterranean coast to Kirkuk in the east. The lands to the north of the line considered as being under French control and the lands to the south under British control. Although the suggestion of 'control', that line-making on maps can assume, was derived more from diplomatic wishful thinking and a political need for clarity; the reality on the ground being much more complex. Actual control more often being in the hands of various kings, princes, muftis, sheiks, sultans, chieftains, and warlords. The exercise that Sykes and Picot were engaged in was an example of top down power-politics at its worst - a process of major military powers picking over the remains of an empire coming to an end (here the 400 year old Ottoman Empire). And undertaking the exercise motivated entirely by considerations of what was perceived to be in the best interests of themselves rather than of the peoples whose homelands they were squabbling over. For most of the next few decades Britain and France would be engaged in efforts to undermine each other's position with Arab states.

The twentieth century foundations of a Jewish homeland in the Middle East, along with its part in the territorial carve-up noted above, was another legacy of British diplomacy exercised during the First World War. The, mostly low-level, (nominally institutionalized) anti-Semitism that was experienced on an almost daily basis by Jews throughout pre-war Europe (highlighted by the notorious Dreyfus affair of 1894) had contributed to forming a movement calling for a Jewish State. Many of these 'Zionists' held influential positions in business, science, and government. One of these was Chaim Weizmann, a scientist who had made a significant contribution to Britain's war effort.[33] He was prominent in the Zionist movement and the esteem in which he was held by senior government ministers, such as Lloyd George and Arthur Balfour, gave him the opportunity to make the case for a Jewish State in Palestine at the highest level. Weizmann, along with other prominent Jews, kept up the pressure for British support for their cause. A cause that Arthur Balfour (promoted to the Foreign Office during the war) in particular was sympathetic towards. Another factor in driving the campaign for a Jewish state was Britain's hope that the US would enter the war and that pressure from US Jews might help to achieve this.

On 2nd November 1917 Balfour, acting on behalf of the cabinet, wrote a letter to the Jewish financier Lord Rothschild; later made public with its publication in The Times newspaper. The relevant paragraph of this letter being: *' His Majesty's Government view with*

---

[33] Weizmann devised a fermentation process that produced acetone - a chemical vital for the armaments industry, the production of which had been a German monopoly.

favour the establishment in Palestine of a national home for the Jewish people, and will use their best endeavours to facilitate the achievement of this object, it being clearly understood that nothing shall be done which may prejudice the civil and religious rights of existing non-Jewish communities in Palestine, or the rights and political status enjoyed by Jews in any other country.'

This commitment (although later reneged on by the British in 1939 - when it withdrew its commitment to a Jewish State) was accepted by the League of Nations in July 1922 and would be included in the terms of the mandate that gave Britain control of Palestine. During the interwar period there was a modest but steady migration of Jews to Palestine - but from the start there were antagonisms between the local population and the in-comers. The basic issue was the fundamentalist Zionist long-term ambition for occupying all Palestinian lands. But the sale by wealthy Arabs of large tracts of land to Jews, and the subsequent forced removal of farmers whose families had farmed the land for generations, was a more immediate source of tension.

By the early 1960s 1.2 million Jews would have migrated to Israel, mostly from Europe. I would think that the imposition, by force, of a new country on lands that had for centuries been occupied by others can have been expected to induce resentment at the gross unfairness, and so lead to conflict. That this new nation was created by countries, not seeking to right any historic injustices, but rather from an attempt to balance their own diplomatic commitments and economic interests in the region. Even the biblical claims for pre-Diaspora (the traditional accepted date for this being from the destruction of the Second Temple in Jerusalem in 70 CE) Jewish occupation are at odds with the archaeological evidence of the actual pattern of tribal occupation of over three millennium ago. And there might also be the need to consider the competing rights of descendents of the Canaanite and other peoples who were so brutally displaced by Jewish migrants from Egypt. But I accept, that what is for me and many historians at best a tenuous claim to historical rights, is a fundamental certainty for many orthodox Jews. And even if the historical evidence could prove that those tribal peoples who adopted the (monotheistic) religion in lands we now term Palestine were but some amongst the many other tribal peoples with whom they co-existed (who occupied the region traditionally termed Palestine) - and even if the diverse genetic roots of peoples now so determinedly claiming 'Jewishness', and familial links to peoples who accompanied Abraham so long ago, suggest such deterministic claims to be dubious - then for sure orthodox (and I expect many non-orthodox) Jews would refuse to accept this. Such is the strength of the psychological commitment to the interpretation of a form of tribal identity that they have been socialized into.

The creation of Israel was a process driven significantly by the European Jewish experience. The roots of Israel is in difference and the systemic persecution of a people endeavouring to live amongst others but with a determinedly different identity; one that provocatively included the divisive claim of their being a 'chosen people'. The ambition for a distinctly Jewish homeland began in the nineteenth century with the ambitions of some prominent European Jews for a 'homeland'. The British Zionist Federation (an umbrella organization for a range of Jewish groups) was formed in 1899 and Theodore Herzl founded the World Zionist Organization which played a leading role in promoting Jewish migration to Palestine between the two world wars.

Towards the end of his influential 1896 book, 'Der Judenstaat' ('The State of the Jews'), Herzl wrote: *'... I believe that a wondrous generation of Jews will spring into existence. The Maccabeans will rise again. Let me repeat once more my opening words: The Jews who wish for a State will have it.*'

During the interwar years Britain[34] if reluctantly, at least paid lip-service to the commitment made in the Balfour Declaration and allowed a modest but steady migration of Jews into Palestine. They were also endeavouring to contain Arab nationalist opposition to

---

[34] Exercising their mandate via a military government, a mandate to find a way of partitioning the land of Palestine to allow the formation of a Jewish state, whilst at the same time, in line with the conditional clause in the Balfour Declaration, to protect the civil and religious rights of Arabs - non-Jewish Palestinians.

British (and indeed, further to the north, French) occupation, and their anger with the influx of Jews determined to create a new state within their lands. Relationships between Arabs and Jews became increasingly fractious, and at times violent clashes occurred. One of these, in April 1920 saw five Jews and four Arabs killed with hundreds more on both sides injured when groups rioted in Jerusalem during the Muslim festival of Nebi Musa.

British control of Palestine was tough, and at times brutal, including the collective punishment of villages (burning down and bulldozing homes) thought to have harboured Arab fighters. In 1938 the possession of firearms was made a capital offence but this did little to reduce the wide-spread smuggling of arms and explosives into Palestine. During what became known as the 1936-39 Arab Revolt, different Arab groups were undertaking guerrilla actions against the British, and on occasion against Jews; estimates suggest that possible as many as 5,000 Arabs were killed during this uprising. At the same time Jews were bombing Arab markets and Arab quarters in Jerusalem and Haifa - which in turn led to a murderous cycle of tit-for-tat reprisals. At this stage the British applied their mandate unevenly in relation to dealing with Jews and Arabs, most often favouring Jews over Arabs. In 1938 the newly appointed British intelligence officer, Orde Wingate, set up a special mobile force ('Special Night Squads') that involved Zionists. A force that included Yigal Allon and Moshe Dayan - both of whom became prominent military and political figures in the future state of Israel, who even at this time were also a members of the radical Jewish Haganah.

Wingate himself was, or at least became, a fanatical Zionist and had made a foolishly derogatory assessment of Arabs - that one Jew was worth up to one hundred Arabs, who were 'ignorant and primitive' people. British military operations did little but further provoke Arab opposition and, from early in the war, even previously fairly cooperative Zionist Jews became frustrated by the lack of progress towards a Jewish state. Increasingly from now the British in Palestine had to contend with guerrilla groups of both nationalist Arabs and Zionist Jews.

The British took a pragmatic decision in early 1939 to change their approach on the issue of a Jewish state. They did this mainly in order to ensure a reliable flow of oil from the oilfields in Iraq down the long and vulnerable pipeline to Haifa. One change was to moderate talk of a Jewish state and to appease Arabs more obviously by significantly reducing Jewish immigration and by making the purchase of Palestinian land more difficult.

By some macabre sense of irony the leader of the Jewish Stern Gang, Avraham 'Yair' Stern, made (via the French Vichy Government) an offer to fight for Nazi Germany if Hitler would make a commitment to 're-establish' the state of Israel within what he claimed was its historic borders. With no offer forthcoming from Hitler, Stern nevertheless launched a campaign of action against Britain, in the initial stages of which the Gang managed to kill more Jews than Arabs and also managed to cause Britain to divert military resources to the Middle-East that could have made at least some contribution to fighting the actual war against Hitler and his allies.

At the end of World War II British failure to achieve the primary aim of the mandate reached a point where they considered their continued presence untenable - not least due to their having to confront the tough, determined Jewish gangs of Irgun and Stern, composed of a number of fighters who would go on to become prominent Israeli politicians. In October 1945 David Ben-Gurion Chairman of the 'Jewish Agency' executive instructed the leader of Haganah, Moshe Dayan, to combine with the Stern (then led by Menachem Begin and Nathan Friedman-Yellin) and Irgun (led by Zvai Leumi) gangs as a unified Jewish Resistance Movement. Then followed months of intensive activity including, theft of weapons, shootings, kidnappings, bombings, and sabotage; not least the notorious bombing by Irgun of the British administrative headquarters based in the King David Hotel in Jerusalem in July 1946 in which 91 people were killed.

Finally, in April 1947, the British indicated to the United Nations their intention to withdraw from Palestine in May 1948, and requested that the UN seek a permanent resolution to this issue. The UN set up a Special Committee to progress this and in a short time the committee had drafted a plan (the basis of Resolution 181) for the partitioning of Palestine into an Arab state and a Jewish state. This plan was then endorsed by the General Assembly in Nov 1947, and the State of Israel was declared on 14 May 1948. During the later war years, and at the UN, the US (its government being persistently lobbied by Jewish groups) was directly involved in pursuing the creation of a Jewish state. A state whose border would encompass about half of Palestine and about one-third of its Arab population. The US government formally recognized the State of Israel within 24 hours of its foundation.

So a new state had been created out of a sense of collective European guilt after the genocidal disaster that had engulfed up to 6 million Jews in the Hitlerian-Nazi holocaust, along with the pressure from influential Jews in the US and Europe, and of course the military pressure from belligerent groups of Jews. And this in a land that was also home to about one million Palestinian Arabs who had no influential friends in the west and mostly only unreliable ones in the Middle-East. More than 700,000 non-Jewish Palestinians would early on be driven from their homes by Jewish settlers.

Jewish incomers brought a real sense of dynamic purpose to the land, making fertile farmland out of swamps and productive pastures out of barren wastelands. They brought knowledge of modern agricultural and horticultural techniques, increasing crop yield and building a transportation infrastructure to take produce to internal markets and for export. But many of them also brought a determination to rid the land of Arabs, at any cost.

Atrocities were perpetrated by both sides of the Jewish/Palestinian divide. The animosity hardened as the new state was being carved out in Palestine. A number of wealthy Arabs fled abroad, selling large tracts of land to (well-funded) Jewish settlers who then set about clearing the land of Palestinian peasant farmers whose families had farmed the land for generations and for which the individual buyers had no authentic claim other than that provided by money.[35] The civil 'right' of private property ownership overrode any right arising from long historic connections and generations working the lands; the issue of a more general 'Jewish' right to occupy parts of Palestine is a different question.

Whatever the experiences associated with the creation and consolidation of Israel, it does seem that the reality on the ground today needs to be the accepted base from which any future resolution of on-going conflict needs to begin. Past injustices do have a relevance to considerations, but these would not justify new injustices being perpetrated. Both Palestinians living in Palestine and Jewish and Palestinian Israelis have the right to peaceful living conditions, but also living conditions that provide a reasonable standard of physical comfort and the opportunity to gain economic and personal security. It is these basic requirements that any future settlement must endeavour to address. If these basic rights are not successful maintained then there will be no fair, nor perhaps any lasting, settlement of the Arab/Israeli conflict.

Elsewhere in the post-war Middle-East, Britain had been instrumental in setting up 'puppet' governments (mostly monarchies) in Egypt, Jordan (Trans-Jordan) and Iraq, primarily in pursuance of its oil, trade, and strategic military interests. It would be these three countries along with Syria, Lebanon, plus token forces from Saudi Arabia and Yemen with their somewhat disorganized armies, that would attempt to invade Israel from 15th May 1948. Whilst ostensibly claiming to be defending Palestinians, they were in fact seeking to gain territory for themselves (occupying 20% of what was left to the Palestinians following partition). The 100,000 strong Israeli army (the backbone of which was 60,000 ex-Haganah fighters) was, quite well-trained, very well-led, and fairly well-resourced. This last, thanks

---

[35] I mean here some claimed right that preceded the Jewish Diaspora – The Jewish claim to Palestine is based on familial connection between an imagined community of Jewishness existing today and one of 3,000 odd years ago – when genetics, demographic studies, and more disinterested history, suggests that for many of today's Jews there is no familial connection at all to the earlier peoples.

significantly to funding from Jewish individuals and organizations based abroad and the active support of the US government. But of considerable relevance, they (the IDF) were a highly motivated army fighting what they saw as a war for their very survival; historically, the Israelis term this the 'War of Independence'. The Arab armies were manned by mostly poorly trained and equipped soldiers, generally lacking the survivalist motivation of the Israelis. But their most significant military weakness was probably the lack of co-ordination between each group; Israel was in effect fighting four individual armies on a number of fronts. In terms of conventional military strategy, this should have been a considerable problem for the defenders but it turned out to be a military advantage for the highly mobile Israeli forces.

For Israel, the outcome of the war was a tremendous success. Yes they lost over 6,000 killed and the estimated cost to them of the war was a then massive $500 million, but it was able to show their military strength to neighbouring states, to reinforce support from the west (especially the US), and to extend its borders beyond those of the initial partition. Jewish skill at manipulating the western media was at an advanced level of narrative sophistication - a narrative imbued with the idea of historical rights and of a small nation (people) fighting to survive with bravery and gritty determination, surrounded by hostile 'natives'. Perhaps of even more relevance to the birth of this new nation was the pride in victory that the war had given the Israeli people - as well as boosting its attractiveness to potential migrants. For the Arab allies there was the loss of 7,000 killed, and the humiliation of defeat. A humiliation that would contribute to swift regime change in a number of these countries.

In 1952 a group of Egyptian junior army officers launched a coup, sending King Farouk into exile and setting up a Revolutionary Command Council (RCC) to run the country. Although Major General Muhammad Naguib became the Head of State the real power lay with the charismatic Lieutenant Colonel Gamal Abdel Nasser, who controlled the RCC. Nasser would become Prime Minister in 1954 and then President from 1956 until his death (from a heart attack) in

1970. Nasser's attempts to unite Arabs across the Middle-East, and to embark on a relatively independent path for Egypt, led to him being much admired by the Arab masses across the region. Early on significant land reforms (e.g. the Sept. 1952 'Agrarian Reform Law') were introduced which went some way to break up a pattern of ownership based on large estates.

Nasser embarked on a process of modernization but was unable to attract sufficient private foreign investment to achieve his aims so, from 1961, the government became more directly involved in the economy, with wide-spread nationalization of industry being undertaken; including much of the media. The regime termed this 'State capitalism'. Funding for education was markedly increased, with enrolment doubling from 1952-1970 - although facilities remained generally poor, and even by 1969 only 60% of the adult population were literate. This investment contributed to an increase in the size of the Egyptian middle-class and individuals that, with Nasser's active encouragement, could take up professional occupations that had previously been undertaken by foreigners.

Britain and France secretly conspired with Israel on a plan to invade Egypt and retake the Suez Canal that had been nationalized by Nasser. Israel's relationship with Egypt was already under stress due to on-going, if minor, border skirmishes. With Egypt allowing Palestinian fighters (Fedayeen) to undertake incursions into Israel, and its denying Israeli shipping access to the Gulf of Aqaba; so Israel was a willing co-conspirator. It would be Israel that on 29th October 1956 crossed the border and swept into Sinai, easily rolling back the Egyptian forces. Four days later French and British air-planes bombed Egyptian air-fields. The conspiracy plan unfolded, with the French and British publically calling on Israel to withdraw in line with a UN arranged ceasefire, and on 5th and 6th November they landed troops at Port Said and Port Fuad and moved to occupy the Canal Zone. The US, keen to improve its own image with Arab states, and also aware of the possibility of the Soviet Union intervening on behalf of Nasser, used its influence at the UN to gain a resolution (Security Council Resolution 118, passed unanimously) that called on all nations to respect the sovereignty of Egypt. In effect, in terms of International law, making the occupation of the Canal Zone and the Sinai illegal. In December 1956, the UN oversaw the evacuation of the British and French forces, and in March 1957 Israel withdrew their force back to the border.

Nasser emerged from this crisis as an Arab hero, having confronted, and then humiliated, two of the old imperial powers and with the additional terms of the UN resolution 118 giving him pretty much all he wanted when he had first moved to nationalize the Canal. As a diplomatic bonus, the Aswan High Dam was completed with Soviet assistance.

From this time British and French influence in the Middle-East progressively gave way to the rise of that of the US and the Soviet Union. It would be these two nations that now poured increasingly more technically advanced armaments (including material suitable for making chemical weapons – and the biological 'weapon' of the anthrax virus by US) into the region - as each identified with this or that client regime. The US endeavoured to support Israel and whilst doing so kept at least passable relationships with leaders of the main oil producing states. For these they, the CIA in Iraq and Iran (in Iraq in 1962 it would be CIA support for a Ba'th Party which included a young Saddam Hussein), were directly involved in selecting the leaders. With others, including Saudi Arabia and the Gulf states, being run by despotic regimes aware of the value of maintaining friendly relations with the world's most powerful nation. The US, opted for 'real politics', and prioritized the need for a reliable supply of oil, for opportunities to contain the feared spread of communism, and the regionally strategic and domestically politically useful support for Israel. For the Soviet Union, there were its long-held ambition for gaining influence on its southern flank. Between the wars it had mainly channelled these ambitions into more subversive support for local communist organizations. Then, after WW II, this involvement was expanded to offer diplomatic, military and economic support for nationalist movements, especially in Egypt, Iraq, Syria, and Yemen; but decisively excluding Israel.

Similar to Britain and France before them, neither the Soviet Union nor the US were much concerned (other than rhetorically) with the wellbeing, or even democratic rights, of the masses as they cynically pursued their own interests. The limitations on personal freedom, lack of democratic rights, and for most, economic impoverishment, would later on become key factors in driving the spread of radical Islam; especially amongst the educated young. Human rights abuses were to be ignored if the perpetrator was a 'friendly state' but were loudly condemned (and indeed exaggerated and used when required to justify military intervention) if the perpetrator was perceived as unfriendly. But perhaps it was the legacy of the involvement of the imperial powers in the region, along with the more recent imposition of the state of Israel, which served as more potent sources of resentment, fostering a strong sense of injustice. Radical (Jihadi) Islam or more secular terrorism offered outlets for the frustrations and anger of those not prepared to easily concede control to overt power and not strong enough to engage in conventional warfare - terrorism draws much of its popular support from the embittered poor, if mostly led by middle-class individuals.

With the collapse of the Ottoman Empire during WW I, the Middle-East had experienced a period of upheaval as various regional factions, along with the imperial powers, endeavoured to stake claims or otherwise to protect their interests. In 1920 Britain had been provided with a mandate from the League of Nations for the Mesopotamian territory that makes up most of Iraq. Soon after this Sunni and Shia Islamic fighters overcame traditional hostilities and united for an attempt to end Britain's occupation. But, reinforced by troops from India, Britain managed to suppress the insurgency. It was in 1921, during this insurgency, that the then British Sec. of State, Winston Churchill, actively favoured using chemical weapons against the insurgents, and had to be dissuaded on this by advisors.

In 1921 the British put the Hashemite Faisal ibn Husayn (ex king of Syria who had been expelled in July 1920) on the Iraq throne. Faisal was a scion of the Hashemite Royal family claiming descent from the Prophet Muhammad; that, since the 10th century, had political control of the most holy Islamic cities of Mecca and Medina. Britain was determined to control Iraq's oil and with the formation in 1929 of the Iraq Petroleum Company they were able to achieve a virtual monopoly of oil exploration and extraction across the country. Throughout the period minority groups including, Kurds, southern Shias, Yazidis, and Christian Assyrians, rebelled, with the British using their own forces and playing one minority group against another to maintain their control. Under an Anglo-Iraqi Treaty (signed in 1930) the British were able to maintain a strong military presence in the country.

Iraq gained independence in 1932 when, as the 'Kingdom of Iraq', it became a member of the League of Nations and the Faisal's regime was to control the county, brutally at times, until his death in1933 (from a heart attack at the age of 48 - in questionable circumstances). Faisal was succeeded by his only son Gahzi bin Faisal who, as well as becoming king, was also appointed the military head of Iraq's army, navy and air-force - becoming an Admiral, a Field-marshal, and an Air-Marshal on the same day. Gahzi ruled until his death in a car crash in 1939. This left Gahzi's three year old son, Faisal, to become King as Faisal II. Given his age, his uncle Abd al llah was made regent, a regency that lasted until Faisal (having been educated in England - Harrow School - along with his second cousin Hussein bin Talal - later King of Jordon) came of age in 1953. It was Faisal's friendship with Hussein, and the Hashemite heritage in Syria, Jordan, and more recently Iraq, that were combined in their shared aspiration for a greater Hashemite Kingdom encompassing the three countries - not least, this monarchical merger would aim to counter the more republican threat of Nasser's pan-Arabism.

Iraq had experienced a series of military coups from 1936 but it was one in 1941, following which Abd al llah was briefly deposed from the regency. This, the 'Golden Square' coup, was led by four Sunni military officers from a group of seven senior officers (the 'Circle of Seven' - who maintained close ties with Germany) determined to end Britain's direct involvement in Iraqi affairs.

The new National Defense Government, with Rashid Ali as prime minister, was virulently anti-British and pro fascist Germany. It wasn't long before the relationship with Britain deteriorated and from early May 1941 war began (Anglo-Iraq War). The British had the military advantage and were able to deploy both internal allies such as Kurdish and Assyrian Levies from northern Iraq, as well as troops from the Indian sub-continent; this included the Gurkka mercenaries from Nepal that had become an integral unit within the British army. The new government was encouraged in their anti British stance by Germany, who would also supply them with arms sent via the French Vichy government through Syria.

By the end of May the outcome of the conflict was clear and, as the British forces advanced on Baghdad, the National Defence Government collapsed and Rashid Ali, along with the Grand Mufti of Jerusalem (then a refugee in Iraq) and senior members of the government, fled the country. The British victory, in effect their re-occupation of Iraq, was resented by much of the Iraqi population. Following the ending of the war, Baghdad was rocked by a series of violent riots and looting in which Jews, and Jewish properties, were targeted; with estimates of 120 Jews being killed within a few days of the war's end. Britain would control Iraq until October 1947 and during this period they (at times in cooperation with their war ally the Soviet Union) sponsored (via the Iraq Command force) attacks on Vichy France controlled Syria. Along with a Soviet force, Britain invaded neutral Iran (the Anglo-Soviet Persian War) in August 1941 in order to secure both its oil-fields and the overland routes along which US supplies were sent to the Soviet Union.

In neighbouring Iran the then Shah of Iraq, Reza Shah Pahlavi (who had ruled Persia/Iran since 1925 and had overseen the country's name change from Persia to Iran - 'Land of the Aryans'), being perceived by the Russian and British allies as friendly toward the Axis powers, was forced to abdicate and in September was replaced by his son Muhammad Reza Pahlavi.

The new Shah - a constitutional monarch with legal immunity - had to rule with an, at times, uneasy relationship with the National Consultative Assembly He progressively sought to gain more power and to obtain US financial, as well as diplomatic, support. In 1949 he was able to take advantage of an assassination attempt made on his life to gain the right to dismiss the Assembly. This was conditional on his then organizing an election - even accepting that the Shah's supporter's involvement in rigging elections was well known. He also moved to suppress the opposition of more radical religious leaders, of organized labour (and especially the communist Tudeh political party), and to close down newspapers critical of his actions. Aware of the electorally successful politician Mohammad Mosaddegh's (then leader of the National Front) increasing popularity with the people, the Shah accepted his nomination by the Majlis's and appointed him as Prime Minister in April 1951.

In 1951, following the refusal of the British (who had controlled the Iranian petroleum industry since 1908) to allow an audit of the Anglo-Iranian Oil Company, the strongly nationalist Mosaddegh - who was also seen as an obstacle for the US and Britain given his support for democratic values and respect for human rights - gained the support of Parliament to nationalize the petroleum industry. An industry up to then controlled, on very favourable terms for British and US interests, by the Anglo-Iranian Oil Company[36].

The US and Britain's response was initially the imposition of economic sanctions but when this proved ineffective (and possibly due to their wishing to send a message to leaders of other oil states) the American Central Intelligence Agency (CIA), along with their counterparts in the British Secret Service (MI6), organized a coup, using Iranian fighters from groups opposed to the elected government. This first attempt to bring down the government failed and, due to his role in offering some spurious constitutional legitimacy to the coup, the Shah fled to luxurious exile in Italy. The general disorganization within the government, and rifts in the military, enabled a second coup (Operation Ajax) attempt to be successful; with Mosaddegh being deposed and the Shah being brought back and re-established on the

---

[36] Much better oil deals - 50/50 profit share rather than Iran's and Britain's 25/75 - were being agreed elsewhere in the Middle-East.

throne of Iran. A position he was later to make even grander by adding the tiles 'Light of the Aryans' and 'Head of the Warriors' to that of 'King of Kings' - as he endeavoured to exercise his predilection for showy, faux-medal and gold braid strewn, uniforms, and to establish a dubious Pahlavian link to the Persian Achaemenium Empire of Cyrus (and its consolidation by the fourth king, Darious) circa. 2,500 years previouly. The Shah headed a repressive regime, considerably aided by his feared secret police the 'National Intelligence and Security Organization' (SAVAK). Established in 1957 it became one of the worst government security organizations in history, renowned for its fearsome brutally. Its first head, General Teymur Bakhtiar (in 1970 he would himself be assassinated by SAVAK agents when he was deemed to be a threat to the regime), the military governor of Tehran, worked closely with US and Israeli advisers on the operational design of SAVAK. The new organization had the freedom to operate in any way it thought best as it pursued its central task of ruthlessly crushing any opposition to the Pahlavian regime. Torture and arbitrary execution were common, with groups of religious and communist dissidents being identified as the main targets for the attention of this unsavoury body - they fairly easily compare with the Nazi SS in terms of the cruelty of their methods. The regime's approach to maintaining power was well known to government (and media) in countries such as Britain and the US but that did not prevent these selling Iran armaments, and indeed even torture equipment.

Western politicians were aided in support of the Shah by a compliant media offering the images of a modernising Iran as presented in western mass media. Especially in the global broadcasting of the absurd, and costly, celebration in 1971 of a claimed 2,500 year-long imagined 'Persian Empire'. A veritable Shah-fest costing $10s of millions, with the Shah (as noted above) claiming some spurious family links to 'Cyrus the Great', founder of an empire in 550 BCE.

Western leaders were prepared to accord the Shah the highest honours, observing diplomatic supplication before his 'Peacock Throne'. An absence of moral assessment was deemed to be a fair price to pay for a Western-friendly regime in the Middle-East and for a reliable supply of oil. Nothing new in morality being absent from international politics but in the case of dealings with the pretentious, callous, and at times delusional, Shah, it was a starkly drawn and obvious admission.

It would be a combination of Shia religious fervour and left-wing political opposition that would, in 1979, bring an end to the Pahlavi dynasty. And, post the success of the revolution, it would be the religious leadership that brutally turned on their left wing (primarily communist) revolutionary allies to gain control over the whole country as they set about publically executing any members of the previous regime that had not managed to escape from the country. A government was established, with Medic Bazarjan appointed by the Ayatollah Khomeini (newly returned from exile) to be post-revolutionary Iran's first Prime Minister. But it was the 'Islamic Revolutionary Council', led by Khomeini that exercised real power in the country - and on 1st April 1979 it would be Khomeini who declared the founding of the 'Islamic Republic of Iran'. The Shah himself fled to an exile spent primarily in the Koubleh Palace in Cairo, Egypt.

Moving from Iran back to Iraq, from 1941-1948 the British had operated to prop-up the Hashemite monarchy and to maintain its hold over the oil industry. In 1945 Iraq become a member of the UN and would later be a founder member of the Arab League. In 1948 Britain and the Iraqi government, led by Prime Minister Nuri al-Said, concluded negotiations and signed the Anglo-Iraqi Treaty (generally a revision of one signed in 1930). A treaty that nominally established Britain's withdrawal but only on the basis of Britain remaining responsible for Iraqi foreign affairs and military planning.

The tensions over Israel's occupation of Palestinian lands continued throughout the 1960s to then erupt in the six-day conflict of 1967, when a well trained Israeli army humiliated the poorly co-ordinated armies of Jordan, Syria and especially Egypt. The war began when Israel responded to some threatening actions taken by the Egyptian government by launching strikes at it airfields – destroying most of the Egyptian air-force (and also killing 15 UN Peacekeepers). Much of the short war was pretty much a series of routs and at the War's end 20,000 Arab and 1,000 Israeli troops had been killed. Israel had extended the land under its control....taking the Golan Heights from Syria, the West Bank from Jordan, and most of the extensive Sinai Peninsula from Egypt. The four armies were variously equipped with weapons primarily from the Soviet Union, the US, Britain and France, whose arms dealers, encouraged by their governments, had been pouring armaments into the region.

But the residual resentment of the defeated came to a head again in October 1973 when Syrian forces invaded the Golan Heights and Egyptian forces crossed the 1967 ceasefire line and advanced across the Sinai dessert. These coordinated actions, began on the holiest of Jewish religious festivals (Yom Kippur), took the Israelis by surprise and it was some days before they could mobilize their air-force and army and so halt the Egyptian advance and begin to push the Syrians back. The fighting was fierce; with the Soviets and the Americans each supplying their own favoured side (the Soviets Egypt and Syria, and the US Israel) with a range of modern weaponry. The casualties on each side were heavy, but UN attempts to arrange a ceasefire were successful completed in late October.

Although strategically Israel retained most of the territory gained during the earlier (1967) war, the relative success of two Arab nations in at least holding their own against the Israelis restored at least some sense of Arab pride. Diplomatically, the display of the growing military strength of the Arab states bordering Israel gave their leaders a stronger negotiating position. Negotiations that produced the Camp David Accord and a peace treaty between Egypt and Israel signed in March 1979. These diplomatic efforts continued and developed into a series of 'peace' talks - Madrid Conference of 1991-93, the Oslo Accords of 1993, and another round of Camp David Accords in 2000. Perhaps the most tangible outcome of these negotiations has been the production of a 'Road Map' (clear time-lines, target dates, benchmarks, etc) with a two-state outcome that probably remains the most likely basis for gaining some level of Israeli/Palestinian peaceful co-existence, even if its original 'arrival' date for peaceful co-existence, being 2005, has now long past. When the initial plan was submitted to the Palestinians and the Israelis by President George Bush in April 2003 it had the support of the United States, Russia, the European Union, and the United Nations. If the more recent right-wing governments led by Benjamin Netanyahu have pretty much undermined the likelihood of a two-state settlement, the plan remains to possibly be updated and returned to.

In Iraq in 1961 a serious issue arose when the Kurdish people attempted to fulfil a traditional ambition to create a Kurdish state in the north of the county. This conflict, (in fact a civil war), involving about 80% of the Iraq army, continued until 1970 by when each side had reluctantly accepted that neither could defeat the other. The subsequent peace treaty allowed the Kurds a degree of regional autonomy and at least a promise of some Kurdish representation in central government.

In 1972 the government of Iraq signed a 15 year 'Treaty of Friendship and Cooperation' with the Soviet Union, clearly indicating its rejection of the US. In response, the US, using the Shah's pro-US Iran as a facilitator, had directed generous funding and arms supplies to the Kurdish rebels in the north of Iraq and so was in part instrumental in encouraging the outbreak of another brutal civil war, pitting Kurds against the Arab government.

In September 1980 Saddam turned on the neighbouring country of Iran. During the ensuing war, Saddam initially received considerable US support. Indeed there is evidence to support the claim that Saddam had been on the CIA payroll as early as 1959 - and that he had liaised with the CIA during the 1963 military coup. During the bitter and bloody confrontation with Iran the US supplied Saddam's regime with funding, weapons[37], and valuable satellite intelligence information about Iran's military installations and troop movements. Up to 90 US

---

[37] This included precursor material for making chemical and biological weapons - both types of which were used during the war.

military personnel were also deployed to Iraq during the war to provide guidance on targeting missile attacks. It was the US envoy, Donald Rumsfeld (yes, the same Rumsfeld so keen later on to go to war against Saddam) who, during a number of secret meetings with Saddam and his advisors, facilitated the transfer of considerable funding, plus armaments and chemical and biological weapons material; the latter including the virus's of Anthrax and Bubonic plague, and the toxin Botulism. Following the use of chemical weapons in the Kurdish town of Halabja, the US Regan administration, fully aware that it had been carried out by the Iraqis, tried to blame Iran - In international politics the 'ends' (basically the national interest as perceived by ruling elites) justify any means, whatever the cost in human lives and the destruction of infrastructure and other property. The US was officially neutral in this war, it also had Iraq on its list of 'State Sponsors of Terrorism' (which, given the US activities in central America at this time was itself ironic), but in early 1984 it conveniently considered that it could remove this status and so offer covert support to Saddam.

During the war the US sold Iraq 500 million dollars worth of dual use equipment - such as computers that were used in Saddam's nuclear program and the materials that were used in chemical warfare. Chemical weapons were used against the Iranians in at least 16 actions during the war.

Most western nations had in place an official embargo on arms sales to Iraq. But policing of this policy was at best loose and at worst inoperative. Aware of the increasing influence of the Soviets in Iraq, and in order to continue the cold-war's bleak military choreography, the US also provided (both accurate and purposefully inaccurate) intelligence to Iran and, via Israel, were complicit in providing it with arms. A turgid mess, with the more powerful nations offering a hollow rhetoric of neutrality, while pouring weapons into the region, rather than endeavouring to use their influence to promote conditions for peace.

Although the US offered generous military support for Saddam's regime, it was Russian companies that supplied even more (in funding terms), and private companies of other nations including: Britain (parts for high-tech artillery and for the nuclear program), France (Mirage jet fighter-planes and Exocet missiles), Germany (chemicals and chemical weapon expertise), as well as mixed armaments from Brazil and Czechoslovakia - this bonanza for the world's arms industry was funded by Iraq's oil revenues (oil mostly sold to the west) and by funding from Saudi Arabia and Kuwait.

Saddam was able play a deviously clever game in accumulating a $50 billion arsenal of modern weaponry by taking advantage of the at best indifference, at worst collusion, of governments to companies dealing with Iraq and the complex network of shady arms dealers (and accommodating intermediate governments - such as Jordan, Egypt, Kuwait and Saudi Arabia), who, vulture-like, circle the globe in search of profitable deals.

We need to bear in mind that each bullet, artillery shell, landmine, missile, and bomb, produced is more likely to kill a civilian than a member of a military unit (conventional or guerrilla) and indeed, their products could well end up being used against soldiers and civilians of the same arms producer nations! Are workers in the arms industry, and the TU leaders that represent them, prepared to address the moral implications for their work? Especially when alternative work, for these mostly highly skilled workers, could be provided. Indeed, such is the level of public subsidies of weapons manufacture in most industrialized nations that it would cost governments less if it just paid the workers the same wages to stay at home.

Saddam's push for industrial and agricultural modernization continued, including the extension of the road and rail networks. Funding was available to markedly improve the education and healthcare systems which, by the 1980s, would compare favourably with any in the Middle-East. But also continuing was a drift towards dictatorship, aided by the expansion of Saddam's internal intelligence service; any opposition was soon exposed and swiftly dealt with. Saddam was close to the Russian intelligence agent Yevgeny Primakov, who is thought to have been a valued advisor on domestic security strategy.

Although the Ba'ath party was officially secular many of its members (including Saddam) were Sunni Muslims and some of these held the most senior positions in the government, civil service, and army. Traditionally, it was the Sunni that ruled in Iraq even though the majority of Iraqis were Shia Muslims. But most Shia, especially those in the military were strongly nationalist and maintained their loyalty to Iraq, and so to Saddam.

Two of the more active anti-Saddam Shia groups were SCIRI and Ad-Dawah, and it was the latter that was accused of sponsoring an assassination attempt on Saddam in July 1982 (during the war with Shia run Iran). As a reprisal for this, Saddam ordered an attack on the Shia town of Dujail (strong-hold of Ad-Dawah) with a population of 75,000, an action that destroyed hundreds of homes, with dozens of orchards and date plantations being razed. Up to 800 men women and children were arrested and following staged trials, many of which relied on 'confessions', 148 people were executed. Saddam was involved in a number of massacres of Iraq people - notoriously, the chemical attack in 1988, on the Kurdish town of Halabja, in which 5,000 people were killed with many injured. But it was the attack on Dujail that was one of the 'crimes against humanity' with which he would later be charged, and would in December 2006, be executed.

From 1985 the conflict took on a new dimension as civilian areas and industrial facilities became intended targets for both sides. So the war continued, becoming even more bitter and bloody. It would be ended when by July 1988 Iran's repeated failed attempts at a 'final offensive' had sapped the peoples' commitment to the conflict. The fighting ceased when both sides accepted a truce based on UN resolution 598.

Throughout the war, and continuing afterwards, the CIA was channelling funding to almost any half-viable group that was opposed to Iran's regime (even if at the same time the US military was providing intelligence and military support to the Iranian military). In particular, the Paris based group 'Front for the Liberation of Iran', and at least two para-military groups based in Turkey - all of these three having strong ties to the deposed Shah's regime.

By the war's end approximate 1,000,000 people had been killed, with many more injured, billions of dollars worth of industry and infrastructure had been destroyed, and extensive pollution of the land and the waterways was obvious and is continuing. Who or what was gained at this cost? Well, if anything Saddam's own position was stronger, as was that of the radical clerics running Iran; the very outcome that neither participating national leaders would have wanted for their enemy. And of course armaments companies, chemical companies, financiers, arms dealing middle-men, and the politicians involved in the arms industries of the US, Britain, France, China, the Soviet Union and some other countries........ made a great deal of money out of this brutal conflict; then I guess, these many representatives of an unsavoury world clique, just turned away to sniff out the next source of potential conflict, for which read 'profit'!

If anything, Iraq's military machine came out of the war even stronger, it's having been equipped with a range of high tech. weaponry by the international arms trade. And Saddam's ambitions to expand were undiminished by the experience of invading Iran. Indeed, domestic issues including, rising unemployment (not least soldiers demobilized after the war), massive indebtedness to Saudi Arabia and Kuwait, and uprisings of the southern Shia and northern Kurds threatening the unity of the country, prompted him to embark on another costly military action.

It seems that Saddam considered an invasion of Kuwait would provide the opportunity to dispense with some of the nation's debt, and to gain further oil revenues from the still substantial Kuwaiti reserves; as well as obtaining improved access to the sea. It would also be a possible way to foster national unity behind a cause. And so the 'cause' was made known to the Iraq people, including a propaganda campaign based on claimed past injustices and current unfairness. Publically, Saddam resurrected a traditional right to Kuwaiti territory as being a 'natural' part of Iraq, and he also accused the Kuwaitis of stealing Iraqi oil, with their horizontal drilling into the vast oil field of

Rumaila (just 32 kilometres from the Kuwait/Iraq border - subsequently Kuwait did offer $9 billion compensation but Iraq insisted on $10 billion).

Saddam's forces crossed the border into Kuwait on 2nd August 1990 and its battle-hardened troops soon (taking12 hrs) occupied most of the state. Within days a puppet government, 'The Provisional Government of Free Kuwait', had been set up. Iraq had in effect annexed Kuwait.

While groups of ordinary (non military) Kuwaitis quickly formed an underground resistance network (by the end of the occupation more of these had been killed than were killed of the US-led coalition liberation force) the King, Royal Family, most leading politicians and wealthy Kuwaitis fled - in effect deserted - the country.

When the issue came before the UN the Security Council passed Resolution 660 that demanded the withdrawal of Iraq forces. The UN also advised a policy of economic sanctions against Iraq[38], but this intended policy of persuasion was in effect prematurely trodden underfoot as the US industrial/political military machine mobilized for war, and US influence at the UN obtained a second resolution worded in a way that made military action permissible.

This, Resolution 678, passed on 29th October 1990 called on the Iraqis to withdraw by 15th January 1991 and directed UN member nations to use '......all means necessary to uphold and implement Resolution 660'. The US immediately deployed a significant force of naval ships, air-planes and troops to Saudi Arabia; fearful that this would be Saddam's next territorial objective. They then moved to co-ordinate a multinational force to retake Kuwait. Prior to the US-led force moving to directly confront the Iraqis it was made up of troops and/or supplies of 34 nations; although of the nearly 900,000 strong force 700,000 were US military personnel and only 200,000 from the

---

[38] The same economic and trade sanction policy that would lead to the deaths of as many as 500,000 Iraqi children over the next 10 years as the people of Iraq were punished by the international community for the crimes of their leaders, who were themselves unaffected by the sanctions.

other 33 nations.

The US government, in conjunction with a leading US PR agency employed by Kuwait's government in exile, also mobilized a slick propaganda machine seeking to demonize the Iraqis for the US population. Included in this propaganda campaign (in which much of the national media organizations meekly colluded) was the claim of Iraqi troops being massed on the border with Saudi Arabia (so threatening this even more important oil supply state) - this turned out to be a totally false claim, as no such build up had taken place. Similarly, General Schwarzkopf, the US commander, knowingly doubled the estimate of the number of Iraqi troops in Kuwait. On the other hand, there was a truthful accusation of human rights abuses, but of course this had been happening when the US and a range of other nations were supporting Saddam as a friend to the west. Indeed human rights abuses were also common practices perpetrated by the regime that had run Kuwait, as well as the one in power in neighbouring Saudi Arabia. Then there was the 'outrage' at Iraq using chemical weapons on Kurds and others, and the threat of its working towards a nuclear capability - again true, but much of the material and technical expertise that made these (chemical weapons and nuclear capacity) possible had been supplied by many of the nations now making up the anti-Saddam coalition.

On an even cruder level, the mainstream America press ran a PR supplied story of a woman named Nayirah, claiming to have been a volunteer in Kuwait City Hospital when the invasion took place. Nayirah offered a graphic description of Iraqi soldiers pulling at least 300 very sick newborn babies from incubators and leaving them to die on the floor. This was an oft repeated story (broadcast by US news agencies across America and around the world), one that was found to have had a significant impact on US public opinion. But it was one that had been entirely made up. The woman turned out never to have been a volunteer at the hospital and she was in fact a member of the Kuwaiti Royal Family - even after the story was shown to be false President George Bush still mentioned it in a speech. A body named Citizens for a Free Kuwait (set up immediately following the invasion), who had hired the PR agency Hill & Knowlton (well-connected on Capitol Hill, Washington), showed pictures of bodies, seemingly victims of horrible atrocities - but the 'bodies' in these slightly unsharp photos turned out on closer examination to be dummies (mannequins).

This is but a selection of the lies, exaggerations, and misrepresentations, to which the people of America (and those of other coalition nations) were subjected to in the build up to military action. The old saw of: 'truth being the first casualty of war', was clearly illustrated at this time and yet populations continue to be vulnerable to government, PR organizations, and media propaganda - it seems that we 'want' to believe what we see and hear on the T.V. radio, and internet news and what we read in news-papers!

As we were to see again in the second Gulf War......indeed during all 'modern wars' propaganda, is a weapon used by all sides. We need to consider the question: do we want our agreement to be party to the widespread destruction and mass killing caused by war to be based on politicians, senior military personnel, and a complicit media, knowingly seeking to mislead and intentionally lie to us? It does seem that the financial (and class) interests controlling the mass media, and the pre-condition of 'embedding' for journalists, are engaged in the permanent task of the shaping, if not actually forming, public opinion.

As I write this in March 2023 we see the Russian government controlled media maximising the use of propaganda to influence public opinion as to its invasion of Ukraine. The fact that they have closed down foreign media, and any internal media that would challenge government misinformation, suggests that they were aware that the claims being made could be easily proven to be false.

The crusade to combat the Nazification of Ukraine, of Russian-speaking citizens being murdered by the Ukrainian government, of western attempts to 'destroy' Russia, that Russian weapons target only the military not civilians, and such lies. Lies similar to those told by western governments when they engage in conflict in foreign lands – if these are at least sometimes liable to be challenged by a range of more or less independent media. The same Western governments that took advantage of the break-up of the Soviet Union (1988) to move NATO eastward to push up against the borders of Russia, and to site more nuclear missiles in Turkey. Moves that could understandably have been seen by egocentric Russian leaders as threatening the country. Indeed, western governments strategically friendly to Ukraine and ignoring the less savoury aspects of pre-war Ukraine's internal conditions involving official corruption, shady right-wing political influence, and serious human rights issues.

Faced with the UN ultimatum to withdraw by 15th January 1991, and aware of the massive military build-up of the coalition forces, Saddam offered a conditional withdrawal from Kuwait. Conditional on foreign military forces leaving the region, that agreement was reached to resolve the Palestinian issue, and that both Israel and Iraq agree to dismantle any weapons of mass destruction they held. This offer was rejected, and on 17th January operation 'Desert Storm' was launched. Within hours 30,000 soldiers of the occupying Iraqi forces had been killed and the rest had fled Kuwait and were in disorganized retreat back along the roads through eastern Iraq.

A ground war followed, with coalition forces moving in from Saudi Arabia and sea-borne landings launched from a US battle-fleet stationed off-shore. The coalition ground forces included a range of 'special forces' units, sent in to infiltrate Iraqi lines. Then followed 150,000 troops and 1,500 tanks (US and British made, each superior in fire-power and manoeuvrability to those, mainly Chinese made, deployed by the Iraqis), supported by overwhelmingly superior air cover. A massive bombardment preceded the advance including 14,000 artillery shells and 4,900 MLRS rockets that, along with the heavy bombing, significantly degraded Iraqi defences and its general military capability.

Within 100 hrs of the ground war starting President Bush announced a ceasefire and that Kuwait had been 'liberated', but then the US-led coalition re-installed what was in effect an illiberal royal dictatorship.[39] If the coalition had intended to 'liberate' Kuwait should they not have passed power to the mass of the people who, unlike the royal family and leading members of the government, had remained in Kuwait? And indeed, some of whom formed the underground resistance movement, with many being killed when undertaking actions against the occupying Iraqis.

This was a media war with real-time engagements broadcast across the world, news sent by embedded (so particularly liable to bias in favour of the coalition) news reporters setting the scene and interpreting rapidly moving events for the public - graphic images of Iraq soldiers, exposed to air attacked as they retreated down the 'Highway of Death', forever stilled in charred, twisted rictus, as they slumped in burnt-out lorry cabs and tank turrets.

A number of Arab nations opposed the intervention of non Arab countries in this dispute – except, that is, for the vulnerable dictatorial monarchies of Saudi Arabia the Gulf States, Egypt (later to be relieved of $7.1 billion of US debt in return for its support) and Saddam's Ba'ath run Iraq's bitter enemy President Assad's Ba'ath of Syria.

Apart from the thousands of deaths and many more wounded, the destruction of infrastructure, the extensive pollution that is a (largely unspoken) enduring legacy of any form of military action, compounded by the burning of the oilfields, there has also been an legacy of harm to the troops that seemed initially to have survived but have subsequently taken sick. Not only the many suffering from 'post traumatic stress syndrome', but also those affected by some form of radiation-like sickness, probably caused by the depleted uranium used to coat the tips of tank and artillery shells. These new forms of post-conflict illness, with symptoms that include debilitating gastrointestinal and nervous system disorders (as well as birth defects of babies born to returning service personnel), being specifically

---

[39] The Emir/ King appoints the prime minister - who has also to be a member of the Emir's Al-Sabah Royal Family - who in turn appoints the 16 unelected members of the government - there is an elected National Assembly with very limited political power.

labelled 'Gulf War Syndrome'. The full economic, environmental, and human costs of modern military conflict are suppressed by those who order warfare.

As they retreated through Kuwait the Iraqi troops obeyed orders from Saddam to open the taps of oil storage units and to fire about 700 oilfields, causing extensive pollution. Up to 11 million barrels of oil poured into the sea and on land the release of millions more created vast black lakes. Thousands of wild birds died, with extensive damage being caused to marine life. Vast tracts of land were contaminated, making previously fertile soil unusable, with pollutants seeping through the surface to despoil precious natural underground freshwater reservoirs, and with the burning oil contributing to levels of air pollution that threatened human health. Taken all together, the Iran-Iraq War, followed by the two Gulf Wars, caused extensive environmental damage across the region, with effects continuing down to today.

Initially intended to pressure Saddam to leave Kuwait, from August 1990 until March 2003 Iraq was subjected to a UN Security-Council agreed set of sanctions (Resolution 661) - with some relaxation in 1997 of a food for oil arrangement. Sanctions having minimal to no impact on Saddam and his ruling cronies who, due to corrupt deals with overseas companies post the oil for food arrangements, were able to accumulate considerable personal fortunes - as did the French, Russian, Arab, and other nation's businessmen that they were dealing with. But sanctions that did have a massive detrimental impact on the mass of the Iraqi people such as: the lack of medical supplies, fertilizers, and even basic foodstuffs (not least powdered baby milk), leading to the deaths of up to an estimated 500,000 children.

The US, and its anti-Saddam allies at the UN, seems to have been prepared to persevere with economic sanctions and to accept the ongoing frustrations with the UN weapons inspection program. Although subsequent events suggest that this assumed patience was due to a war mongering team of White House politicians, and their civilian and military advisors, reluctantly having to accept a then lack of national enthusiasm for all-out war. But when up to 3,000 people were killed[40] in the attack on the World Trade Centre in New York, and the headquarters of the Pentagon near Washington D.C., on 9th September 2001, the situation changed dramatically. An attack perpetrated by 19 members of the terrorist group Al-Qaeda.

Since 9/11 the US government and mass media has squeezed every possible gram of patriotic propaganda from this horrible terrorist incident - used to justify two ill-advised invasions (Iraq and Afghanistan) as well as many non-judicial killings and a number of incremental US internal security measures to advance the surveillance 'state'. America's approach to what its government characterized as the unruly 'rogue states', especially Saddam's Iraq and an Afghanistan controlled by the Islamic fundamentalist Taliban, was to become even more belligerent. Al-Qaeda had been formed as a breakaway group within the fractious (if united in their Islamic fundamentalism) alliance known as the Mujahedeen (those who fight in a Jihad - holy war) who had fought, with covert US military training and financial support mostly channelled via Pakistan, against the Russians during their occupation of Afghanistan from 1979-1989.

It was from one of Al-Qaeda's camps in Afghanistan, that its leader, Osama Bin-Laden (Saudi Arabian born - and avowedly anti-Semitic), claimed the attack was undertaken in response to America's support for Israel. The day after the attack President George W. Bush made a speech to the nation vowing that those behind the attack would be relentlessly tracked down and that: 'We will make no distinction between the terrorist who committed these acts and those who harbour them' and he vowed to 'win the war against terror' - naming this task 'Operation Enduring Freedom'. The 9/11 attack took on the symbolism of a simplistic polarity between good (America) and evil (terrorism, as selectively identified by US political leaders), with a media frenzy that contemplated little but naked revenge - Bush, early on, even used the term 'crusade' but was persuaded to drop this due to its suggesting historic connotations thought to possible weaken

---

[40] Compared with an average of about 30,000 Americans killed by fellow Americans using firearms each year – about 3,000 of these being children.

support for military action from otherwise US-friendly Arab nations.

The initial US action was to demand the Taliban-run government to hand over Bin Laden, but when this was refused, they launched missiles attacks on what were thought to be al-Qaeda camps. Such was the domestic pressure, and no doubt his own inclinations, that Bush soon escalated military action and, joined by Britain, began a bombing campaign. Bush also used the prolific Afghan crop of opium producing poppy plants as another justification for his going to war. But, such is the economic reality for most Afghan farmers, that the extent of poppy growing would actually increase within a few years of the later (post invasion) US withdrawal, and by 2005 90% of the world's heroin producing poppy crop was being grown in Afghanistan.

When the Russians had withdrawn from Afghanistan in February 1989 they left a legacy of mostly post-apocalyptic urban landscapes. An extensive US-led bombing campaign generally just shifted the piles of rubble around, if causing more disruption to the lives of ordinary Afghans than damage to the Taliban. From late September 2001, U.S. and U.K. 'Special forces' infiltrated into the country to undertake a range of actions. This was followed in October by a UN/UK invasion force allied to an indigenous Afghan group called the 'Northern Alliance'. A collection of various, often mutually antagonistic, militias led by local war-lords, who composed the majority of ground troops.

The decade-long attempt to re-construct Afghanistan, a country that had suffered over two decades (1980-2001) of war and at least four years of severe drought – the US committed $88.5 billion with more contributed by some other countries: reconstruction by UN agencies, various NGOs and Afghan transitional and elected governments - has shown that it was far easier to destroy the country by warfare than it has been to rebuild a viable (democratic) state from the widespread human misery, degraded infrastructure, and with extensive piles of rubble strewn across the land.[41]

---

[41] Although war is arguably more profitable - large profits were also made on reconstruction-related contracts awarded to many US and western European

Even by 2020 only about 60% of the population had access to clean water and attempts to re-settle up to a million families dislocated during the conflict has been generally disorganized and in places chaotic. The mortality-rate for pregnant women is as high as the worst in the world, and thousands of civilians continue to be killed in internecine conflict each year; the GDP per capita, at about $600, rates Afghanistan with the world's very poorest countries. Even more enlightened measures such as advancing women's rights, and introducing democracy, have proven to be problematic. The former giving rise to cultural dislocation, the latter setting the conditions for sectarian party politics, often played out in violent conflict.

The retired Army Colonel Hy Rothstein (served in US Army Special Forces for 20 years) was commissioned by the Pentagon to assess the war in Afghanistan. He concluded that on the ground, the conflict had left behind a situation that '…….offers warlordism, banditry and opium production, a new lease on life'.

The situation for much of the population hardly improved in the following two decades of a US supported Afghan government (although the situation for women did improve if more so in the cities) and was then made even worse by the resurgence of the Taliban that, from about 2019, had progressed from insurgency to conducting all out civil war. A conflict that the incompetently led and poorly motivated Afghan Army (supplied and advised by the US) were unable to contain. The lack of motivation of the Afghan forces could have been expected given the county being run by an inept and mostly corrupt government led by then President Ashraf Ghani. The Taliban took control when, in August 2021, Kabul fell, and since then they have borne down even more harshly on women's rights (indeed on human rights more generally). And their Leadership Council (the Rahbari Shura) has been unable to provide even basically effective administration. In addition, they have had to manage an economy in tatters (significantly exacerbated by economic sanctions from the West), and poor harvests.

---

companies.

Going back to 2003, George Bush and his militaristic (warmongering) coterie moved on, to construct a legally dubious[42] justification for action against Iraq. No coincidence that Iraq was estimated to hold the world's fifth (possibly the second) largest reserves of oil in the world, and also no surprise that at the war's end a number of (western, mainly US based) oil companies would sign a series of lucrative deals with the corrupt interim government led by Iyad Allawi. These 'Production Sharing Agreements' locked the country into deals that in effect privatized the oil industry with an estimated loss to the people of between $75-$200 billion (assuming oil priced at a then very conservative $40 a barrel) and giving a return on investment/capital to the companies of between 42%-162%, in an industry with a standard return at the time of about 12%.

Amongst the reasons given for launching an invasion of Iraq were:
- Early on some US officials conceded that that access to oil was a factor, but this was later denied.
- Human rights abuses by Saddam - but as we know, the US and Britain have been happy to deal with countries such as Pinochet's Chile, Argentina, Guatemala, China, and Saudi Arabia, to name but five regimes who have at times shown little respect for the human rights of their own citizens.
- That al-Qaeda groups were being haboured by Saddam - subsequently no evidence for this was found but al-Qaeda did infiltrate into the country after the war had started to join indigenous forces operating against the coalition and Iraqi government troops.
- That Saddam had developed Weapons of Mass Destruction (WMDs) - this was a particular claim of Britain's Prime Minister Tony Blair (supported by Jack Straw Foreign Secretary) - if this

---

[42] Such is the semantic flexibility of the UN-associated legal system - that the world's most powerful governments can claim UN-based legal justification for pretty much any aggressive act - even, as with Iraq, the outright invasion of a sovereign nation.

claim had been true it would have shown Iraq to be violating UN directives, but it was another claim that turned out to have no substance.

The U.S. had also been prepared to support Saddam and supply him with weaponry during the conflict with Iran. And the US setting up of an 'off-shore' prison-camp at Guantanamo Bay (assumed to be beyond the US legal system) to house individuals who have never been put before a civilian court - and the later Abu Ghraib prison (west of Baghdad) where abuses of prisoners by US personnel, as well as US occupation forces 'standing back' as Iraqi security personnel carried out numerous acts of torture - (only known thanks to the 'WikiLeaks' information - WikiLeaks, the 2010 release of cyber interceptions of 400,000 US military documents revealing that the US was complicit in widespread torture, as well as the US military knowingly misinforming the US public of the number of Iraqi civilian casualties) - were clear abuses of human rights.

Discussions over how to interpret UN resolutions continued during early March 2003, with France and Germany opposed to military action. But on 17th March, George Bush announced an end to diplomacy and issued an ultimatum to Saddam. The ultimatum demanded that Saddam leave Iraq immediately; a demand unsurprisingly rejected outright. The invasion - the 'Shock and Awe' campaign - began on 20th March with a massive aerial attack (cruise missiles, 'bunker busting' bombs, and long range shelling from off-shore navel craft) tearing into the military capability and degrading the civil infrastructure of Iraq's principle cities. Within a few days the ground forces (overwhelmingly US and British - with Kurdish militias fighting in the north) moved into Iraq and progressed quite swiftly through the country, overcoming the disorganized, demoralized, and poorly led Iraq forces. Resistance was mainly from local Fedayeen and other irregular militias as the US forces drove towards Bagdad and the British forces endeavoured to occupy the region around the city of Al-Basrah.

On 1st May - just over two weeks after the invasion began,

Bagdad had been taken and the conventional stage of the conflict was at an end. The second stage, that of occupation and reconstruction, then began. Throughout most of this second period large areas of Iraq became lawless wastelands, where religious and other sectional differences were violently progressed and insurrection against the US/UK occupation forces was relentlessly expressed in daily death tolls.

Leading members of the Ba'ath regime who had managed to avoid arrest fled abroad or sought refuge amongst their supporters in the countryside. Saddam himself was captured on 13th December 2003 during operation Red Dawn (with two follow-up operations being named Wolverine 1 and Wolverine 2[43]) and subsequently tried before an Iraqi Special Tribunal, on a charge of crimes against humanity; with conviction being followed by his execution on 30th December 2006.

During the initial invasion, the end of Iraq's Ba'th regime was symbolized in April 2003 by the widely broadcast (later proven to be staged by a US PSYOPS unit) scene of a US military vehicle pulling down ('toppling') the impressive 12 metre high statue of Saddam, located in Al-Firdos Square, Baghdad. With an assembled crowd of Iraqis cheering the statue's destruction (symbolic dethronement), some slapping the fixed face of the fallen dictator with their slippers, an insulting gesture in Iraq. One enduring, media image being the camera of an 'embedded' news-team zooming in on a US marine covering the face of the statue with a US flag.

Post Operation 'Enduring Freedom', as played out in Afghanistan and Iraq, there remains a bitter legacy of internal conflict – primarily involving local Sunni and Shia militias and in Iraq Kurdish forces, Yazires, and the national army of each country. In addition, within the Taliban there are various antagonistic

---

[43] Named after a 1984 Hollywood film 'Red Dawn', an apocalyptic fantasy in which eight all-American teenagers – name the 'Wolverines' - foil a communist invasion of their town by Nicaraguan, Cuban, and Soviet troops at the start of a supposed WWIII – such is the movie-infused mindset of leading US politicians and military.

factions each drawing financial support (equipment and recruits) from religious groups based mainly in Pakistan. Against the Taliban were ranged a poorly trained and equipped, as well as mostly illiterate, Afghan army and police force - both forces liable to traditional factionalisms and led by senior officers, many of whom are thought to be corrupt. There are also a number of militias operating at a local level, and these have often been more effective than official government forces. Since 2014, in Iraq and neighbouring Syria, there is the added element of the extremist (Jihadi) Sunni group IS-Dash. The disorganization of Iraq, including the destruction of its indigenous military capability, provided just the conditions that IS-Dash had been able to exploit.

In 2008, Iraq was number 5 on the list of 'Failed States' and in 2015 Iraq and Afghanistan remained high on this list. As of 2022, Afghanistan 8th, and Iraq 23th – out of 179 countries - on the now renamed 'Fragile States' index. If the intention of these massively costly misadventures was to make 'freedom endure' (as in operation 'Enduring Freedom') then they were a complete failure - but those who ordered these wars have now moved on, knowing they have raised their historical profiles and in the knowledge that mainstream historians will be quite circumspect when assessing their legacy[44].

Naomi Klein, in her 2007 book 'The Shock Doctrine', uses the experience of the Iraqi war to illustrate how fortunes are made by armaments and military logistics companies (the big ones being BAE in Britain, and Boeing, Blackwater, the Carlyle Group, Halliburton

---

[44] In terms of human lives: 4,266 coalition troops killed, 31,107 wounded - possibly as many as 1 million Iraqi's killed, up to 170,000 civilians killed in Afghanistan to 2010. A 2007 report noted that in Iraqi 655,000 deaths were directly due to the invasion and its aftermath -, infrastructure destruction, 4.7 million Iraqis alone displaced, 2 million of these refugees in neighbouring countries, and financial costs of over $1 trillion for Iraq and $468 billion for Afghanistan - just imagine what these resources could have been used for - instead of being 'wasted' in military funding and in creating vast profits for a range of armament/munitions, material suppliers, and 'conflict services', companies.

(the latter made $20 billion of US taxpayers dollars in Iraq alone), and Bechtel in the US – '....the corporatist project at the heart of the invasion' Klein, 2007, p351) as war and security have become increasingly more outsourced to private contractors. Often with the same personnel circulating between the government (and senior military) that had decided to go to war and who were involved with assigning contracts, and the large corporations who benefit from them - a revolving network of individuals seeking to progress their own career ambitions or otherwise advance a ideology of corporate-capitalism, with gross evil as the pervasive and predictable externality.

How can we accept warfare as one element of the collateral impact of the operation of global corporatism, speculative trading, (and military, corporate, and political career advancement) as integral aspects of the world's insidiously freeloading financial system? For Klein (ibid. p314) 'In the Bush administration, the war profiteers aren't just clamouring to get access to government, they are the government; there is no distinction between the two.'

Post the invasion of Iraq, the US Special Envoy, Paul Bremer (a consultant from the private sector, ex aid of Henry Kissinger, and disciple of the notorious if economically discredited Chicago School), intent on progressing the task of reconstruction more as a payback directed to the needs of corporate US, than of rebuilding a more viable mixed economy able to support a sustainable civil society, introduced a range of economic measures tailored to provide the profitable arrangements sought by foreign investors. Bremer oversaw the wholesale privatization of Iraq's industrial base. As of 2016 there were few signs that the Bremer 'plan' had done much more than draw billions of dollars from Iraq and made a few well-placed Iraqi politicians, businessmen, and warlords, very rich.

Little has been done to re-settle the 2.25 million Iraqis displaced by the conflict. As recently as 2021 up to 50% of Iraqi children were suffering from chronic malnutrition - 40% of healthcare staff had left the country and of the pre-war 34,000 physicians, 12,000 left the country and 2,000 had been killed.

Even after the US 'wars of liberation' involving Iraq (Operations 'Dessert Storm' and 'Shock and Awe') the traditional divisions: Shia/Sunni/and other Moslems, Arab/Kurd, Bedouin nomads/settled peasants, the more recent division of tribal chieftains/regionally elected politicians, as well as the enduring division between rich and poor - continued to expose the fragility of national cohesion.

Living under a tyrannical dictatorship, such as that maintained by the Saddam-led Ba'ath regime - a regime at times supported and armed, for their own strategic aims, by countries such as the US, Saudi Arabia, the Soviet Union - means the suppression of political, as well as a range of other personal, rights. Not least, those freedoms of speech, of movement, of association, of the right to a fair trial if arrested; and invariably of the opportunity to take part in electing a government. A public life pervaded with a wary fearfulness of authority and of arbitrary arrest for self, family, friends, and more generally, a life lived with the suppression of the human spirit. So yes, the international community, if it were to care about these denials, should operate foreign policy in ways that would encourage basic human freedoms, and ways that deter dictatorship, than, as now, operating a foreign policy of narrow national self (i.e. elite group/corporate) interest. Not least, the international practice of publically condemning corruption and yet in practice allowing a corporate approach that is prepared to cooperate (so collude) with the corrupt and allowing the international financial system to manage (in effect 'launder') the massive gains made by individuals as they, in effect, loot disrupted states.

Klein perceptively highlights a phenomenon she terms 'disaster-capitalism' that includes the direct involvement of large corporations (and corporate-friendly governments) in both causing disasters and massively profiting from the militaristic ways in which they are addressed. In terms of future 'disasters' Klein notes: 'All indications are that simply by staying the current course [corporate capitalism's 'business as usual'], they will keep on coming with ever more ferocious intensity. Disaster generation can therefore be left to the market's invisible hand. This is one area where it actually delivers.' (Klein, ibid, p427)

The conflicts in Afghanistan and Iraq, with their suggesting at least some sense of space for democratic processes (along with a number of global mass protests at dictatorial regimes) encouraged people in Syria to protest at their own dictatorial government. The result being a massive military reaction by the al Assad-led regime (backed primarily by the Russians) that has brutally crushed this fractured rebellion over the last few years. A period of civil-conflict that saw the built infrastructure of cities such as Aleppo, Damascus, Idlibe, Raqqu, and Homs, reduced to rubble.

At 2022: 50% of the country's hospitals were closed, nearly 50% of its children are not in school, and about 80% of the population are living in poverty. Of a total population of 22m, nearly 5m fled the country and 6.5m are internally displaced. The conflict has resulted in 470,000 killed and nearly 2m wounded: in but four years average life expectancy had fallen from 70 to 55 years.

It was a coup in 1963 which brought Hafez al Assad to the Presidency then, post his death in 2000, power past to his son, Bashar, to rule over a nation under close control. Control sustained by the operation of the feared *Mukhabarat* security organization that uses intimidation, torture, and killing, to suppress any sign of dissent against the regime. The recent period of conflict was sparked when in March 2012 15 children, aged 9-15, caught up in a national (and international) mood of 'Arabic Spring' protest, graffitied some walls in the southern town of Darra with anti-regime messages. The children were arrested, detained and taken to a prison in the city of Damascus where they were subjected to torture. A series of peaceful protests spread across the country with the regime's forces responding violently; from when the conflict escalated. With the regime being supplied with arms by the Russians and others, and the disparate opposition forces being supplied with arms by the US and others.

Situated in the most southerly region of the Arabian Peninsula, Yemen is another Middle-Eastern country with a troubled history and a country currently involved in an on-going, bitter, civil war. Apart from Palestine, Yemen is probably the poorest Arab nation (nos. 1 on the

2022 Fragile States list). It is a country whose post WWII experience has been defined by a north-south split. In 1839 Britain (British East India Company) took control of the southern territory of Aden, the port that became of strategic importance when the Suez Canal was opened in 1869, from when it became a major re-fueling station for the British navy. To the north as the grip of the Ottomans weakened, along with the more general decline of its empire, Northern Yemen (as the Hashemite Mutawakkilite 'Kingdom of Yemen') was able to gain its independence - the two territories mostly co-existed relatively peacefully between the two world wars. Iman Ahmad bin Yahya ruler from 1948 was an autocratic head of state, nursing an ambition to create a greater Yemen. As they seemed to be the main obstacle to this, he called for the British to leave Aden. On the King's death in Sept 1962 his son Prince Muhammad as-Badr was in line to inherit the throne but even before his coronation a group of young (Egyptian trained) military officers staged a coup d'état, deposed the crown prince, and declared the Yemen Arab Republic. The north was now plunged into civil war, with the royalists supported by Saudi Arabia, Jordan, and later on Israel, and the opposing republicans supported by the Soviet Union and Egypt; with the latter sending up to 70,000 troops. The fighting lasted until 1970 when the combatants agreed to end the fighting and the key neighbour, Saudi Arabia, reluctantly recognized the Republic.

Although the full-blown civil war had ended lower-level conflict continued. Throughout the 70s and 80s a range of insurrectionary activities were undertaken by groups of extreme to centre-left political parties aligned together within various umbrella groups; starting in 1976 with the 'National Democratic Front', which in 1979 re-grouped into the 'Yemen Popular Unity Party'. From 1978 Ali Abdullah Saleh became President of the northern 'Yemen Arab Republic', a position he would hold until unification in 1990. He would then go on to be the president of a united Yemen until 2012. During the 1980s the government led by Sahel was able to benefit from generous foreign aid and also from the revenues of oil discovered in the north.

Recent history of the south was characterized initially by

overcoming colonial control. It was Britain, endeavouring to bring some sense of unity to the south and west of the country, that sought to form a federation of the provinces in the south. This led to the creation of the 'Protectorate of Southern Arabia'. From the early 60s the Marxist National Liberation Front (NFL) undertook a range of insurrectionary activities in an attempt to force a British withdrawal. In response to increasing NFL guerrilla attacks, the British in 1965 suspended the government and declared a state of emergency - imposing direct colonial rule. Around this time another left-wing grouping formed as a breakaway from the increasingly extreme NFL communist grouping. This, the socialist 'Front for the Liberation of Occupied Southern Yemen' (FLOSY), had leaders with roots in workers organizations, and the situation was then that the NFL and FLOSY were fighting each other as well as both fighting the British. With many civilians becoming victims of the conflict.

The British position became increasingly untenable and it officially withdrew from the colony in 1967 leaving the NLF to form a new government and establish the 'Peoples' Republic of Southern Yemen'. This brought an end to the federation of provinces under the 'Protectorate of Southern Arabia' and began a period when the NFL waged a brutal campaign to bring the provinces under their direct control.

Loss of Egyptian military support following its defeat in the six-day war with Israel left FLOSY militarily weak, and a combined force of NFL and the regular army led to it having to concede defeat; with the surviving leaders fleeing the country. In 1969 a hard-line (Marxist) faction within the NLF took control and established the 'People's Democratic Republic of Yemen', making close links to communist regimes in the Soviet Union, communist China, and Cuba. The Soviet Union in particular - adopting the usual (default-mode of) superpower approach of ignoring human rights, here of the Yemeni people - helped to equip and train the new republic's army. In return gaining access to a strategically useful naval base with direct access to the red sea.

From the early 1970s conflict between north and south Yemen

broke out on a regular basis and, following more extensive fighting in 1972 (Soviets supporting the south and Saudi Arabia the north), representatives of some of the main groups met in Cairo in October 1979 to arrange a ceasefire, which also drew up a constitution for a united Yemen. A constitution that would commit Yemen to free elections within a multi-party system, the protection of private property, and for the people to be entitled to basic human rights. Following a period of continued conflict, a united Yemen was finally achieved in May 1990. This brought the northern YAR and the southern PDRY together in the government of the 'Republic of Yemen', with the northerner Ali Abdullah Saleh as its first president and the southerner Ali Salim al-Baid as its vice-president. Sadly, political unity did not bring lasting peace and southern dissatisfaction with what was felt to be its marginalization within the new country (including a claim of northerners being given preference for filling civil service jobs) erupted into civil war in 1994. Saleh announced a state of emergency and sacked southern ministers. From a base in Aden al-Baid declared the establishment of the 'Democratic Republic of Yemen'. But Aden was soon overrun by northern forces with al-Baid and other southern leaders fleeing abroad.

The late 1990s and throughout the 2000s saw continuous tensions between a range of groups. If this was mainly between each of the two government forces and then, from about 2004, also involving northern-based Houthi rebels seeking a return to the century-long rule of Zaidi Shia. In 2011 the calls for democratic reforms that characterized popular demonstrations across the Middle-East also enthused (mainly younger) people living in Yemen's cities. As well as this generally peaceful popular unrest, leading politicians were targeted by more extremist groups; President Sahel was injured in a rocket attack, seeking healthcare in Saudi Arabia. In Nov 2011 he handed power to his deputy, Abdrabbuh Mansour Hadi, who set about establishing a unity government. In February 2012, following an uncontested election, Hadi became President. Then, following nearly a year of deliberations a National Dialogue Conference produced a draft document intended to form the basis of a new constitution. But conflict continued, with rebel tribesmen blowing up oil pipelines, al-Qaeda launching suicide-bombing attacks, and with on-going Houthi and government security forces repeatedly clashing.

The Houthis rejected proposals for a new constitution, as they increasingly became the dominant military group. They took control of the capital Sanaa in Sept 2014 and in February 2015 they set up a 'Presidential Council' to replace the government. It was about this time that Islamic State (IS-Daesh - dedicated to the creation of an Islamic Caliphate encompassing all Arab nations) began to undertaken violent attacks in Yemen, including the bombing in March 2015 of two mosques in Sanaa, killing 140 worshippers.

In March 2015 (Sunni) Saudi Arabia, in effect, went to war with the Houthis, launching a bombing campaign that has killed over 10,000 Yemeni civilians (most victims of air-strikes) and degraded whole neighbourhoods - destroying hospitals, schools, factories and other parts of the infrastructure that supports civil life. A destruction made even worse by the Houthi rebels regularly firing mortars into civilian neighbourhoods. Dr Riaz Karim Director of the respected NGO 'Mona Relief Organization' noted that the Yemen is in turmoil and is a 'humanitarian black hole'. And a UN Human Civil Rights Committee report highlights: '...systematic warfare against the civilian population'.

The diplomatic influence and financial power of the Saudi regime has been brought to bear on foreign governments and on the international mass media, to ensure that their key role in this conflict is at best suppressed or at least misrepresented. Whilst it seems to be quite a stretch of the imagination (even in the context of the Orwellian language used by governments), the autocratic Saudi monarchy claims to have become involved in Yemen due to its 'noble' wish to support progress towards democracy!

Yemen is currently a conflictual mess of a country, with a population experiencing high levels of unemployment, shortages of food and of vital medicines, weak and corrupt governance, and minimal access to education and healthcare, as well as to the longstanding issue of access to land - whilst warring factions vie for power. The main factions being the Zaidi Shia, 'Houthi', rebels who have been fighting the government forces on and off since 2004. The official security forces are divided in terms of support for the government and their allies of the Popular Resistance militia, or for the Houthi rebels - a division broadly set in terms of Shia/Sunni. Within Yemen there are a number of tribal-based groupings fighting at a local level; especially the powerful Hasid loose confederation of tribes. Then there are the externally based groups such as al-Qaeda[45] and Islamic State, each pursuing their own murderous extremist Islamic aims.

Behind this toxic mix of warring factions there is on the deposed government side a coalition led by Saudi Arabia (armed mainly by the US and Britain), including the Gulf States, and Jordan, Egypt, Morocco and Sudan. As well as being a supplier of military equipment and intelligence to this coalition, the US has also carried out numerous drone strikes, primarily targeting the al-Qaeda leadership, in support of the deposed president and his Yemeni supporters.

Although the Shia Houthis (whilst officially denied, there is evidence that they are receiving arms and training - plus possibly fighter pilots - from Iran) are militarily more effective than the government forces, they do not have widespread support across this predominately Sunni country, so it is unlikely that they will be able to sustain any form of national rule.

The European parliament has voted overwhelmingly for an arms embargo to be applied to Saudi Arabia but, as yet, even Britain when an EU member state (and a major supplier of arms to Saudi Arabia) did not responded to this vote. From 2017 a Saudi naval blockade has been preventing medical and food aid reaching the country – with children as victims.

Talks to settle the conflict have been taking place in Saudi Arabia

---

[45] Since about 2000 – al Qaeda has been responsible for a series of attacks on the economically important oil installations and notoriously the suicide bombing of the US guided missile carrying destroyer USS Cole whilst moored in the port at Aden in Oct 2000 - killing 17 US servicemen.

but, given the underlying issues, including the enduring Islamic religious fault-lines, set in the context of the recent history of Yemen, it is unlikely that lasting peace can be found in this fractured land any time soon (as of 2022 the warring factions are 'more or less' observing a UN overseen truce). Any possibility for lasting peace would seem to be based on some form of loose federation (perhaps some arrangement with a structure of governance somewhere between a federation and the loser confederation) of the provinces, with a central/federal government ideally free from corruption and committed to oversee the fairer regional distribution of revenues from natural resources, along with significant land reforms. It would also require foreign powers such as Saudi Arabia, the US, and Iran, to change from funding destruction to funding re-construction. Even these steps would not necessarily neutralize the extremist groups of al-Qaeda and IS-Daesh[46] but it might contribute by making local recruitment much less successful, and national security in a unified, if federated, nation more effective.

The political conditions of much of the current Middle-East generally continues as a complex intermixture of potentially significant issues. Within Islam there has been the traditional, often bitter, division of Shia/Sunni, and in places there continues to be some legacy of historic antagonisms involving Islam, Christianity, and Judaism, and in others Islam verses the secular. Most Middle-Eastern countries have young well-educated populations but with many of these facing fairly bleak employment prospects. Economic inequality, corruption, nepotism, and bureaucratic inefficiency, continue as systemic issues in most countries. Then there are the more common problems for nation states created as part of some larger great-power games (mostly directly related to securing access to resources, especially oil supplies), with neighbouring

---

[46] This grouping presents a challenge beyond just one country. Divisions are emerging within IS-Daesh over interpretation and adherence to Shia law - this also seems to be the case in Yemen, with an IS faction rebelling against the IS governor (wali) in the 'IS Province of Yemen'.

nation-states at odds over seemingly endless border disputes and various ethnic groups seeking greater autonomy within countries (the Kurds stand out).

Into this veritable cauldron of potential conflict there has been the enduring conflictual legacy of the non-Arab state of Israel being imposed on the region; with a bitter, divisive, process of displacing much of the indigenous population. If we then allow that the whole region has been providing yet another setting for great power hegemony, as the predominance initially of France and Britain gave way to that of the United States and the Soviet Union. Each pouring billions of dollars worth of modern armaments into the region, including material that can be used in the manufacture of biological, chemical, and nuclear weaponry.

Given the steaming complexity of divisions, group rivalries, and personal ambitions, the ways in which the sad post-war history has played out can hardly have been a surprise. But, of more relevance to the future, it was a series of outcomes that could have been predicted. These last five words should serve as a mantra for those involved in international affairs......'that could have been predicted'..... perhaps changing the 'could' to 'should', and so become a cautionary suggestion. It seems reasonable to follow an approach to conflicts along the lines of: 'consider a situation you are faced with; think about the relevant past; act to do whatever you can to avoid repeating the mistakes of history.......' and bear in mind that in this globalized world the '...any of those involved in international affairs' includes each single one of us.

The foundations of the rise of Islamic fundamentalism, with its more militant activists - themselves prepared to die for the cause identified by mainly clerical leaderships - has as many causative factors as the number of, mainly young, people involved. Each individual takes their own personal route towards conceiving then operationalising a belief in the justification for violent action. But within the uniqueness of personal experience we can perhaps identify correlative, and possibly even plausibly causative, factors that are part of the shared experience of those who take up an 'Islamic cause'. The individual uniqueness of experience overlaps and fuses into a mutuality of perspective in local interactions (not least in the Islamic Madrassas - of which there are as many as 30,000 in Pakistan - that many of the poorest children attend.....partly incentivized by the offer of free food) and in internet forums and the many sectarian web-sites, accessed by believers; and of course, this aspect of fostering support for confronting non-believers (especially those considered to have themselves challenged Islamic interests) can be accessed by any Moslem (or other) anywhere in the world.

The frustrated and angry young man/women in Birmingham, England or Birmingham, Alabama (USA) alone in their bedroom, perhaps feeling alienated from lives lived in an overly materialistic society. Societies so strongly focused on heightening identity dissatisfaction in order to sell products and services. Within which their own identity is degraded rather than respected for its ordinariness. Angry at what they see on the daily news programmes (especially what is happening to fellow Moslems), and aspiring to make a difference in the world.

Across the primarily Arab states of North Africa the legacy of great power involvement (Britain, France, Soviet Union, Italy, USA) continues as bitter national memories. Sharing, with other economically developing nations, a disadvantaged position in a global economic system progressively designed to serve the needs of the powerful elite groups of the nations early into industrialization. And with the almost universal fault-line inherent in imposed national borders. In addition to the legacy of violent imperialism and more recent cold-war hegemony, there are the local cleavages such as, religions (Sunni/Shia), lifestyle (between nomadic Tuareg and other Berber tribes-people, and more generally between settled peasantry/herders and farmers), between rich and poor, and in localities where tribal rivalries abrasively rub together.

Across most of North Africa and the Middle-East, combinations of the factors noted above, where they meet conditions of high levels of unemployment, poverty, gross inequality, and a bitter, frustrated, sense of primal injustice (anti-Moslem - anti-Arab persecution -

pervading the lives of generations), are being expressed in various forms of religious or civil strife. With Syria, Libya, Egypt, Afghanistan, Iraq, and the Yemen, being especially vulnerable to religious fundamentalism. Relatively more stable countries include Saudi Arabia, Kuwait, Oman, the smaller Gulf States, Morocco, Tunisia, and Algeria, have been looking to the US and Western-Europe for security and partnership for exploiting oil and natural gas resources; with all of these countries being run by more or less repressive regimes. A number retaining despotic neo-medieval monarchies (and their congeries of sycophantic retainers), and the others having governance controlled by various combinations of self-serving politico-military-business elites. But each having to cope with a range of internal problems, whether these come from Islamist political parties, Islamic fundamentalism, high birth rates, high levels of youth unemployment, protests at lack of democracy and personal freedoms, and of gross economic inequalities.

In some ways the post-war history of the Lebanon represents the chaotic experience of the Middle-East more generally, and yet it also stands alone in terms of its political complexity (70 legally recognized political parties and 36 banned parties circa 2016). It has for centuries been a refuge for minority (mainly religious) groups fleeing persecution elsewhere in the Middle-East. Up until recently it has managed to, if at times uneasily, accommodate a range of different political/religious groups (accepting that the 2016 election 'stalemate' was followed six attempts to form a new government). It has been continuing a reconstruction process necessitated by damage caused during a bitter civil war lasting from 1975-90 and the 1982 invasion by an Israeli army intent on destroying the Palestinian Liberation Organization (PLO) then based in the country. An operation that was extended to the bases of militant (Shia) Islamic group Hezbollah (Party of God – the military arm of Islamic Resistance) that had been funded by Iran and has exercised a significant power-broking, role in recent Lebanese politics. The Israeli action was cynically termed 'Operation Peace in Galilee', and apart from being a clear breach of international law the Israeli army, commanded by then Minister of Defence Arial Sharon, was complicit in the September 1982 massacre of thousands of civilians (including many women and children) in the Palestinian refugee camps of Sabra and Shatila - when they stood back and allowed their murderous Christian militia (Phalange) allies into the camps.

If we pick up developments in China towards the end of the 1930s we see this vast land broadly separated into three areas. The Japanese were occupying extensive areas in the north-east, inner Mongolia, then, following the 'Marco Polo ('Lugou') Bridge Incident' of July 1937, a number of the major cities down the eastern seaboard; as well as having annexed and maintained a colonial occupation of Korea since 1910. The west of the country is mainly under communist CCP control (the 'People's Republic of China') with Mao Zedong as the most powerful of a group of leaders, steadily consolidating his position. From its base in the west the Red Army was undertaking guerrilla-type activities beyond its border into Japanese controlled China. These forays became increasingly effective, leading to the setting up of 'liberated areas', and by 1945 there would be 19 of these. An extensive range of the south of the county was under the control of the nationalist - Kuomintang (National People's Party - NPP) - government that had been governing China from 1928, with Jiang Iesha (better known to the west as Chiang Kai-shek) as leader. Since the early 1930s the NPP had been seeking first to repress then, from about 1935, to crush the CCP and its Red Army. Jiang captured Shanghai in 1927 and set about terrorizing any potential opposition..... thousands of CCP activists and trade union leaders were murdered and similar 'tit for tat' massacres happened in CCP controlled areas against Nationalists.

Significant groups of the population, including many university students and sections of the army (Fujian revolt), in nationalist areas felt that the government was more focused on defeating the communists than on fighting the Japanese. The United States had been offering some fairly modest support to the nationalists. But following the Japanese surprise attack on the US naval base in Pearl Harbour in December 1941, this military support was markedly increased and a formal US/ Nationalist Chinese anti-Japanese alliance was agreed. It would be the defeat of the Japanese in the Second World War that would see them finally removed from China and from the Korean Peninsula. During the Sino-Japanese war, the nationalist government had become increasingly more dictatorial and repressive. This approach was not compensated for by efficient economic management or indeed military competence. Mainly in order to pay the army, but also to sustain widespread corruption, taxes were steadily increased. The inflation rate grew and the value of wages fell. In the countryside 1535 peasants were taxed up to 50% of the value of their crops. There were shortages of commodities such as oil and basic foodstuffs. The generally poor economic situation was, in 1942, exacerbated in Hunan Province, by drought, infestation of locust, and the depredations of Japanese attacks in this border region. One outcome of this combination of circumstances was a very poor harvest and so widespread food shortages. In the resultant famine 2-3 million people died and another 4 million fled to the south and the west. In sum: the nationalist-controlled areas were rife with corruption, black marketeering, and with living conditions for the most peasants and urban workers continuing to be pretty miserable. In contrast to the corrupt, incompetent nationalist regime, in the years just prior to and during the war (the 'Yan'an years), the communists built a range of political institutions, and developed an approach to administration, that contributed to their claiming to be a government in internal 'exile'.

From February 1942, an intensive training programme ('zhengfeng') was introduced intending to create a large body of ideologically informed and politically determined cadres ready to spread throughout the population to act as local teachers and leaders. The communists gave economic priority to increasing agricultural productivity, and they also accumulated a reserve supply of grain, available in the event of a poor harvest. A more progressive tax system was introduced and some relatively modest land reforms undertaken. All measures that gained the support, or at least a level of cooperation, from the population in the areas under their control as well as enhancing the image of the communists across most of China. Such was the improving reputation of the communists that the US sent a diplomatic mission, led by John S. Service, to take a closer look. Service reported quite favourably on what he had seen - reporting high morale of the people along with a general respect for the leadership in CCP areas - and this later on, in 1945, encouraged the US (Gen. George Marshall) to attempt to persuade the Nationalist and Communists to stop fighting each other and come together to form a coalition government. But drawn out negotiations intended to achieve this floundered on basic differences on how to share power and on deep mutual suspicion of motives.

At the end of the Second World War the US predictably, and the Russians rather perversely, supported the Nationalist (Kuomintang) government. And in terms of numbers the Nationalists, with an army of over 2.5 million soldiers (against the Communist one of about 900,000), and with many more tanks, airplanes, and artillery pieces, had the superior military strength. But their army did not have the high morale, self-belief in their 'cause', and level of organization comparable to the Red Army; the 'People's Liberation Army'. The nationalist army was led by generals, noted by Harman (ibid, p555), as mostly being '......motivated only by the desire to grow rich at the expense of their soldiers and the peasants whose lands they passed through.' So even in the context of the seeming military superiority of the nationalists, the outcome of the civil war, with its resounding communist victory, cannot be a surprise. It was a victory achieved after four more years of fighting, with the communists initially adopting a more mobile strategy - raiding nationalist bases and stretching the nationalist supply lines - rather than engaging in conventional battles. This was an approach that proved to be effective in the northern provinces and in Manchuria. In June 1947 the communist army (PLA) crossed the Yellow River and steadily advanced south. By the start of 1948, when the communists felt the balance of military power had shifted decisively towards them, they became increasingly prepared to take on the nationalists in large-scale engagements. In one of these, in November 1948, at Huai-Hui, the two armies, each of about 500,000 troops, faced each other and for nearly four months they fought in quite bitter weather. As the fighting progressed, a number of nationalist units joined the communist side and the engagement ended on 10th January with the surrender of the remaining 300,000 nationalist soldiers and with the communists in control of all the land north of the Yangzi River. During the final months of the civil war the communists pursued a still substantial, but demoralized and disorganized, nationalist army towards the southern coast, from where 2 million of them the fled to the large island of Taiwan. Where they acted as a brutal occupation force, killing and imprisoning thousands of Taiwanese.

The People's Liberation Army entered Peking in 1949, led by Mao Zedong, Zhu De and Lin Shauqi, and on 1st Oct that year, symbolically standing at the entrance to the 'Forbidden City', Mao proclaimed the inauguration of the People's Republic of China, with its capital in Peking, now renamed Beijing. The years immediately following the revolutionary victory were ones during which the new government endeavoured to create a sense 1537 of China (including Manchuria and from 1950 Tibet) as a nation-state, rather than a land made up of various large, generally autonomous, provinces. In 1951 'Residents Committees' were introduced in the cities with the purpose of involving citizens at a very local level, along with the CCP-trained cadres functioning as a means of communication between people and government as well as between government and people. If the former more in theory than actual practice. Key texts were produced, not least the transcription of Mao's June 30th 1949 speech in commemoration of the 28th anniversary of the founding of the CCP. This text - 'On peoples democratic dictatorship' – an oxymoronic title which gave an overtly ideological analysis of the conditions facing the government, including the class structure of post-revolutionary Chinese society; it was something of a peon of praise for Marxism-Leninism and for the dictatorship of the proletariat. Two other important documents were 'The Organic Law' and 'The Common Programme' - The first, outlined new constitutional arrangements (with at least some allowance for political opposition), the second, sought to outline guaranteed human rights in areas such as free speech, religious belief, movement, and the equality of treatment for both genders. Although an emphasis was on centralized planning and top-down authoritarian control there was also a range of devolved powers operating at the provincial and local levels where an extensive body of cadres helped to ensure that a CCP ideology directed deliberations. Determined initiatives were undertaken to clamp down on prostitution and on opium consumption, both rife in cities along the coast. A quite ruthless approach was taken to the treatment of exKuomintang supporters, with prison and 're-education' for the more fortunate, and execution for thousands of others.

Control of Taiwan was an on-going ambition (it being an ever-present political irritant) but one deterred by the still substantial military strength of the nationalists (with Jiang Jieshi continuing as the leader), their strong defensive position on an island, and the committed support of the US. Economically, the new government took a relatively cautious approach (relative to later developments), extending the, popular with peasants, land reforms (40% of the land was redistributed 1949-50) that had previously been introduced in CCP controlled areas to the newly 'liberated' areas, and giving priority to developing a base of 1538 heavy industry. A combination of modernization and communist ideology was the driving force determining economic policy, with agrarian reform and industrial development being the two more significant challenges facing the post-revolutionary government. Up until about the last two decades of the twentieth century modernization in industry was more successful that in agriculture, even though a significant transfer of land ownership had been carried out. The process of nationalizing foreign businesses began in early 1951 with the take-over of the assets of Shell Oil. The first 'Five Year Plan' was introduced in 1952, and markers of industrialization considered over the five years (to 1957) indicate some steady progress in industrialization: oil consumption increased by over 200%, pig-iron production by 200%, and steel production by 300%. A progress benefiting from the presence of specialist advisors from the Soviet Union. But advances in industry were not accompanied by any advance in agriculture, and even after the dramatic change from cooperative units to collectivization began in 1955, agricultural productivity continued poor. In 1952 the 'State Statistical Bureau' was established to quantify a range of economic and social features of Chinese society. A population census took place between June 1953 and November 1954, recording nearly 600 million people, almost 40% of these being under 15 years of age.

In terms of international relations, during the final months of the civil war lukewarm support of the Russians for the Nationalists had changed to much warmer support for the new CCP government. A friendship formalized by a treaty signed in 1950. But whilst the Peoples Republic's relationship with the US had been significantly challenged by US/Kuomintang alliance, the Korean War would transform antagonists into enemies. As Gen. MacArthur's nominally UN force, supporting the South Korean government, reached close to the Chinese border, Chinese troops in the form the 'Chinese Peoples Volunteers' (a title depending more on diplomatic convenience rather than military reality) moved to support the North Korean army. Chinese casualties would be as many as 900,000, with Mao's son, Mao Anying, being one of them. Towards the end of the first five year plan there was a noticeable groundswell of dissent in some major Chinese cities where university teachers, students, and some artists, called for more freedom and democracy, as well as voicing mild criticisms of the authoritarian 1539 application of the form of Marxism adopted by the government. At least partly to divert public attention from the poor economic performance, Mao blamed these 'bourgeoisie-revisionist-intellectuals' for undermining the government (and so by implication the masses) and he called for 'continuous revolution'. Possible as many as 700,000 intellectuals were sent to work on farms and in factories and, in an effort to continue the revolutionary dynamic, with the 'Great Leap Forward' being announced to follow the 5 year plan. This new plan set out a number of key agricultural and industrial production targets, these being increases on those of the earlier plan. The higher targets were to be achieved by workers working harder, being managed more effectively, and with many of them being formed into locally based, mutually supportive, 'communes'; often a commune was composed of workers in just one factory. There was a drive to reduce illiteracy and more generally to expand primary, secondary, and higher-level education. At the same time there was a campaign to purge any bourgeois elements from within the education system and to include 'suitable' students in the management of schools. But economic problems continued and divisions began to appear within the leadership. The Minister of defence, Peng Dehuai, wrote a letter to Mao that offered a fairly balanced assessment of the successes and some failures of the revolution. Peng was particularly critical of the exaggerated claims for levels of output that bore little relation to what was actually being produced. By this time Mao's leadership position was strong and Peng was dismissed from his post and replaced by the Mao loyalist, Lin Biao. Now Mao felt able to elevate himself somewhat above the day-to-day affairs of the government and he resigned from the Chairmanship and moved into semi-retirement, with Liu Shajoqi taking over the official leadership.

It was from 1959 that the poor agricultural performance became catastrophically obvious, a problem exacerbated by inefficiencies in distribution and with the continuing export of grain (to gain foreign currency), and this even during the worst of the famine that blighted China between 1959-1961.The range of estimates of those that starved to death in this situation is between 14-28 million (at its worst in the north and the west of the country).....it seems so insensitive for me to offer a death-toll with a 14 million human-being 'gap'. But even if we only accept the lower estimate the magnitude of this human disaster can be seen, a disaster, the extent of which was throughout denied by the Chinese government. And this taking place in a country that was sufficiently technologically advanced to have been testing atomic weapons since 1957.

The Sino-Soviet relationship deteriorated markedly in 1958, with Mao initially not being consulted before Khrushchev had in 1956 denounced Stalin, and so for Mao by implication Marxism-Leninism. Mao also felt that the Soviet leadership was becoming too accommodating to the West, especially the US. These differences were exacerbated by the Soviet Union siding with India over Sino-Indian disputes on the western border of Tibet. By the early 1960s the break in relations was clear, with the thousands of Russian technicians, and other specialist advisors, being recalled. During the mid-late 1960s modest progress was made in industrialization, especially in manufacturing and construction, but agricultural productivity continued poor, and this in the face of a rapidly growing population. During this time it was Mao and his close supporters within the leadership that determined policy with others, such as Deng Xiaoping (Gen. Sec. of CCP) and Zhou Enlai (founder of the CCP in 1923, and Premier of the Peoples Republic of China from 1949 until his death in 1976), conforming if not agreeing. China, as well has other communist governments (Russia, Albania, Cuba) that had leading personalities, often allowed these to develop into 'Heroic Leaders' - and Mao became just such as hero, a benign father-figure who had led his people into socialist freedom and now worked tireless for their good. It would be from this position of populist esteem, along with support of key political allies, that made his position unassailable and which allowed him to launch the 'Great Proletarian Cultural Revolution'. An action intended as an initiative to revitalize the revolution and perhaps also to divert attention from deteriorating economic conditions. If Mao, and those close to him such as his fourth wife Jiang Qing and the military leader Lin Biao, also used this cultural revolution as a means of purging the party and the country more widely of bourgeoisie elements and revisionist ideas.

It would be the military, in the form of the Peoples' Liberation Army, along with the 'Socialist Education Movement' (which Mao had himself set up), that would take the lead in operationalizing the revolutionary dynamic. From the mid-sixties this movement, with Maoist hardliners (including thousands of students seen in the media proudly waving copies of Mao's 'Little Red book') in the vanguard, invaded schools, colleges, universities, hospitals, government offices, 1541 factories, the military itself, seeking out any teacher, manager, officer, even CCP cadre leader, judged to not be sufficiently committed to the revolution. Condemning even the slightest form of ideological deviance and any adherence to the 'Four Olds' - old customs, old habits, old ideas, old culture. The accused were usually subjected to public humiliation, sent to undertake manual work in factory or on farm, and were expected to undertake intensive 'self-examination' and 're-education'. Many individuals were badly beaten, some even killed. Within a couple of years even Mao became concerned at the level of social and political upheaval resulting from these activities and endeavoured to restrain the Red Guards. The cultural revolution slowly petered out and by the time of Mao's death in 1976 had effectively come to an end, drained of revolutionary enthusiasm. Since 1947, China has been ruled by an elite group composed of individuals drawn from the higher ranks of the Communist Party. Competition for control has been more about conflicting ambitions of CP leading members and groups of supporters than the 'will of the people' which was and is assumed as synonymous with the 'will of the Party'. What amounts to a new ruling dynasty was created in 1947 from when it has expanded in size and with each member increasingly reaping a bounteous harvest of personal wealth and political prestige. The high level of within CP conflicts at the end of the Mao period was but a variation on earlier imperial dynastic intrigues. During the twenty-first century decisive, if measured, moves toward a market economy, have seen the inclusion of some leading business and military people join the ranks of the ruling group. An 'elite' has coalesced around the idea of a China on the rise. If the seeming unity in shared (personal and familial) interests has been disrupted in the more recent move by Xi Jinping's crackdown on high-level, more obviously rampant, corruption – with up to 100,000 officials and some others being arrested: so more a politically astute purge than any active reform.

China today has the economic means to claim a global presence and so align its international political stance to that of the US – a stance including an hegemonic approach to the neighbouring lands its leadership coverts. These include a number of islands in the south China Sea, not least disputes with the US over the Chinese construction of artificial islands to be used as military bases. But the most critical current issue is over Taiwan and its independent status. The Chinese leadership is but one of the, national now become global, 'elites' that in effect set the conditions for international political (and indeed economic) relationships.

An even just brief consideration of post-war Central and South America would, in general, show a similar pattern of internal strife exacerbated by the involvement (interference) of the leading (19th century) imperialist nations and the two (20th century) super-powers, as they determinedly pursued their own financial and political interests in line with their own elite-group and wider corporate priorities. For Latin America the US was by far the main foreign influence on national affairs – regional politics in the decades following WWII have been played out within a wider antagonistic polarity of US/USSR (and either's various allies) relations. The US was determined to maintain its own political and economic neo-colonial hegemonic control over much of Latin America. It would see its influence threatened by 'communism', and for the US in the cold-war period communism was a simplistic label applied to any organization, even if only just mildly left-wing. At no point did any US administration seem to seriously contemplate using its influence to address the reasons why left-wing groups gained support mostly from the poorest sections of a country. It would be too easy to exaggerate US influence, and it was at times mercenary, anti-democratic and harmful, especially to the interests of the poorest. But the historic cultural influences such as machismo, caudillios, strong military leadership, the personal favour-ship system of compardrez/compadrazgo, the Catholic Church, peasant-based agriculture on large landholdings, each continued as strong influences. With the descendents of native peoples also maintaining a significant presence in some countries - Bolivia, Mexico, Peru, Paraguay – and the historic framework of what were Iberian social institutions. For countries such as Brazil, Mexico and Peru, there has also been a significant if generally integrated African heritage, giving social and political developments a decidedly Latin American form.

The continent has been characterized by extreme economic inequalities, with a wealthy elite made up of land-owning and big business aristocracies based on families descended from, mainly Spanish and Portuguese (but also some other European) immigrants, and at the other end of the income scale masses of peasants/peons, and an urban underclass. Most of the latter being descendants of slaves (imported from Africa) and a wide range of indigenous native peoples. In between the wealthy elites and the poor and very poor masses, were a relatively small but growing middle-class. The latter being a conservative class often unsure whether to offer political support to politicians from the traditional elites or to argue for some level of populist reform; what happened usually depended on the extent to which a country was progressing industrialization and so to what extent the middle-classes felt empowered as a group. Alleviating the causes of popular dissident were not part of an operational agenda primarily designed to protect the interest of traditional and emerging elites as well as those of corporate America. The latter included ensuring the uninterrupted flow of raw materials and other primary products, as well as debt payments, to the US.

During the 70s, US support for the most unsavoury of dictatorships was at its height - however fabulously corrupt and inhumanly brutal, these regimes were either actively supported or at least accepted by the US providing they were seen to be keeping communism at bay. Bear in mind that for most dirt-poor Latin Americans (rural peasants and urban workers) all that communism really meant was some possibility of relief from poverty and oppression - not some through-going deep-rooted commitment to any version of Marxist ideology - a desperate hope rather than any profound ideological commitment.

US favourites included Alfredo Stroessner in Paraguay, Augustus Pinochet in Chile, Anastasio Somoza in Nicaragua, and Carlos Arana in Guatemala.... for each of the regimes led by these four human rights were denied as a matter of policy and intimidation, torture, and extrajudicial murder were simply population control mechanisms within an overall strategy of sheer terror (national domination).

T.H.Donghi's (1993, p324) assessment of Guatemala's government at this time was that: 'The unrestrained brutality suffered by Indian peasants and urban opposition elements during Arana's rule foreshadowed the inauguration of similar tactics by the right all over Latin America during the decade to come.' An assessment that could apply to all four dictators, they led in a vanguard of terror where others followed.

Some evidence of the active involvement of the US in facilitating illegal abductions, torture, disappearances, and extrajudicial killings became known when US documents relating to its 'Operation Condor' were declassified. Operation Condor was based upon an early 1970s agreement between six governments of the then worst human rights offending countries - Brazil, Chile, Bolivia, Argentina, Paraguay and Uruguay, with Ecuador and Peru joining later on. The right-wing regimes in these countries, alarmed by the rise of populist and socialist opposition to their control (a threat to the economic and social dominance of privileged elites), agreed to co-operate in the coordination of repression. The cooperation focused on exchange of surveillance and other intelligence information, on cross-border operations by multi-national special forces, and on a multi-national team of assassins tasked to travel anywhere in the world to murder 'subversive elements', especially opposition politicians in exile. All, yes all, of these activities were supported and facilitated by the US, mainly via the CIA. The CIA played a key role in providing ICT-based telecommunications equipment and expertise. And US embassy staff in the Condor countries were regularly complicit in the identification and targeting of 'subversives' – estimates are of between 60,000-80,000 left-wing sympathizers being murdered in this coordinated project.

The US covert operations were based in Panama City at the headquarters of the US Southern Command (SOUTHCOM), which also served as a base for US special forces, and in the US run Army School of the Americas (in 1984 it was renamed and relocated to Fort Benning, Georgia) - many graduates of which went on to become notorious torturers and murderers. The US government felt it could justify (although not make public) its convert complicity in terror due to their viewing Condor as a 'legitimate counter terror operation'.

Most South American nations had emerged from the World War II, yes with significant inequalities in relation to land-ownership and wealth distribution, but at least with some form of democratic constitution. Even if it was only at the end of its civil war in 1948 that Costa Rica established the region's first legitimate democracy. But the steady increase in support for political groups with more moderate democratic socialist, to more radical left-wing, policy plans offered a threat to powerful interests and led to a series of military coups. Of the 11 Latin American countries (so excluding those 7, plus Mexico, of Central America) all had some post-war experience of rule by military dictatorship - the least, Columbia covering 4 years the most, Paraguay 38 years. Dictatorship, whether in the form of a military regime or of an unelected civilian government (supported by the military), in a context of gross economic and social inequality, invariably creates the political conditions for the formation of more radical left-wing opposition. This is more so in countries lacking a sufficiently large industrial base to provide the conditions suitable for organized industrial action by groups of disaffected workers. The 1959 Cuban revolution served as a model for angry, mainly young, people across the continent who took to armed opposition and sought out bases in the less accessible countryside. The right-wing groupings did not generally need underground guerrilla groups as they could generally rely on the indigenous military leaders (including para-military 'death-squads') to protect their interests. An exception being the directly US funded Contras in 1980s Nicaragua - who mounted attacks into Nicaragua from safe havens in Costa Rica and Honduras.

US foreign policy since WWII has exhibited a clear mismatch between stated international aims and its actual behaviour in South America - it's as if the US political elite, and its public and private security establishment, have assumed a right (and yes, with some delusional politicians even elevating this to a 'god-given' right) to interpret the world using alignment with US corporate and military interests as a guide to what is acceptable. An interpretative framework that seeks to excuse, misinform about, relativize, or simply ignore any abuses of international law, or even of basic human rights, if the culpable nation has a leadership (however murderous) that is friendly towards the US interests. A framework imbued with an implacable sense of its rightness in whatever the US does, but one with a significantly etiolated sense of morality.

This approach has dominated US relations with Central and South American countries, where there has been a stark disjunction between US publically stated aims and its actual behaviour. Its public aims have been stated as encouraging and actively supporting progress towards representative democracy. But in reality, its post-war governments have never been able to accept the social and financial reforms necessary to achieve an authentic democracy. And also that a country's people (especially in countries with extreme poverty for most and extreme wealth for the few) might express their own aspirations by electing a government prepared to progress reform programmes that would threaten the power of the army and the influence of the land-owning aristocracy, the accumulation of wealth for already wealthy industrialists, and of even more concern..... might threaten the financial interests of US banks and private corporations.

Throughout the region there had been some signs suggesting the prospect of progress towards more enlightened democratic forms of governance. In the late 40s and early 50s countries such as Honduras, Guatemala, Costa Rica, and to a lesser extent Argentina, Mexico, and Venezuela, were led by governments committed to reform and for some the development of mass education and a level of welfare provision. In all but Costa Rica - a country that continued to follow a social reformist programme up to the early 1980s – the aspirations of the masses for improvements in both standard of living and for stronger constitutional rights was short-lived. Crushed by the reaction of traditional elites - large landowners, wealthy merchants, big business, along with senior military officers drawn from these two groups - determined to protect their own privileged economic and political position. Elites supported by a succession of US governments that together prioritized anti-communist action over democratic, and indeed often even basic human, rights.

In Venezuela, the moderate reformist government of the left-wing but anti-communist President Rómulo Betancourt (the 'Father of Venezuelan Democracy') had introduced agrarian reforms, progressed industrial development, and widened the franchise. But in 1948 his immediate successor Rómulo Gallegos, was removed by a military coup that placed Gen. Marcos Pérez Jiménez in the Presidency. Whilst Jiménez continued to progress most of the Betancourt reforms, his regime favoured US corporate interests, and was brutal in its repression of any opposition.

In Guatemala, the US administration actively conspired to remove the elected President Jacobo Árbenz; indeed declassified documents reveal the CIA advocating the elimination of both communists and any sympathizers of the Árbenez regime - in effect it being complicit in the murder of thousands of innocent people. Árbenz, and his predecessor Juan José Arévalo, had introduced policies such as: the abolition of forced labour and the introduction of a labour code offering some protection for waged-workers, the beginning of land reforms (including nationalization of land belonging to the US United Fruit Company), and the extension of social reforms to Mayan Indians who made-up about 50% of Guatemala's population. Árbenz and his government had been publically denounced by the US representatives at a meeting of the Organization of America States (OAS - held in Caracas), as they pursued their government's obsessive concern to eliminate the threat of communism, or indeed any even modest progress towards democratic socialism - simply ignoring any country's right to self-determination. The Caracas Declaration classified communist activity in any South American country as foreign interference in American affairs, and went further by stating that the establishment of a communist government would be a threat to regional stability.

The US government was prepared to accept that stability meant oligarchic rule or military dictatorship, and for these to be as corrupt and brutal as necessary to maintain the business as usual type of stability suited to big business. Mexico and Argentina abstained from the vote and Guatemala voted against. This move (the Declaration) embodied the US's unwillingness to understand that support for communism (or indeed any reformist political party) might not be part of some world-wide conspiracy but instead could be but the legitimate expression of the frustration and anger of the masses having to bear such injustices as gross economic inequality, oligarchic or dictatorial governance, slum living conditions (and uncertain supply of utilities), poor welfare provision, sustained unemployment, and the lack of constitutional rights.

By the early 1960s a series of military-backed coups had removed most of the more enlightened regimes in all but Puerto Rica.

As noted above, it is easy to exaggerate the US influence in Latin America as a whole - undoubtedly, the US's willingness to co-ordinate its business and political interests and to serve as de-facto power-brokers in countries such as Guatemala, Honduras, Panama, Chile and Nicaragua made it a key determinant of governance, but countries such as Brazil, Argentina, and Uruguay, have powerful indigenous groups that have been able to mobilize popular support for national self-determination.

Assuming that they were faced with the binary choice of support for democracy and possibly significant social reforms, or support for military dictatorship and aristocratic oligarchies (supported by the military) and so the economic status quo, US governments have fairly consistently opted for the latter. I note 'fairly consistently' as, for a brief period in the 1960s, a US government led by a President in John F. Kennedy did attempt to promote circumscribed forms of democracy, if ones that specifically excluded socialist and communist political parties (so in effect any left of centre grouping). Democratic systems that would elect governments whose approach to reform would be gradual and moderate in extent – ambitious pre-election promises were made to the poorest sections of populations whilst post-election delivery would see but very modest, if any, change. Kennedy's attempt to progress this change of approach was embodied in the Alliance for Progress. Measures intended to achieve the same end of protecting US financial interests but by a politically less embarrassing and potentially economically more effective method. A plan initiated by President Kennedy in 1960 as a ten-year, billion-dollar if somewhat vague aid program for economic and social development. Kennedy promoted the idea of a clear link between political freedom and material progress. The 1960s were a time of the masses trying, from a low base, to gain some measure of material progress but even modest attempts at reform were met throughout most of the sub-continent by brutal suppression. In the 1960s military action removed thirteen constitutional governments, to be replaced by dictatorships.

The three years 1989-1991 saw the break-up (disintegration) of the communist bloc in Eastern Europe[47], and so a significant renegotiation of the hegemonic balance of the post-war period of the 'cold war'; including some international realignment of the countries involved. This event had an adverse impact on Cuba's economic situation and further isolated the various guerrilla groups still operating across mainland Latin America. This was a development that contributed to the US public and members of Congress increasingly voicing concern about the nature of US overt and covert intervention in countries to the south. Public confidence in US foreign policy was further undermined by the exposure in the late 1980s of the criminal activities of the Regan administration, in particular the continued funding of the Contras in Nicaragua. Revealed to public scrutiny during the prosecution of Col. Oliver North the Assistant Deputy Director for Political-Military Affairs with the National Security Council. North worked out of the White House and was actively involved in a series of clandestine operations, in particular the illegal diversion of money raised from arms sales to Iran to fund the Contras - ironically termed by North 'Project Democracy'. The personal narrative of Oliver North could serve as an interesting study in showing just how insidiously self-righteous a proportion of US politicians and senior military show themselves to be – North used the

---

[47] Indeed the demise of the last vestiges of 'neo communist' - i.e. never genuinely communist in the Marxist sense - regimes that had pertained in Eastern Europe.

phrase in relation to moral issues that: 'I was authorized to do everything I did' – so covertly arranging the sponsoring of a murderous organization was for North was acceptable because he was, in effect, '….only following orders' - a chilling defence for a military officer given 20th century history.

Funding and other support for the Contras was a particularly nasty aspect of US policy. During the Somoza dictatorship the Nicaraguan National Guard became notorious for brutality with the routine torture, rape, and intimidation of anyone linked to opposition groups, as well as extra-judicial killing of 10s of thousands of civilians. In 1974 President Carter did at last respond to (US domestic) public pressure and belatedly withdrew overt US support for the Somoza regime; indeed the West Point graduate Somoza would later on blame this action for his downfall. But when the sheer weight of internal opposition forced Somoza to leave the country Carter was instrumental in providing US assistance for members of the National Guard fleeing abroad. Many of these being transported in US supplied air-planes carry Red-Cross markings; a war crime in itself - according to the Geneva Convention. Initially based in Argentina then later in Honduras, the US brought various groups together, including remnants of the National Guard, members of the military wing of the right-wing political party Nicaraguan Democratic Union, and anti-Sandinista peasant groups. Offering training and generous financial support as they endeavoured to build a viable anti-Sandinista force in exile. Between 1979 and the early 1990s the Contras launched over 1300 terrorist attacks into Nicaragua. During these incursions the Contras undertook the bombing of gatherings of civilians and carried out attacks on healthcare clinics, along with the targeted murder of healthcare staff, teachers, journalists, and elected local politicians. The US government was well-aware of the Contras strategy of terrorizing the population whilst endeavouring to avoid direct contact with armed Sandinistas. The charity OXFAM, unusually for them, made the cynical observation that the aim of the Sandinista government to improve the living conditions of the mass of Nicaragua's people offered the '…….threat of a good example' to other

Latin American dictatorships. An example of something to be avoided in the view of the US administration. The extent of Contra violence reached a level that even the US Congress could no longer accept and it voted to end all US support for the Contras. But, as was later revealed (noted above), the Regan government continued to use covert (illegal) methods to channel support to the rebels. The US government's behaviour in supporting Somozan regimes and in later organizing and funding the Contras revealed its willingness to disregard some of its own publicly stated principles of governance (especially those related to human rights) in the pursuance of its perception of economic interests and of a wider hegemonic political agenda.

Public concern about involvement and the easing of the cold-war did lead to a marked reduction of US support for more extreme right-wing political parties and to their cessation of training and funding of the most unsavoury Latin American security forces. This, along with indigenous developments - disillusionment with military regimes, the expansion of a more democratically minded middle-class, a somewhat more organized urban working class, and in some countries peasant classes prepared to resist gross exploitation - provided conditions suited to support governance based on multi-party democratic elections. And from the early 1990s military and obviously oligarchic governments were replaced by more representative regimes.

Over the following 20 years countries such as Nicaragua, Venezuela, Brazil, and Argentina, have adopted democratic governments, even if in most the institutional roots of democracy still seem to be worryingly shallow.

In recent years we had the 'Bush Doctrine', based on a policy document, issued in 2002, signalling a significant ramping up of the international declaration of US's assumed entitlement to take military action. An entitlement that had for over a century been a core aspect of its mainly covert, but sometimes overt, modus operandi across the world, would now be official policy and so, (preparing the US people of the justification for action) domestically easier to undertake and to internationally admit to. The role of a right-wing owned US mass media, with its reluctance to seriously challenge the neo-conservative inspired international aggression – following its stated aim of spreading 'liberty and capitalism' throughout the world which, shorn of the deceptive nobility of (high-flown) abstraction and actually applied, means at best closely managed forms of liberty circumscribed within a form of corporate benefit-capitalism. An aim that becomes sinister when considered in terms of its implications.

In 2001 Bush made the absurd threat to the nations of the world that 'Either you are with, us or with the terrorists' - and his assuming the right for America to take pre-emptive military action against any nation it deems to be a potential threat to America. Not just to America as a nation but to 'American interests', for which read financial and corporate interests.

The George W. Bush's Doctrine has its roots in policy initially drafted by two close advisors to his father George Bush Snr. These, Paul Wolfowitz and Lewis Libby (two neo-conservative Defence Department officials), produced a 1992 draft policy document suggesting the need for a new (post cold-war) approach to national security. That America should move from a broad policy of 'containment and deterrence'[48] to one of proactive action. Their draft concluded with the recommendations that:

- 'The United States must remain the world's only superpower, unchallenged by any other nation.
- The United States may need to use pre-emptive force (attack an enemy first) in self-defence.
- The United States will, if necessary, act unilaterally (and alone) to confront and eliminate threats to American security.'

At least George Bush Snr. saw the pointlessly confrontational nature of such a publicly declared change of policy and instructed his Defence Secretary, Dick Chaney, to revise the document and take out

---

[48] A policy that had in practice been over-ridden by the ways in which the US had become pre-emptively involved in a number of South and Central American countries in the preceding decades.

references to 'pre-emptive' and 'unilaterally'. The next President, Bill Clinton, returned policy to that, at least officially, of 'containment and deterrence'. But when George W Bush became president in 2001 he proved to be susceptible to the prompting of aggressive neo-conservative advisors in a group that included Libby, Cheney, Wolfowitz, and Rumsfeld. A susceptibility to preferring aggressive, if simplistic, policies that came naturally to Bush; combined with the opportunistic political assessment that in the post 2001 al-Qaeda attacks on mainland America, the public mood was sympathetic to a more robust approach to foreign affairs. A change of policy set out in the document: 'National Security Strategy of the United States' issued on 20th September 2002.

When I write of US-interests, it can been seen that throughout this extended essay that this encompassing descriptor refers to 'interests' as assessed by an elite group constituted by the US politico-military-industrial-financial-media complex, and those in control of the nexus of vast personal wealth that has accrued to a relatively small cohort of individuals. I identify a distinction between these interests and the interests of the mass of the US nation. The interest of the masses (and indeed I would argue the elites if a longer-term perspective is taken) is in a peaceful, more economically equitable world, a world with environmentally sustainable economic conditions, a world of cooperating rather than competing nations (peoples). Unfortunately, the mass media that interprets the 'world' is owned and controlled by the elites frightened by the prospect of systemic change. Even democratic governance, or rather especially this, is bound to elite interests; historically and currently no-one in the US can become president unless they can generate the 100s of millions of dollars required to run a successful campaign, and it is to big pharma, big agri, big oil, big armaments, and the NRA, and of course the big private investment groups, to which they mostly turn to garner this funding[49]. A clear incentivizing of any would-be and actual administration to

---

[49] In the 2016 presidential election Donald Trump's campaign spent $950m and the Hilary Clinton's campaign spent $1.4bn.

view the interests of these powerful agents as being the operational determinant of 'US interests'. The same power of funding pertains at the state as well as wider (Congress and Senate) national levels. The American system of governance is systemically in hoc to elite interests. When you then put the revolving door of individuals moving from government administration to big business and vice versa, into the power mix, we can see the further interlinking of interests. And of course there are the thousands of lobbyists metaphorically and actually 'tapping on the shoulders' of elected representative to remind them of their obligations and to present them with propaganda (information – in the form of selected facts and figures - and implicit threats in relation to investment at state-level) to both present the best case for a elite-interest supporting policy and to frame the range of narratives on any issue to exclude even moderately radical alternatives.

The electoral public relations 'key' is to manufacture the necessary connections between elite and mass interests - this usually takes the form of threats to employment, to economic opportunity, to healthcare, to 'freedom'..... in general the denial of access to the 'American Dream', unless this or that approach is taken. The management of public relations seen in the way in which the Bush administration managed the terrorist attack on the World Trade Centre and the Pentagon (9/11 2001) - by launching highly profitable, for some, wars in Afghanistan and Iraq. And also its artful management of the 2007/8 financial crash - by massive subsidy to big finance and austerity for the masses; including homelessness for many. A financial bail-out that resulted in a significant increase in long-term debt for the nation. In these two situations the public relations machine of the leading politicians, the mass media, the military, and conventional economic 'experts', can be seen to operate quite effectively on behalf of the elites.

Those in control of the US rely upon a number of entrenched collective behaviour states of the many Americans. A collective mindset involving the inclination of its population to accept the messages of leadership of a narrative expressed in 'Americanese' – a form of political discourse drawing ideas and images from an imagined 'western' past, created by the Hollywood film industry and the mass media, absorbed during childhood being reinforced throughout life. This includes a systemic belief that there is a high-value entity termed the 'American Dream', somehow accessible for Americans as individuals and that this Dream, if attained, can offer personal fulfilment and draw social admiration. It finds embodiment in the US flag and national anthem, being sustained by personal hopes confounded in a socially constructed jingoistic totemic milieu which is the fragile contextual presence within which many American citizens live out their lives.

Of crucial relevance, with the change of international policy, is the assumed right of the US government to be able to decide what and who is a potential threat to some idealized version of the American way of life - in practice, for US-client states this generally means any political (or even religious or social) group campaigning for measures to alleviate the living conditions of the poor and the oppressed. Any nation challenging US military or corporate interests or those of one of its client states would often be placed in the category of 'rogue state'. A category which the Bush Doctrine would then decree to be open to (indeed 'deserve') economic sanctions or even military action - and when this anti-American categorization is signalled the mainstream mass media deals with client and un-American state (especially the 'rogue' states) in very different ways in relation to how news events involving them is reported. Just compare how the US government, and so it mass media, has treated the governments overseeing equally poor conditions of the populations of Venezuela and Honduras – one when the US is seeking to remove the elected leadership (sanctions) the other where it provides support (military).

The US mass media knowingly co-operates, indeed is a central pillar of an elite 'conspiracy' (the conflation of a multi-faceted consensus incorporating the spectrum of elite group self-interest) to deceive the American masses. A media offering a selected type of news and biased interpretation of international events.

Returning to consideration of the Bush Doctrine, its essential points were initially being mentioned as early as 2001 by the Bush regime, later to be clarified in Bush's 2010 memoir published the year after he left office.

They are the following:

1. "Make no distinction between terrorists and the nations that harbour them--and hold `both to account."
2. "Take the fight to the enemy overseas before they can attack us again here at home."
3. "Confront threats before they fully materialize."
4. "Advance liberty and hope as an alternative to the enemy's ideology of repression and fear."

The fourth claim is especially ironic, not to say hypocritical, in the context of US actions with its client states such as El Salvador and Guatemala in South America and those such as Israel, Saudi Arabia, and the smaller Gulf States, in the Middle-East – Unfortunately, while Barak Obama promised much for the gullible in relation to American governance he delivered little (being in hoc to the interests noted above), whereas Donald Trump promised much less and he easily delivered on this. Little surprise given that both Obama and Trump are themselves members of the US elite and also that they were politically dependent on support from the elites in big business and finance.

In the twentieth century alone, nations such as - Russia, China, Britain, Japan, France, Germany, etc. - where they held power, have been little better in terms of brutally pursuing the (hegemonic) self-interest of their own elite groups. The would-be empires of China and Russia have been and are politically controlled by elitist regimes responsible for significant evils. Evil expressed in the relentless repression of their own people, in the imprisonment and killing of members of internal opposition groups, and also in the millions who died due to ideologically generated economic inefficiencies. I have mainly focused on the US because increasingly since 1945 it became the ascendant world power (in terms of military and economic power) and so has the ability to continue to cause great harm or to realize a profound change by creating the conditions for great good to pertain. All three global powers - China, Russia, and the USA - exhibit a marked mismatch between the language of politics in relation to motives and intentions and their actions. But the marked dissonance between rhetoric and action of the US is so wide that a veritable industry of media, PR, and political spokes-people, are employed to produce an endless stream of movies, news interpretations and other types of more sophisticated propaganda intended to mislead.

Conclusion

'The greatest problem for the human species, whose solution compels it to seek, is to achieve a universal civil society administered in accord with the right.'

Immanuel Kant 'Idea for a Universal History with Cosmopolitan Intent' (1784)

So my sweeping if very selective overview of humankind's history suggests a strong tendency to resort to violence to achieve what are primarily elite-group determined ends. In terms of international politics, these ends have been articulated over the past three centuries in progressing or defending some notional entity termed the 'national interest'. My outline has mostly focused on the headline warring but conflict more generally has been a defining characteristic of civil life when elite-group interests have clashed. A steaming brew stirring together elements of greed, ambition, ignorance, and power ill-used. The generating conditions for the tracery of evil that has pervaded the human species time on earth.

It is estimated that in the 5,000 years since the beginning of recorded history, from 3,000 BCE onwards, only about 268 years had no recorded warfare, with 14,300 wars having been fought. Just consider the material destruction and human dislocation, death, and general misery caused by this seemingly systemic collective human behaviour.

In the more modern period we have seen that the twentieth century alone was characterised by destruction – of property, government finance, of lives, and of hopes for humanity's future - in a series of wars interspersed with numerous more localised killing fields as nations - and within nations, ethnically, religiously, or politically, divided groups - clashed on the battlefield and also the on the streets of towns and cities. Is there something deep within the nature of humankind that will invariably find expression in violence? Or are we led into conflict due to institutions of governance and the patterns of international relations, and more generally of global political tropes, inherited from the past, made even more terrible by the advancing technology of weaponry? Provisionally we might assume that elements of both could be involved, and so our focus would be on mitigating the influence of our human nature and reconstructing our inherited civil institutions. In our addressing the twin sources creating the pre-conditions for warfare.

The Janus-faced countenance of our species – a moral side suited to co-operation and peaceful co-existence and a more aggressive side prone to competition and conflict – was clearly seen in conditions of international relations in the first half of the twentieth-century. The utter futility of WW I with its mud-curdling, blood-curdling, insanity followed by the enlightened setting up of the League of Nations (1920) to arbitrate between nations in dispute. The preamble to its constitution noted that its aims were: 1) To promote international co-operation 2) To secure international peace. Aspirations reinforced with the signing of the Kellogg-Briand Pact in 1928 (more formally: 'The International Treaty for the Renunciation of War as an Instrument of National Policy'). Initially based on an agreement arranged between Aristide Briand (French P.M) Frank Kellogg (US Sec. of State) that the two states would agree to renounce war. Given theoretical substance in a multi-lateral agreement signed by: India, Turkey, Germany, U.K., France, Spain, Soviet Union, USA, China, Norway, Canada, Australia, Japan.....and about 50 other countries.

The authority of the LoN was terminally eroded with its attempts to mediate being in effect ignored on a regular basis throughout the 1920s and 30s, and the noble aspirations of the K-B Pact being ignored by the world's most powerful signatory nations as the world was plunged by them into yet another war engulfing much of its population. At this war's end, many European towns and cities were devastated, Japan had been scorched by visitations of hell, and much of the globe was still being argued over by European nations only being at best grudgingly prepared to accept the post-war surge for independence across much of the ex-colonial territories.

At this second global war's end we again see the moral side expressed in the establishment of the United Nations in 1945.

The purposes of which was noted in its constitution as:

'The purposes of the Organization should be:
1. *To maintain international peace and security; and to that end to take effective collective measures for the prevention and removal of threats to the peace and the suppression of acts of aggression or other breaches of the peace, and to bring about by peaceful means adjustment or settlement of international disputes which may lead to a breach of the peace;*
2. *To develop friendly relations among nations and to take other appropriate measures to strengthen universal peace;*
3. *To achieve international cooperation in the solution of international economic, social and other humanitarian problems; and*
4. *To afford a centre for harmonizing the actions of nations in the achievement of these common ends.'*

Then followed about 100 more wars, including India/Pakistan partition, Korea, Vietnam, Afghanistan, Iraq, Iran, Kosovo, Israel/Palestine from 1948 on......actual wars often involving the world's more militarily powerful nations or what were, in effect, proxy wars fought with their support. It seems that we have the wish (and the moral intuition) to realise the futility of warfare and the need for international institutions to prevent these, but powerful elements of national leaderships have considered an easy recourse to violence as being a legitimate way to conduct international relations; to progress their perception of their nation's interest.

The costs of war in just human terms (omitting the massively destructive impact on built and natural environments) is significant, with the two World Wars of the 20th century alone taking 95 million lives (50 million of these being civilians – WWI 20m dead with 10m of these being civilian, WWII 75m dead with 40m of these being civilians). Since WWII came to an end there has only been 2 days when there has been not conflict between at least two nations; these being the 2nd and 28th Sept 1945. Since 1945 warfare has added about another 10m casualties (again disproportionally civilians) - Korea, Vietnam, Algeria, Russian invasion of Afghanistan and Ukraine, Chinese invasion of Tibet, American invasion of Iraq and Afghanistan, etc. In sum: 200 million plus have died as a result of 20th and early 21st century warfare, over half of these being civilians.

Just consider the economic resources poured and continuing to pour into military preparation and the actual expression of international conflict. Today the global spending on the military is running at $2 Trillion per year (2021), with the three highest spending nations being Russia $62 Billion (2021), China $252 Billion (2021), UK $62 Billion (2021), Saudi Arabia $58 Billion (2021 est.), and the USA $778 Billion (2021); these all on rising trends. A waste of resources on a vast scale each and every year – just consider what could be done with such funding for good rather than as preparation for evil in the world.

What sense can there be in young people from different countries, who have themselves never met, coming together with the intention to kill each other? What sense is there in launching missiles, and dropping bombs on cities, towns, and villages, when experience shows that most of the casualties will be non-combatant civilians, including many children? What sense is there in turning civil infrastructures into rubble, farmland into wasteland, and waterways into toxic flows? All being just the more obvious impact of military conflict.

The consequent question to engaging in such a nonsensical activity would be........Whose interests are being served by fostering such inter-nation conflict? Who benefits from our living in a world where international diplomacy is pervaded which an overwhelming aura of between-nation antagonisms and background conditions of aggressive economic competition and political hegemony? I would like to, just briefly, consider some of the more obvious aspects of this question.

In recent centuries the most obvious interest would the vast fortunes made by arms companies, various types of 'security' companies, and invariably financial speculators. Then there are political leaders endeavouring to deflect opposition to domestic economic and/or political failure. Or due to the more insidiously mundane fact that for our current national leaders an alternative perspective (one based more on the longer-term 'interests' of the whole world's people) does not form an aspect of their mindset. Today's leaders have been politically nurtured to interpret international relations primarily in terms of aggressive economic competition and threatened or actual military conflict. This is their psychological 'comfort zone', one infused by an intentional perspective based on assumptions gained during their socialization within this or that, usually quite privileged (elitist) socio/political context. And these represent just the primary interests served by the conflictual milieu that pervades international relations. A crude but clear set of correlations can be made between the decisions taken by national leaders and the means of furthering the interests of their own elite class and in some countries the even more specific interests of their own family.

I wish to focus on international relations here, but of course within-nation civil wars have been and are also significant expressions of evil. In places such as Yemen, Mali, Afghanistan, Somalia, Myanmar, Tigray, DCR, Libya, and Turkey, communities are currently being torn apart by inter-group violence: groups divided by religion, ethnicity, tribalism, or by political ambitions. I would expect that if we can outline a viable alternative to global governance than that which currently pertains, this would also contribute to providing conditions, including political mechanisms, conducive to at least easing within-nation conflict.

If international relations based on sovereign nation-statehood at least pretend to be suitable for overcoming the primary issues facing the world's people then recent history alone suggests that this is a seriously flawed assumption. It probably seems obvious but should we not have aims for world peace, the end of poverty, access to decent healthcare, housing, and education for all being quite minimal aspirations for the world's people. The obviousness stems from the repeat claims made, from at least mid 20th century, by a series of mendacious politicians in whose speeches these aims have had the substance sucked out to become mere husks containing a residue of but empty promises.

And failure in any one of the four critical issues will impact on significant numbers of the global population.

- Environmental degradation.
- Warfare (military conflict), both conventional military engagement and the possibility of nuclear catastrophe.
- A.I. and its implications
- Significant and increasing economic inequality (of more importance, significant poverty).

This text has a focus on warfare but each of these critical elements impacting on our species can be considered as interrelated

An evil activity closely associated with warfare is the act of massacre, sometimes to the point of genocide. And even just the twentieth century saw a series of massacres, a list that began with the Saan, Namaqua, and Herero peoples of West Africa between 1904-08 (about 100,000 killed). Those that followed included: the Armenian massacre of 1915 (1.5m killed); the Nanking atrocities during the second Sino-Japanese war in 1937; the relentless killing (100million) often amounting to massacres...... of service personnel in the sea, air and land battlefields and of civilians in the villages, towns, and cities - especially the Russian military and civilian casualties on the eastern front - the extreme carpet bombing of German and British cities, and equally destructive fire and nuclear bombing of Japan - during the two World Wars; the murderous dictatorships of Stalin, Suharto, and Mao Zedong, the many 'death-squads' tasked with the elimination of those who have opposed dictatorships such as those of Videla (Argentina), Pinochet (Chile) and Somoza (Nicaragua) in South America, and those bands of state-sponsored murderers in Nazi occupied Europe, and more recently in Africa - and the multiple bloody acts of terrorism throughout the century - the 'holocausts' perpetrated by the regimes led by Hitler/Nazis (6m – Europe 1939-45) and Pol Pot/Khmer Rouge (1m - Cambodia/Kampuchea 1976-79); the communal strife killing over 1 million during the birth of India and Pakistan in 1947; the killing fields of Rwanda with 800,000 people massacred in but 100 days of 1994.

Then there are what were in effect massacres of populations due to indifference, including the millions that died due to famines in Russia, India, China, and Eastern Africa, in a world of sufficient food; the estimated (UNICEF) 1.5 million children who do not reach the age of 5 annually due to vaccine preventable diseases (over 4,000 per day), with another 1200 dying each day of malaria and 2 million children dying each year of diseases contracted due to contaminated water.........and the too many similar macro expressions of avoidable evil together representing the very bleakest aspect of humanity. A systemic evil with effective foundations in global economic and political arrangements.

In part, a sense of collective amnesia perhaps induced by disaster overload – we are (or choose to be) but impotent witnesses as history unfolds in shapes determined by the more powerful in ways strongly influenced by the past. We, being more passively entertained than actively informed by brief if repeated exposure to vivid media imagery and conventionally impotent interpretations. Interpretations that only make sense within the artfully constructed frameworks of our own social relativities.

Milan Kundera tellingly notes how news of each new atrocity

obscures the preceding one '.......as so on and so forth until ultimately everyone lets everything be forgotten.'[50]

The generalized socialization processes to which we are subject, including any society's normalized value system not only influences how we view events but also offer some assumed context for how these events are presented to us by political and economic interests and by the media; the power-bases of modern society. When individuals, whether they be Hitler, Stalin, Pol Pot, or Suharto, or more recently Saddam Hussein, Radovan Karadžić, Bashar al-Assad, and Vladimir Putin, are in fact but elements of the – historical, social, economic, political - conditions in which any evil is expressed. Psychotic individuals might well play a key role in an evil action but it is systemic dysfunction in governance that allows them to rise to positions of power.

In evil acts such as the carpet bombing of the German city of Dresden or the fire-bombing of the Japanese city of Tokyo in 1945 or the spraying of the toxic defoliant Agent Orange over farmlands and villages in Vietnam in the late 60s and early 70s, most 'westerners' would be reluctant to classify Britain's then Prime Minister Winston Churchill, or the then US Presidents Franklin D. Roosevelt, Lyndon B. Johnson and Richard Nixon, as psychopaths. And yet the outcomes of their decision-making – the killing of thousands of non-combatant, men, women, children, babies - were surely pure evils.

Eric Hobsbawm noted that in relation to the 20th century: '...more human beings had been killed or allowed to die by human decision than ever before in history.' He references an estimate of 187 million killed up to 1993 made by Z. Brezezinski (Brezezinski 1993, cited in Hobsbawn, 1995, p12).

Twentieth-century conflicts have more often involved neighbouring countries. With obvious current between-nation disputes being:

---

[50] Cited in J.Glover, 2001, p4 – the original being Kundera's 'The Book of Laughter and Forgetting', 1982.

India/Pakistan - China/Japan - China/USA - NATO/Russia – Russia/Ukraine - Palestine/Israel – Serbia/Kosovo - China/Taiwan - Venezuela/Honduras – Armenia/Azerbaijan - USA/Iran. And in addition a range of civil wars, with the more significant being; Libya, Yemen, Turkey (Kurds), Mali, Burkina Faso, Niger, Mozambique, Syria, Somalia, Ethiopia. These too many situations with the potential for minor, border or other, clashes to escalate into more significant, even possibly nuclear confrontation. In any conflict between antagonists heavily invested in complex computer-based technology there is also the potential for error.

Even during periods of the hegemonic normality of international relations the danger of escalation is an ever-present possibility - As recently as June 2021 HMS Defender, a British warship was on passage through the Black Sea, off Cape Fiolent on the Crimean coast, in what the UK considers to be international waters but Russia views as being within its own territorial waters. A Russian coastguard vessel moved to intercept the warship and a number of Russian S24 jet aircraft flew low over the ship. There were different claims, not just on the legitimacy of the passage, but also on the context of the confrontation. Whoever ordered HMS Defender to take the route it did (and conveniently took the highly unusual step of inviting a number of journalists to join the voyage) was well aware of the potential for confrontation. Globally, these sort of hostile/provocative contacts seem to happen on a fairly regular, pretty much 'tit for tat', basis by countries in dispute over some aspect of their assumed sovereignty.

We might ask why British warships would be exercising in the Black Sea, or why the Russians have increased their own activity in the Arctic Sea. No doubt part of the general provocative activity engaged in by both 'sides'; the military element of hegemonic diplomacy. We might even pose the question..... why 'sides' in a world we share?

And of course – similar types of provocation (brinksmanship) are regularly engaged in by other nations: China and Japan with islands in the south-Chinese Sea, China and Taiwan, India and Pakistan over

Kashmir, North Korea with South Korea and Japan, Ukraine and Russia over the Crimean Peninsula and more recently the whole of the Donbas region. With most neighbouring unfriendly states undertaking intentionally provocative sabre-rattling military manoeuvres in their border regions.

For egoistic nation-states, the narrowing politico/military mindset leads to easily making threats and issuing warning that are difficult to draw back from. The current language deployed in international relations is suited to contributing to quite easily transforming an issue into a crisis and on to escalate into open conflict.

Conventional warfare has been truly terrible......wasting lives, spreading misery, degrading environments, and using vast amounts of economic resources that could have been available to do good rather than evil. We now also live within the shadow of thermonuclear warfare and a sense that it could begin imminently, as the many more local conflicts involving nuclear powers progress incrementally and irrationally to the highest level of politico/military tensions.

Such are the weapons now available that the next global conflict could see the elimination of millions within but a few days of a nuclear exchange and with a global environment unable to support human (or much other) life. And for sure, if we continue with the same malfunctioning – competitive, conflictual, and hegemonic – international system, and do not adopt some form of global governance in relation to international conflict, it is highly likely that such an exchange will soon engulf us.

Just nine of the world's 210 countries together hold a sufficiency of nuclear weapons to render our planet uninhabitable for human life.

As of 2023 there are a total of about 12,700 nuclear warheads in store or readied for use. These to be carried by bombers parked at military airports, at sea on aircraft carriers, by intercontinental missiles nestled in numerous deeply buried silos sited across the continents, and in nuclear armed submarines on continuous patrol in the silent depths of the world's oceans.

The atomic warhead – 'Little Boy' - used to destroy the Japanese city of Hiroshima in August 1945 had an explosive power equivalent to 15,000 tons of TNT. The US has tested and deployed warheads such as the one named 'Castle Bravo', with an explosive power equivalent to 15 megatons of TNT, so 1,000 times more powerful than the bomb used at Hiroshima. The Russia has tested and deployed a warhead named the 'TSAR Bomba' with an explosive power of a staggering 50 megatons, so equivalent to 3,300 times the power of the Hiroshima warhead. 'TSAR Bomba' has a killing zone of 1,000 kilometres from the initial blast and potentially lethal levels of radiation as clouds drifting way beyond this. There has over the past 70 odd years been a veritable escalation in a macabre competition between the world's leading nations to find the means of killing as many human beings – men, women, children and babies - as possible. And of course in doing so they are, via the attempt to maintain a balance of mutually assured destructive power (MAD), also increasing the threat to their own peoples.

We have been exposed to images of mushroom-like clouds rising serenely over unseen terrain – from which we can hardly gain any realistic sense of just what the cloud represents in human terms. For Britannica (online – 23/05/2022): 'When a nuclear weapon detonates a fireball occurs with temperatures similar to those at the centre of the Sun.'

Within the first minute of an initial explosion about 85% of the thermonuclear energy released is air pressure blast and thermal radiation and about 15% is in the form of radiation 'clouds'. The air pressure blast expresses itself as a nuclear fireball that explodes at ground zero and in seconds would expand out to engulf the surrounding land for hundreds of miles around. Almost all life within the immediate killing zone is burnt off the face of the earth within a couple of minutes, but the highly ionised radiation then forms a nuclear wind that will drift way beyond the immediate killing zone, to degrade the environment and inflict often fatal doses of radiation sickness as it spreads. The immediate killing zone for a single thermonuclear device could easily destroy a city the size of London, New York, Moscow, Islamabad, Mumbai, Buenos Aires, Mexico

City, Jakarta, Manila, Tokyo, Jerusalem, Jerusalem, Paris, Beijing, Pyongyang, and leave their extensive hinterlands as but radiation wind-blown wastelands.

If just 1% of the currently held nuclear warheads were to be used (so a 'relatively' low-level exchange) the likely desolation impacting beyond the immediate killing zone would lead to 2 billion people dying of starvation as a result of a global famine caused by the ensuing nuclear winter.

A more significant and probably more realistic scenario of conflict between Russia and the US would be the exchange of about 3,000 warheads (Russia has 4,477 warheads readily available and the US has 3,708). The explosive energy released would generate millions of tons of soot rising into the atmosphere, this happening within but 6 minutes, would reduce the amount of sunlight reaching the earth's surface to about 35% of current amounts. Consequently, the earth would enter a nuclear induced winter lasting for decades, during which food production would be cut by about 90%. Within two years 75% of the world's population will be dead and those that remain will be living on an irradiated planet with conditions inducing, still births, deformed babies, and a veritable eruption in the number of cancers for decades on.

Of the nine currently nuclear-armed nations, each has an identified 'enemy' to threaten and to be threatened by. All of the global nuclear powers are involved in some level of inter-nation tension that highlights the possible costs in human terms of allowing an issue to escalate into armed conflict and so the potential to progress to a nuclear exchange if one side appears to be 'losing'. And the losing will be judged as such by egocentric leaders who will themselves be safely ensconced deep underground in well-provisioned nuclear shelters when they launch a nuclear Armageddon.

These same leaders who are at least assumed to be tasked to protect the populations they represent currently allow international conditions to pertain that are based on conflictual and competitive relationships rather than on the recognition of mutual interests – their primary interest should surely be the maintenance of peace.

However sophisticated are the measures designed to prevent an accidental launch of these fearsome weapons the risk of human, or more likely technical, error remains. Since 1950 there have been 32 documented accidents involving nuclear weapons (and these only the ones known of in a context of obsessive secrecy – coded as 'national security') – these 'broken arrow' events highlight the risks involved in maintaining such weaponry.

In the 1960s the world was taken to the brink of nuclear war over the Cuban Missile Crisis, an egocentric argument over the siting of Russian missiles on the Caribbean Island of Cuba (the US already had nuclear-armed missiles sited in Turkey, close to the Russian border). – We know that some US generals were arguing for a first strike nuclear launch, I think that we can fairly assume that Russian generals have been doing similar urging of their political leadership, and we can be certain that if one side launched then so would have the other - millions killed, extensive infrastructure damage. Because two nations were engaged in a macabre provocation/reaction diplomatic game the consequences of which could have been far in excess of any rational evaluation of the issue.

As US President Ronald Regan and USSR President Mikhail Gorbachov agreed when they met in 1985 'A nuclear war cannot be won and must never be fought'. And yet the leadership of both nations have continued to prepare for just such an event as each nation continued to build its nuclear strike capability.

In a context of rising military tension, mutual suspicion, inflated egos of the politico/military leadership, a wide range of true and falsified information to be evaluated and this continuously added to the mix as well as numerous 'what if' scenarios having to be considered - consequently we have politicians and the heads of armed services being potentially overwhelmed by streams of information and having to assess competing pressures from an aggressive military and more moderate advisors whilst having to assess streams of often new and usually quite complex information – the emotions could easily come to override any rational decision-making. We can see a reflection of this during the 1960s Cuban missile crisis (noted above) where, if a significant nuclear exchange had occurred as a result of the Russians sitting missiles on the island of Cuba, then potentially hundreds of millions of civilians would have been killed in initial the strikes, with hundreds of millions more dying during subsequent years from burns and radiation poisoning – whereas even if missiles had been sited on Cuba (as the US itself had already sited missiles in Turkey within a few miles of the Russian border) this would not have any significant impact on the defence or attack capability of each superpower. The mutually assured destruction (MAD) balance would have been maintained.

So whilst, if we step back we can accept the sheer irrationality of thermonuclear confrontation, we would, at least in the short-term need to introduce some protection, some 'trip switch' to prevent an immediate decision to launch missiles due to politico/military agents reacting emotionally in the heat of escalating confrontation and of information overload as an event plays out rather than stepping back to take decisions in a calmer setting. And bear in mind that the extensive – global – impact of a thermonuclear exchange would include the possible extinction of humanity and indeed of most other mammalian life on earth.

The necessary 'trip-switch' could be embodied in a form of international governance. Just a no first strike commitment would be something. But even better would be a commitment of the nine nuclear-armed nations to allow the Head of (a reformed) UN to order a suspension of verbal exchanges and any conflict on the ground that is escalating towards a potentially immediate uplift to the nuclear. This to allow a pause in confrontation and so a chance to recalibrate the response to what has been assessed by each side as aggressive action by the other party.

Many of the World's leaders and senior military just do not seem to get what Mutually Assured Destruction actually means.

The threat of nuclear conflict is real, with the major powers still, even post START (began 1980s), bristling with nuclear weaponry in conditions of rumbling international conflicts, each with the potential to conflagrate into warfare. Even relatively lowly nuclear armed

Britain has access to some formidable weaponry – it has a nuclear fleet composed of four Trident submarines each armed with 16 missiles, each one of which is eight times as powerful as the weapon dropped on Hiroshima in 1945. With this weaponry alone Britain has the capability to destroy 64 major cities within 7,500 miles of its mobile craft. There is an estimated 10,200 nuclear warheads in the hands of the World's military. That's over 10,000 of the world's cities that can be totally destroyed – with the loss of hundreds of millions of lives in an immediate exchange and no doubt similar numbers subsequently dying from radiation sickness, and many more from the extensive damage that would be done to civic infrastructure and to the world's environment.

More generally, the technology of war-making is progressively involving artificial intelligence – advanced drone technology, robotics, and other computer-based innovation has been a primary feature if 21st century life. The world's military has sought to both drive this advance and ensure that it can be applied to battlefield weapon systems, intercontinental missile design, and intelligence gathering.

The advance of all forms of artificial intelligence are developing at an accelerating pace, primarily driven by the search for evermore financial profit, by the military itself, and by governments and security companies seeking the means for ever greater observation and control over populations. The potential human benefits are merely used to 'sell' the idea to populations rather than these actually leading the development and control of the technology. Conflict, in its planning, preparation, and engagement, is becoming evermore reliant on types of A.I. So a potential source or real harm to human beings. (see Appendix 3 'Artificial Intelligence: a possible scenario', for more on this)

The journey through some of the history of conflict outlined in this book has identified that a most critically obvious feature of conflict is 'difference'. Of one group of people.... be it tribe, clan, class, ethnic group, religion, nation, or federation of these, identifying another group as being different and possibly holding to views on an issue that differ from their own. The evolutionary mode of self-consciousness tends towards favouring the world-view and more general descriptive and explanatory tropes of one's own group and rejecting or being suspicious of alternatives expressed by outsiders – the 'others'. There does seem to be a natural propensity to auto-consciously gravitate towards within-group identity. At times the theoretically neutral acceptance of difference can become antagonist and even to escalate into conflict. Throughout civil history ruling elites have known how to manipulate this seemingly natural propensity toward 'othering' via the fostering of suspicion, and the use of propaganda and other forms of persuasion. Underlying any group difference is of course a unity in our shared species identity and if we are to find an alternative to intergroup conflict, not least warfare, we need to design ways to socialise people into transcending the relativity of group identity (more often an accident of time and place of birth).

Nation-statehood (along with religion) is probably the most powerful, and currently for the World the most dangerous, entity fostering the identification of difference between peoples. Difference being the basic originating marker of separation that so easily spreads and erupts into the pathological fault-lines upon which conflict between peoples is founded. States and Nations are different concepts – the concept of state merely represents some form of political sovereignty over a geographic area, whereas the concept of nation most often includes this but in addition we invariably have an archly selective version of history, usually a common language, and all the other social and economic elements that constitute the 'imagined community' noted by Benedict Anderson (1983). You can have nations without statehood as in the pre-Israel Jewish Diaspora, The Kurdish peoples, and certain Moslems sects which believe in a global Ummah where the gravitational pull of Islam draws in some primary characteristics of nationhood traditionally treated as secular.

It might seem to be obvious, but at least one group has to see a difference between themselves and another group for conflict to ensue. And nation-statehood (as well as tribe, caste, class, religion, and ethnicity more generally) is a seemingly automatic marker of difference that we are each born into – and within which we are subjected to the powerful socialization processes that are (implicitly and explicitly) designed to emphasize the good aspects of one's own country and the bad aspects of others. The inherited form that relationships between nation-states have taken is of competition and conflict rather than cooperation and an enlightened acceptance of mutually shared interest. Any between nation-state co-operation has been more about gaining support for competing with another nation or groupings of these, or part of some superficial pretence of some common values.

We have inherited an international political and economic system that assumes conflict and competition but can we learn to re-set how we live together as nations? Is there an alternative way of organizing international relationships? Or is humanity condemned forever to drag the divisive political and economic institutions created in conditions of greed, aggression, avarice, suspicion and fear, into the future? When from the earliest time of civil life such conditions being primarily promoted by elite groups and subsequently maintained by their descendants and others who have since joined the elites. If 'forever' might be dramatically foreshortened by human species extinction...... perhaps in some nuclear conflagration or due to making the world's environment progressively unable to sustain a viable human population.....or even a combination of these. The point being that if conflict, tipping into warfare, is based on choices, individual and collective, then there is always the option to choose peace rather than war. We can, at least potentially, find an alternative way to live together. A key element if we aspire to some form of peaceful world governance would be the need to address the role (purpose) of the nation-state.

Nation states in their modern types are a relatively recently established form of political organization (for Jürgen Habermas 1969, p109, 'State and nation have fused into the nation-state only since the revolutions of the late eighteenth century.'), with institutions effectively designed by generations of elite groups. Those who, as a class, have accumulated both hard and soft power to themselves. Institutions designed in their own perceived interests, as aided initially by the printing press and national education systems each contributing to creating and spreading the use of common versions of national languages, and assumed national histories. And more recently aided by a xenophobic mass media controlled according to corporate interests, often as guided by billionaire owners who assume the privilege to interpret news and produce info- and enter-tainment in line with their own reactionary political views. Mass populations, from earliest childhood until old age, are now being drenched with information in forms redolent of the competitive, conflictual, mindset that determines international relations. The mendacious construction of external enemies can be used to reinforce control by elite groups over national populations.

Obedience, at times jingoistic enthusiasm, has more often been realised as the default behaviour of the masses, so allowing divisions to be fostered by elite groups able to gain advantage from this fracturing of the potentially unifying resources available for the masses - resources that include the potential to transcend national borders which were afterall mostly only created on the basis of fiefdoms of local or regional exploitation.

The world's peoples' have over the last 500 years been progressively and artificially divided ('separated') into nation-states, each with a range of ideas that congeal to create some assumed sense of a 'national interest' which can include the economic (markets and resources), claimed territorial rights, and a self-reflective (too often oversensitive) national ego saturated in selected versions of history.

The early civil history of political organization, circa 3,000 BCE, was characterised by city-states as circumscribed units of centralized power; if with some at times expedient regional confederations of these. As certain cities, or federations, became more powerful (in terms of ambitious leaderships and surplus material resources available to equip and support armies) they sought to expand their control, and more widely their hegemonic influence. This in places developed into empires, some more prominent ones have been: Mesopotamian, Macedonian, Mauryan, Roman, Islamic, Gupta, Han, Inca, Aztec, Mogul, Axum, Benin, British, Ottoman, and Hapsburg. Empires, each constituted by a multiplicity of ethnic groups, with most being run by an elite section of a dominant one of these.

In addition to the contribution of both printing in promoting national languages and the development of national education systems, to the formation of nation-states noted above, the $15^{th}/16^{th}$ century voyages of 'discovery', and associated mapping of the world, provided a territorial perspective serving to provide graphic representation of potential areas of trading or more directly controlling interests (exploitation). The processes of forming the large volunteer or, from about the 1790s conscripted, military units developed to fight European wars, also contributed to forming national mythologies – with impressive statues and other monuments constructed to remind populations of this archly edited past. These, and some other less obvious processes, created the cloying notion of a national identity which could then generate the idea of some 'national interest' and for providing some assumed justification for an aggressive approach to foreign policy.

Noam Chomsky (2012, p196) noted the 'national interest' as being a form of nation-state international perspective that is something '....abstracted from [the] distribution of domestic power.'
So highlighting how this national interest is created in any country primarily to reflect elite group priorities – those who have domestic power. Be they from: corporations, the mass media, the military, landed aristocracy, political groupings, oligarchs, religious leaders, financiers, speculators and the armies of lobbyists (and Franz Fanon's other types of modern 'bewilderers') who so determinedly represent them.

The European types of nation statehood provided models to be adopted, if more-often only awkwardly adapted to local circumstances, by ruling groups across the world. And, primarily for European elites, nationalism became an artful means of legitimising imperial expansion and exploitative forms of colonialism. It was the

European nation states, increasing influenced by powerful merchants and financiers that enthusiastically engaged in a shameless international conflict over land, trading rights, and other resources in the Americas, the Middle and Far East and, by the 18th century, Africa. European nation-states were created in conditions of military conflict, economic exploitation, and often violent between-nation competition over trading rights and in seeking primary resources. It was these intentional elements that served as core determinants constructing national institutions and shaping the approach taken to foreign policy. The perception of the world as being there for the taking, assuming competition over valued goods in what were assessed as being a zero-sum game, with each nation determined to gain as big a share of the bounty as possible. Seeking to advance its elite constructed notions of national self-interest, at whatever cost in sweat, blood, and lives, to indigenous peoples.

It is the 19th and 20th versions of strategic military, economic, and diplomatic, strategies based on systemically operative notions of national self-interest primarily serving the interests of elite groups that have set the scene for today's international political arrangements. Arrangements, prominent in which are the more powerful 'empires of influence' (China, USA, and Russia, today) – if underlying these there is the dislocated empire of global finance. All of the world's people are now inveigled within a global conspiracy of assumed division.

Up to about 1500 C.E. by far the majority of the world's people, even within empires, had lived their lives within an identity based on the quite local and in accepting the power (control) of some more regional or city-based hierarchy with a variety of types of feudal lord or chieftain at its head. In Europe, it was from this class of lordships and chieftains, along with a wider aristocratic class, that sought to dominate the earliest of states being formed during the almost continuous conflict that characterised medieval Europe. By the end of the sixteenth century much of Europe had been divided into individual 'states' run by elite groups, gaining authority by assumed heredity rights, by the power of arms, and by the disinterested or fear driven obedience of the peoples they sought to exploit.

International politician–led diplomacy has been characterised by a dysfunctional trope compounding suspicion, power, greed, and aggression. This is our heritage of international politics. Even in a simple form we can understand how symptoms of the consequent disfunctionality can be quite easily identified in various international incidents and in their variable interpretation by the nations involved.

I want to digress to just briefly consider the idea of elite groups due to my using this concept as conceptual shorthand for the powerful national and international groupings of people that are able to deploy power and so garner material and social rewards significantly beyond those of most people. Simple national-based elite groups would be constituted by different proportions of individuals drawn from top civil servants, politicians, prominent agents in the financial sector, top criminals, business people, large land and property owners, and senior members of the military and security services, religious leaders; and, as a generalization, the wealthy. Nation-based groups of these more obviously competing against each other on many inter-national affairs but perversely also cooperating to protect and advance interlinked personal interests on a global scale. At times and on certain issues they are fully aware of the value (not least in controlling national populations) of selectively emphasizing competition even with the associated risk to their own nation's well-being (indeed in a nuclear age their very existence) but they are also aware of the intertwined aspects of their personal economic interests.

Sections of these elites have been various termed such as: Oligarchs (Russia and eastern Europe), Crony Capitalists (most obviously of sub-Saharan Africa and South America and the Far East), Aristocrats, War-lords, Mafia-type cartels and Cybercriminals, The Party, The State, the Davos class, the Business Roundtables, Plutocrats, Top bankers, speculators, and Hedge fund managers; in sum the Ruling Classes as a generality.

Any specific boundary that separates an elite group from the rest is usually quite difficult to determine, unless using crude, if often perhaps instrumentally quite useful, wealth and/or power-holding position. As the politically reactionary philosopher Plato was aware 2,400 years ago, there has to be some capacity in any hierarchical politico/economic system for 'bright' (so potentially disruptive) individuals to ascend from the masses to the elite. Suffice to note that, even given potentially permeable masses/elite-group boundaries, there are significant barriers to joining any elite (including at least some acceptable degree of conformity to the dominant ideology); if in most countries today the ability to become wealthy in itself usually serves as an elite group ticket. It was U.S. President Eisenhower (himself an elite-group member) who on leaving office warned of the power of the Military-Industrial-Complex and the danger of its progressing its own institutional interests even where this conflicts with a wider national interest.

So elite groups progressing both institutional and personal interests as they and their precursors have more or less strongly contributed to the design and identified the purpose of any institution be it political, military, business, media, finance, criminal, intellectual, or religious. There is a considerable commonality of institutional and personal interest of those in control. And it is the control (power) aspect of elites that is of fundamental relevance for global governance and economic conditions.

As with a number of collective concepts used in this book that of 'elite' is not intended to circumscribe an easily bounded collectivity. I can't offer a ridged definition of what can seem to be an amorphous body, rigidly fixed at its core, but with an element of ever-changing personnel at its margins. A body that at a national level can, on very rare occasions, be subjected to revolutionary change.

Twentieth-century sociology has seen a number of attempts to define and consider elites within a debate stimulated by Marx's conception of classes and Weber's of interest-groups; with useful contributions. initially from V.Parato, G.Moscha, M.Kolabinska, and later C.Wright-Mills and T.B.Bottomore.

For the economically developed countries elite-group homogeneity has included selective forms of education experienced by most elite-group members themselves and for their children. For elite-groups in the economically developing countries this aspect of elitism has been the experience of elite-groups members often being educated abroad. An exclusive education is usually but one (if very important) aspect, along with the family milieu and normative acceptance of hierarchy in any social setting, of psychological preparation for elite-group membership. This privileged intermixing also lays the basis for the accumulation of the very important 'social capital' that will help to facilitate a person's transition from privileged childhood, through gilded youth, into an elite-group power-position. A commonly implicit intention of elite group socialization being to instil a sense of justified entitlement – of any individual being a member of a privileged grouping due to some innate set of abilities (some superior faculties) rather than the set of social and economic advantages that have provided a conducive framework for their upbringing. Social intermixing, marriage, kinship obligations, and occupational networking, allow opportunities to gain reinforcement for a shared interpretation of their own experience and affirmation for their privileged position. Individuals each situated within a tangled density of interrelated social capital and economic advantages from which they can draw.

If it is difficult to define the minimum qualifications required for inclusion in any elite, the necessary conditions for membership are at least sufficiently clear for my purposes. The notion of elite will serve as a useful heuristic for understanding the operation of power in our world; and it is power than matters. I am sure that any citizen of any of the world's countries would be able to recognize the members of the elite running their own land, and so their own country's participatory ties to global power[51].

---

[51] In the African country of Tanzania, the second half of the twentieth century saw the rise of a wealthy elite popularly known as the 'wabenzi', or 'people of the Benz' due to their liking for luxury Mercedes Benz motor cars. Similar nouveau-rich groupings have arisen in many post-colonial settings –and whilst their wealth and associated conspicuous consumption is only indirectly relevant to elite control the power they hold over both governments and national economic systems is of vital relevance.

Elite groups, representing a privileged layer of individuals located at the political, judicial, economic, criminal, and social status apex of any hierarchically stratified society, have been a defining characteristic of civil life since its inception – initially as aristocratic, religious and military. The 19th, 20th, and 21st centuries have seen the emergence of financial, political, criminal, business, and media elites, that to some extent have displaced the more traditional types of power holders.

I would concede that, in the absence of some system of effective bottom-up participatory governance, mass societies do need some political and administrative 'leadership'. But of more relevance to my own considerations the core issue is…… in whose interest any elite group wields the political and economic power it has been able to accumulate and so deploy.

As early as 1956 the perceptive social scientist C. Wright-Mills, referring to the US power-elite, noted that 'As the means of information and power are centralized, some men come to occupy positions in American society from which they can look down upon, so to speak, and by their decisions mightily affect, the everyday worlds or ordinary men and women.'

And even more so in the twenty-first century it is naked wealth rather than prestige or other forms of social status that generate power; for Raoul Martinez (2017, p224): 'The more wealth a person controls, the greater their capacity to determine the [our] future.'

If the global elite is comprised of about 5% of the population of 7/8 billion, then we have about 400 million individuals with (relatively) disproportionate access to power. A significant proportion of these would be voluntarily disengaged from active participation in politics, finance, business, or the military. Such a proportion qualifying for elite group membership by wealth alone, prepared to concede control of their source of potential power (wealth) to various (institutional) investment managers; be these CEOs of companies or to managers of hedge or other types of investment fund. Their being a leisured class of rentiers set within the wider elites. These are of little interest to my own analysis as, although they operate via a mostly parasitic relationship with society, their place in any country (especially their various tax avoidance schemes) could quite easily be reformed.

So, leaving these groups aside, we can then identify a body of about 200 million individuals. At the top of global: politics, finance, business, religious, media, crime, and the military (a seven-fold power nexus). These – the actual 'rulers of the world'- in effect interpret the past and set the political and economic conditions within which we all live.

If there is any relevance to the accusation of elite conspiracy it would be more in terms of small discrete groups (e.g. some generously funded alt-right US groups, the inner cabinet of one-party dominated states, the large hedge and vulture funds, religious leaders, along with co-ordinate groups of currency speculators, and in some developing countries the military cliques) rather than some interlinked process of wide-spread, internationally coordinated, planning. But if outcomes are considered we would at least be able to identify the extent of the conjunction of approach taken by sections of the global elite's quite obvious pursuance of its own self-interest. The current situation of group members experiencing similar socialization processes and having a shared (if fairly broad) social and economic ideology, means that conspiracy-type co-ordination is unnecessary as the 'hidden hand' of these 200 million individual decision-makers, designing and adjusting institutions in their perception of their own interests reveals an unplanned but convenient coordination of purpose – the not so 'hidden hand' of elite-group activities has produced a significant shift in wealth and control over the past 30-40 years, with any improvement in the living conditions of sections of the masses being but a by-product of elite group individual and institutional activity. Direct co-ordination is unnecessary where intentionality is shared and key institutions have been designed to facilitate these intentions.

This un-conspired co-ordination receives continuous reinforcement, not just in terms of financial success but also from the collegiate/clubable nature of family, friends, and associates, coming together – elite group members are enmeshed within a nexus of self-affirmation and specialized sense of entitlement; with the egos of leading representatives being stroked by a mass-media created sense of public admiration and normalized approval. For T.B.Bottomore (1964, p130): 'The major inequalities in society are in the main social products, created and maintained by the institutions of property and inheritance, of political and military power, and supported by particular beliefs and doctrines.'

Even as early as mid nineteenth century Marx identified a monopoly on the control of the '……production of ideas' as being an important factor in maintaining the dominance of the ruling class. A combination of media persuasion, intellectual justification, and the tendency of populations towards obedience, have supported and provided ideas that conveniently serve elite interests. The media tends to dumb down complexity (rather than clarify this), suppresses information on viable economic and political alternatives to the status quo, and more generally takes a patronizing view of the masses.

As the neo-liberal economist Friedrich von Hayek noted (Hayek, 'The Road to Serfdom' 1944): '….the great majority are rarely capable of thinking independently ……on most questions they accept views which they find ready-made.' - a view pretty much shared with Adolf Hitler and noted in his book Mein Kampf.

For C. Wright-Mills ('The Power Elite', 1956, p3): '…..they [the 'Power Elite] are in command of the major hierarchies and organizations of modern society. They rule the big corporations. They rule the machinery of state and claim its prerogatives. They direct the command posts of the social structure, in which are now centred the effective means of the power and wealth and celebrity which they enjoy.'

A celebrity daily reinforced at the local level during their smoothed passage through the exclusive hotels, clubs, restaurants, first class air and train travel, the T.V. studios, plush conference centres, and luxury shopping outlets serving to pamper the wealthy; all emphasize their specialness, and provide some comfortable distance from the masses. They can experience the continuous flattery of a large service class closely attuned to their needs – the turned heads and admiring (if perhaps often covetous) glances of some of the public as the privileged glide by in expensive cars, yachts, and private jets. A group defined for the public more by their conspicuous consumption, and seemingly glamorous lifestyles, rather than by how they are able to fund this and the contribution their economic and political activities might make to the wider social good.

Such is the growing dysfunctional social impact of increasing economic inequality that the wealthy increasingly seek the security and distance of gated estates, and private security groups, as parts of some cities become ever more dystopian terrains of disadvantage than the relatively integrated communities that many had once been.

But the serious issue for my own purpose is the assumed right of a relatively small number of the world's people – most of whom begin life with significant social and economic advantages, as will their own children – to wield political and/or economic power and, for what any even-handed consideration of the evidence would suggest, by progressing their own interests. My own use of the term 'elite' is as a heuristic device employed to encompass the relatively small national groups and conjoined global groupings that in effect 'rule our world'.

A significant source of division (and so evil) has been an outcome of historical events mostly re-presented in ways from the partial and narrow to the invented and malign - and these have formed the narratives of imagined injustice and oppression upon which tribal, ethnic, religious, and national hatreds have been secured - the insidious group-specific collective memories of but partial facts set in narrative contexts structured according to motivations too often projecting difference in terms of suspicion, competition, and more general antagonism.

Throughout civil history elite-groups would not have been able to deploy power to malign ends without the World's people being divided. And now I touch on a key aspect of ethnic, tribal, and national, types of group memory that is of crucial relevance to our future. Given what we know of human psychology and human history, as this impacts on inter-group relations, we can be fairly confident that none of today's identifiable collectivities, be it tribe, ethnic group, clan, religion, or nation, has a history free of evil perpetrated by its ancestors. It is extremely doubtful that human inter-group relations have been peaceful for more than a relatively short time.

In some locations groups may have made accommodations that have at least contained intergroup violence, showing that intergroup conflict is not inevitable. Peaceful co-existence can be negotiated if conditions of agreed fairness, trust, and mutual good-will pertain. But history is replete with massacres, genocides, raiding for women or other valued resources, ethnic cleansing, enslavement of others, conflict over water and over hunting territory, pastures or otherwise fertile farmland, gross economic exploitation, the destruction of neighbouring town or cities, religious conflict, and of course nation-based warfare. And this only externally directed evils – internally, few groupings have refrained from persecuting the different, the rebel, the otherwise awkward individual or minority

. My selective outline has been primarily about the history of warfare with an increasing focus on the US and Europe. This due to the significant influence of these areas over the last two centuries, as today's global political/economic system was being established. The politico/economic interests of these countries (as formulated but national elite groups) has been a significant determinant on how the global economic system and international political relationships have come to be constructed and so conducted – with these being competitive (economics) and conflictual (as in international political relationships).

It is of fundamental importance for the future that we recognise that indigenous peoples of all the habitable continents have been involved in on-going conflict and at times organized warfare from long before any contact with western nations. Historical events must be acknowledged but we are alive today and if the world is to work toward a peaceful future then the contested past has to be left there. Today's conflictual issues, such as: Palestine/Israel, India/Pakistan China/Taiwan Iran/US, Russia/NATO Kurds/Turkey, Yemen, Ethiopia, Sahel, Myanmar, etc etc... each need to be considered in today's forums of just global governance and assessed according to human rights and group self-determination as set out it in terms similar to the UN Charter.

The ancestors of all nations and most ethnic groups have been involved in the perpetration of evil whether as warfare, or indeed most also as in slavery. The interpretation, of facts and implications, of each conflictual event are liable to irresolvable contestation. If we want to create a peaceful world we need to move forward unhampered by an invariably contested past and assess current disputes in the context of today values about human rights and international law - accepting that the constitution and application of the latter do need reform.

If the World's people are to work towards a more peaceful future we have to accept and share the past but use it to, in a sense, begin again informed by knowing the conditions in which evil can find expression. We were not the past, we do not need to fight entrenched genealogical battles embellished and otherwise distorted by partial collective group memories. The sense of 'begin again' noted is a preparedness to frame past evils as fearsome lessons to be learned, so bracketed as an element of self-consciousness that can be overcome. The 'can' conveying a sense of optimism, of what might be achieved, is more an imperative expressing an urgent and necessary task to be taken up. There is a need to re-imagine the past as past and to live the future without variously interpreted versions of the past determining how we live together as collective units. To acknowledge that group identity can be a sustaining mode of existence for an individual – a comforting fit, with the socialized known offering emotionally enriching relationships and cultural practices – but recognizing that the types of collective identity (nation, tribe, clan, religious, and ethnic group) are in fact more often accidents of birth progressively embodied and reinforced as an outcome of intensive socialization. If we reflect closely on our existence, we can peel off the layers of personality primarily accrued from any more specific collective modes and reveal an underlying connectedness to all humanity. A connection enriched by deeply personal commitment to a willingness to transcend the socialized self and identify with the expansive potential of world-consciousness.

Historically, individuals have been but more or less significant agents in the expression of avoidable evil – key decisions are made by individuals - but it is the wider conditions within which they come to power and the national and international conditions in which they operate, that also need to be examined. If to do so would be seen as a threat by the various centres of power – financial, industrial, military, dynastic, political – that have historically exercised control in the world and those that continue to do so.

We can characterize human civil history as being a 6,000 year-long journey of developing the latent awareness of how we should live together alongside a more dominant motivation seeking to fulfil baser needs realized through: domination, threat, conflict, enslavement, aggression, gaining coercive control, and other forms of exercising power over others.

A primary task must be to seek to understand the construction of circumstances that provide a context (the conditions) in which evil is more rather than less likely to be expressed – including the economic, political, and social structures within which people are socialized. The interconnecting web involving: structural inequalities and existing forms of exploitation, no realistic opportunity to find any personal fulfilment, a social environment based on aggressive competition and social status being gained for succeeding in such an environment, with economic and social structures that create and maintain class-based division, ethnic division, religious divisions, inter-nation division, polarized political division…....and other such potentially divisive characteristics. Societies whose collective mindset values superficial achievement such as the mere accruing of wealth, or overvalues relative achievement (in many areas including business, military, political, academic, as well as music, sport, art, entertainment) that all contribute to the dehumanization of our social relationships and to shaping our perspective on the 'others' we know of but never really know.

Immanuel Kant noted that: 'For peace to reign on Earth, humans must evolve into new beings who have learned to see the whole first."

In evolutionary terms the species Homo sapien developed from about 150,000 y.b.p. taking a more modern anatomical form about 50,000 y.b.p. In the introduction I suggested that the underlying dynamic driving evolution is information processing. That from the very first single-cellular life-forms we can, if crudely, identify levels of development (with example species at each level) arranged in a hierarchy based on ability to process evermore complex patterns of information and so activate the complexity of the behavioural repertoire exhibited by species within each level. With human-beings (Homo sapien) and the level identified as 'self-consciousness' currently the species at the apex of the hierarchy.

The behaviours that characterise self-consciousness have amongst other things produced, modern medicines, legal systems, land, sea, and air transport, a range of other technological innovations, modern medicine, philosophy, the sciences, and other developments associated with civil life. Unfortunately warfare was also one of these.

In terms of understanding the world and interacting with others self-consciousness means a narrowing of view, primarily linked to personal and group interests. Self-consciousness tends towards seeing the other as friend or foe, and the foe usually being the unknown other. Self-consciousness tends towards stereotypic categorization of others, tends to notice difference rather than recognising underlying sameness, self-consciousness at home in an industrializing consumer society tends towards a focus on self rather than on common interests. Tends towards reductionist thinking; if not the reductionist analysis of the sciences - more the silo-like narrowing of, me, myself, and of my family, my tribe or group, my nation.......my 'kind', rather than more holistic thinking ('...seeing the whole...' for Kant). Generally a tendency towards essentialist and stereotypic thinking, of reducing issues to simplistic explanations often sanctioned by tradition and, in a post-modern mass society of accepting the interpretations of experts and other influential individuals whose views have a more general coherence with an individual's own intentionality; basically a tendency towards intellectual laziness and therefore a milieu that mitigates against much personal commitment to the clarification of moral implications.

Note my repeated use of the word 'tends', this indicates that the characteristics I am describing express core aspects of self-consciousness, but that at anytime aspects of our next evolutionary level[52], 'world-consciousness', can intrude. We can rise above the limitation of a narrow self-consciousness; tendencies can be resisted. Reflective thinking – with an assumption of rationalism and more logical considerations – can serve to provide hope for our species, that we do potentially have the psychological resources to think beyond the immediacy of self-hood and group-hood.

It is this originating, personally interpretive, aspect of our experience that offers hope for change. This capacity for creative agency (allied to the human imagination) offers the basic psychological conditions for the construction of social, economic, and political systems that can provide some humanity-affirming structures and so is our hope for humanity. Each one of us has a hold on kindness, has the potential to be in touch with our humanity. An economically comfortable upbringing in an acquisitive consumer society - with an over-emphasis on having rather than sharing, or even on being itself - can leave a child deficient in social empathy. But for most the potential to do good rather than accept evil, to get involved rather than maintain a detachment from the world, is present within the depths of our individuality. And, given the complexity and palpable flexibility of the human psyche, no human is irredeemably beyond the potential for some precocious sense of world-consciousness.

What would the evidence for the soon to appear level of 'self-consciousness' have been at the pre-Homo sapien point – this could surely only have been based on identifying the primary direction of

---

[52] This next level is of course offered as a notional idea – and it might be that the species Homo sapien becomes extinct prior to fully attaining the 'world conscious' level.

evolution, and so a focus on the information processing model of biological adaptation. A prediction made then, and my own being made now, of a new form of 'consciousness' (self-consciousness then, and world consciousness for me), gains validity if considered in relation to the mass of biological, paleontological, and neurological evidence, showing the progressive appearance of information processing modes – action/reaction, awareness, consciousness, self-consciousness.... - in the evolutionary journey of all life on Earth.

I suggest that the past offers persuasive empirical support for a future evolutionary stage/mode expressed as 'world consciousness'. This being one that would allow us to aspire to economic, political, and social relationships beyond the competitive, the conflictual, and the more generally evil. That we can use the concept of world consciousness, and its potential for moral enlightenment as it transcends the self-conscious mode, to stimulate the design of economic and political institutions that would sustain humanity into its future.

If it has taken about 1.8 million years since the first Homo forms of consciousness evolved from earlier primates, then the 50,000 odd years from the appearance of modern Homo-sapien down to the past 6,000 years of the development of more mature forms of civil life, then surely even another 1,000 for a more definite transition towards 'world-consciousness' would seem to be reasonable. But only if the mode of self-consciousness that dominates today's world does not lead to the early eradication of life on Earth; a distinct possibility.

We cannot identify a specific biological transition point between each of the four crude modes of information processing noted above – but using a metaphor involving a colour, say red gradually changing to brown as the wavelength of radiation is adjusted. If normal colour vision, we would quite easily see the distinction between red and brown but as we observe the original redness fade and the brown gradually being revealed, the point somewhere between the two when we can say that the change actually occurs would be quite difficult to identify – although each end would be clear. Unless, that is, we chose to identify colour (red or brown) by a specific wavelength. But even choosing this quantifiable point would still be a subjective decision, as would any attempt to identify a specific primate species whose information processing capacity is assessed to be a new form of 'awareness' becomes 'consciousness' or 'consciousness' becomes 'self-consciousness.' Each progressive mode of information processing subsumes some primary characteristics of the preceding modes and some individuals in each mode show aspects of the next.

The pre-Homo sapien development of self-consciousness can be traced by the increasing sophistication of tool manufacture over about 2 million years and by skull (brain) development (especially the 'bulge' just behind the left-hand eye socket related to speech) – both aspects of evolutionary development appearing from species such as Homo habilis (circa. 2 m.y.b.p), and more modern forms of Homo erectus down to Homo neanderthalensis and Homo sapien.

I acknowledge that what has (perhaps up to the time of the innovations of numeracy and literacy) been primarily biological evolution - assessed in relation to information processing capacity - became increasingly more complex, in that, as a species we have an information processing capacity significantly enlarged; supplemented by having the underlying form of biological evolution overlaid by humankind's intellectual achievements, as increasingly aided by the technological developments that have been central aspects of civil life. Biological evolution became overlain with civil development (with its production and accumulation of knowledge), and the progressive intensification of this being compounded by IT-based information processing; with today all three woven together as they each contribute to the expanding Reality within which humankind exists.

In the twenty-first century, the power of IT-based information processing is a key driver of the development of civilization, in ways qualitatively different to past technological innovations. So whereas I am here positing my concept of world-consciousness as being in the progressive line of: stimulus/response, pre-conscious, conscious, and self-conscious, evolutionary modes, I do need to acknowledge that this is a gross simplification. We can identify 'ideal' species (forms) for each of these modes but between each of these are thousands (possibly millions) of species exhibiting more of an incremental progression than clear points of separation. But the idea of 4/5 primary modes of information processing is useful to illustrate the bio-teleological potential for humankind - especially in relation to reducing the evil in the world – one with a range of practical scientific, and some profoundly philosophical, implications.

I am not suggesting that this is a connection to some biologically inevitable process of evolving consciousness - the stark epistemological reality is that it is a dubious assumption to conclude that evolution has a direction, some pre-determined teleology related to a particular species; that it is inextricable drawn towards some end-state. As I have been endeavouring to show, we can trace a progression in terms of information processing capacity, but a continuing place in this for humankind is not inevitable - any species can become extinct and so its information processing capacity becomes irrelevant, becomes but an aspect of the overall evolutionary lineage. The concept of bio-teleological merely reflects the direction expressed by the evolutionary dynamic of increasing information processing capacity.

World-consciousness, as I have outlined it, is a direction for humanity that challenges the evils of human self-conscious history to not be repeated – for modern humans, a 50,000 odd year tale of the increasing expression of evil. World-consciousness is a possible direction for humanity, and only in this sense is teleological, the extent to which we align our lives with the implications of this possibility is the extent to which we are living morally authentic lives.

We humans as individuals, groups, nations, and as a species, might appeal to some personalized god, some idea of the entry requirements for eternal bliss, or some range of human ideals for guidance on how to behave. But I believe that the information processing mode of 'world-consciousness' can only evolve (find expression in the world) if we, each of us as individual human beings - in an act of reflective authenticity – decide that world-consciousness is a morally based mind-set to be fostered by today's individuals - it is an expression of moral autonomy at its most critical.

As a slight digression to consider a more metaphysical implication of my positing information process of adaptation to an ever-expanding Reality……just imagine the cognitive capability of the type of organism that would evolve into anatomically modern Homo circa 50,000 y.b.p. …..perhaps of some primate species one million years ago? How much could they have 'known' beyond their immediate geographic locality and emotion-laden relations within their small primate social groups? Can you grasp the implications of the information dynamic model? The very emergence of Homo sapien from an earlier primate species was one of those implications!

Individuals of that pre-Homo sapiens primate species might occasionally have gazed up at the stars with some primitive sense of curiosity and some obviously did start manipulating materials (stones, bones, and sticks,) in what we came to recognize as tool usage – but just consider the difference in cognitive ability and imaginative world-view (perspective) between advancing primates species over just the past 1 million years to realize what might be possible over the 1 million years to come. Just how much will they (some intelligent species of the future) 'know' about say the Universe; or indeed how will they know in terms of metaphysics more generally? I am not just suggesting some accumulation of knowledge by our own (aided by computer-based technology) species but rather what will in fact be a new super-intelligent (by our own standard) biological species; if possibly one evolved from our own.

Or will some self-replicating A.I. entity have by then taken over the leading information-processing role, with any surviving humans (in the unlikely event that our own species can survive such a scenario) living on the margins of some super-intelligence-dominated world; surviving due to their presence being irrelevant to the dominant information-processing forms that had displaced them.

A third alternative for 1 million years hence would be a planet denuded of the means to support any form of intelligent life due to humans long having destroyed themselves, presumably by some combination of nuclear conflagration and/or environmental degradation.

The A.I. takeover is a realistic possible scenario, as is the end of all intelligent life on Earth, but for now humankind holds its future in its own hands. How we order the world by taking a necessary global perspective on economic planning, environmental protection, and on governance, requires urgent consideration. In all three areas we seem to be on route to disaster......and this within but 50-100 years – a potentially terminal disaster brought about by our inability to move beyond the narrow parameters characteristic of the self-conscious level of decision-taking – to what I term world-consciousness in order to capture the sense of the global perspective required.

Being human in its-self is not a pathological condition - The uniqueness of individuality is a fundamental opportunity to 'be'. For some this be-ing is in suffering, for others in creative becoming, and for most be-ing in a more 'mundane' sense from which we can each seek to develop our own level of consciousness. For us, that the tendency towards evil can be mitigated by the realization of more transcendentally possible ways of living together.

As individuals and as collectives we humans tend towards expressing a mix of behaviours, at worst we would term these our colluding in evil – wars, massacres, raping, enslaving, killings, ethnic cleansing, and gross economic exploitation. During more enlightened times people have been aware of this raw tendency and of the need to maintain a level of social order. So public institutions have been devised to mitigate our more anti-social behaviours. These institutions have included systems of representative governance, of legal codes, religious and secular moral injunctions, and of economic arrangements seeking to balance different interests within a wider context of consensual acceptance. Internationally, I would highlight the United Nations and the range of human rights guidelines that it has generated as the global institutional, if too often seriously flawed in operation, modern expression of humankind's collective ethical wisdom.

The twenty-first century Reality is now so vast in terms of information (especially knowledge content), and its rate of expansion so great, that humankind as a species risks being terminally overwhelmed as it becomes unable to assimilate the more material and technological impact on such aspects of Reality as: the biosphere, the human implications of the internet, the armaments industry, and robotics and automation more generally. The elusive, uneasy, complexity of the 'liquid modernity' noted by Zygmund Baumann.

So much information pouring over and through us, eroding the relatively more secure psychological foundation of the relatively more stable traditional. Our psychological constitution has over centuries generated an interrelated uber-complexity of discovery and invention. But with each human being born anew with a psychological constitution showing little progress in cognitive capacity on the human born 20,000 years ago – a mismatch between what we can now do (technologically) and our seeming inability to manage the probable consequences. A mismatch possibly revealing the conditions for an evolutionary dead-end and so extinction for our species. Invention has accumulated, as has complexity, whereas wisdom has remained static (if certain moral truths retain a continuing relevance) – as a species we are struggling to manage technology in sustainable, human-sense ways. Some, such as Arthur Koestler, have described this mismatch in terms of brain physiology, highlighting the lack of functional integration between the 'more intelligent' neo-cortex and the 'more emotional' central areas (older in evolutionary terms) of the brain.

In terms of universal values, in the context of the urgent problems facing the world, we need some agreed set of human values. Those already outlined in the Charter of the United Nations could provide a good base for the constitution of global governance. Experience of the UN suggests that interpreting the provisions of the Charter in terms of actual practice would, given the current arrangements of that body, be susceptible to variable self-interested motivations of governments and the globally powerful elites. But we can at least imagine comprehensively reformed UN forums serving as potentially useful interpretive bodies for the application of the Charter's provisions. Forums ideally composed of individuals that have a proven record of non-factional wisdom. How this qualification can be assessed is another complex challenge, some others include being to determine to what extent individual nations would be prepared to cede sovereignty (a base-line necessary condition for effective global governance), and what would be the scope for sectional lobbying and public representations to such a body.

We are not necessarily discussing a World Government here – just a global body established to apply even-handed wisdom to complex social and political issues, as guided by the provisions of the UN Charter; a globally-appropriate level of governance designed to address global-wide issues. Two primary factors led to the UN Charter being initially drawn up, one positive the other less so. Positively, it was a response by the heads of leading nations to public demand for something to prevent yet another drift into the experience of warfare following the deaths of over 100m in WWs I and II. More cynically, I would suggest that at the time when the UN's aims were established in their perceptive ('world conscious') form, agreement was reached due to the world's most powerful nations knowing that they could use these when deemed necessary to condemn the action of other nations and ignore (or artfully relativize) them if they were critical of their own actions. The lack of a willingness to cede sovereignty to the new body and the previous experience of international diplomacy (especially the LoN and the Kellog-Briand Pact) made this a certainty, one repeatedly and depressingly confirmed by the subsequent development of the UN.

Given this, those drafting the provisions were free to use their significant intellectual resources to outline a truly enlightened range of human rights provisions. The cynical, self-interested actions of nations making up the body of the UN should not detract from the inspirational nature of the Charter's provisions; indeed the Charter stands as a written monument to humankind's collective enlightenment that would shame the subsequent actions of national leaders: see the Appendix 1 below for some tentatively drafted ideas for a re-imagined, re-constructed, UN.

In terms of power on a global level, the assumed authority of nation-states to represent the interest of the populations of the 193 full member-states of the UN is illusory. And this without even considering the extent to which nation-statehood itself actually represents the interests or even the wishes of each nation's population, rather than those of the elite groups who in effect run these countries. The primary 'global interest' is surely peaceful co-existence between and within nations.

Leaving this fundamental suggestion aside, I want instead to focus here on global 'governance'. The concept of global governance (rather than global government) better captures the purpose of designing and introducing a layered system of administration able to operationalise how best the peoples of our world can live together – ideally sharing resources in a world with improving environmental and fairer economic conditions, and one avoiding wars and minimising other forms of conflict. The concept of government suggests static representation and assumed power, whereas governance assumes on-going interrogation and a more dynamic approach to co-existence.

Governance suggests design (implying purpose) and invites continuous questioning on any system's value and possible scope for improvements – the best form of governance would be enlightened by a sense of purpose and any related political system would be but a supplementary means of operationalising this.

Nation-states have been constructed out of political and social processes and so can in theory be deconstructed and remodelled; or indeed global governance could be designed without the divisive presence of nation-states (of a tier of nation-statehood). Perhaps a world without countries would be more of a longer-term ambition than immediately realizable, especially given the nation-based enculturalization currently being experienced by most of the world peoples.

The conflictual tropes generated to advance elite group interests currently pervading international relations should give way to the language of negotiation, in a wider context that assumes a global interest in peace and co-operation. The mass media and populist politician's terminology – mostly sourced from the xenophobic movie industry, the comic book, the barroom and on the sports-field - and the mendacious language of diplomacy must be set aside to allow space for the language of negotiation, understanding, and mutual co-operation. And these set within a framework prioritising justice and peace. The forum for the coming together of would-be antagonists must include some judicial/political body tasked with framing issues within a wider global constitution. A constitution not dissimilar to that set out in the UN charter – but unlike that one, a constitution, determinedly infusing international relations rather than being some set of abstract ideas retained as a residue of some more enlightened expression of hope only invoked as but another source of assumed linguistic support to justify short-term national interests. Another layer of deracinated verbiage deployed to veil the hegemonic geopolitics that currently pertains.

If a fair and inclusive system of world governance, based on some tiers of genuine participatory democracy, were ever to be established, it would need to be alert to attempts made by disaffected elite group members seeking to return to nation-statehood by undermining global unifying processes. And the natural inclination of genuine participatory democracy, in relation to communication and the sharing of ideas, will open-up the space for this. The only realistic option (if the curtailing of valued freedoms of expression is to be avoided) is: the efficient management of administration, obviously open and uncorrupted governance, and continuous vigilance. All in order to continuously prove and promote its worth.

But in the anarchic terrain of global communications it does seem that the promotion of dangerous/harmful ideas and false claims ('alternative facts') would require some open media-editing process. Ideally, this would be undertaken by a respected body operating separately from government as it interprets pre-establish guidelines arrived at following a public debate informed by multiple perspectives (so participatory democracy), tending towards openness and inclusivity, on what was acceptable to be shared in any relevant public space. Guidelines to be regularly revisited in order to amend if required in response to ongoing social and technological developments.

Is humanity destined to trudge relentlessly and sightless towards its extinction as a species, or can we find an alternative? Any alternative can realistically only be viable if national interests are seen to align to some transcendental aims infusing global economic and political justice and the interests of future generations.

Robust alternatives to nation-driven hegemony can realistically only be based on the recognition of a shared 'international interest' requiring the need to cede sovereignty in areas of primary international concern – be these economic, environmental, or in terms of conflict. National interests encompassed within an intentional milieu of mutual respect and genuine co-operation, expressed in a language of unity and collective hope. The intentional element determining global governance should discard elite determined notions of national interest and replace these with governance in the interest of our children and the generations that we hope will follow.....and will do so in peace.

We can note six necessary conditions for international peace:

- Fundamental reform of the UN.
- Committing to the terms of the UN Charter (as a Constitution).
- Accepting the authority of those charged to interpret the Charter in relation to particular issues – so agreeing to accept any 'rulings/decisions', perhaps with a right to appeal?
- Ceding sovereignty over key issues, including the right to threaten or wage war.
- A sufficient proportion of the global population committed to a new enlightened form of governance.
- The willingness of each community, be this nation state, religious sect, ethnic group, etc.to concede that few if any such communities have a history entirely free from some form of aggressive action against others. And so to be prepared to eschew historic antagonisms and, in a sense begin again. To build a new form of world governance rather than retain the festering and invariably contested claims of past injustice.

Those elements which differentially contribute to forming any particular (individual, group, tribe, nation) perspective are not fixed, they are more tendencies towards interpretations, and as such are socially constructed. Historically influenced as but a part of any current elite-group's interpretive framework. But human beings have the ability, more a constant liability, to reflect. And it is within this reflective capacity where lies the potential to transcend the socialized circumscription of our approach towards understanding our own lives.

My sweep through humanity's conflictual history revealed both its extent and complexity. The extent is fairly obvious – the destruction, of built and natural environments, and of millions of people - killed and crippled - whose lives have been ended early or significantly degraded. The solidly sticky strands of evil that have trailed though human civil history. There are few grounds for arguing the extent of this. As to complexity now we do have the challenge of identifying causes. What is pretty obvious is that few if any groups of peoples living today, whether nations, religions, tribes, or other can honestly claim that their ancestors have been entirely innocent.

Even in crude religious terms: Hindus' have killed Moslems, Moslems have killed Hindus, Buddhists have killed, and been killed by each of these and also by Christians who have also killed and been killed by Moslem, Hindus and Buddhists. And those without any religion have killed all of those with a religion and have been killed by each of these. A veritable melting pot of killing of the 'different' by the 'different.'

Even groups that have suffered awful treatment during the 20th and 21st centuries alone have ancestors that have been involved in the most evil of actions.
- The Armenians ......have been involved in killing Turkish Moslems.
- Kurds have been involved in killing Armenians

- The Jews during the synthetic formation of their nationhood murdered those already living in what were, for the group self identified as Jews, a land promised to them by their god (Yahweh)
- Uigers have raided across border regions of China in the past.
- Ukrainians – massacred Poles during WWII (1943)

Just a few examples of the ancestors of the oppressed having themselves been oppressors.

Are there some aspects of human nature that would invariably lead to conflict? Or has conflict more simply been due to more rational assessments made by people/leaders seeking to enhance their own group's access to valued resources? Some more rational cost-benefit analysis determining irrational action. Irrational when considered in terms the harms associated with evil acts. If we are to design the form of international relations in ways that mitigate such evils we would need to set some agreed standards and then design in the conditions for their application. This has been an ongoing problem with peace treaties and non aggression pacts since the dawn of civil life shown most obviously in the 20th century failure of the LoN and the UN to prevent between nation conflict. We do know that the international political and economic institutions have developed during humankind's civil history has been to a significant extent designed to favour the interests of elite groups.

I noted at the start of this extended essay that as individuals we in a sense 'find ourselves' within existence – most of us experience consciousness as of ourselves within and the world more generally as being out there – a external source of the information realised as personal experience. Many of us in more affluent countries are fortunate enough to grow up in fairly benign family and social settings, feeling loved and being loving. An almost cocoon-like period of childhood but one that becomes evermore infiltrated by awareness of the harsh facts of the world beyond our more immediate circumstances. The realization that other children's lives are degraded by poverty, hunger, poor housing and medical care, as refugees and being more directly involved in the horrors of civil or inter-nation conflict. Children forced into crime, prostitution, begging, garbage-picking or sweated labour, just in order to survive from day-to-day. So many of the world's children growing up in fear-inducing conditions, painfully aware of the poverty of their circumstances.....that they are but the detritus of civil life.

It is difficult to avoid the images of others suffering seen on TV/smart phone/iPad – and these of only the surface of global suffering that those in control of the mass media choose to show. We increasingly become aware of just how difficult are the lives of others in the world.

But why should I feel that I have any responsibility towards others beyond my family, class, tribe, caste, country...etc? Why should I not just get on with my own relatively comfortable life? In some ways I do just get on with my daily life but a core part of me is aware that we - as in all people in the world - need fundamental change in the ways in which the international economic system and the international political institutions operate. My earlier book 'The Human Condition' (Dyer, 2021) included an analysis of aspects of the global economic system before going on to tentatively suggest how the system could be re-designed in ways that would: end life-threatening poverty, reduce economic inequality, provide opportunity, and maintain environmental sustainability. This present text has focused much more on international political institutions – accepting that the current economic arrangements strongly influence the conditions for international politics.

The 'we' that have a need for change is not just an appeal to help the poorest, most exploited, most oppressed, in the world, or to introduce a bit more economic justice in terms of equality of opportunity... No the 'we' is all of us, those on the crude scale ranging from the poorest to the richest and all those in between. Without fundamental change in the economic system and the international political institutions the future of the whole of humanity is threatened. Relentless environmental degradation threatens the mid-to-longer term viability of the planet as a habitat for human beings. And of more immediate concern, the sightless behemoth of the conflict industry progressively accelerates the world towards warfare potentially involving a significant exchange of nuclear devices.

The idea of 'finding ourselves in existence', is used to express the possibility of a meta-awareness whereby we can view the relativity of our own particular situations within a nexus of pre-established relationships and social institutions, and also realising the uniqueness of each of our experientially formed perspective on life. This perspective can include an awareness of being on a relatively fragile (in terms of its being a human life support system) blue/green planet spinning lazily on its axis as it traverses an elliptical passage around the more substantial Sun. These two bodies of the Solar System providing the material means to sustain humankind's journey through time. Echoing Kant ....allowing us to gaze with curious wonder upon the starry skies - and for our imagination to roam through our lived experiences forming ideas of the possible.

The suggestion that we 'find ourselves within existence' – implies the finding of the already there as well as the realization that most of us have the agency to transcend the limitations of the socialization processes that we have experienced.

Being prepared to stand exposed to our own reflective self, a mode of self-hood informed by deep consideration of a life sub-specie aeternitalis. I am suggesting that we have an existential responsibility to purposefully decide on how we should live, not in term of personal career, close relationships, day to day attitudes, etc (although these would also probably come to be involved) but a deeper level of considering our lives in the context of humanity itself rather than the individual as myself.

There is a correspondence between perspective-taking on your own life within Reality in terms of self-creative engagement with a future involving others – the cognitive bridge to world-consciousness - and the key task of endeavouring to take-up the perspective of this other in relation to this situation or that issue. Each requires us to adopt processes determined to transcend two aspects of our individuality, the first the individual as socialized, the second as an individual prepared to assume a level of social responsibility beyond their more immediate relationships; and each of these as processes of open-ended engagement. Both directed towards transcendence – moving beyond the narrowness of the accidentally socialized and of the limitations of self-consciousness.

In our personal lives we can feel a depressing sense that there is an ontological absurdity in the very fact of our existence. The world is so unjust – some born into comfortable lives some born into the misery of poverty – some dying young, some living into old age. Most of us uneasy with trying to find some sense of purpose beyond material ambitions.

Our cries for justice and peace echo around an unresponsive universe. The immensities of space and time magnify my own helplessness, my aloneness. When we consider our flickering existence in the silent immensities within which our lives are set we can quite easily lapse into despair. To seek some solace in family, religion, work, hobbies, or in the distractions of entertainment, or some comfort in the superficial satisfaction of material goods and services so pressingly available for those with sufficient income.

My own life has been felt as a investigative journey seeking answers to the injustices so obvious in the world; the $20^{th}/21^{st}$ century's bounteous expression of evil. I progressed from curious childhood to questioning and angry young adulthood to more reflective, if still angry (now tinged with despair) middle age. And throughout this journey having progressively formed a strong sense of what needs to be done to end, or at least significantly mitigate, the expression of evil in our world.

The primary conditions, reflecting directly upon each one of us, is to accept the relative conditions of our lives in local social settings – those experienced within a family, class, caste, religion, ethnic or other group, nation, etc. More often the source of our prejudices and stereotypes, the formation of our general outlook and more specific interpretive frameworks within the psychological processes involved in our socialization – i.e. the accidental setting of our within existence. We need to accept this randomly experienced lived relativity but to seek to transcend it in order to acknowledge our singular collective species identity within humanity more generally. To foster an outlook that prioritizes issues such as poverty, inequality, environmental sustainability, justice, and conflict......facing humanity as a collective.

Consider each of our own genealogies – reverse engineer our own unique presence in the world - the very incalculable (statistically improbable) odds against our ever existing. And even more so of our experiencing our being in the here and now.

Let's leave aside the metaphysical perspective involving the very improbability of life itself – that profound mystery of why humanity is here at all. But rather than this let's consider how our ancestors negotiated our ignorance of the meaning of the our existence......that enigmatic mystery that the religions have each attempted to explain using ideas imagined by some people at some time long ago, those who compiled the various 'holy' texts: Bible, Koran, Torah, Vedas, Tripitaka, Kojiki, Guru Granth Sahib, Avesta, etc.

Authors of these texts assumed that they lived on a flat earth being circled by the Sun, whose sky was but a material cover beyond which was a bright light glimpsed through star-shaped 'pinholes' in the fabric of the sky.

The sacred texts were written for people whose ancestors had relied on 'hope' to avoid the many difficult and dangerously unpredictable vicissitudes of pre and early historic lives that they were liable to encounter on an almost daily basis. From hope, allied to imagination, came the gods – even the mystery of death could be re-imagined from hope, as but a continuation of life in some other form, if only for the 'chosen'. Those peoples whose gods were often depicted by those who wrote the holy texts from their imaginations, and for their own purposes, as often cruel and always demanding. Their being able to induce awe in believers by claims of acts and miracles that suspended the laws of nature as we came to learn about them, and demanding of total obedience. Gods whose earthly representatives required social elevation and for most quite generous material rewards.

So setting aside the substantial 'why at all' of life, and also hope allied to imagination producing the religious attempts to resolve the mystery..... What we do know is that our planet was formed from rotating cosmic dust-clouds about 4.5 billion years ago. By some particular combination of its position (distance from the Sun, rotational speed) and material and climatic conditions it provided just the circumstances suitable for chemical complexity to increase to a critical point when we can judge that 'life' on earth had begun.

These 'Goldilocks' conditions are predicted to also be a feature of numerous planets elsewhere in the universe. Recent (2013) calculations, using up-to-data, suggest that possibly up to 10% of the 100 billion star systems within just our own Milky Way Galaxy could provide conditions potentially suitable for life to have evolved – This is of course quite speculative (not in terms of the conditions, but more in terms of likelihood of any life actually beginning) and simple life is one phenomenon, with civil life being something much more complex.

The Earth has seen life from about 3.8 billion years ago, with the simplest of cells (Prokaryotes) appearing from about 3.5 billion years ago, and then more complex cells (Eukaryotes) from about 1.6 billion years ago – then with multi-cellular life evolving in evermore complex ways, following an adaptational dynamic based on the development of organisms able to process increasingly complex forms of information.

Some type of nervous system is the primary means by which an organism engages within its environment as it processes incoming information streaming from the environment and processes a selection (each species has its own informational 'bandwidth') of this internally; with species-specific behaviour being the most obvious outcome. We can quite easily see the advance in information processing ability if we compare any species of the genus paramecium (evolved approx. 715 m.y.b.p.) with a human-being (evolved approx 150,000 y.b.p., as already noted, to a 'modern' from about 50,000 years ago). The paramecium is a single-celled creature that uses up about 50% of its total available energy output in moving around in its watery habitat. Fortunately, being a grazer (on algae, bacteria, and yeasts) and not a hunter, it does not have to move too far or too quickly. It is a single-celled organism without any neuron-based 'nervous system' but with its primary behaviours.....of movement, grazing, and digestion, being coordinated via a macronucleus with a micronucleus controlling reproduction and the passing on of genetic material to the next generation. Then compare this to the species Homo sapiens with its approx 86 billion neuron-based nervous system potentially sensitive to millions of bits of information streaming in from its habitat per minute. A stream from which is selected (mostly auto-consciously) information which is then processed, consciously and unconsciously, within the organism. But, unlike the paramecium, we can realistically describe human information processing as involving intentions, motivations, memories, emotions, plans, and other concepts embodied in the description of the human psychological system. The resultant behaviours being significantly more complex than those of the simpler organism – a human beings can walk, run, jump, dance, swim, and even fly in machines that members of the species have invented and constructed, it can perform complex surgery, read a map, invent the internal combustion engine, the particle accelerator, the computer, the wheelbarrow, tin cans and the tin-opener, can travel to the moon and beyond – it can also kill and devise the means of doing so in forms unimaginable even but 100 years ago.

So in evolutionary terms we now find ourselves on a planet conducive for complex information-processing based life, within a universe that possibly provides similar conditions for other conscious life-forms. The bio-mechanisms of evolution also offer another source of our uniqueness as individuals.

Humans reproduce by two individuals coming together to blend an egg (ovum) with a sperm – and in a traditional setting this would take place during a body on body act of intercourse between a female and a male. So firstly we have to have two people whose lives intersect and who also find each other sufficiently attractive to undertake this act (accepting the act of rape). The two that do – our parents – were but two in billions that could, at least theoretically, have formed a mating couple. So having the parents we do have (and being gifted but a tiny quite random selection of the total genetic material they each had available) is an initial source of a coincidental uniqueness for many of us. If we then consider that in a 25 year period of fertility a female could produce between 300 – 400 eggs and a single male ejaculation (about a teaspoon, 2-5 ml, of semen) can contain up to 200 – 500 million sperm – such is the exuberance of nature - the odds of our having the very specific genetic constitution that we do have is quite awesome. All these stages of material and organic processes involving a genealogy of randomness, possibility, coincidence, and I would add an underlying mystery, contribute to the biological constitution of each one of us.

Rather than being overwhelmed by an awareness of these sources of our uniqueness, or simply just ignoring our material and genealogical heritage and getting on with life, I feel a strong sense of responsibility – my uniqueness is a fundamental source of my autonomy, and exercising my autonomy makes me stand forth – not stand out, as if seeking elevation above others – but stand forth having reflected deeply on how I should live in this world in a way that transcends the relativity of the accidental circumstances (in terms of place and time, and so social setting) of my presence …….here and now. Our sense of self comes from within and enwraps us as we grow into adulthood – our individuality is sourced in our awareness exposed to what we experience.

I would urge you to assume responsibility linked to the opportunity that your uniqueness and a life to be lived in the here and now has gifted you. To seek to transcend your own social setting, and to thoughtfully reflect on how we can together seek to improve the world for the whole species of Homo sapien. Although 'improve' suggests a modest amount of reform, whereas the improvement required to achieve a world without conflict would be significant. Requiring, in effect, a fundamental resetting of the conditions of international relations. To move away from today's conditions of world governance based on hegemonic economic competition and political conflict to one based on co-operation and peaceful co-existence.

An individual human life might be simply expressed as being but a '...sigh between two eternal silences' (noted earlier in this book) but as the connection we each have to humankind as a collective entity, generation following generation, we are part of an ongoing evolutionary phenomenon. Let's collectively endeavour to ensure that this '......sigh between two eternal silences' is not the fate of humankind as an entire species, on but a longer timescale – to be self-consciously driven to extinction.

A fundamental aspect of our lives inextricably involves the idea of reflective choice, and this in the context of accepting the responsibility that accompanies this sense of agency – an important aspect of being what it 'feels like' to be human. An aspect of existence effectively denied to individuals of any other species. And this potential for individuality, for some sense of being an autonomous agent, is the step we can make between unreflective conformity and the post-reflective personal decision-making on how we should live. Within this self-directed personal narrative a thread of authenticity can emerge to be woven into a life of moral substance.

My giving priority to the concept of authenticity as an existential aspiration is intended to express some deeper connection to all the potential good that inheres within the human condition. Authenticity as a form of transcendent achievement realized as an outcome of world-consciously directed engagement with life. The lived outcome of a decision to assume a fundamental level of personal responsibility for the implications of the mystery of finding oneself in existence. The question...... authentic in relation to what? Stands out.... bear with me.

I have traced the rise of consciousness in terms of the increasing potential to process evermore information and I point to human self-consciousness as being an advanced embodiment of this ability. Human history shows that the gross expression of evil has been a fearsome and bleak feature running through the social processes and cultural institutions that have characterized civilizations associated with self-consciousness. But another aspect of civil life has been the refinement of morality, given a symbolic and ordered form in scriptural commands, civil laws (codes - injunctions), and in collectively stated aims informed by enlightened humanistic aspirations. In relation to these types of codified (formalized) morality - in the context of world consciousness - we now have various human rights acts and I have highlighted the UN's collective version of these as set out in its charter. A charter that can embody hope for the human species.

Since the earliest time of civil life some of humankind's political and religious leaders have been able to outline the types of ethical code that we should adhere to - and this offers a glimmer of genuine hope. The problem throughout history being that the tensions between abstract moral priorities and particular issues where vested interests are challenged have almost always been resolved to the detriment of morality and in favour of narrow minded self-interest. Most often the interests of powerful elites (if with the obedient compliance of the masses) and this in the pursuit of wealth, land, or increasing power. The interests supporting war have tended to be stronger than those endeavouring to make the case for peace, the distribution of the material benefits of civil life have tended to favour various types of elite group that have been able to obtain power and who have had no compunction in using it to benefit themselves. Mostly to the short-term detriment of the masses and the long-term detriment of all.

We can characterize human civil history as being a 6,000 year-long journey of developing the latent awareness of how we should live together alongside a more dominant motivation seeking to fulfil baser needs realized through: domination, coercion, threat, conflict, enslavement, aggression, various types of institutional control, and other forms of exercising power over others.

Let's see if I can do a bit more with the concept of authenticity on an individual level because without the engagement of committed and determined individuals the systemic tendencies towards the expression of evil are more likely to prevail. Striving for authentic understanding, and to act authentically in ones encounter with-in existence, means being 'honest' in the best possible sense i.e. existentially rather than legally. Honest as in being true to certain self-formulated ideas, gained during the profoundly personal solitude of self-reflection, to take responsibility for one's own life – an unconditional commitment to seek existential truth. Trying, whenever possible, to go beyond surface understanding and explanations, and also to attempt to separate your own self-interests and potential for bias from your commenting about or understanding any contested issue. It does not mean that you should be seeking to eradicate personal and intellectual bias[53], it just means you should endeavour to acknowledge these, take them into account, and ensure that any bias (which is a natural propensity) is regularly subject to open scrutiny.

Authenticity is intimately related to personal and intellectual integrity. It is about how each of us in our individuality looks life with its multi-shifting complexity, dangers, joy and sadness, and the ontic absurdity of our lives that the writer Albert Camus so clearly drew attention to, squarely in the 'eye'. Trying to be authentic, and searching for authenticity in our understanding, is the thread of humanity running throughout our task of facing absurdity with all of its uncomfortable existential implications. On the personal level to stand-forth, determined to live rightly in relation to the human values that have been revealed; not least by a number of past and present religious leaders and secular thinkers in both the 'East' and the 'West'. And on the intellectual level to strive for deeper understanding, valuing the power of rational thinking, ever prepared to genuinely reconsider your views in response to the reasoned arguments or suggestive insights of others, or of new information becoming available.

Finally, being personally authentic, and searching for intellectual authenticity, is to be prepared to follow the implications of experience to its core and to accept responsibility for one's own involvement. Thomas Nagel wrote in relation to the absurd: 'What he [Camus] recommends is defiance or scorn. We can salvage our dignity, he appears to believe, by shaking a fist at the world which is deaf to our pleas, and continuing to live in spite of it. This will not make our lives

---

[53] Bias can be the outcome of accumulated experience and allows a necessary shorthand understanding of issues – but when these are contentious then the matter of bias, and the need for a deeper consideration/analysis comes to the fore.

un-absurd, but it will lend them a certain nobility.' For Nagel, Camus's is a '...romantic and slightly self-pitying' view. But the insight that allows us to understand the absurd nature of human lives highlights the limits of the human condition, for Nagel, knowing this: '......we can approach our absurd lives with irony instead of heroism or despair.' (Nagel, 1979, pp.22-23)

For myself, the process of confronting the seeming absurdity of our lives, reveals the fundamental nature of moral concerns – we come to the conclusion via a comparison of a world of random unjust circumstances for some and equally random unjustified good fortune for others – and of course, to the lack of any reply to our cries of despair about this......the world just continues to enigmatically turn, trailing evil as it does so. We must aim to create a sense of a moral nobility by acknowledging the absurd but seeking to transcend this by assuming a life lived in defiance of its seemingly depressing finality, brushing its negative (nay saying) implications aside – it merely serving as a stimulus to our overcoming its pessimistic contaminants. The absurd is not a conclusion. It is but a provisional assessment, denying the continuing personal realization (as authentic) of our confronting evil, and also an assessment lacking the consciousness-raising potential inherent within evolving humankind.

We must be prepared to risk exposure to the full blast of a Reality that constantly buffets the limited certainties to which we cling, as individuals and humankind, like shipwrecked mariners might desperately cling onto drift-wood. The touch-stone of 'human values' – is a key source of an authentic perspective, authentic because these would be values formulated following a reflective consideration of the circumstances of a person's life - as a wider guiding intentional framework from which ones attitude in relation to each particular issue is drawn. The extent to which these align expresses the authenticity of a person's life. Each person commits to their own conscience-driven values as they progress the interrogation of a moral basis for their own lives. The conditions for authenticity include: clarity of values (and the implications of these for a person's life), personal autonomy, critical self-reflection, consistency, but most of all in assuming responsibility.

As I approach the end of this text I turn back to a concept introduced at the beginning, that of reason (or rational thinking), a concept synonymous with the best work in philosophy. How best (most effectively in relation to purpose) to apply the organizing framework of reason is probably the most useful thinking process to arise from philosophical speculation. I would argue that it is only of any real use when it is aligned to the realities of everyday life and that the representations generated are accessible to any person motivated to make some effort.

Reason could be described as the 'guided seeking for understanding', guided by the intellect in relation to a purpose; there are good or bad purposes but ideally reason initially aims at a neutral evaluation of the facts arising from the consideration of any subject matter. The concept of reason expresses the ability of humans to interrogate and interpret an issue in particular ways. Involving assessing the veracity of facts and clarifying relationships between these, the justification of any associated claims, examining the logical consistency of arguments, and identifying the implications of judgements and suggested actions. The application of a skill - reasoning – is, at least theoretically, a neutral activity but it is a process that can be significantly influenced by the purpose of those undertaking any exercise in reasoning. Reason has its own determinants of intellectual acceptability that can allow explanations and arguments to be set out or challenged within a mode of credibility. The expectation of intellectual acceptability running throughout reasoning processes, especially in relation to conflictual issues, is the best means humans have to gain an understanding of any issue but also for seemingly competing views to debate these in terms of facts and implications – if these debates must necessarily have to take place within a background context of agreed ethical parameters (some presumption).

Even a cursory glance through human civil history and its accumulated results can induce despair – the mostly seemingly rational expression of but narrow national self-interests producing an irrational story, and dismal prospects; even if humanitarian values have continued throughout history at least as a presence (so a potential) for the human condition. Rationality infused with humanistic values can be called upon in the service of human truths.

A significant issue with promoting the activity of reason is that traditional Western interpretations have overwhelmingly tended to prioritise a form of rationalism that is 'logo-centric'. In philosophy this has allowed description and analysis to assume a certain type of expression that involves the translation of the spoken word into mostly restricted written forms and these with an underlying trope of progression from questions/claims, to facts and, via analysis, to resolution/conclusion. A form of rationalizing that can ignore the meaning-rich power of non-Western (non-logo-centric) language forms. This can be dramatically illustrated in Benjamin Lee Whorf's description of the Hopi Indian language, as being comparable to English as the 'rapier to a bludgeon' – a radically different way to describe (and so constitute) Reality; especially in relation to metaphysics; so opening access to finely drawn imaginative ideas. A number of recent post-modern continental philosophers, notably Jacques Derrida, have drawn attention to this prioritising of log-centrism in traditional Western philosophy, if without suggesting a convincing alternative.

Which only realistically leaves us into seeing at least some potential value in taking an openly rational approach to understanding conflictual issues, whilst retaining a preparedness to reformulate the conditions of the rational as a result of experience or of insights drawn from non-logo-centric sources. Rational processes that involve: clarity of definitions, a coherent form of setting out arguments or views, consistency in ideas, and a willingness to consider criticisms within a more general recursive process of authorial self-examination This last can relate to non logo-centric considerations, and is potentially a key source of redefining the rational process itself if, that is, this process is designed to evermore effectively access Reality and translate its implications into knowledge. Even with his illuminating qualifications, I don't think that Derrida would deny at least some residue of genuine interpretive value in the application of some aspects of rationalism – providing we accept the limitations.

Our enculturalization enwraps us in forms of language regularizing a particular grammatical structure, appropriate phonemic forms, and the use of certain metaphors and analogies, all within an assumed usage. It is difficult to examine the constitution of the wrappings of our 'natural' language if we only have that language itself with which to do so. And yet, critical analysis informed by an understanding of the potential constraints of our language, and perhaps a genuine openness to other language forms, can stimulate our imagination and widen our conceptual horizons even to the point of exposing the '.....vertinginous prospects henceforth opened up for inventive reading.' As noted by Christopher Norris in his 1987 book.

Confidence in the conclusions of any analysis can only ever stand on the foundations of 'faith', but a faith underpinned by a trust in the soundness and intellectual integrity of one's procedures (integrity of the associated reasoning), rather than the type of faith which underpins the dogmatic certainty of all religionists and most ideologues. Meaning inheres within our organicity, even if human cognitive ability provides the means to form a type of awareness we would term 'understanding'; an outcome of a conceived semantic unity allowing us to make sense of our experience.

It seems that social/cultural evolution has provided us as a species with the ability to overcome such threats as are faced by all species, we can use technology to insulate us, at least to some considerable extent, from biological and other dangers. Whether it's that of predatory animals, species threatening disease, or threats to food supplies. But longer-term evolutionary prospects for any species are limited - A species can continue a process of adaptive change, developing in ways (mutational and/or behavioural) conducive to new species formation e.g. some form of earlier Homo (H.habilis, H.erectus, or H.heidelbergensis) to Homo sapien circa 150,000 y.b.p. - Can become 'fixed' and remain stable as a species for 100s of millions of years e.g. alligator, tortoise, dragonfly - Can find itself in a habitat that, due to dramatic change in environmental conditions, it is unable to adapt too and so becomes extinct e.g. the large-bodied dinosaurs circa 65 m.y.b.p. (following a period of ascendancy lasting for over 160 million years). And even some species of Homo who have left but a fossil record of their existence e.g. Homo neanderthal and Homo denisovan – if also some droplets of their genetic inheritance having been gifted to Homo sapien.

One of three possible futures awaits our species:

- Carry on evolving on the developing information processing model to become a new species. Just as the species Homo sapien had evolved from a species of Homo erectus some 150,000 years ago. So to evolve from the information processing mode of 'self-consciousness' into the mode that I have termed 'world consciousness?'

- At some point A.I. develops to the level that it then displaces human-beings.

- That Homo sapien becomes extinct (as have millions of species in the past – the headline grouping being the dinosaurs). This due to making the world unfit for human life......thermonuclear warfare or otherwise dramatic environmental degradation are the two more obvious possible causes.

One of these possible futures will be the fate of our species. I think that the choice is between the first (species change) and the last (extinction). But unlike any other species that has taken one of these two evolutionary paths the introduction of socio/cultural factors, with the corresponding ability to control or destroy, means that the path taken by humankind lies to a considerable extent, in its own hands.

Self-consciousness in Homo sapien is realised in an awareness of itself as a be-ing within a relationship to what is experienced as an external environment separate from itself. Possessing an accessible memory and able to imagine and plan possible futures, with a symbol system (realized in images, expressed emotions, and in language in its widest sense) allowing the re-presentation of information which has led to highly complex scientific and technological advances, to cities, space-craft, the media, mechanised food production, medical-related technological developments, and the means of techno-warfare including nuclear and biological weapons, all the lethal so-called conventional weaponry, as well as imaginative philosophical speculation encompassing both formal philosophies and more traditional sources of wisdom. These developments illustrate the presence of contradictory forces within the self-conscious psyche, past species experience can make one pessimistic about which of the two 'choices' already noted will be made by the human species.

But a close consideration of how evolution operates, the way that socio/cultural factors have greatly accelerated this process, and a little imaginative optimism, allows the possibility of a different choice (a more positive future) being open to our species. Self-consciousness in humans can be distinguished from the self-awareness exhibited by other advanced primates in the capacity we have for 'reflection', the extent that we can hold ideas before the mind and follow-up the implications of these – an ability dependent on a memory capacity and projective imagination significantly beyond those of any other primate species.

In terms of the central consideration of this essay, the question of evil primarily as expressed in warfare, is disagreement at the group (tribe, religion, ethnicity, nation,) levels that in a nuclear-armed world elevates the crucial experiential fault-line in the human condition onto another, a species-critical, level. A fault-line whose sources can be revealed by an examination of the intentional substrate underlying differential perspective-taking for each circumscribed issue where evil is expressed. With this fracture being elevated to species-critical due primarily to the two most substantial issues confronting humanity: Global issues: - Increasingly unsustainable environmental conditions - Threatened or actual armed conflict (even to the point of thermonuclear war), both between nations and within nations as civil wars. War set off initially by competition over valued resources such as: water, land, fossil fuels, rare and valued metals and minerals, power, and knowledge.

What is required if we are to design global institutional structures that will reconstruct the world in the form of a 'home' for humanity rather than various terrains of contestation in which the powerful relentlessly emerge victorious and the poor and defenceless relentlessly suffer:

- The innovative skills of natural and social scientists......tasked with a purpose.
- The analytic skills of philosophers.......tasked with a purpose.
- The wisdom of leaders unfettered by personal ambition...... tasked with outlining a purpose focused on the Global issues noted above, and of designing institutions of governance suitable for addressing these.

  And of course, the actual engagement of mass populations as a necessary pre-condition to stimulate and sustain the requirements just noted.

The challenge for any individual setting out to confront evil today being the disjunction between action at the personal and local levels, and action at the national and global levels. We can at least attempt to resolve this challenge by, as individuals, reflecting and then deciding upon a realistic action-based balance in our lives, but a balance rooted in authenticity, and emerging from a morality based upon world-conscious values. Michel Foucault, commenting on the responsibility and possibility of authentic self-hood in his 'Politics of Truth' (1997 ed, p158), recommend the night-time practice followed by Seneca ('De Ira') who writes of conducting: '…..an inquest on one's day? What sleep better than that which follows this review of one's action. How calm it is, deep and free, when the soul has received its portion of praise and blame, and has submitted itself to its own examination, its own censure. Secretly, it makes the trial of its own conduct. I exercise this authority over myself as witness before myself……..I hide nothing from myself; I spare myself nothing.'

A daily opportunity for the more reflexive consideration of one's life - not some introverted religious contemplation clinging to a self-seeking relationship to a god - not some calculating daily audit on progress towards the achievement of personal material ambitions - but instead, a proactive time located at the end of each day, a time when quietude, and a mode of intense solitary contemplation offers an opportunity for personal life to be considered; the potentially creative opportunity to form an individual's decided ethical stance towards life and lived truth, in which coheres tomorrow's possibilities. It is within this intimate process of personal reflection and decision-making that the resources for authenticity inhere. But it does require some thought-through sense of an appropriate life – of values against which aspirations and behaviour are to be judged. From where does this set of values arise? Foucault (ibid, p156) writes of an: 'hermeneutics of the self' with reference to the ancient Greek Delphic injunction to 'know thyself', set in the wider context of historical processes when at a later time medieval institutions of Christianity and Islam offered an unsatisfactory change in the methodology of self-examination by promoting faith over personal responsibility for others. But I think we could also view this expression ('hermeneutics of the self') as indicating an interpretative boundary between how we do live and how we might formulate the ways in which we should live – reimagining the possible from the actual. The claim that the 'unexamined life isn't worth living' is, in itself a value judgment – the question 'why' stands out. But if we are prepared to rigorously consider the implications of following such an injunction to progress a reflective process of considering the conditions of our lives it becomes a more substantial statement; indeed it offers a direct challenge to our sense of personal autonomy. Any exercise in progressive revelation should not be just some introspective indulgence seeking to peel off layers of personality to expose some 'real' kernel of personhood that the detritus of everyday concerns and distractions have overlain. Of discovering some deep-seated self that has long been present but only in the form of a nascent presence.

Rather, the exercise is more about accomplishment in the sense of being a self-creative revealing of what you might become.

Whilst I would concede that religion continues to play an important support role in the lives of many individuals, the decision to live with the ethical implications of a world conscious level of awareness must be a very personal one - each of us prepared to stand fully exposed to the corscourating blast of lived reality – combining together in action, but to do so as autonomous moral agents fostering the changes, incremental and revolutionary, that can contribute to the construction of a fairer, less evil, world. The emotional and cognitive resources – religious or secular - that we each draw upon matters less than accepting that the outcome is our own responsibility. Indeed doing so sets the parameters within which our authenticity can be defined. It is the originating, personally interpretive, aspect of our experience that offers hope for change. This capacity for creative agency (allied to an aspirational human imagination) offers the basic psychological conditions for the construction of social, economic, and political systems that can provide some humanity-affirming structures, and so is our hope for humanity.

Given the serious and sombre threats of thermo-nuclear destruction, environmental disaster, domination by A.I., and extreme asymmetries of wealth and power, facing the word today, people whose lives are not constrained by the immediacies of poverty and whose primary concern is not in endeavouring to eke out a living on a daily basis, have a responsibility to determine revolutionary change……but then how can building a world freed from the threat of species catastrophe, and a world in which economic fairness pertains, be revolutionary? Isn't it more about necessary rather than revolutionary change? How do we as individuals deal with the global problems that seem to be beyond any of us in a world whose civil institutions have been constructed by historical circumstances in the interests of the powerful? A world now controlled by national and transnational elites.

Each one of us needs the 'courage to be'. Not in the sense of the media-debased currency of overinflated heroism, but rather to garner the courage that would allow us to realize the potential to be fully human in our lives - to carry a sense of world-consciousness and an awareness of how this more transcendental perspective relates to our daily lives. The courage to stand against injustice, against economic exploitation and social discrimination; against the everyday evils we might chose to pass by being suffered by those that it is convenient to not see - where we rationalize our reluctance to engage. For us to more comfortably adopt the vernacular of humanistic values, and to establish frameworks of solidarity that encompass the dispossessed, the socially repressed, and the economically exploited. The courage to take responsibility for lives lived as workers, as consumers, as neighbours, as friends, and as citizens of the more powerful civil societies. Aspiring to world-consciousness would enable each of us to transcend self-consciousness - to connect with the evolutionary potential inherent, if only for now as a latent possibility, in our species.

A difficulty in realizing the constitutive element of courage is to feel that we can be effective - in a world whose institutions are constructed to make us feel discouraged, politically neutered, distracted by entertainment and other forms of wants-based consumerism, and so to be obediently managed. We need to establish and support forums where we can share concerns, reinforce current and create new connections, and build a global sense of common purpose and these at the local, regional, national, and transnational levels. To build a mutually supportive conspiracy of liberation against the forces of control that we must stand against.

A conspiracy initially fostered in our own hearts but one forming and using local, national, and international, connective links, not least those made possible by the internet, to promote and sustain global action. We, each of us, seeking to eschew the everyday accommodations and compromises we might make with obvious injustice. As individuals, we can either obediently align our lives with pathways that just unquestionably accept the normalized relativities of our home society, or we could engage with the world in a significantly different way. To endeavour to use analytic ability and imagination to mentally 'step outside' of the established patterns of our lives - this is the fundamental choice we each have to make. Developing the stance we take to the world following thoroughgoing analysis of central aspects of our lives. It would involve a type of loneliness (or rather 'alone-ness') if we do seek to break free of socialized behaviour patterns; especially if these involve an orthodox religious or politically conservative background.

Bear in mind that I am not suggesting rejection, the discarding, of what we have come to accept, but accepting it on relativised terms and aspiring to transcend this relativity. Each one of us has at least some tenuous hold on kindness, can be in touch with our humanity. Life-denying, cruel and violent upbringings - the child solider, the bullied or battered child, the baby deprived of adequate nutrition, early exposure to religious fundamentalism or relentless racism - can understandably leave a child or adult deficient in the ability to feel empathy towards others, but for most the potential to do good rather than accept evil is irredeemably present within the depth of our personality. Even those many psychologically wounded, so socially dysfunctional, victims brought up in dehumanizing circumstances might be redeemed with a sufficiency of care, and appropriate support.

We, as individuals, are born within a Reality of which we come to be both confronted with in the sense of having to negotiate our passing through it as well as being within it as a uniquely creative dimension. It confronts and yet includes ourselves; an inextricable relationship gaining a dynamic element from its ever-expanding experiential content.

Immanuel Kant noted his wonder at: 'The starry heavens above me and the moral law within me......I see them before me and connect them immediately with the consciousness of my existence.'
This short phrase encapsulates the core aspects of humanity at its best – driven by curiosity to explore the out-there and challenged by our conscience to consider the moral implications of our lives.

This book has had a primary focus on the evil of warfare and consequently a sense of sadness, and on occasion despair, inevitably runs through it and yet no overview of humankind's collective experience on Earth can entirely miss elements of creativity, joy, kindness, and noble self-sacrifice, that have also been an integral part of this experience, even at times and in places where evil has found expression. In the midst of the darkest of times: in concentration camps, living under the cruellest of dictatorships, during periods of civil and between-nation wars, at the scene of atrocities perpetrated in the name of religion or ethnicity, during bitter industrial disputes, even for the very worst of events individual human beings have sought to mitigate evil and to do good: the street child hidden from pursuers, the crust of bread surreptitiously passed from camp guard to prisoner, the machine gun fired to miss rather than to kill, the bomb aimer silently directing a cluster of bombs towards fields rather than the targeted housing, the South American trades union organizer risking her life to foster solidarity and unite exploited workers, the campesino who organizes his neighbours to stand against the large landowners, the poor man in an African village anonymously paying the school fees of the children of his even poorer neighbour, the bystander living under a oppressive regime who points in this rather than that direction to indicate the passage of the victim fleeing captors….the many, many, witnesses who have stepped forward to become involved when injustice or other evils have been expressed.

Numerous examples noted above (rarely witnessed, even more rarely recorded), of the light of human bravery and kindness breaking through the dark veil of evil. The quietude of conscience, the anger at injustice, moving within individuals forced to operate within oppressive political, social, or economic, structures. This represents the golden thread of human kindness that has insinuated itself even at the worst of times, even in the face of the most terrible of evils. This, and in a broader context, the ability to construct social, economic and political systems that can provide some humanity-affirming structures is our hope for humanity.

Nelson Mandela suggested that: 'We have to be taught to hate and if we can be taught to hate then we can be taught to love.' Obvious perhaps, simplistic possibly, but in this short statement Mandela highlights the power of the socialization processes impacting on young people. Currently most children learn about the world in terms of division, of them and us, of our-kind and their-kind, with a global perspective based on economic competition and political conflict. What might pertain if all the world's children were to learn about intergroup co-operation, economic fairness and social justice, and of peaceful coexistence more generally.

Humanity seems capable of so much and yet the same kind of hands that can write a symphony, surgically remove a cancer, carve emotion from a lump of stone, calculate the outcome of a pattern or event observed in a particle accelerator, are also the hands of the same species that have inverted their thumbs to end a defeated combatant's life in the Roman coliseum, wielded an axe to end a life, or fired an automatic rifle to end many more, dashed a baby's head against a rock, held down a women to be raped or a prisoner to be tortured, or pressed a button to release a string of bombs. But behind these actions are human minds; and although the past can foster despair it can also allow hope.

I have noted how we 'find ourselves in existence', doing so in order to express the perspective of a meta-awareness whereby we can view the relativity of our particular situations with a nexus of pre-established relationships and social institutions, and also realizing the uniqueness of each of our own experientially formed perspective on life. This perspective can include an awareness of our being present on an ecologically fragile blue/green planet spinning lazily on its axis as it traverses an elliptical passage around the more substantial Sun. These two bodies of the Solar System providing the material means to sustain humankind's journey through time. Echoing Kant …….allowing us to gaze with curious wonder upon the starry skies – and for our imaginations to roam through our lived experience, forming ideas of the possible.

The responsibility we have as individuals, if we commit to foster 'world consciousness' within ourselves and in our relations to others, is for us to endeavour to understand the world we find ourselves within and then to seek to move beyond our more local (national, interest-group, religion, tribe, ideology, etc.) interests to ones more likely to improve global conditions for all of its 7.5 billion and rising number of people – both in basic material conditions and for all to be able to experience some 'peace of mind' for their lives and those of their children, grandchildren, and the generations that we hope will follow.

I am suggesting that we have a fundamental moral responsibility to purposefully decide on how we should live, not in term of personal career, close relationships, day to day attitudes, etc (although these would also probably come to be involved) but a deeper level of considering our lives in the context of humanity itself rather than the individual as myself. There is a correspondence between perspective-taking on your own life within Reality in terms of self-creative engagement with a future involving others – the cognitive bridge to world consciousness - and the key task of endeavouring to 'take-up' the perspective of others in relation to this situation or that issue. Each requires us to adopt processes determined to transcend two aspects of our individuality, the first the individual as socialized, the second as an individual prepared to assume a level of social responsibility beyond their more immediate relationships; and each of these as processes of open-ended engagement. Both directed towards transcendence – moving beyond the narrowness of the accidentally socialized and of the self-centring tendencies of self-consciousness.

Life within Being is a ontologically mysterious experience, aspects of the condition being (as noted in the introduction) poetically phrased by Blaize Pascal when he wrote: 'When I consider the short duration of my life, swallowed up in the eternity of before and after, the little space which I fill, and even can see, engulfed in the infinite immensity of spaces of which I am ignorant, and which know me not, I am frightened and am astonished at being here rather than there; for there is no reason why here rather than there, why now rather than then……The eternal silence of these infinite spaces frightens me.' (op cit 1976). Within this quote we can realize both the insignificance '……swallowed up in the eternity…' but also our uniqueness '…..why here rather than there, why now rather than then….' And it is within this uniqueness that lies not only the responsibility to contribute to humankind's evolutionary potential but also our chance to step forward and live moral lives even in the recognition of life's seeming absurdity. The last being perhaps the hardest most personally autonomous decision – an existential conundrum to be faced or avoided but always there as a brooding presence in our lives. Possibly the boldest action we can each take as an individual is to question ourselves in the world – to create personal authenticity out of deep, open, reflection. Authentic as being self-created in terms of both: our own interior lives to develop a reflexive, if critical, interpretive mode for our experience and also how we become externally directed towards the world.

In order to gain these facets of authenticated self-hood you would have worked through the central implications of 'finding oneself within existence'. And this by a consideration of your genealogical connection to the evolutionary, become civil, heritage of our species and of your more immediate connection to the present as a citizen of the world. This is a sombre responsibility, but surely also the most creative grasping of freedom. For each of us to Be and so to Become. To Become........entangled with human truth and our human future.

Appendix 1 Global Governance and a re-imagined United Nations

It would be difficult to 'design' a system of global governance that would not be liable to being misused by some vested interest – be they some elite-group, nation-state, global finance, religion, etc. – For most obvious forms of misuse – corruption, bribery, nepotism, promoting a single group's interest, subversive cyber-infiltration - a system can be made quite robust. But any system of governance can only be successful to the extent that it enjoys public respect and ongoing support.

Re-construction of the UN would require the fundamental agreement of nations to concede sovereignty – certainly over the right to go to war, economic arrangements that involve global finance, and environmental matters, and ideally over a whole range of human rights issues.

I am sure that a combination of jurists, constitutional academics, civil servants, and reflective representative politicians, can design a better Global governance system than myself. One that can best balance the various (at times potentially/seemingly competing) interests and asymmetric power available to those whose lives any reconstructed UN would be responsible for – if any balance would need to prioritise the 'voice' of the world's people as this relates to progressing the founding principles and aims of any UN charter. But I will make a few suggestions on the sort of organization that could bring the world into participatory governance more to frame a debate on this than to offer detailed prescriptive guidance.

Balance of interests and powers:

A primary assembly composed of each nation's leader (rotating if a nation has a leadership groups rather than a single leader) or their direct representatives (no Security Council) – so approx 194 delegates – each with one vote.

A second chamber of elected representatives (ideally elected by continents or regions rather than nations) but elected in relation to size of population. I would assume some bottom-up, tiered system, from elected very local representatives to within-nation regional, to national, to inter-nation regions.

This second UN chamber of 300 elected representatives (each representing about 23m people – fixed term of 5 years). Each supported by a back office of 'civil servants' (from a central 'pool' of trained administrators) providing factual information (focused on the regions represented) sourced primarily from a more central, determinedly independent, UN data-producing and advisory office.

In addition to this more representative structure there would also be some judicial body whose primary task would be to assess and declare a ruling on the interpretation of the UN Charter by the first and second assemblies (chambers). Ideally this judicial body would be composed of 5, 7, or 9, 'wise' individuals with some experience of interpretive law i.e. appeal courts or other types of constitutional experience. I would have thought that appointments for this 'High Court' could be made by the second chamber. If from a shortlist identified by civil servants applying some 'objective' assessment combining judicial experience in itself and to some extent some commitment to the values expressed in the UN Charter that has been reflected in applicant's careers/lives. It might be appropriate that these appointments are relatively short-term 3-5 years. These people need to be motivated by an international perspective that is entirely focused on the UN Charter – In the 'normal' course of UN business the role of this body would be to consider First Chamber decisions in a light touch way, but that, if they consider that a decision would be judged to definitely infringe the Charter they can: either advise that it be reconsidered by both chambers: or following more detailed consideration might rule it 'unconstitutional' and so unable to be implemented; or it be accepted, perhaps with 'advisory' reservations. At all stages this 'high' constitutional/charter court would primarily be seeking to work co-operatively with the two principle chambers.

If a decision of the First Chamber was challenged by at least 10% of the membership of the second chamber this could also be referred to the constitutional court for reconsideration – it would be expected that any such 'appeal' would be made on the basis of some identification of where any First Chamber decision being challenged does not comply with the terms of the UN Charter.

Agencies of the UN:

- Global Peace and Security agency (including responsibility for refugees)
- Global Financial/Economic Committee
- Global Environment agency
- Global Health agency
- Global Education agency
- Global Governance committee
- Global Science and Technology agency
- Global Data Coordinating agency

The work of current UN agencies – Maritime, Aviation, Meteorology, Food and Agriculture, Labour, Atomic energy and Weaponry, Tele- and Postal communications, Intellectual property rights, cultural issues, etc. – to be incorporated within the new Global agencies noted above.

I would also suggest a UN public news and information service undertaking in-depth news analysis and even-handed presenting of 'factual' news presented in relevant contexts. I accept this might be contentious….. who judges 'relevant contexts' – I think that the credibility of such an organization will at least be judged against current broadcasters, the quality of almost all of whom it would not be difficult to improve on in terms of both 'factual objectivity' and 'relevant context'.

The work being undertaken by each of the agencies being directly overseen by a small body composed of either only representatives drawn from of the Second Chamber or some balance of these and senior global civil servants.

(The operational approach of the UN's current UNICEF/UNESCO/WHO could perhaps serve as a model for some of the agencies)

Remuneration of representatives:

First Chamber: As these would be representatives of national governments it would be appropriate that home governments determine the pay and conditions of these.

Second Chamber: Each representative's pay should be based on the average income of families of the 23m people they represent, plus 50% to recognise responsibility. All expenses directly applying to their UN work (private office support, travel, accommodation, other living costs, etc) should be paid from a central UN fund.

Global High Court: Judges for this body should be paid the average pay of all the Second Chamber representatives, plus 50% to recognise responsibility.

These suggested levels of financial remuneration might seem quite modest by today's standard but bear in mind the social status of these positions and the central role they would have in global governance meaning that they should set an example of modest material ambitions. There would also need to be some independent body that monitors expense claims and the potential for bribery and corruption – not least to show the represented population that such measures were in place.

The role, if any, for lobby groups would also need some detailed consideration – In terms of relevant information on an issue, the sort of special perspective any company, interest group, sectional interest, and similar could of course be relevant to inform decision-making. But I feel these should be more as ad hoc representative delegations meeting up with sub-committee members from the First or Second Chambers, or even able to address all members of each assembly if an issue is considered as being of particular important.

Funding for the UN (possibly separate from the Global Finance Committee (GFC) noted in Dyer 2021) should come from governments, primarily in line with some formula based on per capita income of each country as a key element. .

PROPOSALS FOR THE ESTABLISHMENT OF A GENERAL INTERNATIONAL ORGANIZATION [1]

There should be established an international organization under the title of The United Nations, the Charter of which should contain provisions necessary to give effect to the proposals which follow.

CHAPTER I. PURPOSES

The purposes of the Organization should be:
1. To maintain international peace and security; and to that end to take effective collective measures for the prevention and removal of threats to the peace and the suppression of acts of aggression or other breaches of the peace, and to bring about by peaceful means adjustment or settlement of international disputes which may lead to a breach of the peace;
2. To develop friendly relations among nations and to take other appropriate measures to strengthen universal peace;
3. To achieve international cooperation in the solution of international economic, social and other humanitarian problems; and
4. To afford a centre for harmonizing the actions of nations in the

achievement of these common ends.

CHAPTER II. PRINCIPLES

In pursuit of the purposes mentioned in Chapter I the Organization and its members should act in accordance with the following principles:

1. *The Organization is based on the principle of the sovereign equality of all peace-loving states.*
2. *All members of the Organization undertake, in order to ensure to all of them the rights and benefits resulting from membership in the Organization, to fulfil the obligations assumed by them in accordance with the Charter.*
3. *All members of the Organization shall settle their disputes by peaceful means in such a manner that international peace and security are not endangered.*
4. *All members of the Organization shall refrain in their international relations from the threat or use of force in any manner inconsistent with the purposes of the Organization.*
5. *All members of the Organization shall give every assistance to the Organization in any action undertaken by it in accordance with the provisions of the Charter.*
6. *All members of the Organization shall refrain from giving assistance to any state against which preventive or enforcement action is being undertaken by the Organization.*

The Organization should ensure that states not members of the Organization act in accordance with these principles so far as may be necessary for the maintenance of international peace and security.

CHAPTER III. MEMBERSHIP

1. Membership of the Organization should be open to all peace-loving states.

Appendix 2 Information

What do I mean by 'information'? Information is that aspect of an environment that is available for an organism, the experiential texture of the 'Reality' within which any organism lives. Information forms a continuum of material and non-material 'substance'.

As the mathematician and cryptographer, Claude Shannon, noted that: 'Nature seems to speak the language of information.'

Organisms process information in order to maintain themselves within an environment. Human-beings (at the top of the hierarchy in relation to information processing capacity) can perceive this 'substance' via the senses and can generate and manipulate more information via their thinking-related activities. Information can be viewed as being a spectrum of complexification ranging from the just noticeable 'difference' in some (external or internal) sensory feature such as temperature, light, appetite, and similar, to the complex nexus of 'difference' that we would encounter with scientific knowledge and more generally the configurations of meaning-infused information that constitutes patterns of our thinking.

The key aspect of information, as it relates to organisms, is 'difference'[54]. Without difference in the stream of internal (bio-psychological) processes and external experience there would be no possibility of awareness. Organisms can only notice differences and this 'notice' could be conscious or unconscious e.g. a molecule in a white blood cell noticing - reacting to - a chemical change such as the presence of a virus in its immediate environment, or a lizard noticing a fly settle nearby, or a human noticing a friend walk into the room. In terms of information content these three examples contain increasing amounts of information being processed.

---

[54] Or as 'differeance' noted by the philosopher Jacques Derrida, giving a more conceptual substance in term of the implications of the narrative context of any difference.

The manifestation of behaviour informed by the processing of information is a defining characteristic of all life. Depending how deeply (the level of analysis) you wish to analyze what 'processing of information' means for the purpose of my book, it is valid to suggest that inanimate matter does not process information. With such matter as rocks, rivers, iron, and ice, although they do undergo changes ('differences') due to changes in environmental conditions i.e. weather, temperature, air pressure, humidity, oxidization, the atmosphere, etc – that do lead to changes in their constitution - this does not involve the processing of information. I accept that inanimate matter does react to environmental conditions in chemical and other physical ways: rocks erode, water precipitates, volcanoes erupt, etc. Vegetable matter (such as trees, plants, fungi, etc) does process information but there is insufficient evidence that such organic life would be 'aware' of doing so, and whether it does so would depend on the definition of awareness. I accept the potential for a detailed philosophical debate on this but for my own more heuristic use of the concept of information processing this is unnecessary.

It becomes more difficult with animal matter (matter that is embodied in organisms). Even the very simplest of micro-organism such as bacteria, and the protista, clearly do process information and I think we can note at least some sense of awareness being present. If that is, 'awareness' is a feature of organisms that can be arranged in terms of a continuum of the ability to respond to evermore complex information. Simple organisms react to simple information with simple behaviours e.g. response to changing temperature/salinity would be movement towards or away. As noted in the introduction, a robust (but simplistic if considered on its own) marker of information processing capacity, as it relates to evolution, can be the amount of neuronal material available. In species terms we can see that primitive organisms such as sponges and tunicates have no specific neurons (although cells in their bodies can react to environmental conditions - 'differences') but the roundworm (caenorhabditis elegan) has about 300 neurons, the jellyfish 800, sea-slug 18,000, fruit fly 100,000, honey bee 950,000, cockroach 1,000,000, rat 200,000,000, octopus

300,000,000, cat 750,000,000 and human over 86,000,000,000 - so in crude information processing capacity we can see how the species means to access Reality has developed as an adaptive strategy.

Evolution depends upon information processing, without this phenomenon there would not have been any life, and the ways in which organisms process information determines the (species) pattern of evolutionary development. If there is a direction in evolution then I suggest that it should be framed in terms of information processing ability. Let's acknowledge, but leave the issue of computing power for now - currently this issue can quite easily be contained with the standard model of organic evolution. In that we could categorize ICT as but an adjunct to the information-processing capacity of the human species. An aspect of humankind's production of 'cultural' innovation and so similar to: mathematics, writing, books, education, TV/Radio, the internet, each also serving to extend humankinds' own information processing capacity. If, or perhaps rather when, computers meet the necessary criteria for self-reflexion (i.e. awareness - criteria that would also presumably be as applied to humans) with self-replicating software, then I think we will be challenged to re-consider the scope of the current model of evolutionary development - or rather perhaps computer programmes will 'write' this for themselves!

I have so far only referred indirectly to what information is actually constituted by (offering notional clarity as an alternative to precise definition), and I think that this at least to some extent reflects the nature of the phenomenon. Yes, simple sensory stimulation conveys information, aggressive animal behaviours convey information, coloration in animals conveys information, bird-song conveys information, so too does printed, screen-based, and spoken, language, Morse (or any) code, facial gestures, graphic images, mathematical equations, chemical formulas, sets of symbolic logic notation and computer programmes.....etc. etc. all convey information...... but what is it? What are the commonalities, the essential characteristics, by which we can usefully define information? Can we only offer indirect descriptions based on the information content, on the means of its transmission (processing capacity), or on the behaviours that are a reaction to stimuli, or that give rise to the psychological creation of information?

At the level of organic complexity we might suggest that information is the currency of communication[55]; from the simple forms of communication, as in micro-organisms, to its more complex patterns, as in human thinking and interaction with others. If money as currency offers a means of the exchange of goods and services (the memory of stored value), then information as currency is the means of internal and external communication – it makes awareness infused with information possible. And in human 'awareness', allied to a background consciousness, processes structured information constituted by meanings. But, taking a slightly different perspective, we might also describe information as an ('open') medium characterized by difference. Bring these two perspectives together and we can suggest that information is a discontinuous medium that actualizes and sustains behaviours, especially those related to communication and understanding.

It would be fair to suggest that even atoms in the process of forming molecules are sharing information and certainly cellular entities such as mRNA and DNA are involved in responding too and in generating information - throughout its material and conscious forms life is pervaded with the creation, exchange, and response to, information. A more thorough analysis of evolution in terms of information could offer a useful framework for understanding the underlying generative forces - but definitely not as a quest for any Bergsonian élan vital!

I will leave a more deeply philosophical consideration of the interconnectedness of information, awareness and consciousness, to others better qualified than myself - my own ambitions are narrower and I only wish to use the concept of information as an heuristic tool deployed to better understand 'life', and more especially the evolution of consciousness. Focusing on the implications of information

---

[55] There is of course a super-complex range of organic information processing systems - most obviously hormonal, viral, bacteriological, neurotransmission, operating below the level of awareness.

processing, of being involved in 'Reality' (in an evolutionary context) for the human condition.

If I can't offer a direct description of information (some autonomous precise definition decoupled from actually usage) that would satisfy forensic philosophical scrutiny we can at least note one processing mode that is amenable to measurement. Computers are a primary means for conveying the material that constitutes information and a unit used to convey computer-based information is the 'byte'. Each byte is commonly made up of eight 'bits' (there can be less for particular usages) e.g. 11011001 or 01100111, using the two basic digits 0 and 1 generated by electrical pulses in various (practically infinite) configurations of eight bits. In my terminology this would be eight potentials for 'differences' - yes just two digits 0 and 1, so seeming just two differences, but as 11011001 or 01100111 etc. there are eight indicators of difference. We also have differences of the position of each digit, hence a significant potential for 'difference' in the form of a byte.

It is the case that a string of 'bits' (and bytes) can be nonsensical in the sense of not expressing any coherent meanings, but this would not make them 'meaningless' – there remains 'differences' and humans will firstly notice the differences and then seek to project meaning - even if only the meaning of seeming nonsense. Even a secret code is nonsense until decoded. Nonsense is appropriately assigned to any form of information only when its meaning is decided as being nonsensical - to assert that nonsensical strings of letters are meaningless is not the same as stating that it does not convey information beyond simple difference. There is difference so there must be information and so/consequently at least the potential for meaning is always present. The eight basic differences are transcended (in fact sublated would be a more appropriate concept) at the level of the byte (international standard - IEC 80000-13). A byte is used to represent a character such as one letter or one number. At this level of letters and numbers we have a new level of 'difference' to that of the 'bits' 0 and 1. This, number plus letter, innovation increases complexity in that a computer generated letter or number contains the configuration of eight digits then adds something more; as do alphabets, words, sentences, texts, and numerical arrangements. With the 'bit' and the 'byte' as basic units, computer scientists have been able to devise a means of quantifying digital information:

an 0 or a 1	=	one bit
eight bits	=	one byte
one kilobyte(kb)	=	1000 bytes
one megabyte(mb)	=	1000²
one gigabyte(gb)	=	1000³
one terabyte(tb)	=	1000⁴
one peterabyte(pb)	=	1000⁵
one exabyte(eb)	=	1000⁶
one zettabyte(zb)	=	1000⁷
one yottabyte(yb	=	1000⁸

With the yottabyte we have a measure of a massive amount of digital information.

As well having been made amenable to quantification, information also has qualitative aspects, not least the quality of 'meaning' that makes human understanding and communication possible. Language is a structured form for conveying information, a form that allows clarity in our thinking and in our communication with others - it allows the potential conditions for meanings to be purposely, if synthetically, formulated. The production of linguistic expression - internally as well as externally directed communication - is a process where 'vague' thoughts (unformed and perhaps infused with emotions) can progress to take relatively clear linguistic forms - but can also remain as part of the continuous blurred background 'noise'. Infused with pre-linguistic - verging on pre-conscious - emotions, motivations and intentional substrate out of which more formed thoughts can be generated[56]. We are information-processing entities located within

---

[56] When I write as if thoughts and language 'arise' from a mind I do acknowledge that 'a mind' is inextricably located within a body and a world (psychological, social,

information-rich environments. I noted above that information can be viewed in quantitative and qualitative terms; as sense-data the quantitative is more relevant (but not circumscribed by this) and as meaning the qualitative is more relevant (but also not defined by this), for humans and some other species these two are blended together in awareness.

One significant implication of the prioritization of information is that the whole of Reality, all that we can know (possible and actual) - all facts, ideas, emotions, states of affairs, indeed all conceived and conceivable phenomena are constituted by their informational content - 'all' is information. I am suggesting that it would be useful to posit this as a key epistemic (as ontological fact and epistemological limitation) condition for human beings. Reductionist, yes but..........to include a reduction in an analysis would only be problematic if this is the whole procedure rather than only a beginning.

Professor of physics Hans Christian von Bayer suggests a more formal (limited) value for the 'idea' of information, noting that: 'If we can understand the nature of information, and incorporate it into our model of the physical world, we will have taken the first step along the road that leads from the objective reality to our understanding of it' (2004, p17). He distinguishes between a colloquial meaning of information and a technical definition that, although closely intertwined, are profoundly distinct. But he suggests that these two '.....must be reconciled'. He also offers a set of indirect characteristics that can express the nature of information as in: 'In-formation - the infusion of form - the flow of relationships - the communication of messages.' (von Bayer, 2004, p27)

When I use the concept of 'processing' as the way in which organisms engage within information-rich environments, I do not mean to imply 'process' in a linear mode (even if including recursive, feedback-sensitive, regulatory, types of linear processing), similar to the way in which computers process information. If there is a sense in which we can say that organisms are genetically programmed this

---

and material).

would just serve as a useful conceptual hook to begin to understand the ways in which organisms are pre-programmed to process information in ways that differ significantly from current types of computer processing. That the genetic programme is subject to considerable and ongoing variation, depending on the outcome of genetic constitution meeting lived experience. The specific details of how human minds (bodies) process information continues as an enigma. But I do think the processing concept, invoking the idea of dealing with information more simply put as 'information in behaviour out', does at least offer a pragmatic means of understanding the behavioural implications of organisms engaging within information-rich internal and external environments.

We are creatures of the creation of informational Reality - not as if 'fish' swimming in a medium of water but rather we are constituted by and constitute the information as a discontinuous medium that just 'is'. The nearest I can get to a philosopher expressing this is Heidegger's concept of Being as Reality, or perhaps just his more personal idea of Dasein's relation to its being, its reality. My capitalization of 'Reality' indicates this as all of the information available in the Universe (so a theoretical idea) – the lower-case 'reality' is that information that is accessible by any individual; so a limitation linked to personal circumstances.

Even just the translation of human biology in terms of computer-type measures of information would reflect the density of the information medium that we are part of. If we consider the human genome: it is constituted by base pairs[57] making up the genetic material in each cell. In the non-sex cell the chromosomes (strings of genes and seemingly non-coding material) take a diploid form i.e. two sets of chromosomes, one from each parent. In 2012 Yevgeniy Grigoryev assumed that each base pair is equivalent to 2 'bit's of

---

[57] A base pair being made of two of: Adenine, Thymine, Cytosine, or Guanine, ATCG - the nitrogenous building blocks of DNA - 3.2 billion bases in the 23 chromosome haploid genome or 6.4 billion bases in 46 chromosome diploid genome.

information (8 bits to a standard byte) and, using this equivalence, estimated that each human genome stores 1.5 gigabytes of information and that a whole human organism stores 150 zettabytes of information. More recently, George Church and Sri Kosuri (working at Harvard's Wyss Institute) offered a calculation that a single gram of DNA contains 700 terabytes (5.5 Peterabytes) of information. Information is the key medium for understanding the primary functional (and the possibly transcendental as a form of non-deterministic teleology) dynamic of evolution - the medium that can be identified in all forms of life.

So, I posit information as similar to space-time, mass, and energy, as being a fundamental characteristic of the Universe as we know it. In terms of evolution on Earth I suggest that life has evolved in terms of organisms adapting to their environments in ways that exhibit an increasing 'capacity 'to process information – both as simple quantity of information and also in evermore 'novel' forms. In human history this can most clearly be seen by comparing the information-based Reality of circa 10,000 y.b.p and the information-based Reality of the today's twenty-first century. Let's leave consideration of information there for the time being and return to tracking the path of species-evolution as it developed on our planet.

Appendix 3 Artificial intelligence – a possible scenario?

Let's consider a possible scenario about 50 years hence: Robotic soldiers, deployed in the field by drone-type guidance systems operated from thousands of miles distance or even self-directed by pre-installed software programmes, are available. Industry, both manufacturing and service, has continued to replace human workers with automated systems. Governments have extended their observation and identification of populations and have the potential to grade individuals according to the extent to which their behaviour aligns with some social 'ideal' (China is already leading in this type of technology). An ideal based on aspects of social acceptability set by governments, or by private industry in line with corporate requirements.

How far could these developments go in but 10, 50, 100 years? Almost all areas of employment will morph from human to machine – just a few being: medical staff, engineers, construction workers, those employed in retail, waste disposal, all forms of transportation, security forces, bankers and those others in financial services, and potentially the most threatening: in the actual manufacture of software and a wide range of robotic machinery. This last including self-replicating A.I. systems, in theory a time when the machines themselves will no longer need humans; noted as 'technological singularity', when technology assumes (and controls) its own momentum and direction[58].

Globally, millions, probably billions, of humans will have become superfluous to the work-place, few if any current areas of work would be immune to A.I.-related technological change. As nations progress

---

[58] It might be that some more culturally colourful 'primitive' groups are allowed to continue to occupy traditional sites so serving as destinations for wealthy tourists.

towards overwhelming observation and control of populations and machines have replaced almost all workers how will those in control manage populations? Some of which would invariable become openly disruptive, or in democratic nations would be inclined to use the ballot box to make their concerns known? There are a variety of sophisticated means of persuasion (informed by internet-based analysis of the mass of data harvested from the activities of individuals and groups) that could be deployed to convince the majority of each population group (nation) that in the longer-term the changes will somehow benefit them; no doubt also mobilising the threat of external competition as an additional persuader.

Another placatory action could be the introduction of a 'social wage' paid to all in order to soften the impact of unemployment and to allow economic demand for goods and services to be maintained. So a wage that would simply be recycled back into the production process, with goods made cheaper by the efficiency of machine and robotic production, and the disposal of the more costly human workforce. With any recalcitrant individuals or leaders of minority groups (perhaps any surviving trade unions or more libertarian or socialist political parties) reluctant to accept this direction of change, being imprisoned or even 'disposed of'; the severity of the means of suppressing dissent will invariably increase as this projected A.I. revolution progresses.

The current advances in communication and control technologies and those that have taken place in global financial control, form the base from which incremental change can continue to shift power towards elite economic and/or political groups. The past 40 years of state subsidised neo-liberal advance has already see a significant shift in power towards the global financial elites especially when (as in Russia and China) these are in direct control of governments. A.I. and its associated robotics offer the potential to vastly increase the power of those who control its development and deployment. Currently, control is relentlessly moving towards global elites, democratic regimes have done little to mitigate this and dictatorial regimes have actively encouraged it.

When the technology has advanced to a time when control can be exercised in a way perceived to be fully in the interest of elites then the question would arise – leaders of elites might ask - why do we need potentially disruptive populations that are not 'of us', or are in the relative small servant-class that we might still need to maintain our luxurious lives? If A.I. based machines can produce the food, construct the buildings, run transport, care for health and attend to all personal needs (even virtual, or otherwise mechanized, sex might become a favoured option – and there would always be the surviving servant class to draw on for this pleasure) why do the controlling elites need the billions who would then do nothing for them, their potential for productive labour being superfluous.

But the masses do contribute massively to polluting the environment, a clear threat even for the super-rich. So there would be a rationale to begin a process of eliminating all but say 100 -200 million individuals making up the global elites and their necessary human support systems.*Allowing an over 7 billion reduction in the population of the world – a powerful, if seriously inhuman, means of dramatically reducing global warming, resource depletion, and pollution!

Who would be able to prevent this elimination gained by global 'holocaust', or gained by just removing all but basic healthcare provision and introducing a no-child policy for the masses? Any resistance at this time could be ruthlessly put down by robotic security forces unburdened by any moral inhibitions. Even if these cyber-troopers are still controlled by some surviving human military (who would themselves be members of elites), I am sure most generals would value being able to deploy these 'ideal' military units: highly efficient killing capability, totally amoral and completely obedient. If there were any 'casualties' these would not be deaths but merely repairable breakdowns in machines, so no bereaved parents to write too, no demoralization of fellow soldiers, no PTSD, only a redirection to some repair facility, one no doubt run by robots!

Is this merely some science fiction dystopia or is it a possible scenario whose catastrophically evil outcome will have been attained by stealth, as power and control is incrementally shifted even more towards global elites and the A.I. based means to enforce obedience has been developed. The numerous gated and high-security patrolled communities enabling the wealthy only having to mix with the wealthy, are already being constructed (and increasing in number at an exponential rate), the 40 year shift in global economic power toward rentier elites, the increase in what are effectively political dictatorships and the mainly uncontrolled frontiers of A.I. development, are early indicators of what could come to pass. The pollution of the planet, the increasing instability with the current capitalist economic system, and the threat these could offer to the current dominant elites, provide the motivational drivers for such change. Who controls our future? Who controls A.I., and how they might do so, could be an appropriate and urgent question for us to address.

Printed in Great Britain
by Amazon